# RAGNARÖK

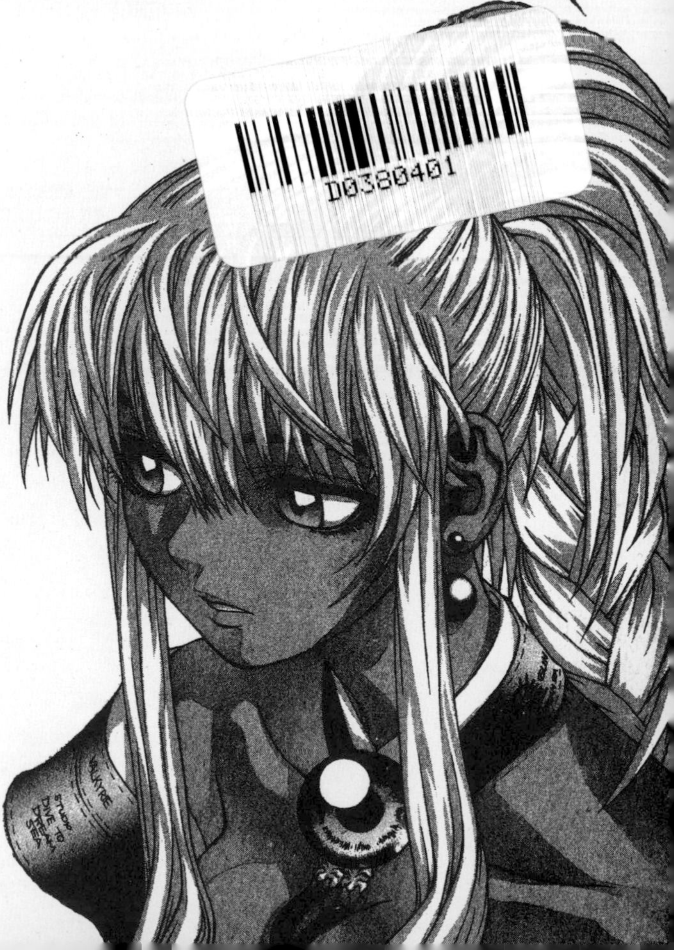
VALKYRIE
STUDIO DIVE TO DREAM SEA

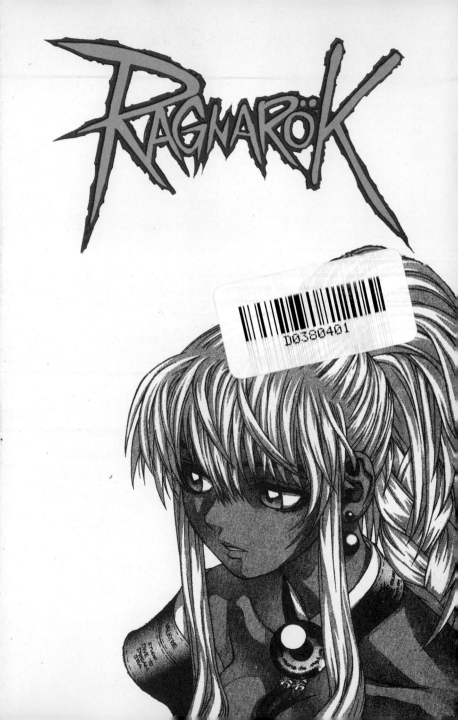

# ALSO AVAILABLE FROM 🔜 TOKYOPOP®

## MANGA

### ACTION

ANGELIC LAYER*
CLAMP SCHOOL DETECTIVES* (April 2003)
DIGIMON (March 2003)
DUKLYON: CLAMP SCHOOL DEFENDERS* (September 2003)
GATEKEEPERS* (March 2003)
GTO*
HARLEM BEAT
INITIAL D*
ISLAND
JING: KING OF BANDITS* (June 2003)
JULINE
LUPIN III*
MONSTERS, INC.
PRIEST
RAVE*
REAL BOUT HIGH SCHOOL*
REBOUND* (April 2003)
SAMURAI DEEPER KYO* (June 2003)
SCRYED* (March 2003)
SHAOLIN SISTERS* (February 2003)
THE SKULL MAN*

### FANTASY

CHRONICLES OF THE CURSED SWORD (July 2003)
DEMON DIARY (May 2003)
DRAGON HUNTER (June 2003)
DRAGON KNIGHTS*
KING OF HELL (June 2003)
PLANET LADDER*
RAGNAROK
REBIRTH (March 2003)
SHIRAHIME:TALES OF THE SNOW PRINCESS* (December 2003)
SORCERER HUNTERS
WISH*

### CINE-MANGA™

AKIRA*
CARDCAPTORS
KIM POSSIBLE (March 2003)
LIZZIE McGUIRE (March 2003)
POWER RANGERS (May 2003)
SPY KIDS 2 (March 2003)

### ANIME GUIDES

GUNDAM TECHNICAL MANUALS
COWBOY BEBOP
SAILOR MOON SCOUT GUIDES

### ROMANCE

HAPPY MANIA* (April 2003)
I.N.V.U. (February 2003)
LOVE HINA*
KARE KANO*
KODOCHA*
MAN OF MANY FACES* (May 2003)
MARMALADE BOY*
MARS*
PARADISE KISS*
PEACH GIRL
UNDER A GLASS MOON (June 2003)

### SCIENCE FICTION

CHOBITS*
CLOVER
COWBOY BEBOP*
COWBOY BEBOP: SHOOTING STAR* (June 2003)
G-GUNDAM*
GUNDAM WING
GUNDAM WING: ENDLESS WALTZ*
GUNDAM: THE LAST OUTPOST*
PARASYTE
REALITY CHECK (March 2003)

### MAGICAL GIRLS

CARDCAPTOR SAKURA
CARDCAPTOR SAKURA: MASTER OF THE CLOW*
CORRECTOR YUI
MAGIC KNIGHT RAYEARTH* (August 2003)
MIRACLE GIRLS
SAILOR MOON
SAINT TAIL
TOKYO MEW MEW* (April 2003)

### NOVELS

SAILOR MOON
SUSHI SQUAD (April 2003)

### ART BOOKS

CARDCAPTOR SAKURA*
MAGIC KNIGHT RAYEARTH*

### TOKYOPOP KIDS

DISNEY CLASSICS (June 2003)
STRAY SHEEP (September 2003)

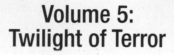

## Volume 5:
## Twilight of Terror

By
# Myung-Jin Lee

English Version
by
# Richard A. Knaak

Los Angeles • Tokyo

Translator - Lauren Na
Copy Editors - Amy Kaemon & Paul Morrissey
Retouch & Lettering - Monalisa de Asis
Cover Layout - Anna Kernbaum

Senior Editor - Jake Forbes
Production Manager - Jennifer Miller
Art Director - Matthew Alford
VP of Production & Manufacturing - Ron Klamert
President & C.O.O. - John Parker
Publisher - Stuart Levy

Email: editor@TOKYOPOP.com
Come visit us online at www.TOKYOPOP.com

A TOKYOPOP® Manga
TOKYOPOP® is an imprint of Mixx Entertainment, Inc.
5900 Wilshire Blvd., Suite 2000, Los Angeles, CA 90036



ISBN: 1-931514-77-1

First TOKYOPOP® printing: January 2003

10 9 8 7 6 5 4 3 2 1
Printed in the USA

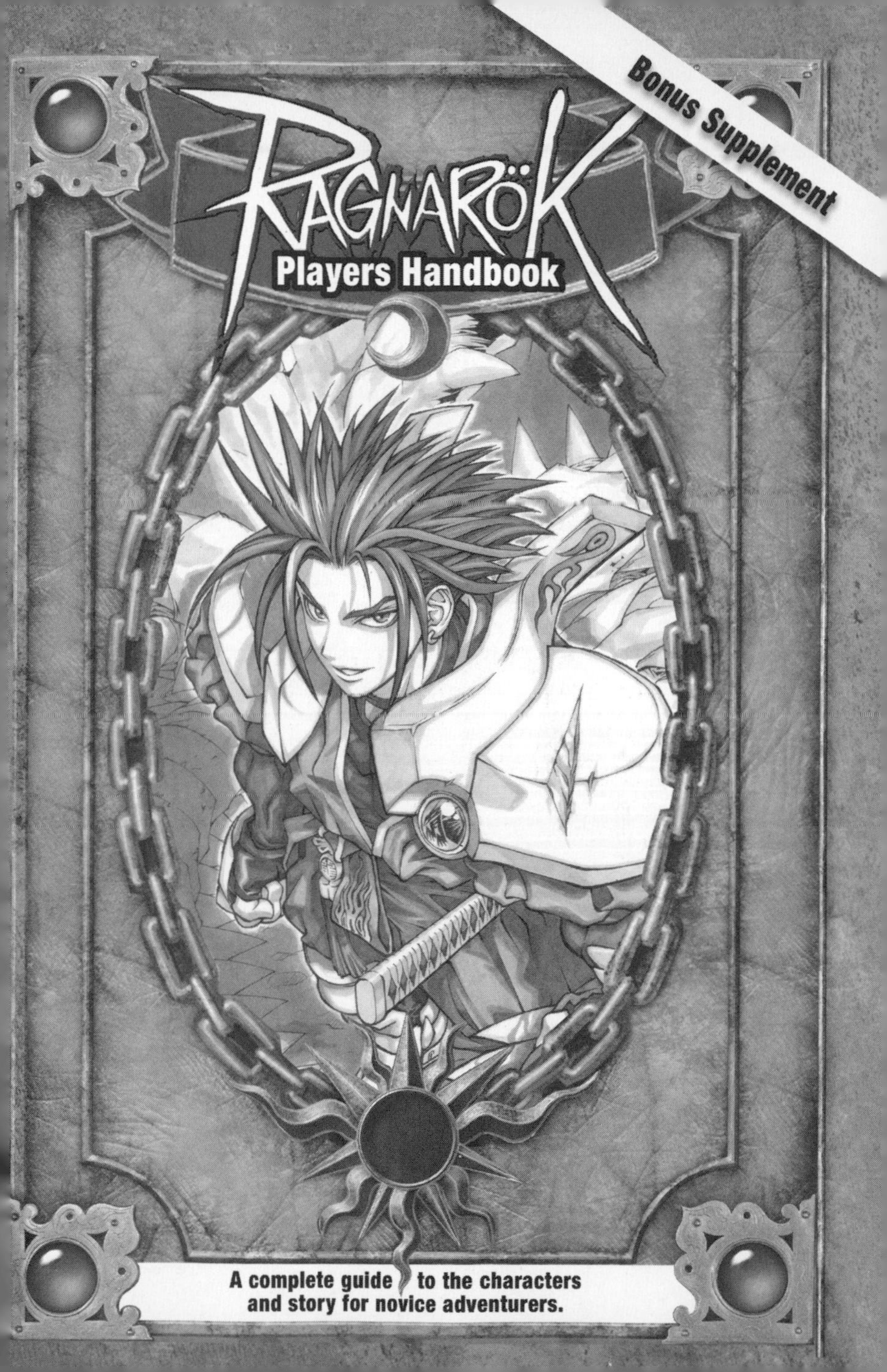
Bonus Supplement
RAGNARÖK
Players Handbook
A complete guide to the characters
and story for novice adventurers.

# HEROES

NOTE: THE FOLLOWING STATISTICS ARE INSPIRED BY THE MANGA, BUT DO NOT REFLECT ANY OFFICIAL RAGNAROK RPG. - EDITOR

NAME: Chaos
Class: Rune Knight
Level: 9
Alignment: Chaotic Good
STR: 17
DEX: 10
CON: 15
INT: 12
WIS: 14
CHR: 16

Equipment:
Vision- Enchanted sword- STR +2

Rune Armor- AC -4, 20% bonus
saving throw vs. magical attacks.

Notes:
The reincarnation of the fallen god Balder,
Chaos has been told by his divine mother,
Frigg, that the fate of the world rests in his
hands. He may also be tied to the legendary
"Dragon Knights."

NAME: Iris Irine
Class: Cleric
Level: 5
Alignment: Lawful Good
STR: 7
DEX: 12
CON: 9
INT: 13
WIS: 16
CHR: 16

Equipment:
Chernryongdo- Enchanted dagger-
STR +1, DEX +1, 1D4 damage if
anyone but her touches it.

Irine Family Armor- AC -5, WIS +1

Notes:
Iris would have become the new leader of the city
of Fayon... that is, if it weren't destroyed by her sis-
ter, the Valkyrie Sara Irine. She now follows her
close friend Chaos.

# HEROES

NAME: Fenris Fenrir
Class: Warlock
Level: 9
Alignment: Neutral Good
STR: 14
DEX: 15
CON: 13
INT: 16
WIS: 12
CHR: 14

Equipment:
Psychic Medallion: Magic compass
which leads its bearer to whatever
his or her heart most desires.

Laevatein, Rod of Destruction- STR+1, extends
to staff on command.

Notes:
The reincarnation of the Wolf God, Fenris
helped Chaos to realize his identity. She now
follows him on his quest.

NAME: Loki
Class: Assassin
Level: 9
Alignment: Lawful Neutral
STR: 14
DEX: 18
CON: 12
INT: 12
WIS: 14
CHR: 10

Equipment:
Sword of Shadows: + 4 to hit, damage +2

Bone Armor: AC -5, STR +2

Notes:
Greatest of the Assassins, Loki's anonymity
is a testament to his skill at going unseen.
When his assassin comrades are killed, Loki
sets forth to get revenge and to discover his
new role in the brewing storm.

# HEROES

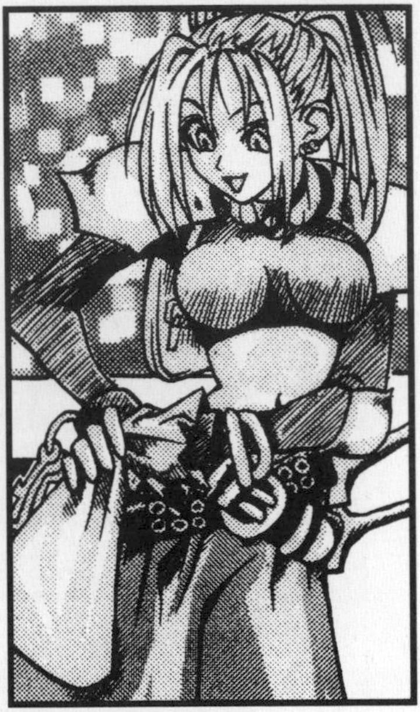

NAME: Lidia
Class: Thief
Level: 4 (level up!)
Alignment: Neutral Good
STR: 8
DEX: 15
INT: 13
WIS: 10
CHR: 15

Equipment:
Treasure Hunter's Bible: 50% chance of identifying magical items

Follower: Sessy, Cat o' Two Tails: +50% saving throw to pick pockets

Notes:
An "expert treasure hunter" by trade, Lidia "borrows" whatever she can get her hands on while she looks for bigger hauls.

# NPC'S

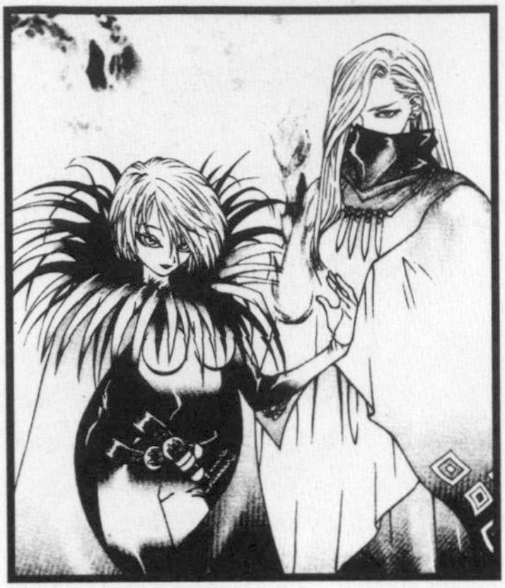

Muninn and Huginn

Odin's Beholders, these messengers can take the form of crows. They seem to be manipulating events, but to what end remains a mystery.

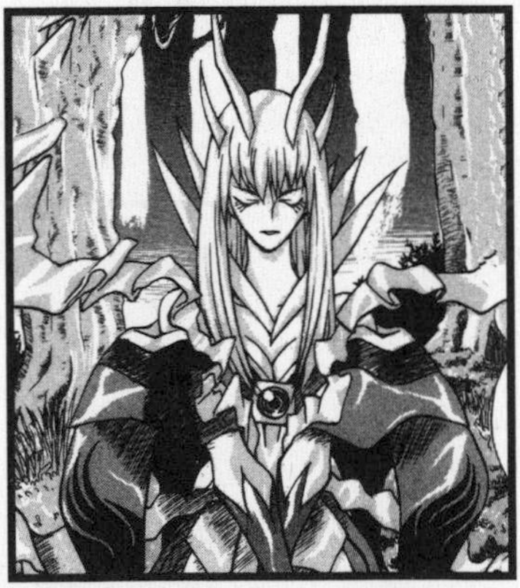

Frigg

Wife of Odin and mother to Balder, Frigg is the queen of the gods. She came to Chaos in a vision and informed him that it is his destiny to save Midgard from destruction. Her final advice was to "find he who is both human and not."

# ENEMIES

NAME: Sara Irine
Class: Valkyrie
Level: 7
Alignment: Chaotic Neutral
STR: 14
DEX: 12
CON: 13
INT: 14
WIS: 15
CHR: 17

Equipment:
Haeryongdo, Sword of Retribution-
STR+2

Enchanted Parchments x 24

Notes:
One of the 12 Valkyries of Valhalla,
Sara Irine was sent to prevent Fenris
from completing her quest. After the
beholders spared her life at Fayon,
she was transported to a place yet
unknown.

NAME: Skurai
Class: Cursed Prosecutor
Level: 13
Alignment: Chaotic Evil
STR: 17
DEX: 16
CON: 19
INT: 15
WIS: 8
CHR: 12

Equipment:
Talatsu- Cursed sword- STR+2, HP
+12- cannot be discarded unless it
tastes the blood it is looking for.

Notes:
Skurai follows the will of his sword,
Talatsu, which seeks the one blood
that will quench its thirst. After meet-
ing Chaos at Fayon, Skurai now seeks
the Rune Knight's blood and tricked
Loki into hunting him down.

# The Story so Far...

The fates work in mysterious ways. Skurai, the Cursed Prosecutor, devourer of souls, seeks the blood of Chaos—he who was once Balder. Knowing Chaos to be too strong a target, Skurai prepared a trap most foul. After slaughtering the Assassins of Morroc, Skurai convinced Loki death-bringer, greatest of assassins, that Chaos was behind his comrades' deaths. After a bout with Loki, Chaos should be weakened to the point where he offers no resistance.

Meanwhile, oblivious to the plots around him, Chaos travels to Prontera, capital city of the Volsug province. Joined by Fenris Fenrir, the war-lock, and Iris Irine, the cleric, he seeks the key to his past so that he might unlock his destiny. Prontera offers no answers, only bloodshed. Cursed Swordsman, Assassin and Rune Knight— three warriors of equal power. Their current battle is a delicately balanced dance, soon to be upset as the sun sets and the Twilight of Terror begins…

# RAGNARÖK

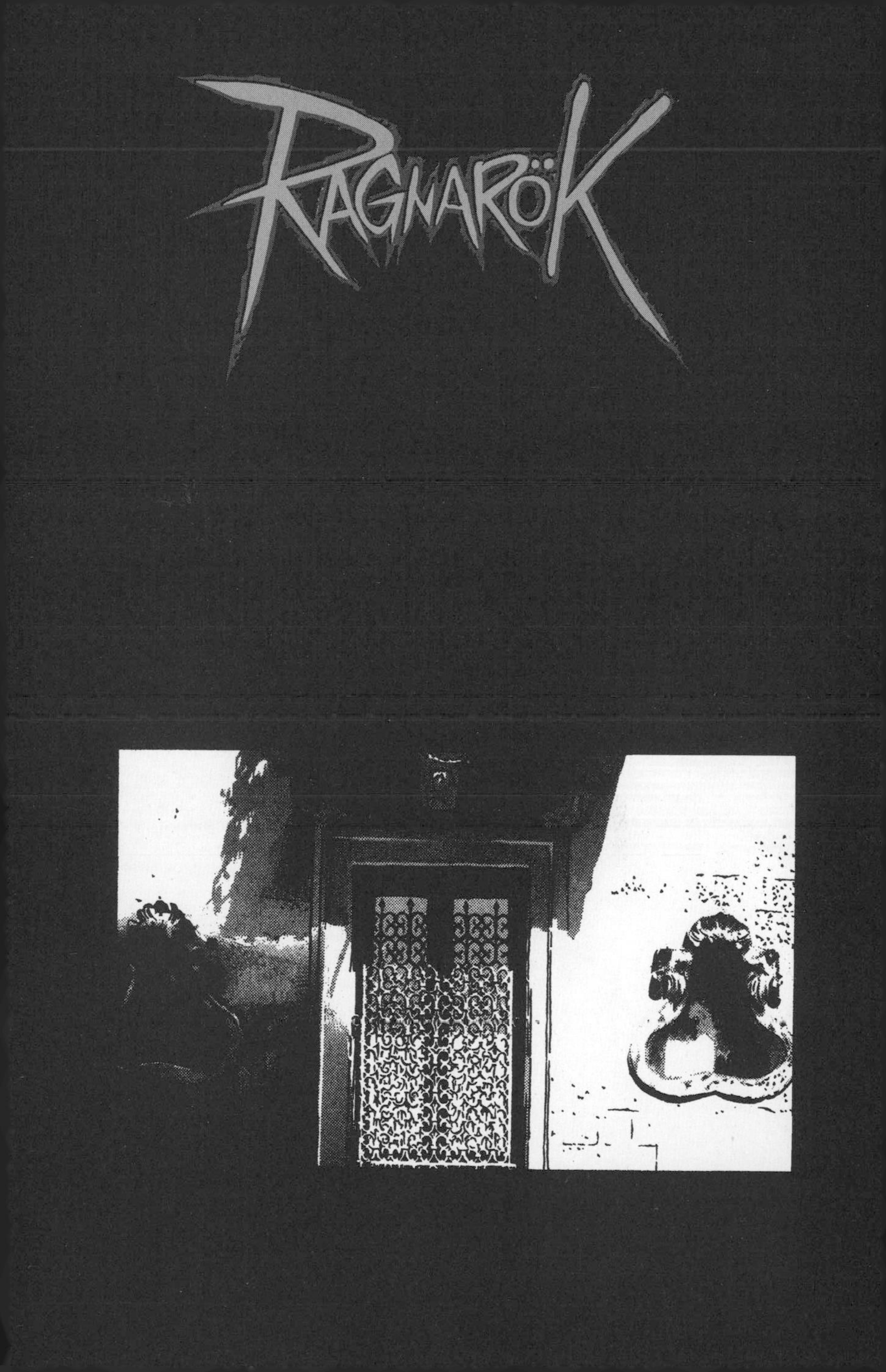

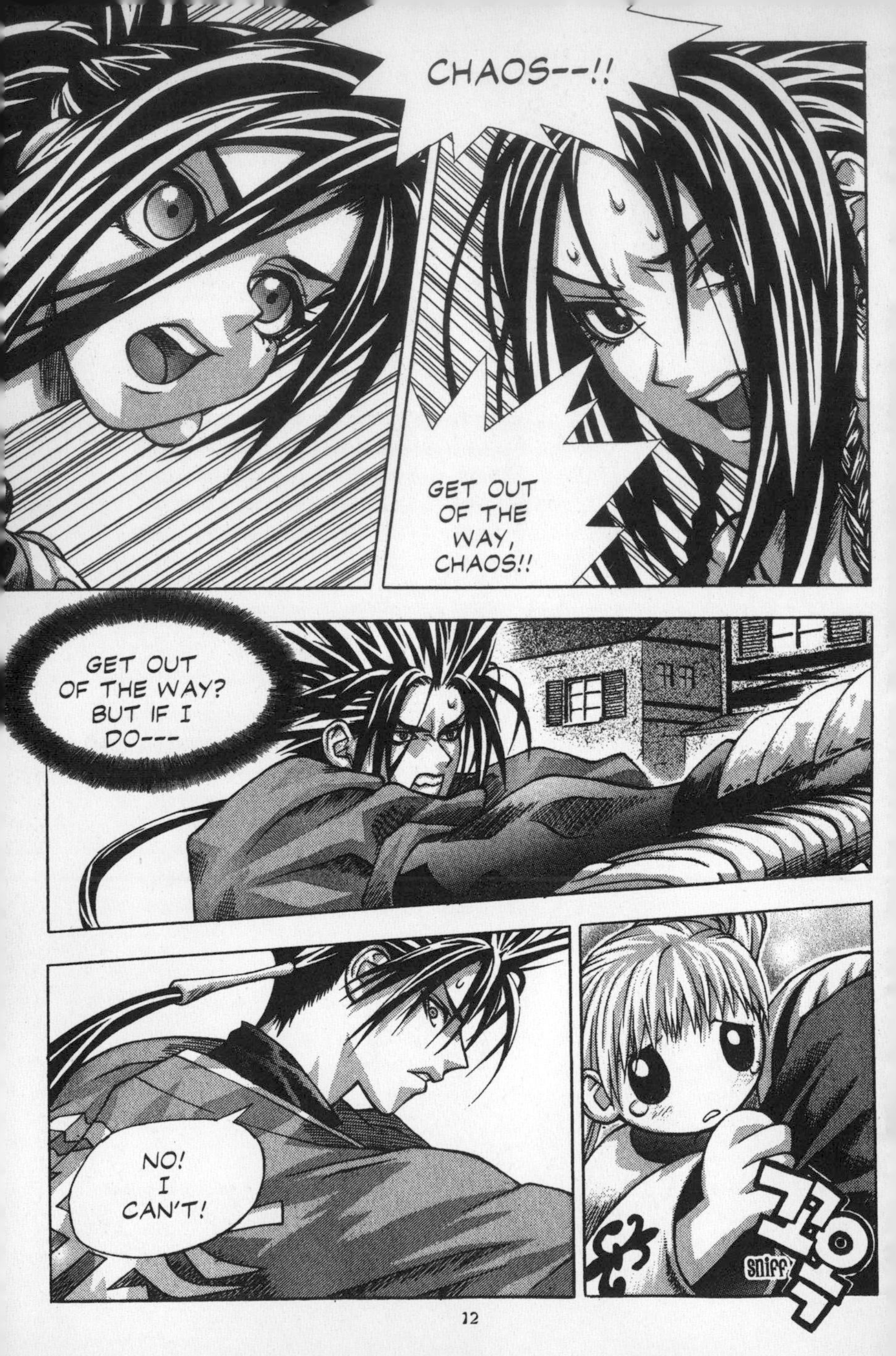
CHAOS--!!
GET OUT OF THE WAY, CHAOS!!
GET OUT OF THE WAY? BUT IF I DO---
NO! I CAN'T!
SNIFF

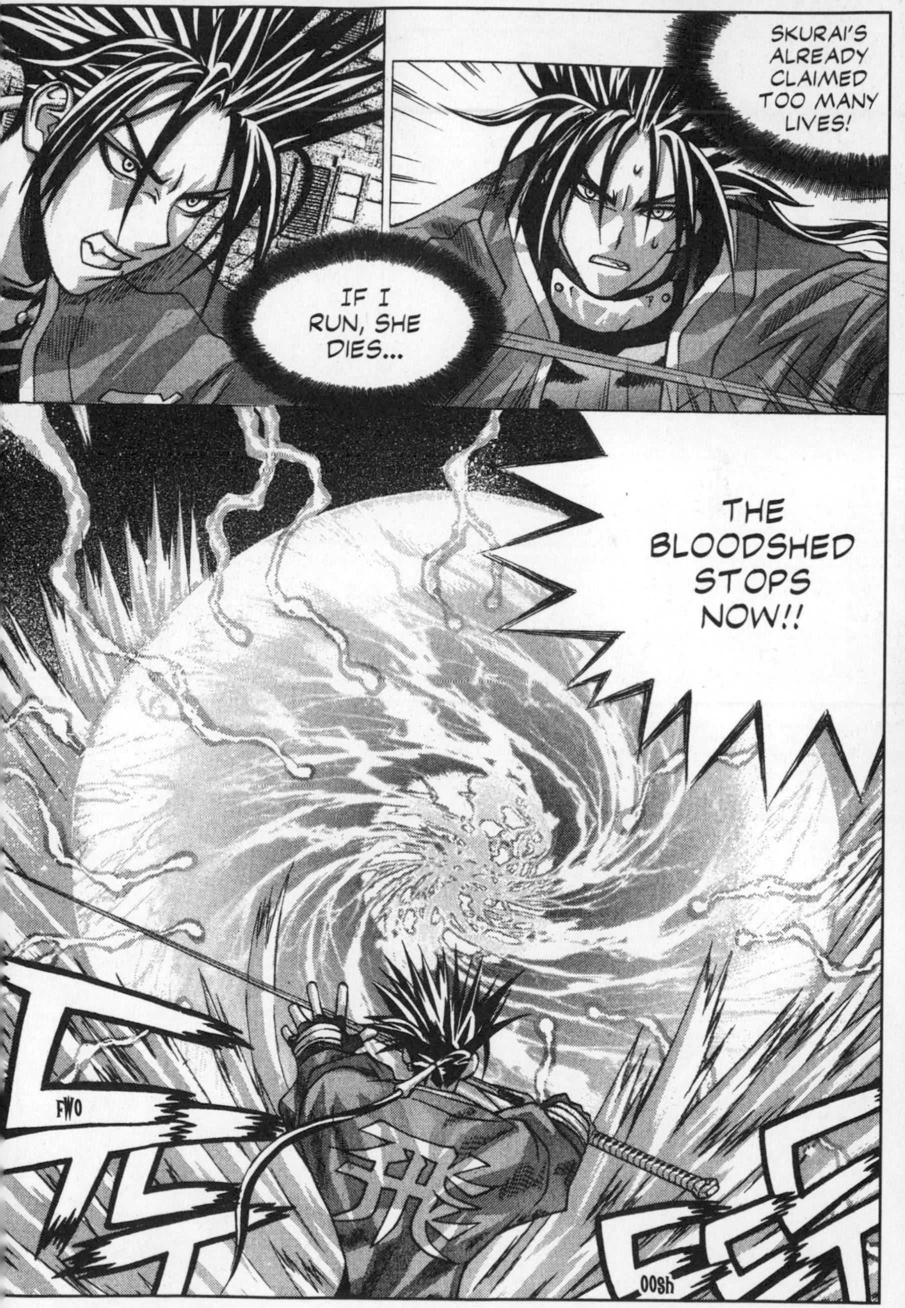
IF I RUN, SHE DIES...
SKURAI'S ALREADY CLAIMED TOO MANY LIVES!
THE BLOODSHED STOPS NOW!!
FWO
OOSH

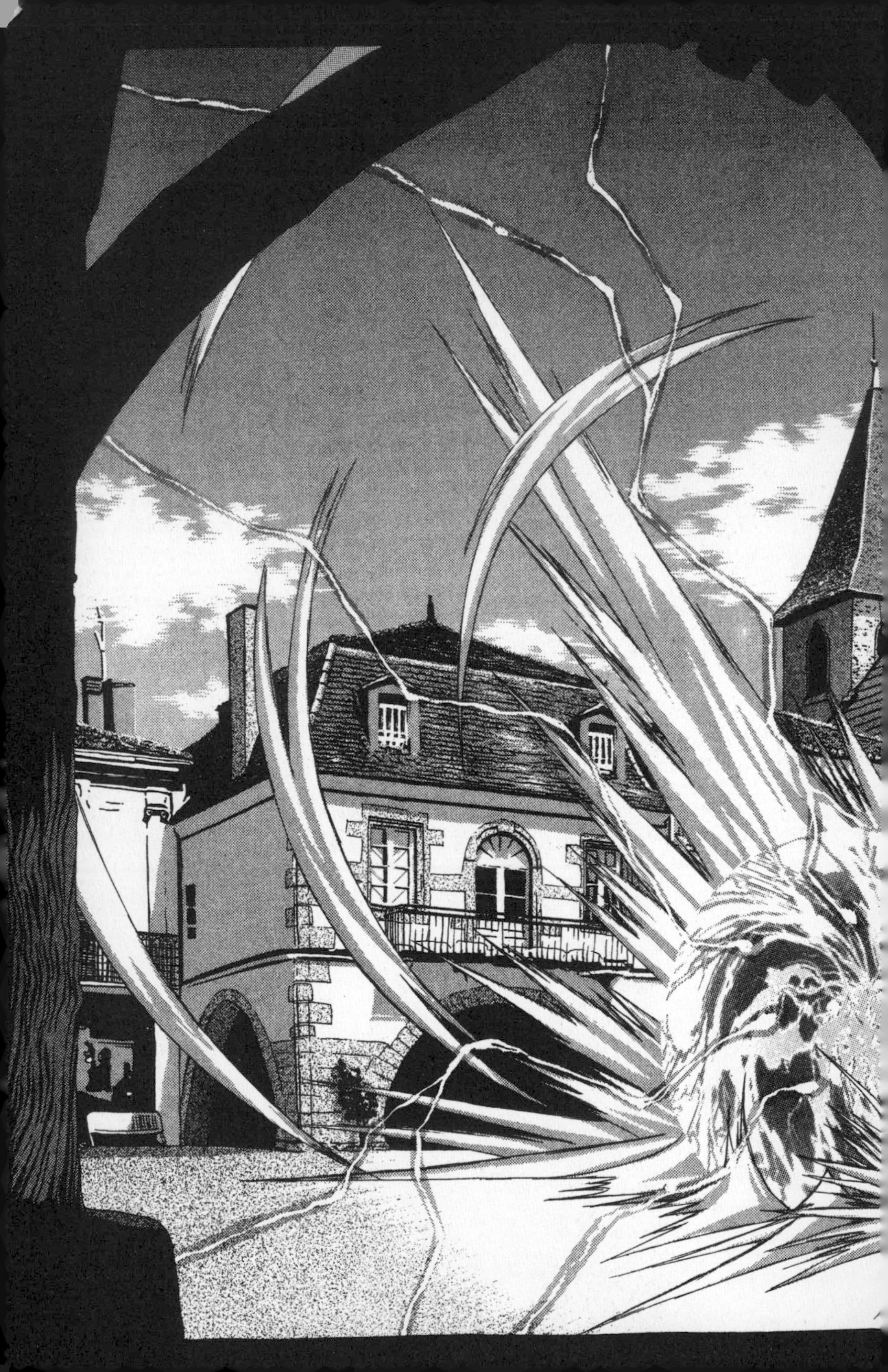

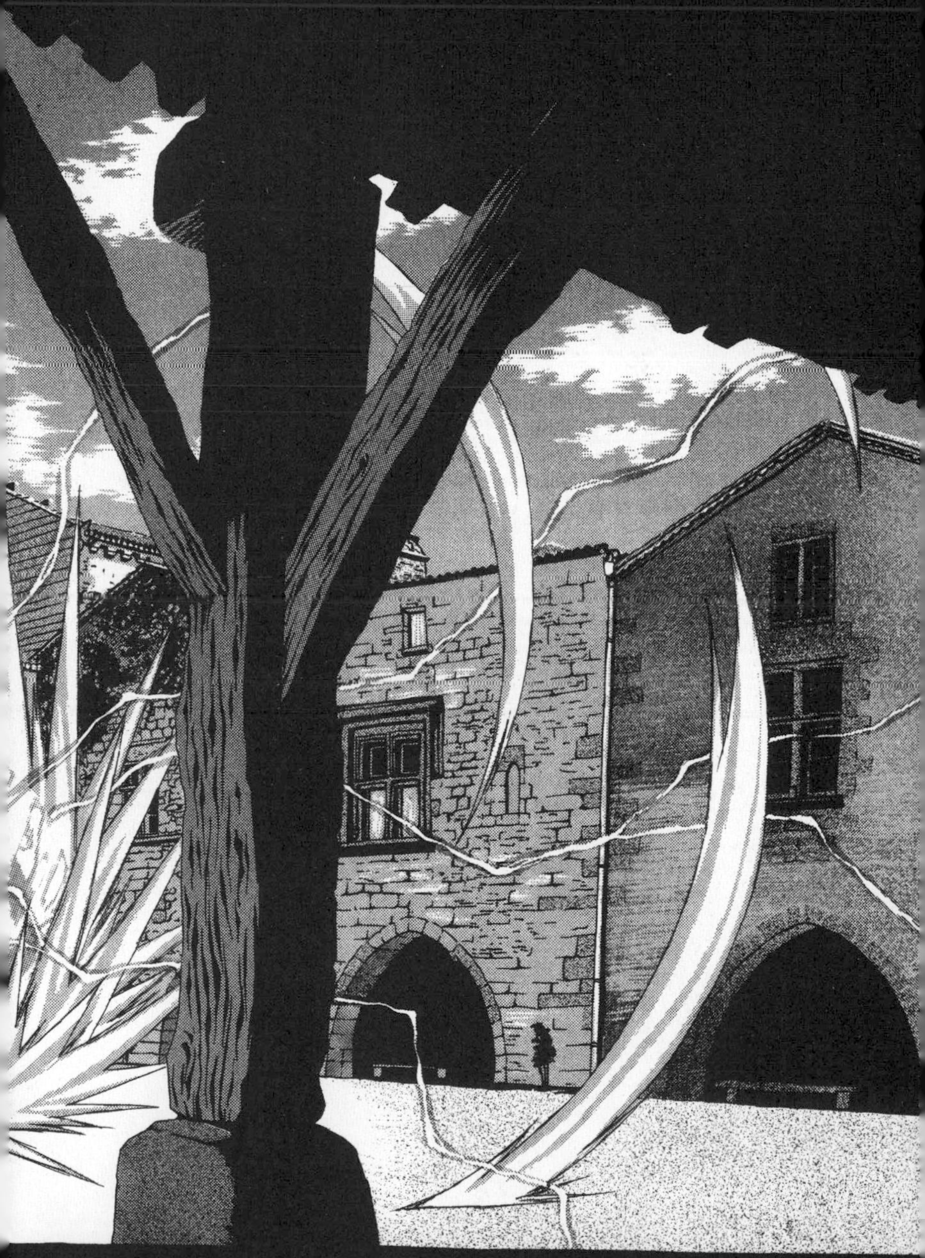

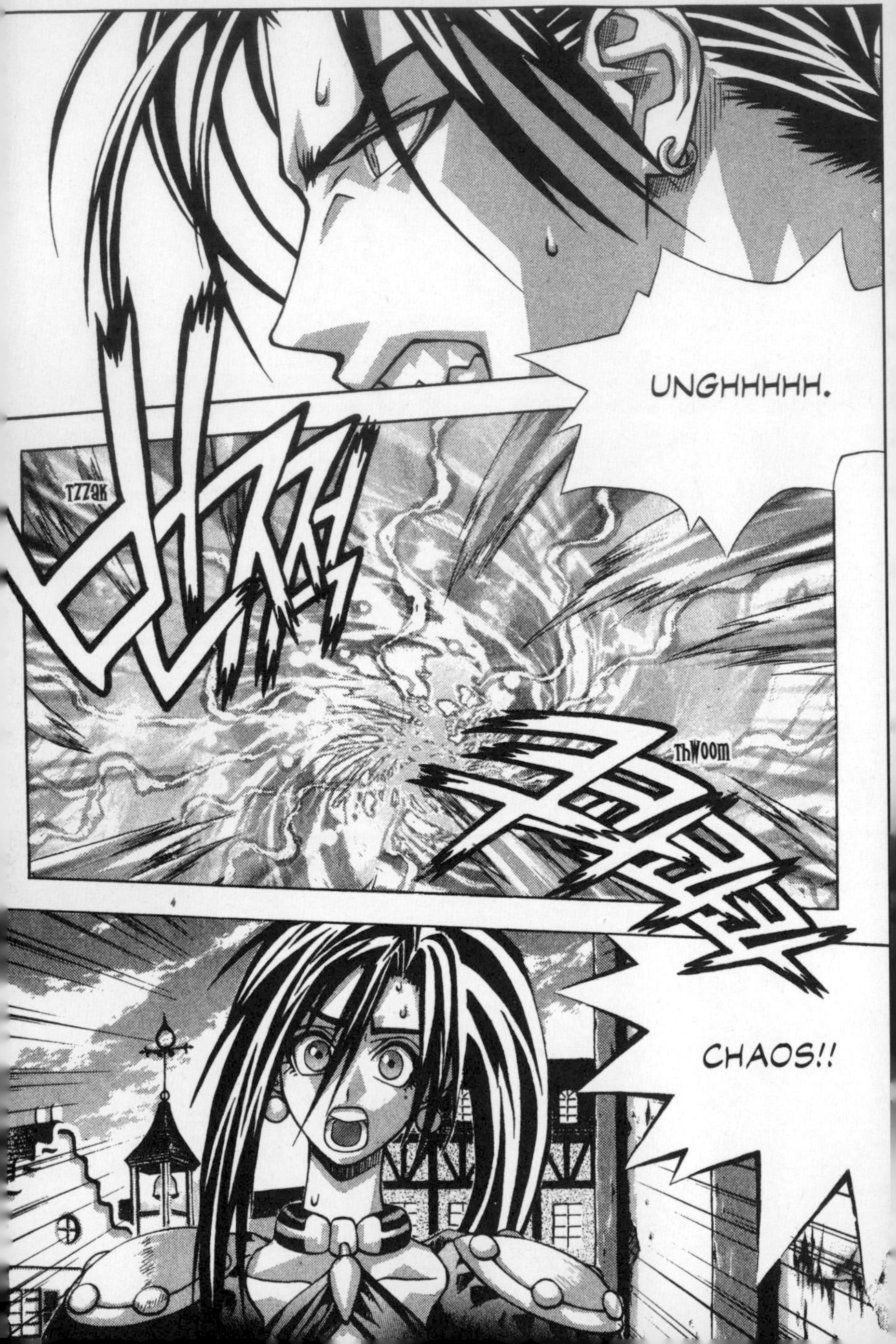
UNGHHHHH.
TZZAK
ThWoom
CHAOS!!

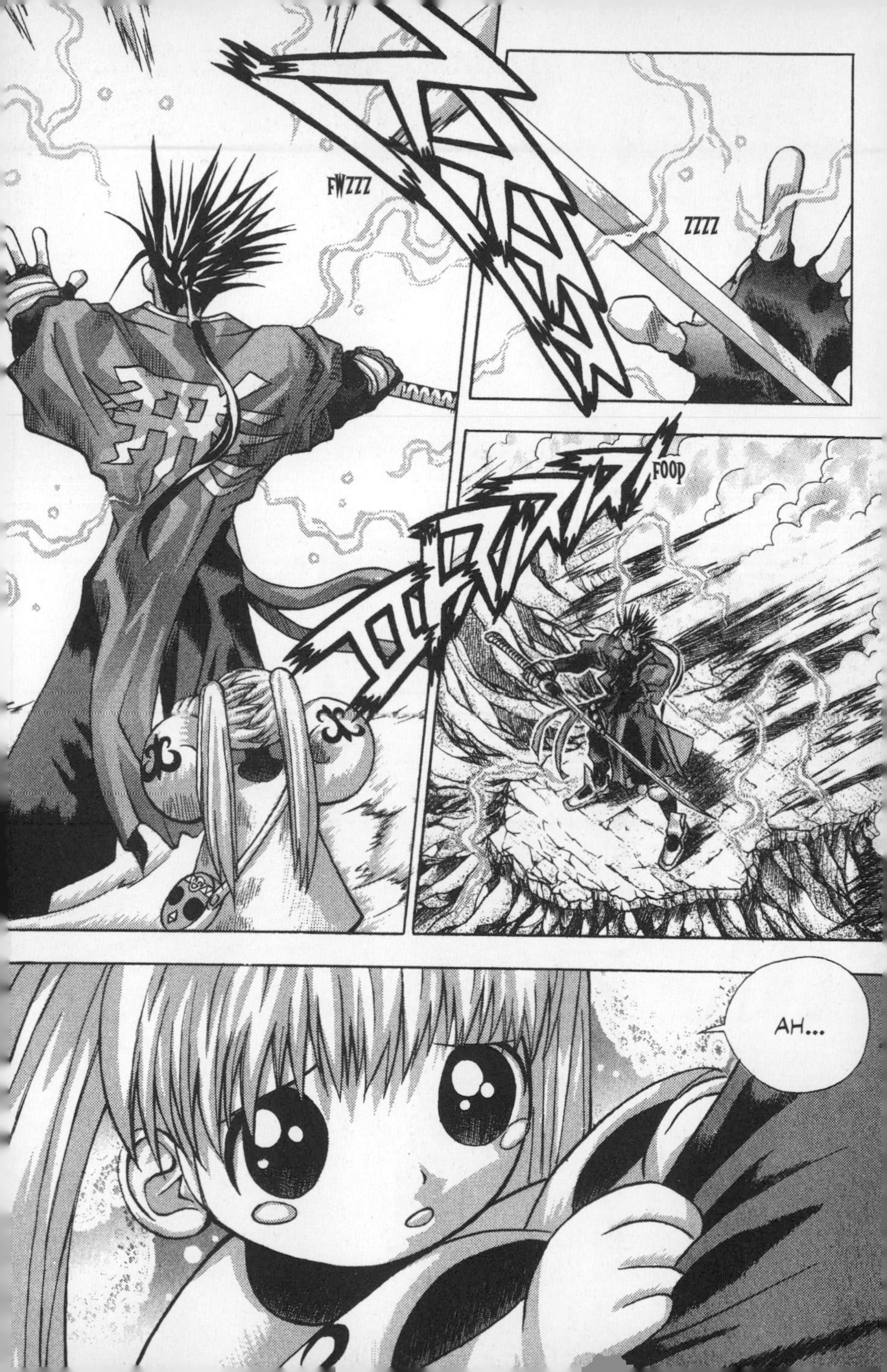
FWZZZ
ZZZZ
FOOP
AH...

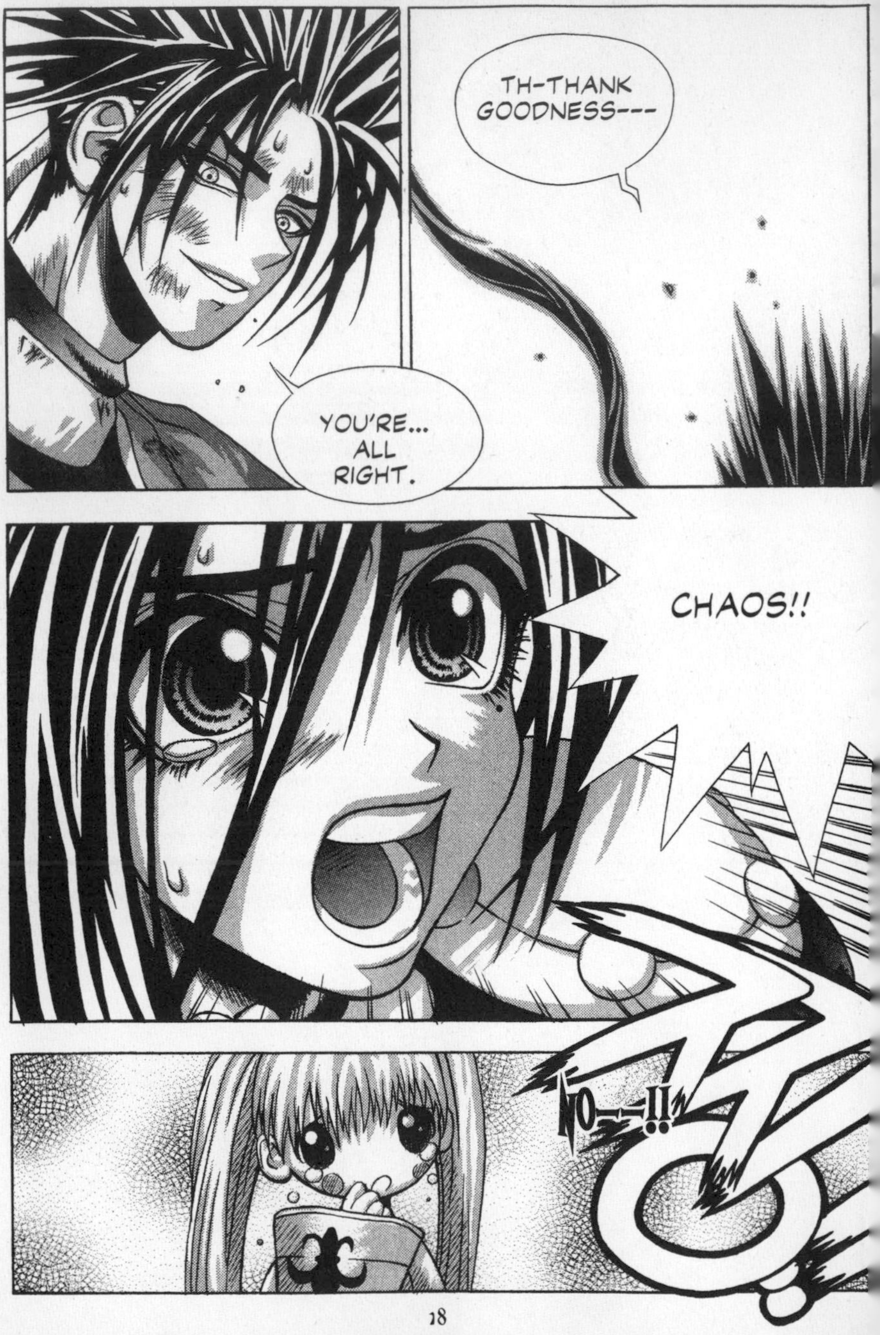

YOU'RE... ALL RIGHT.
TH-THANK GOODNESS---
CHAOS!!
NO---!!

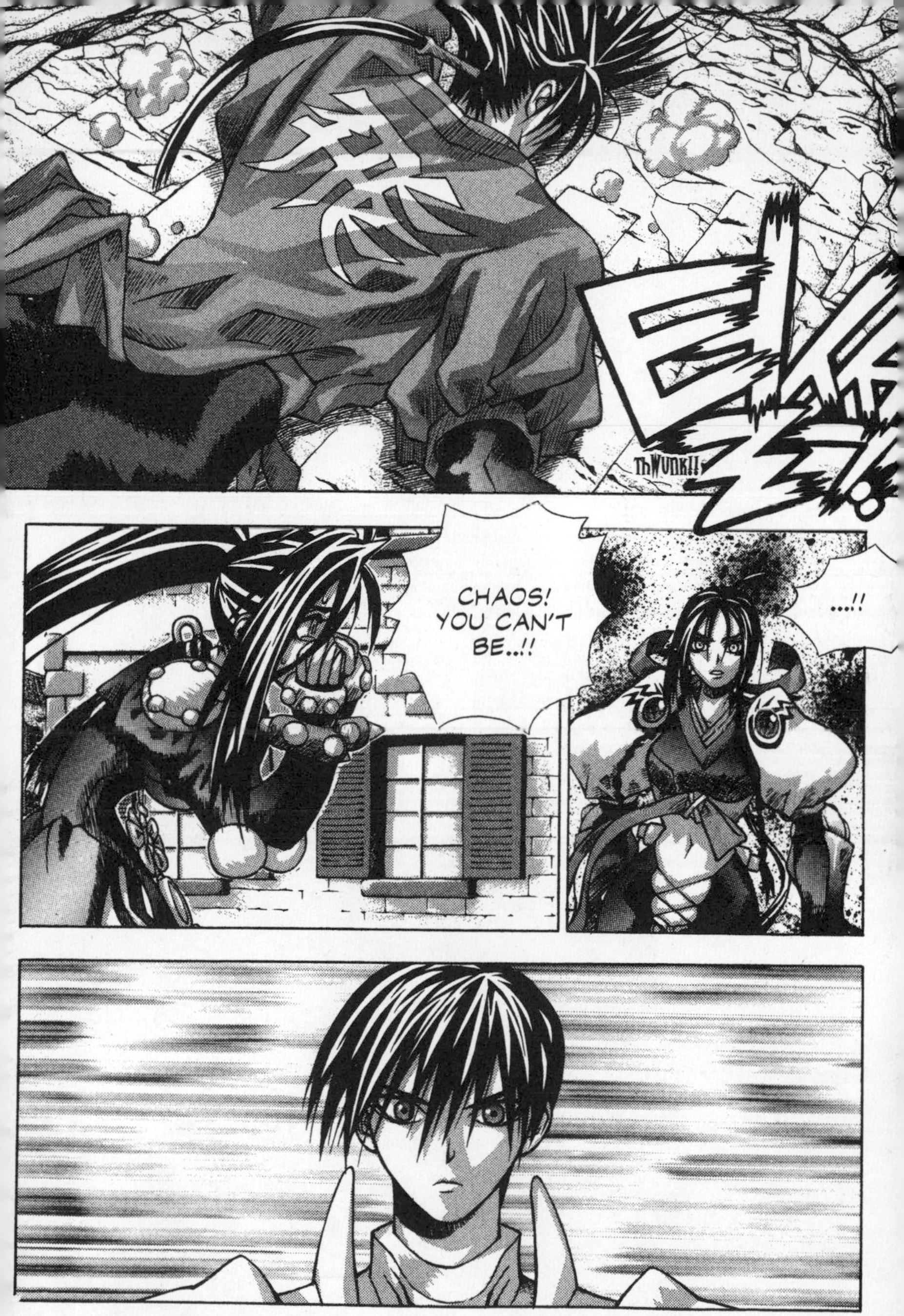
THWUNK!!
CHAOS! YOU CAN'T BE...!!
...!!

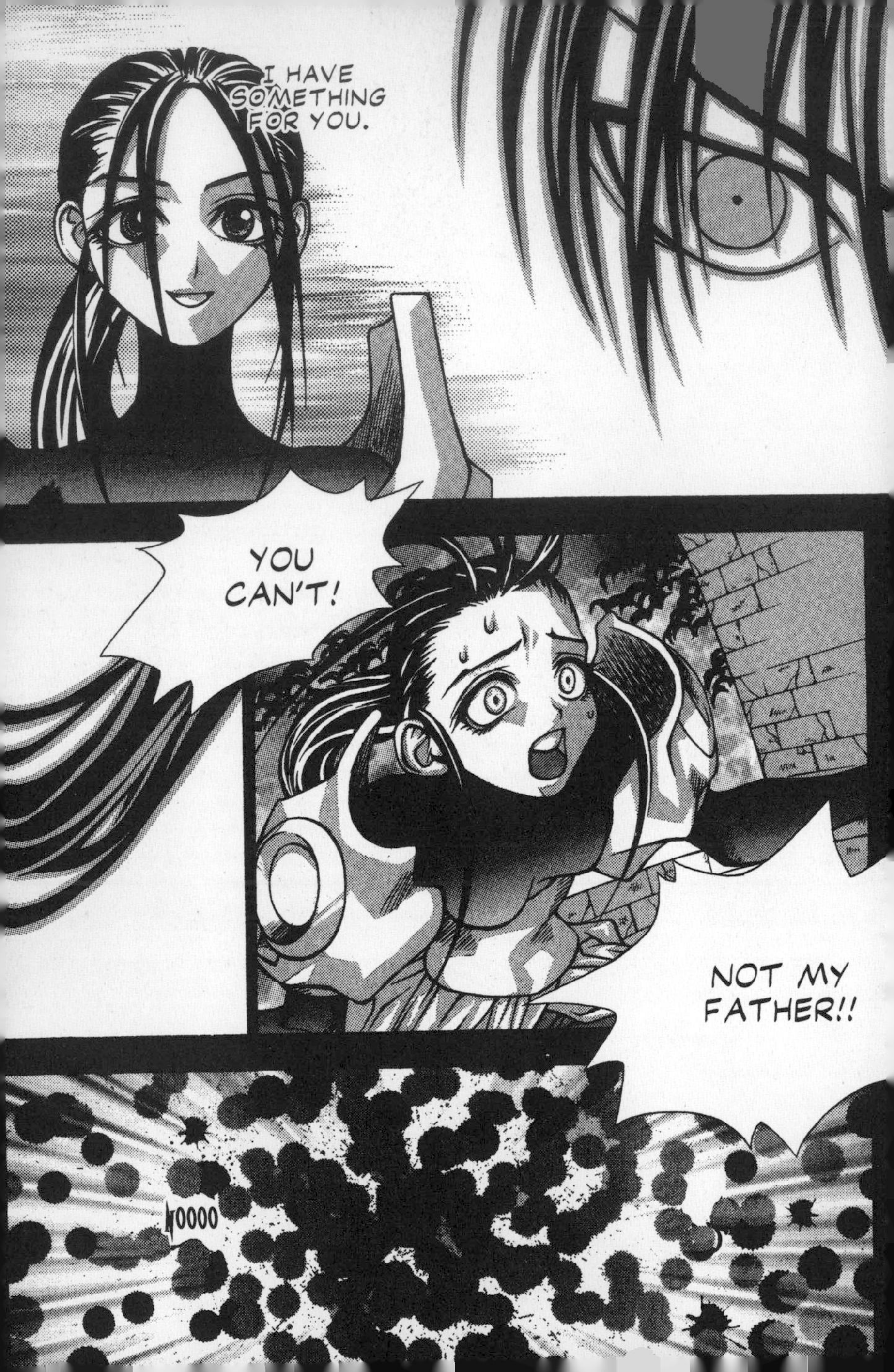
I HAVE SOMETHING FOR YOU.
YOU CAN'T!
NOT MY FATHER!!
NOOOO

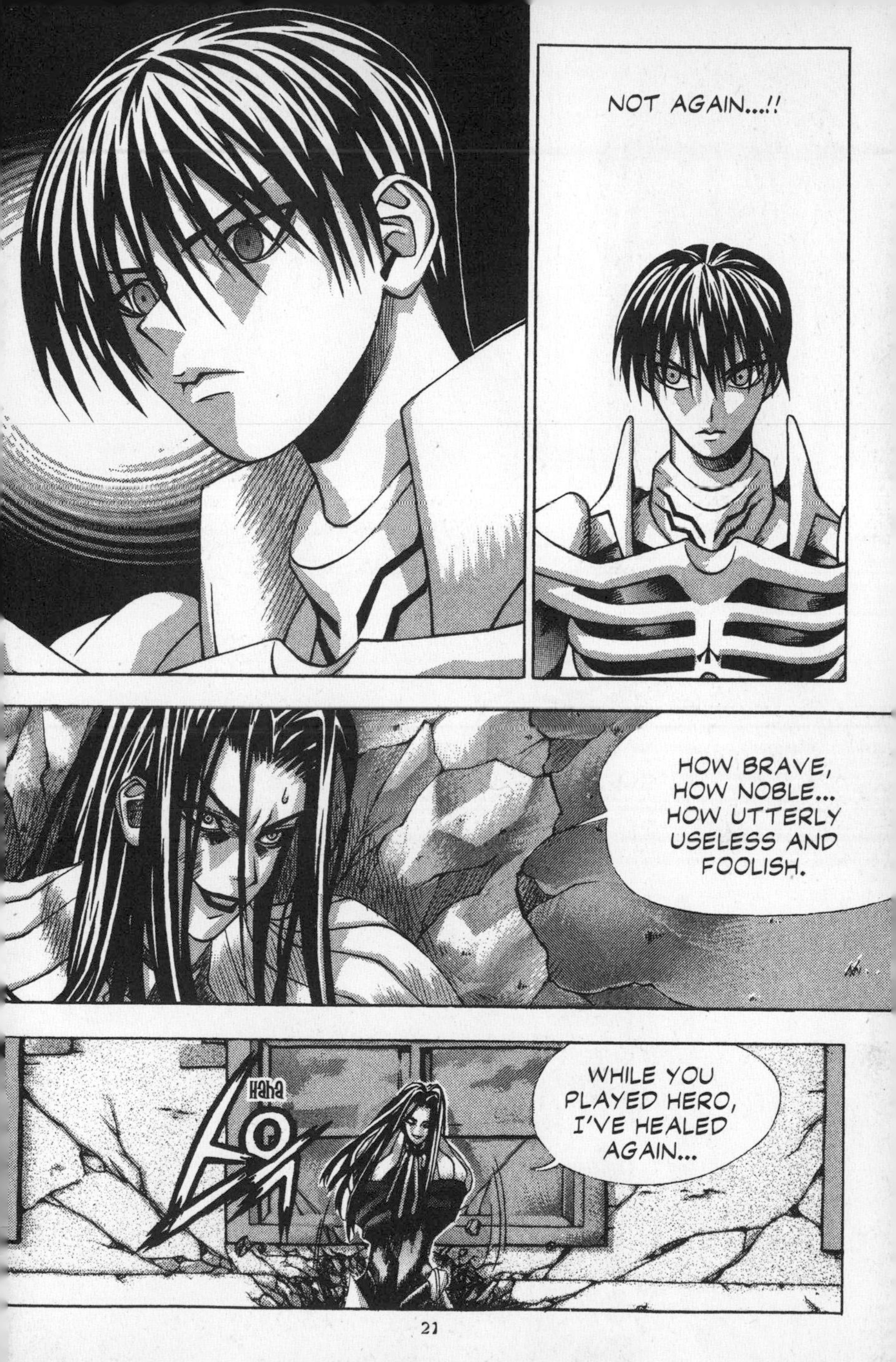
NOT AGAIN...!!
HOW BRAVE, HOW NOBLE... HOW UTTERLY USELESS AND FOOLISH.
HAHA
WHILE YOU PLAYED HERO, I'VE HEALED AGAIN...

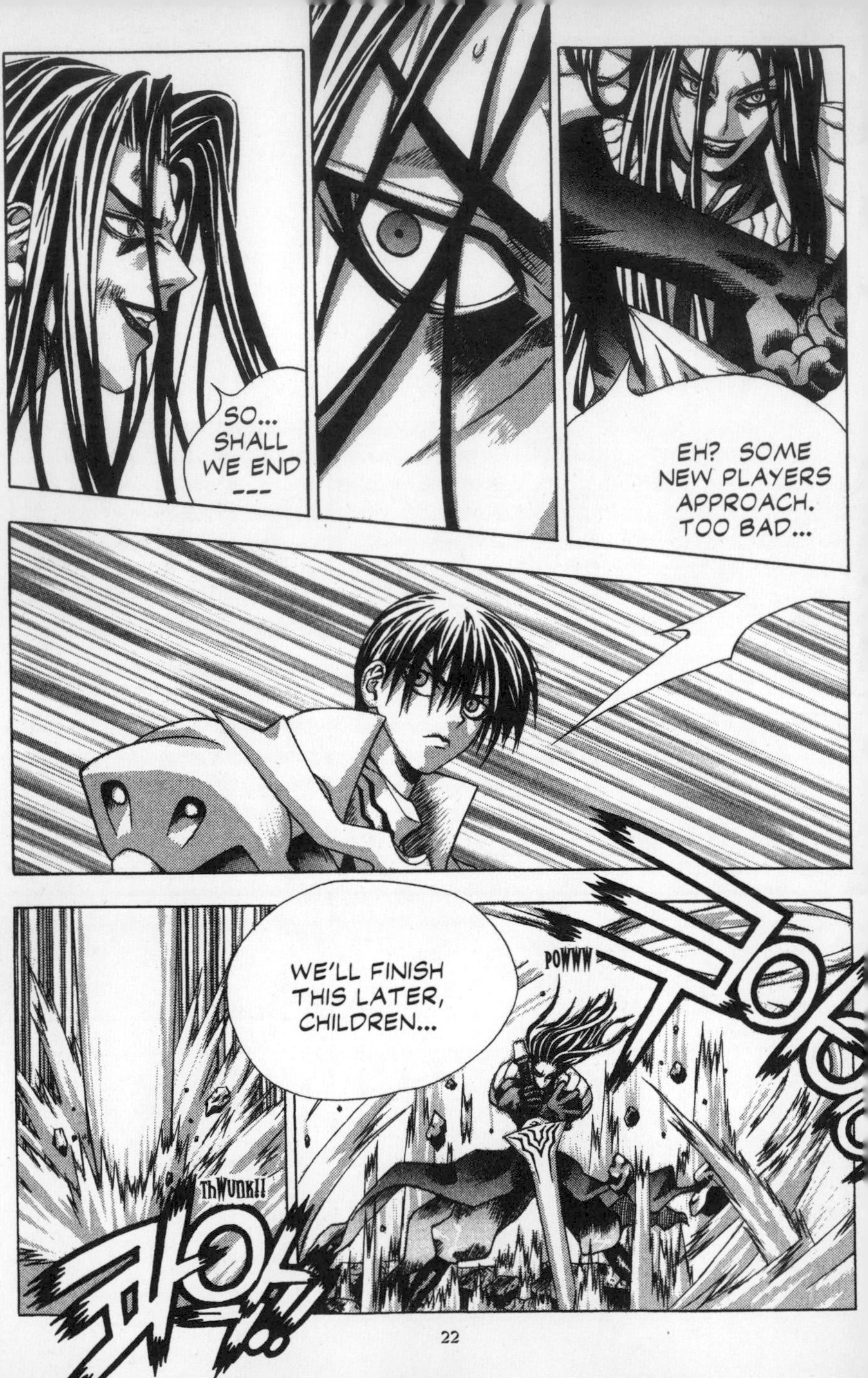
SO... SHALL WE END ---
EH? SOME NEW PLAYERS APPROACH. TOO BAD...
WE'LL FINISH THIS LATER, CHILDREN...
POWWW
ThWUNK!!

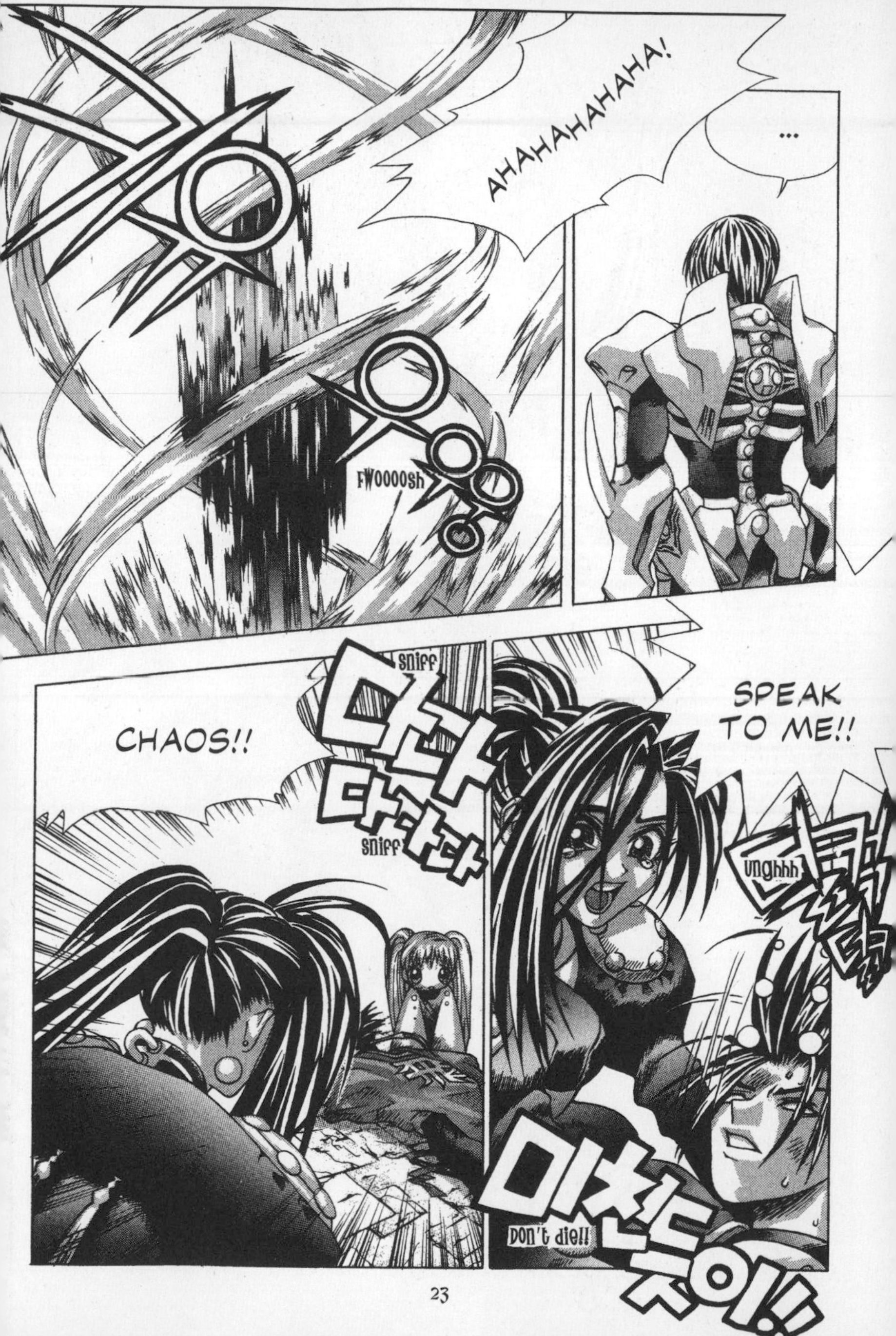
AHAHAHAHAHA!
FWOOOOSH
...
CHAOS!!
SNIFF
SNIFF
SPEAK TO ME!!
UNGHHH
DON'T DIE!!

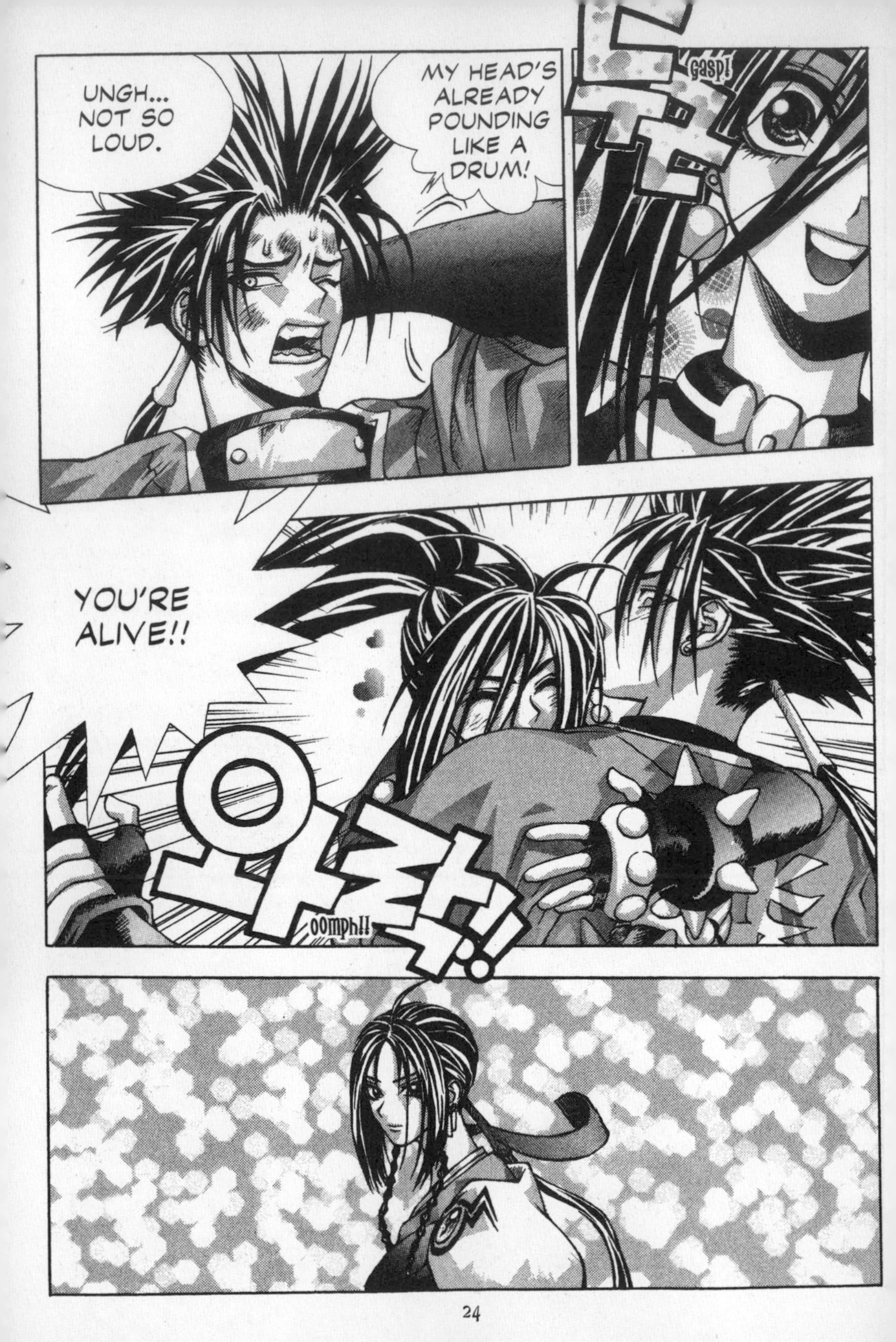
UNGH... NOT SO LOUD.
MY HEAD'S ALREADY POUNDING LIKE A DRUM!
GASP!
YOU'RE ALIVE!!
OOMPH!!

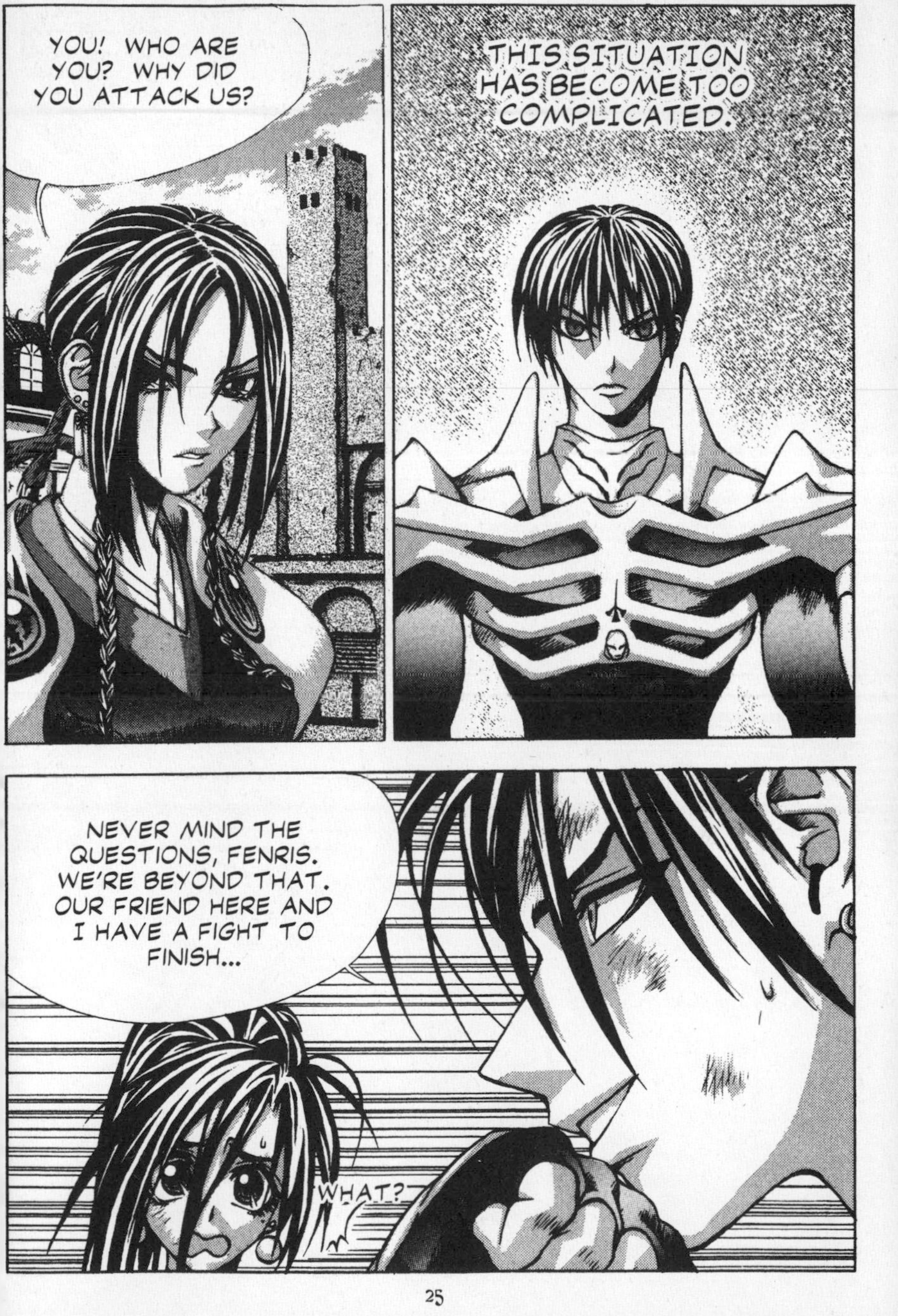
YOU! WHO ARE YOU? WHY DID YOU ATTACK US?
THIS SITUATION HAS BECOME TOO COMPLICATED.
NEVER MIND THE QUESTIONS, FENRIS. WE'RE BEYOND THAT. OUR FRIEND HERE AND I HAVE A FIGHT TO FINISH...
WHAT?

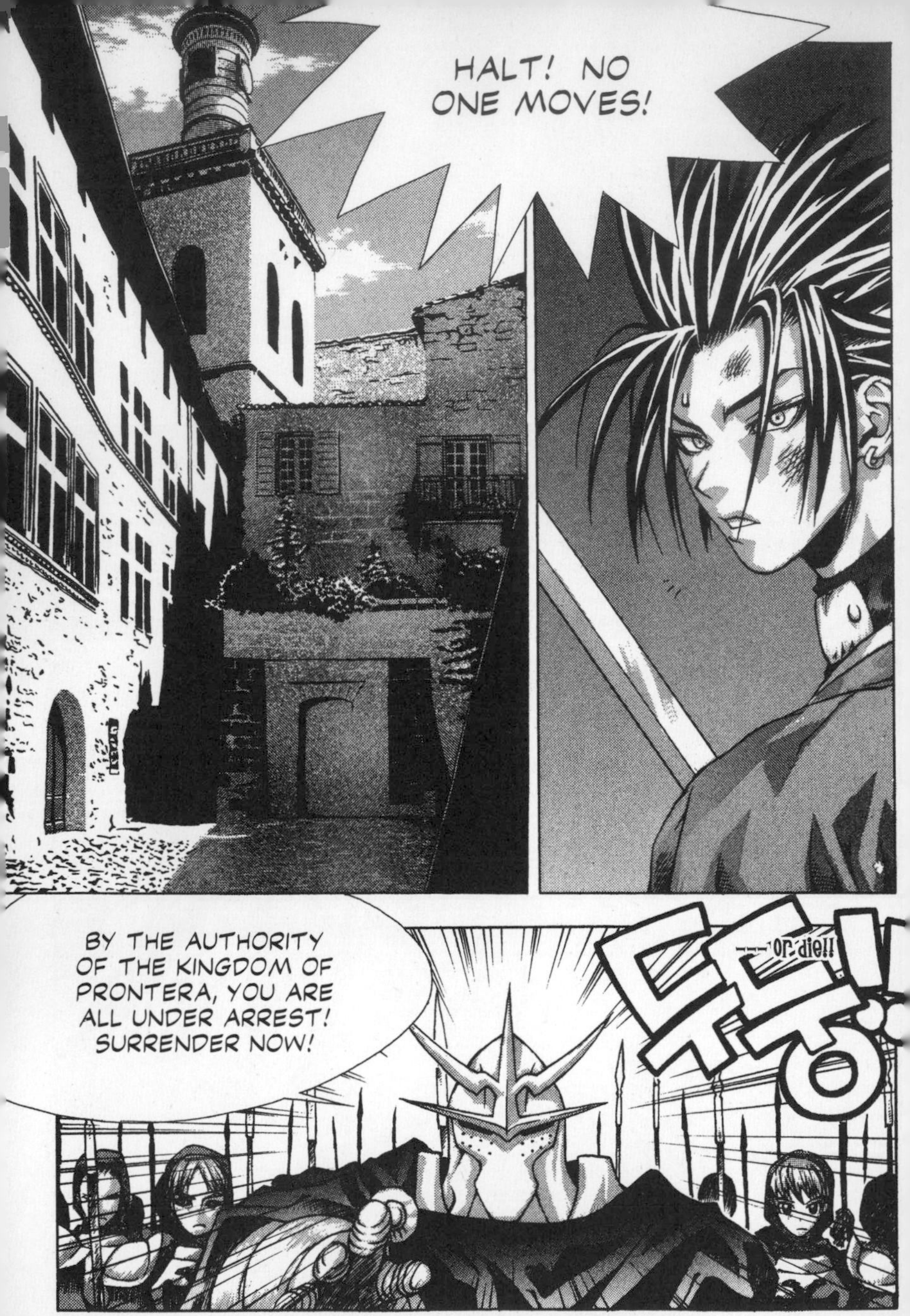
HALT! NO ONE MOVES!
BY THE AUTHORITY OF THE KINGDOM OF PRONTERA, YOU ARE ALL UNDER ARREST! SURRENDER NOW!
---or die!!

RAGNAROK
라그나로크
IN TO THE ABYSS

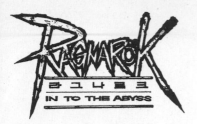

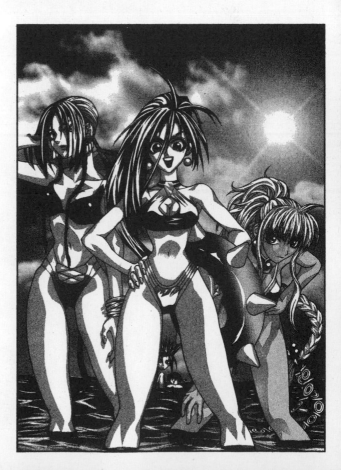

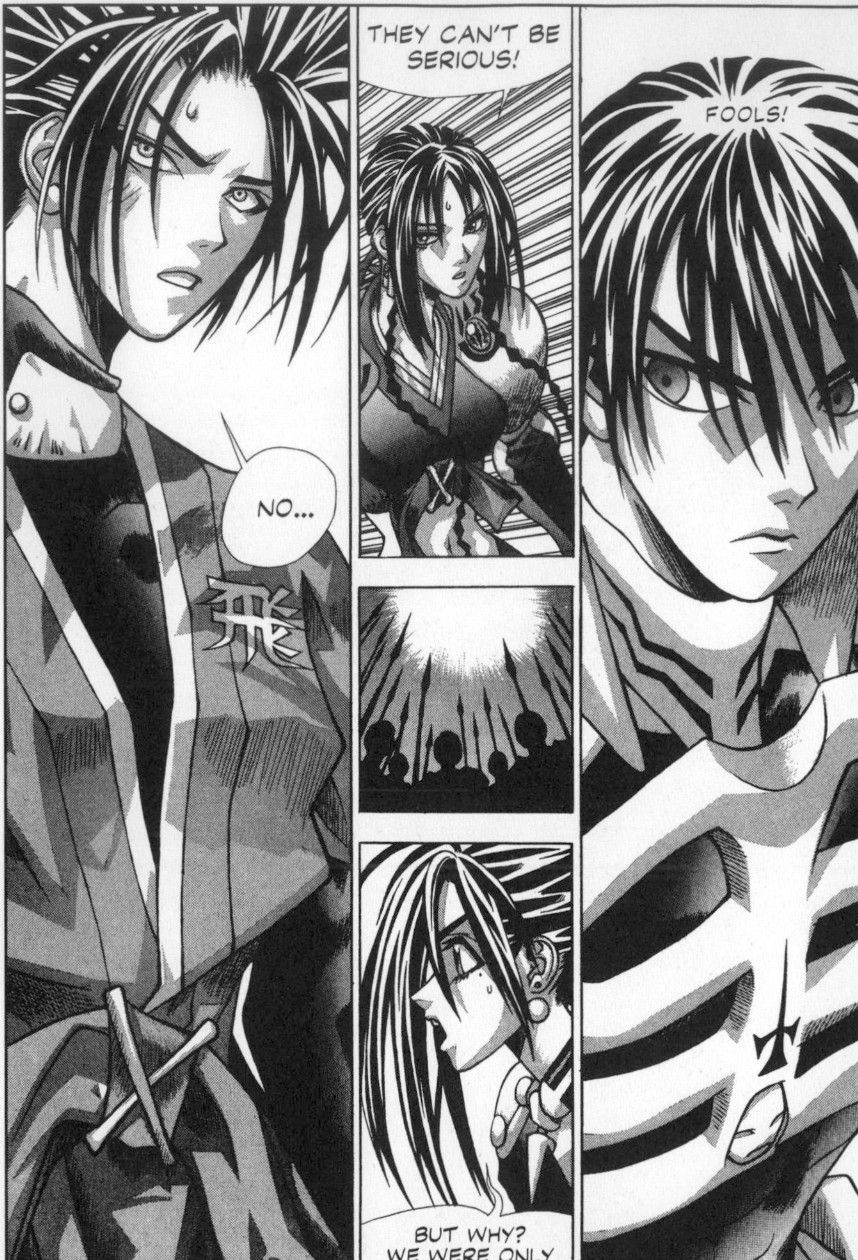
NO...
THEY CAN'T BE SERIOUS!
BUT WHY? WE WERE ONLY TRYING TO HELP!
FOOLS!

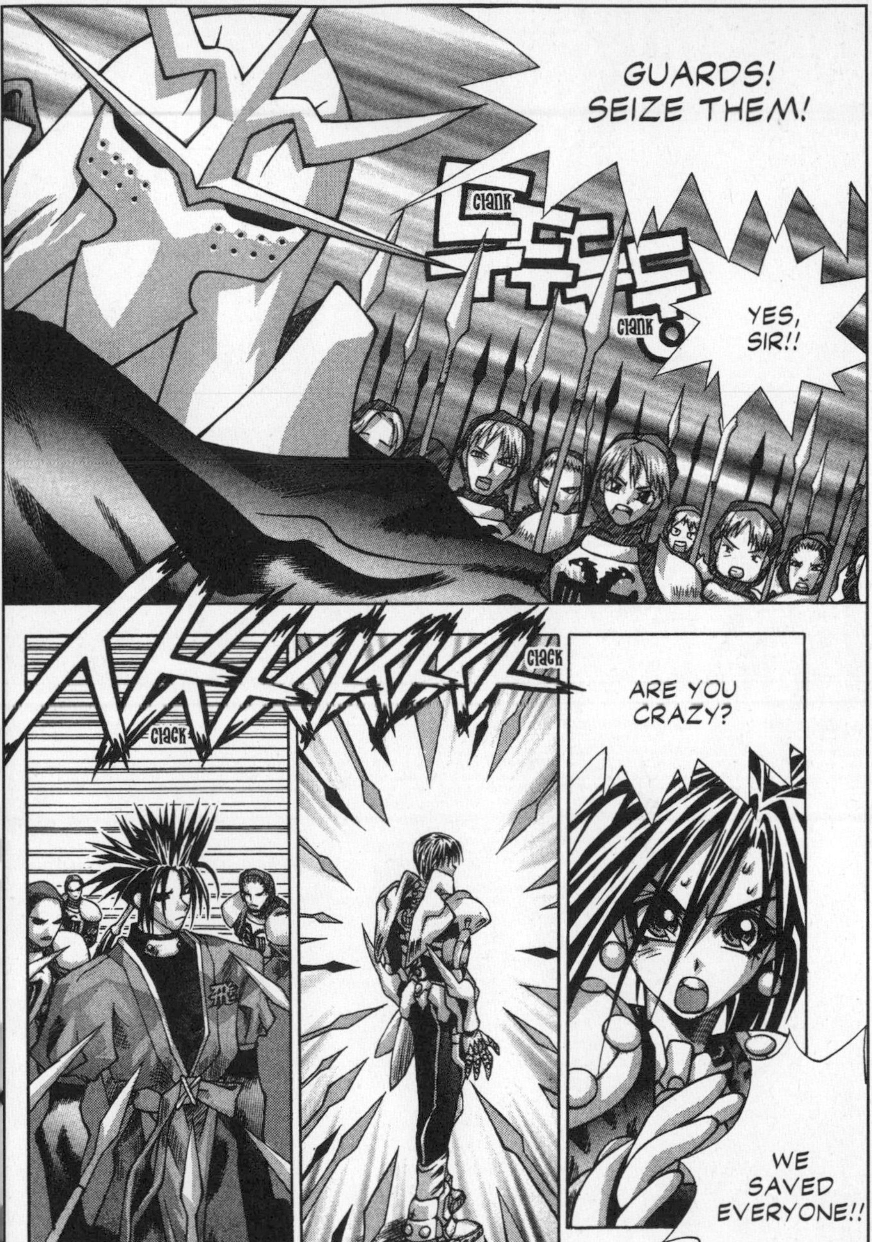
GUARDS! SEIZE THEM!
CLANK
CLANK
YES, SIR!!
CLACK
CLACK
ARE YOU CRAZY?
WE SAVED EVERYONE!!

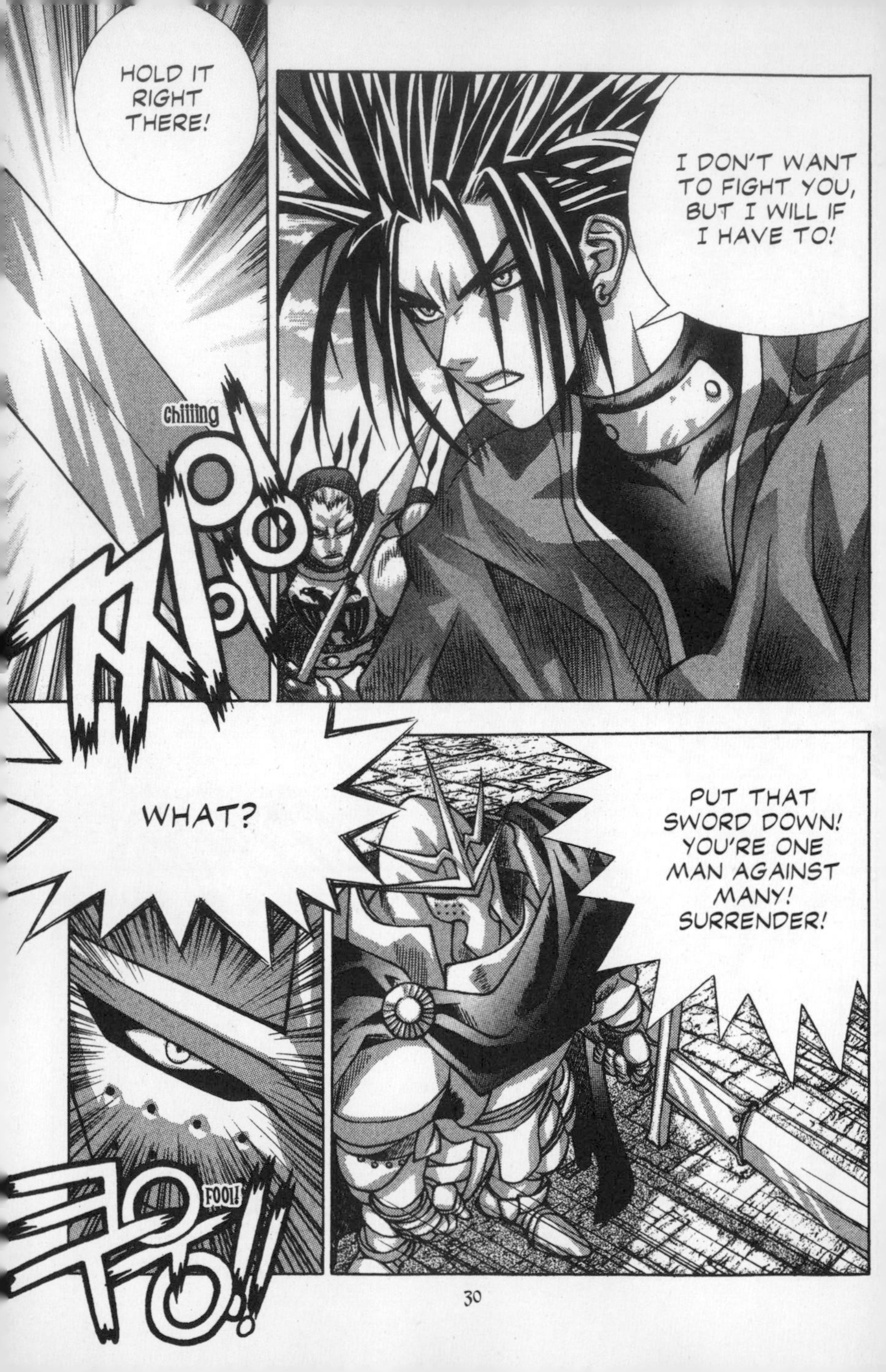
HOLD IT RIGHT THERE!
Chiiiing
I DON'T WANT TO FIGHT YOU, BUT I WILL IF I HAVE TO!
WHAT?
PUT THAT SWORD DOWN! YOU'RE ONE MAN AGAINST MANY! SURRENDER!
FOOL!

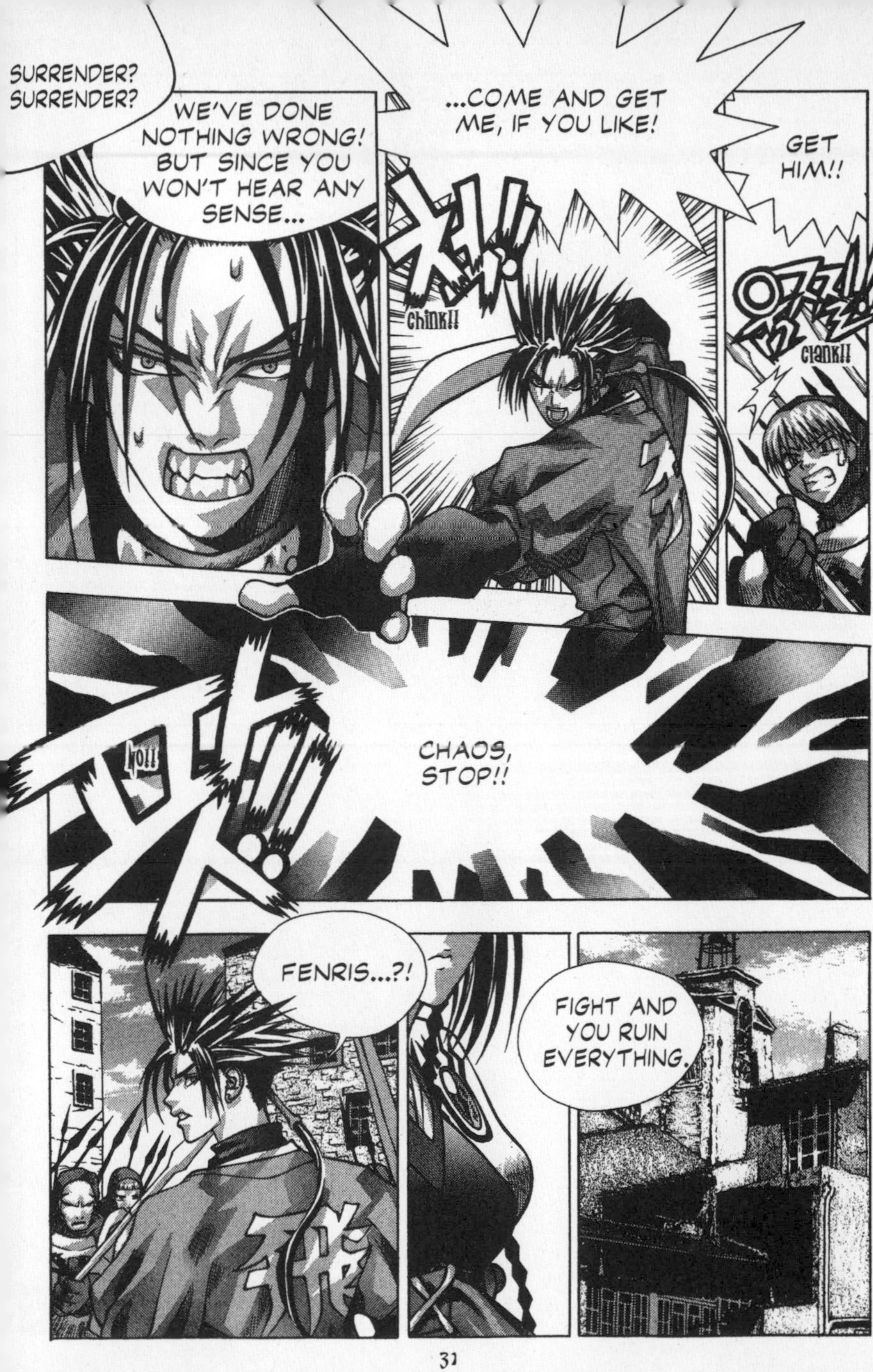
SURRENDER? SURRENDER?
WE'VE DONE NOTHING WRONG! BUT SINCE YOU WON'T HEAR ANY SENSE...
...COME AND GET ME, IF YOU LIKE!
Chink!!
GET HIM!!
Clank!!
NO!!
CHAOS, STOP!!
FENRIS...?!
FIGHT AND YOU RUIN EVERYTHING.

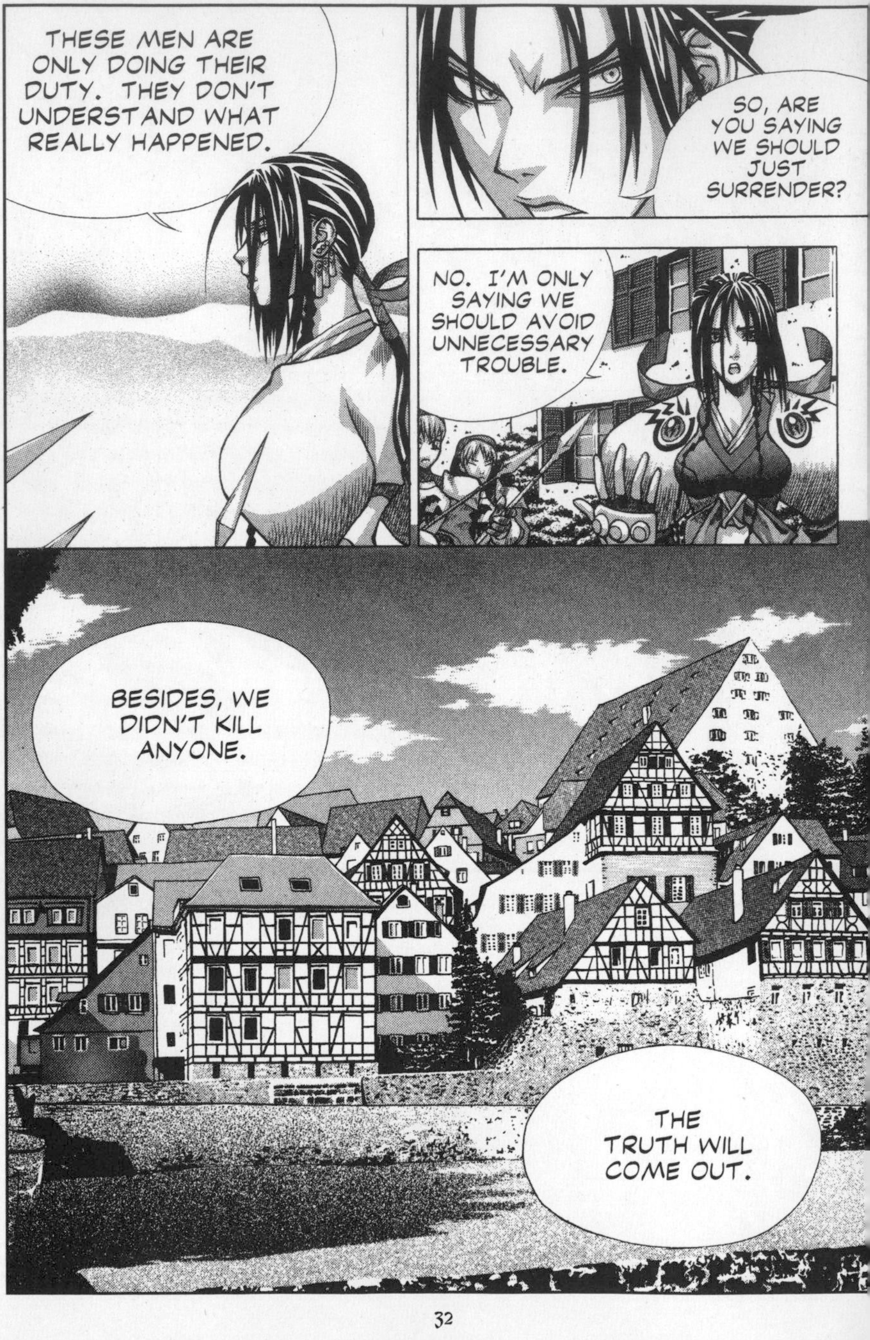
THESE MEN ARE ONLY DOING THEIR DUTY. THEY DON'T UNDERSTAND WHAT REALLY HAPPENED.
SO, ARE YOU SAYING WE SHOULD JUST SURRENDER?
NO. I'M ONLY SAYING WE SHOULD AVOID UNNECESSARY TROUBLE.
BESIDES, WE DIDN'T KILL ANYONE.
THE TRUTH WILL COME OUT.

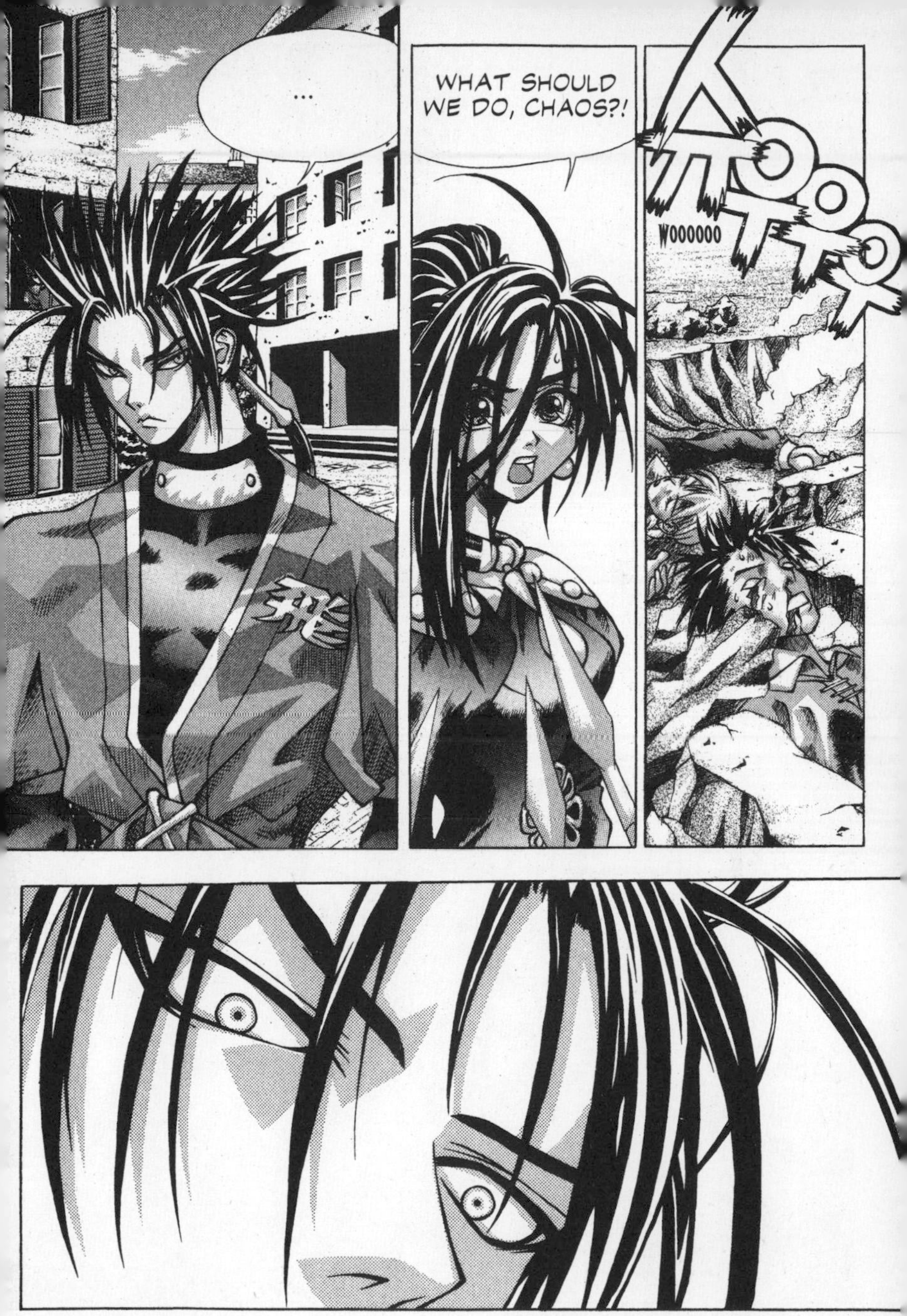
...
WHAT SHOULD WE DO, CHAOS?!
WOOOOOO

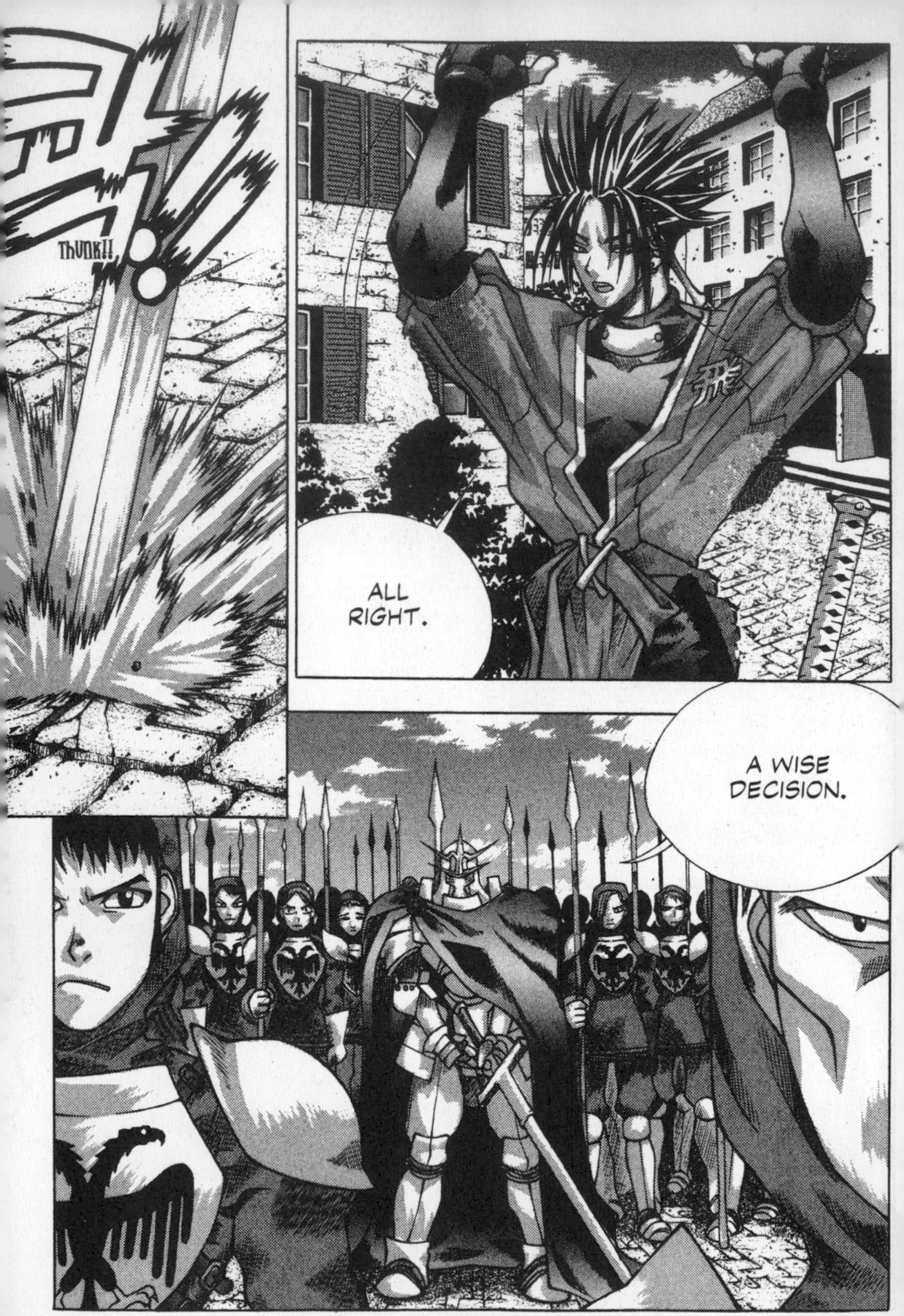
THUNK!!
ALL RIGHT.
A WISE DECISION.

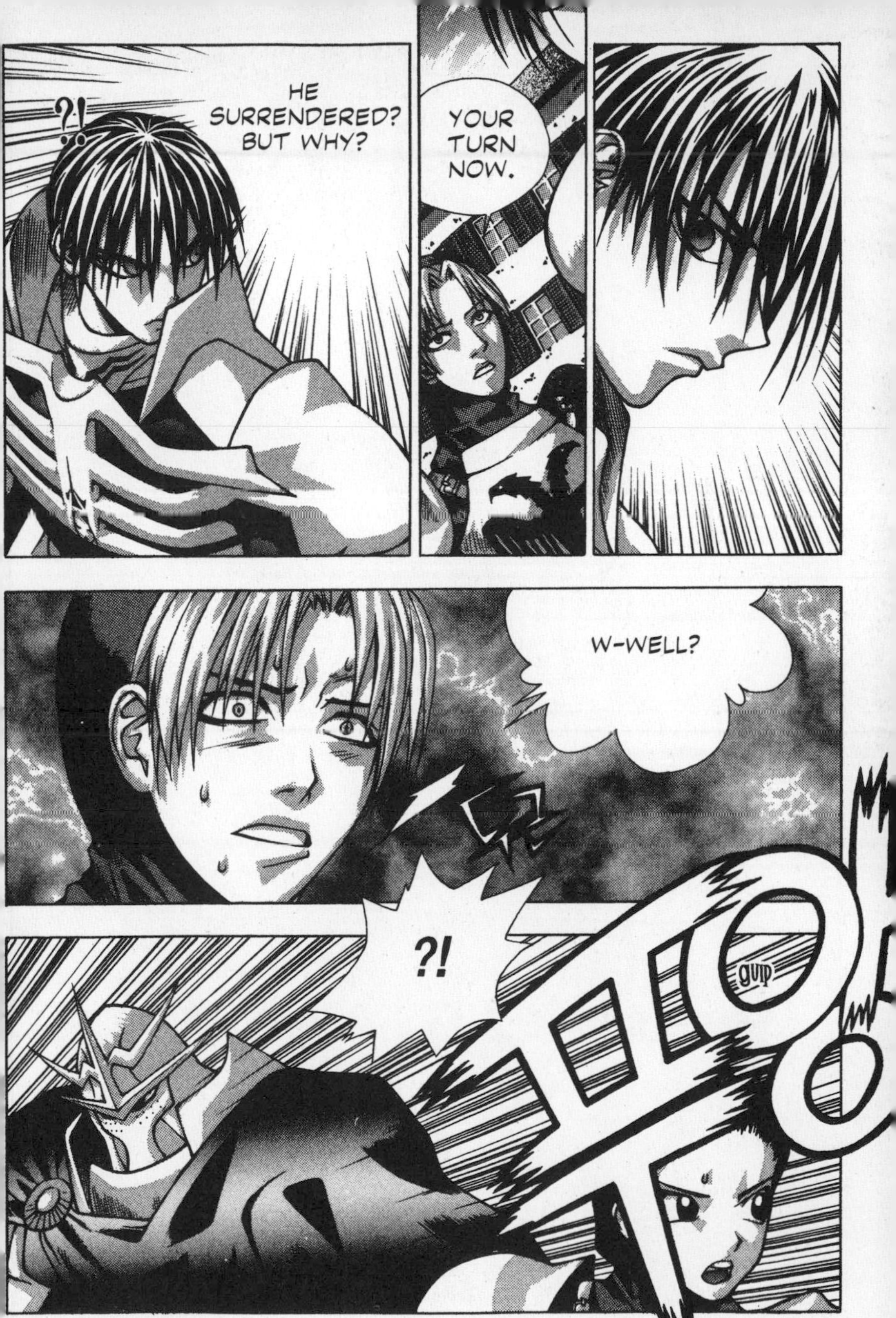
?!
HE SURRENDERED? BUT WHY?
YOUR TURN NOW.
W-WELL?
?!
GULP

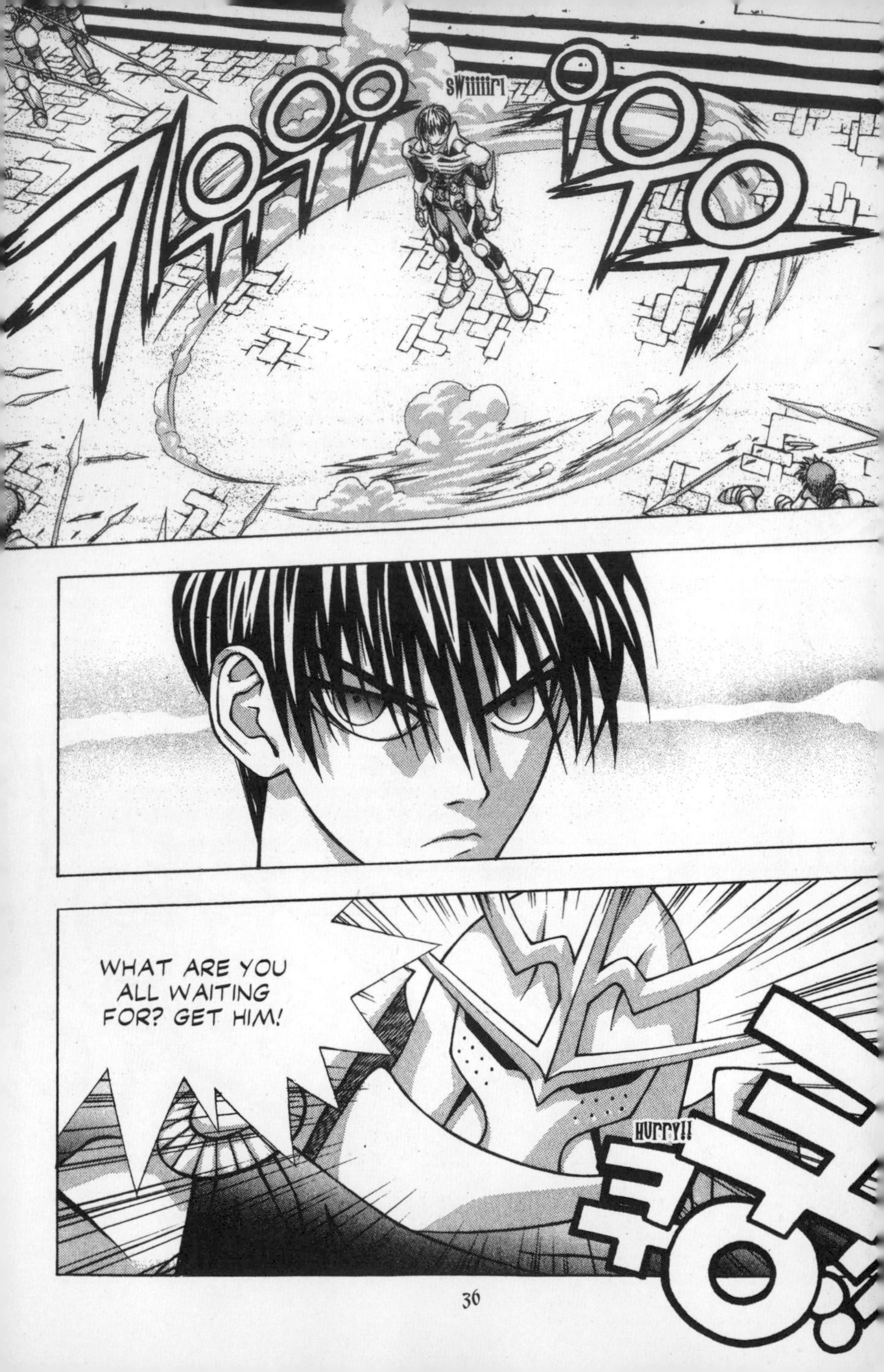
sWiiiiirl
WHAT ARE YOU ALL WAITING FOR? GET HIM!
HUrry!!

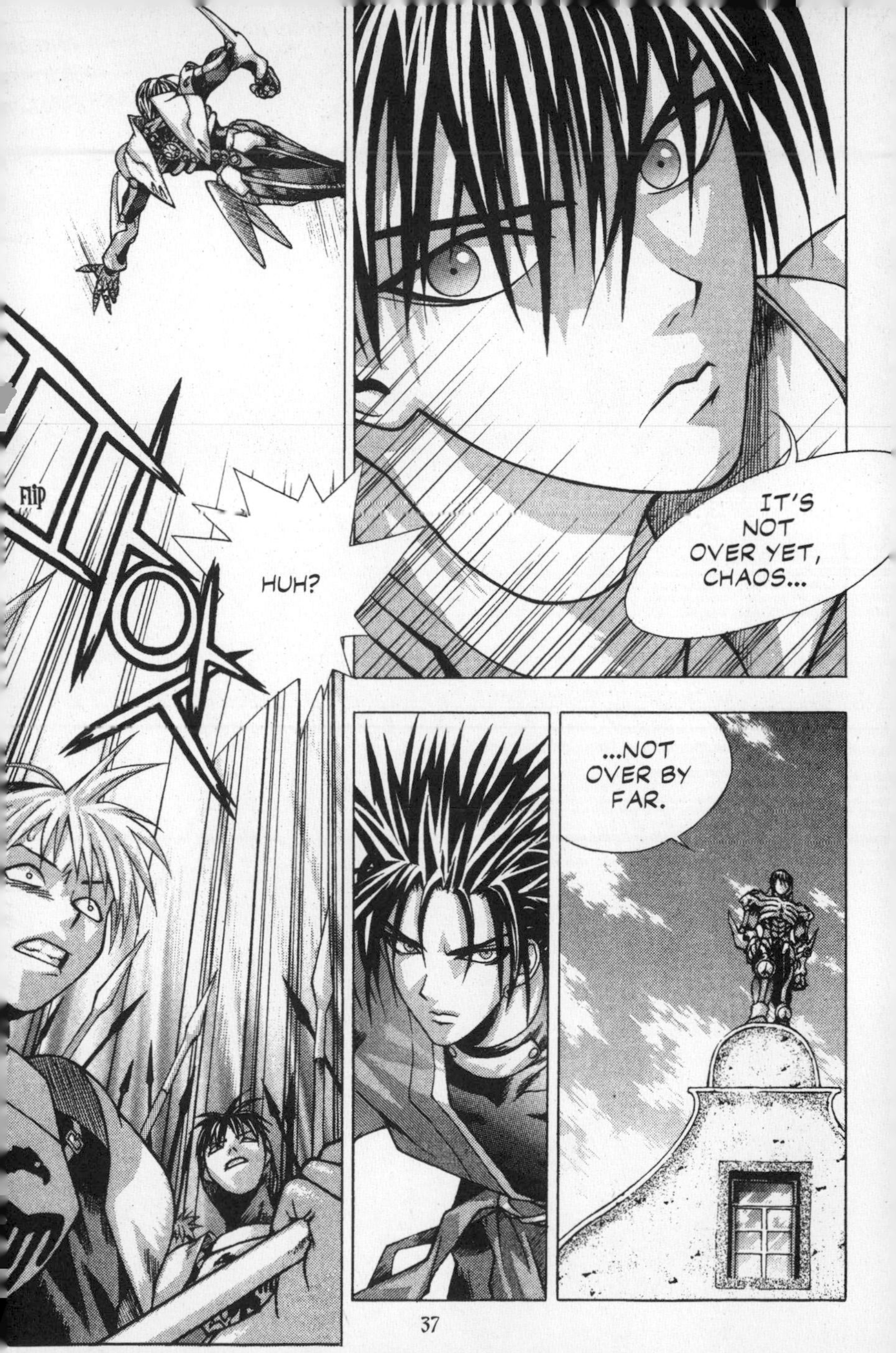

Flip
HUH?
IT'S NOT OVER YET, CHAOS...
...NOT OVER BY FAR.

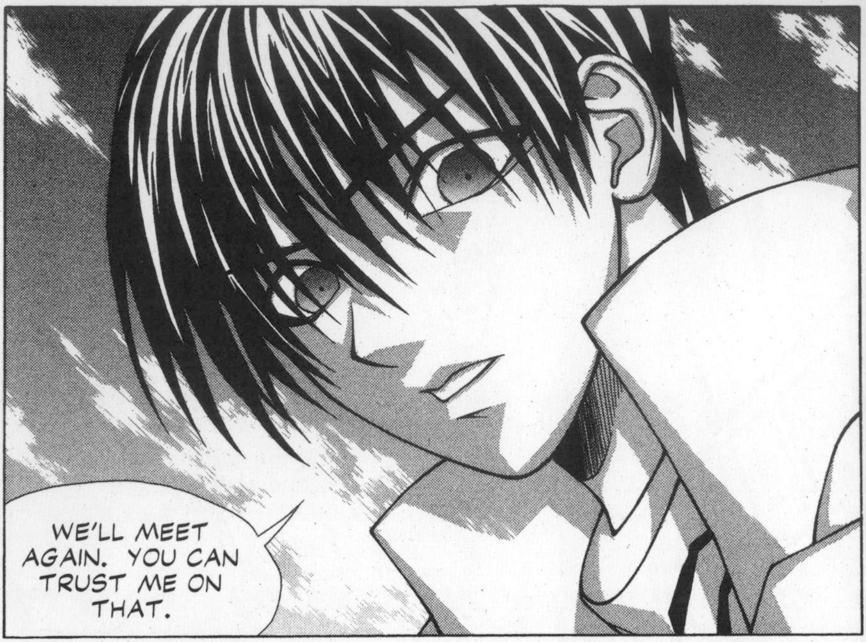
WE'LL MEET AGAIN. YOU CAN TRUST ME ON THAT.

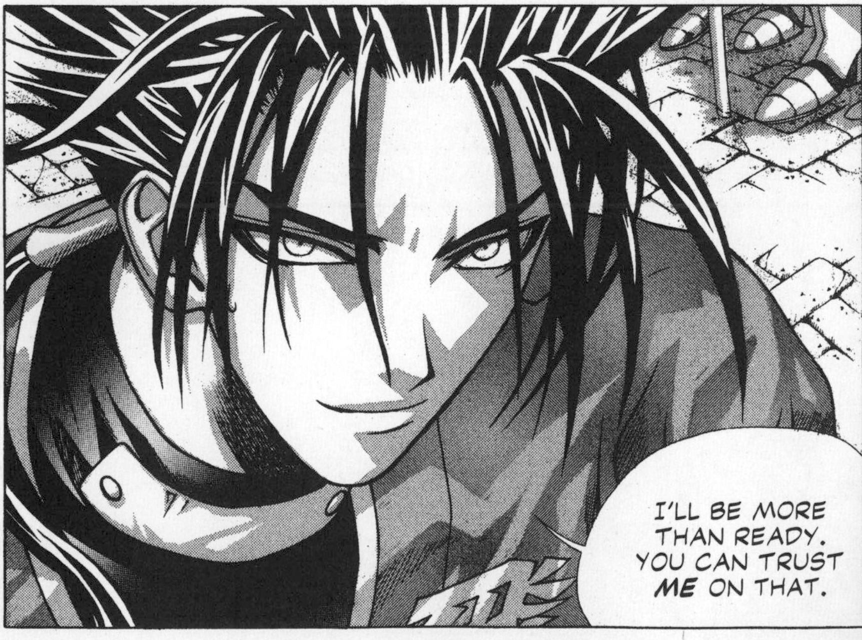
I'LL BE MORE THAN READY. YOU CAN TRUST *ME* ON THAT.

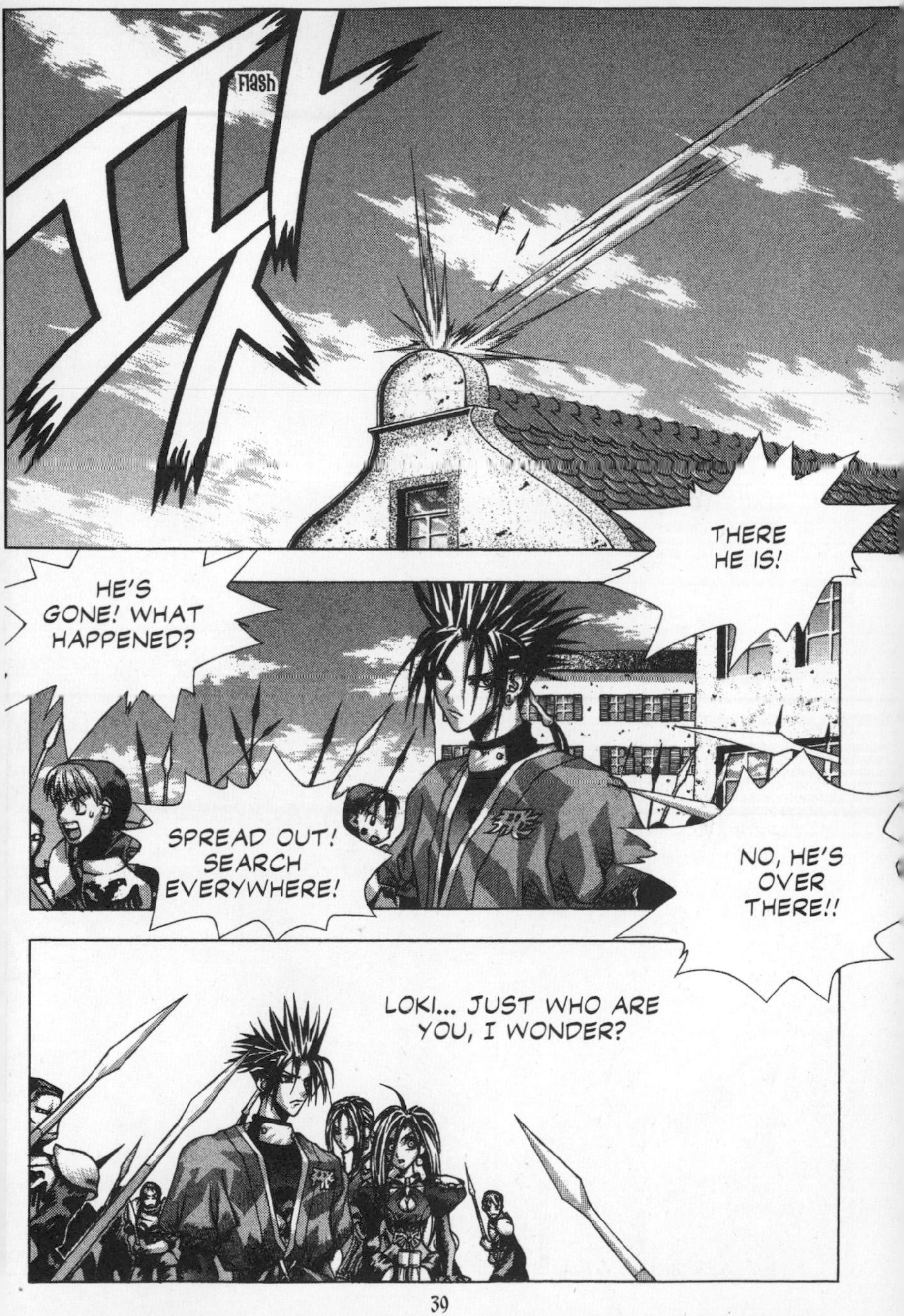
Flash
THERE HE IS!
HE'S GONE! WHAT HAPPENED?
SPREAD OUT! SEARCH EVERYWHERE!
NO, HE'S OVER THERE!!
LOKI... JUST WHO ARE YOU, I WONDER?

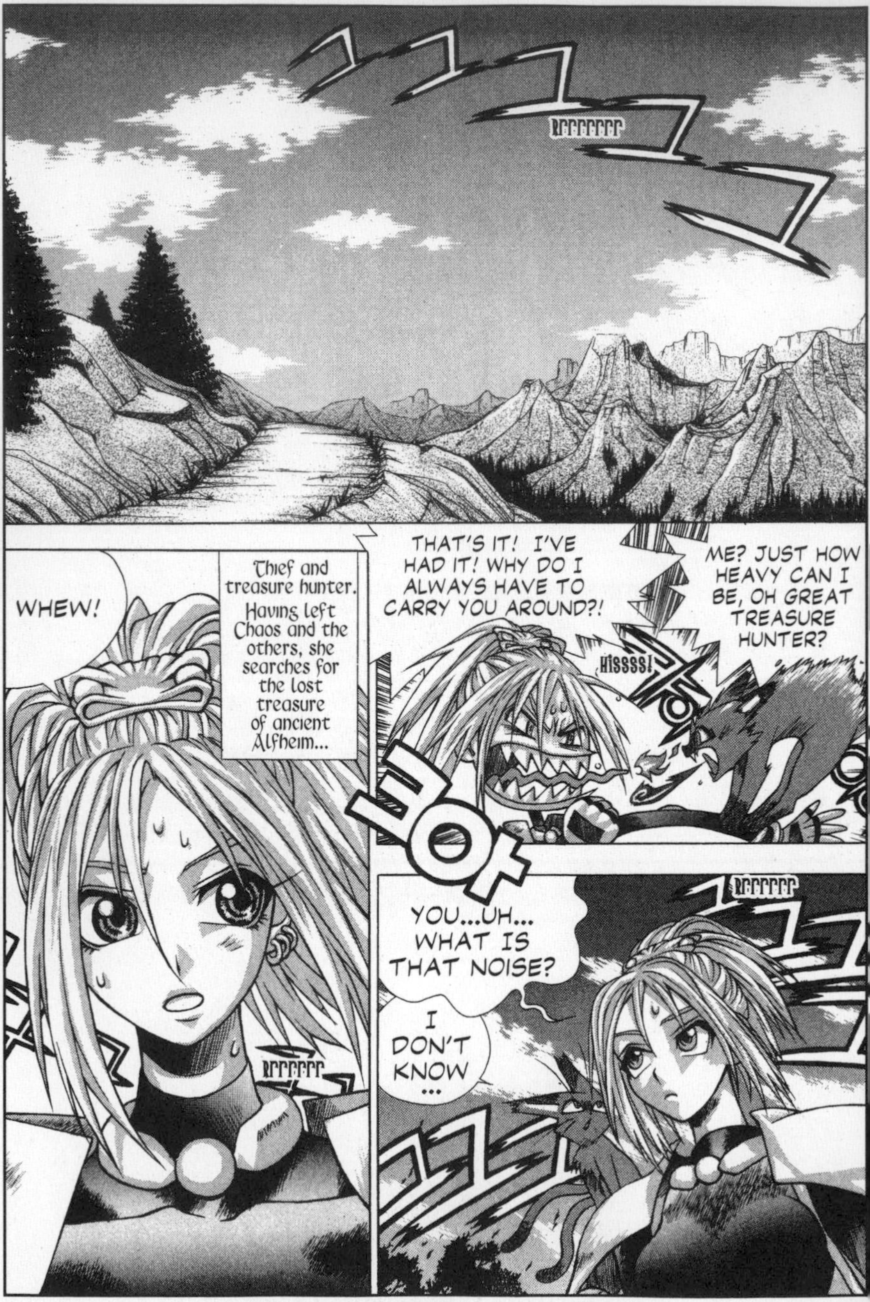

RRRRRRR
WHEW!
Thief and treasure hunter. Having left Chaos and the others, she searches for the lost treasure of ancient Alfheim...
RRRRRRR
THAT'S IT! I'VE HAD IT! WHY DO I ALWAYS HAVE TO CARRY YOU AROUND?!
HISSSS!
ME? JUST HOW HEAVY CAN I BE, OH GREAT TREASURE HUNTER?
BOT
RRRRRR
YOU...UH... WHAT IS THAT NOISE?
I DON'T KNOW ...

RAGNAROK
라그나로크
IN TO THE ABYSS

CHAOS
THE RUNE KNIGHT
STUDIO
DIVE TO DREAM SEA

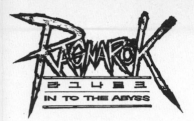

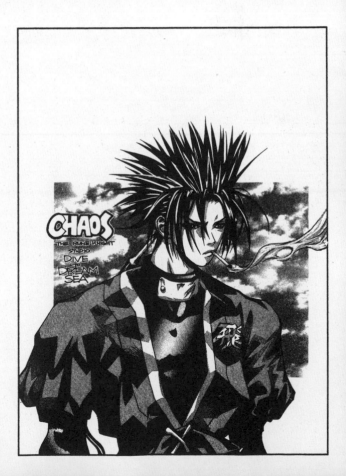

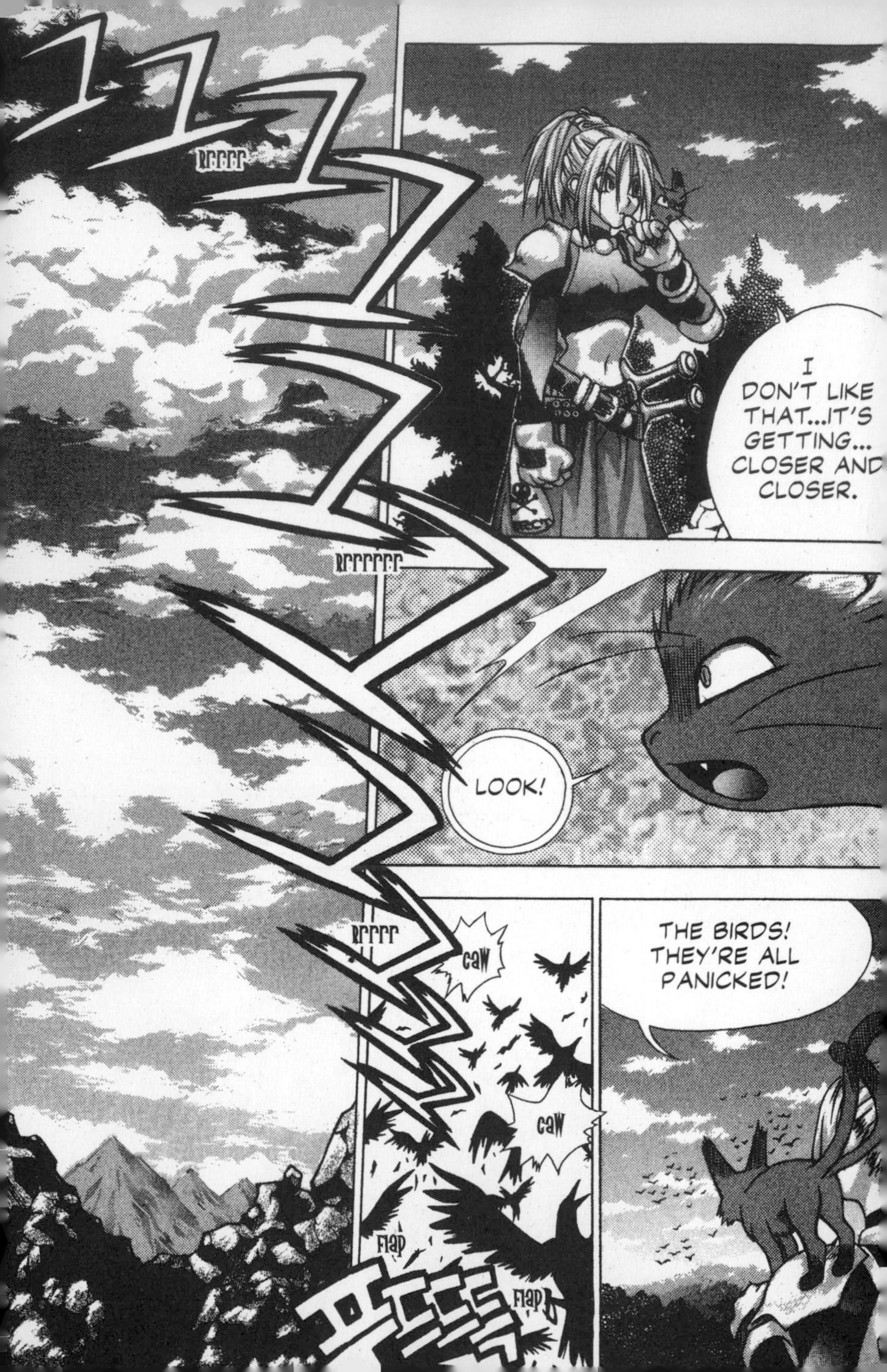
BRRRR
BRRRRRR
I DON'T LIKE THAT...IT'S GETTING... CLOSER AND CLOSER.
LOOK!
BRRRR
CAW
CAW
FLAP
FLAP
THE BIRDS! THEY'RE ALL PANICKED!

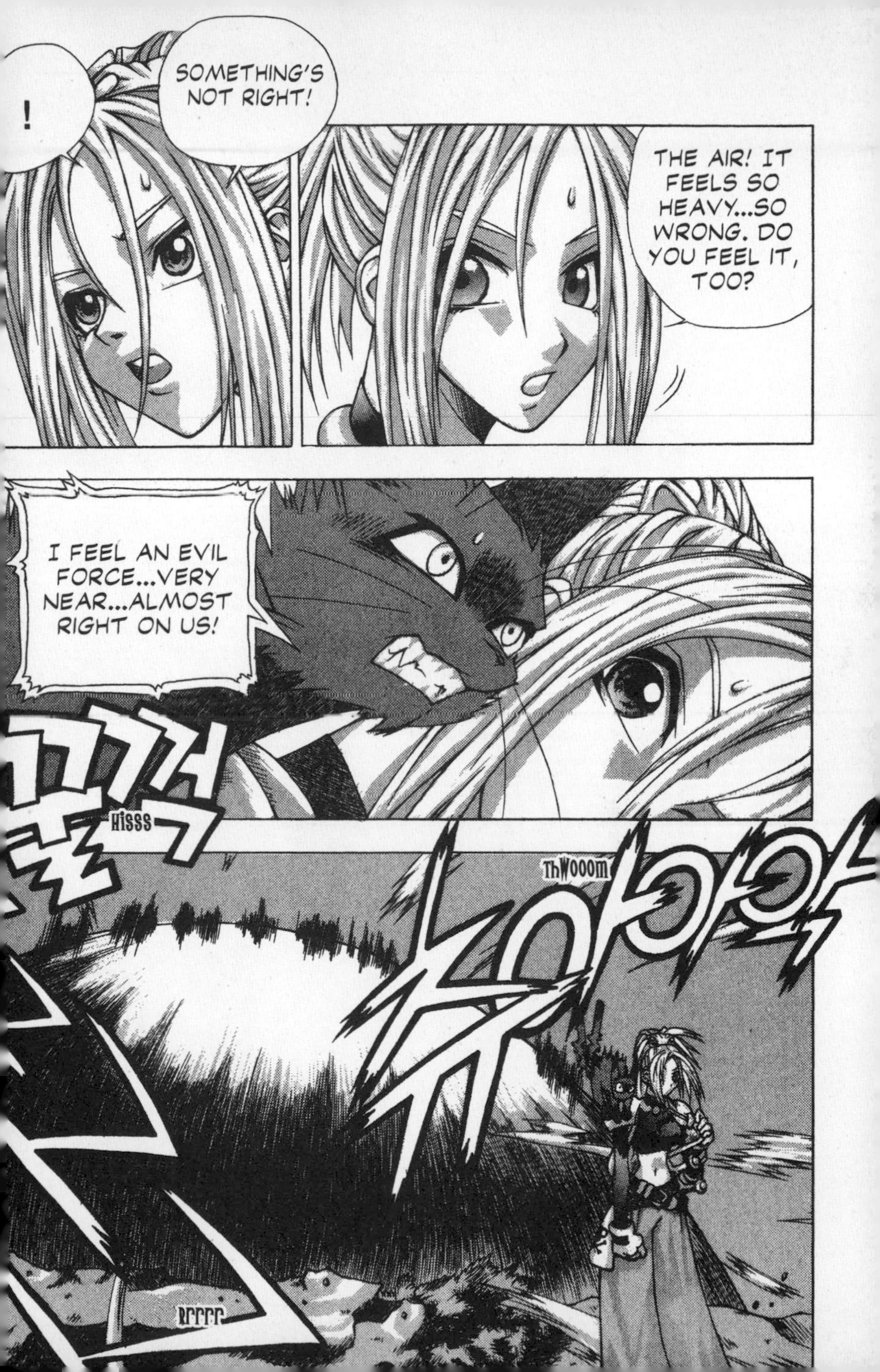
!
SOMETHING'S NOT RIGHT!
THE AIR! IT FEELS SO HEAVY...SO WRONG. DO YOU FEEL IT, TOO?
I FEEL AN EVIL FORCE...VERY NEAR...ALMOST RIGHT ON US!
HISSS
ThWOOOM
RRRRR

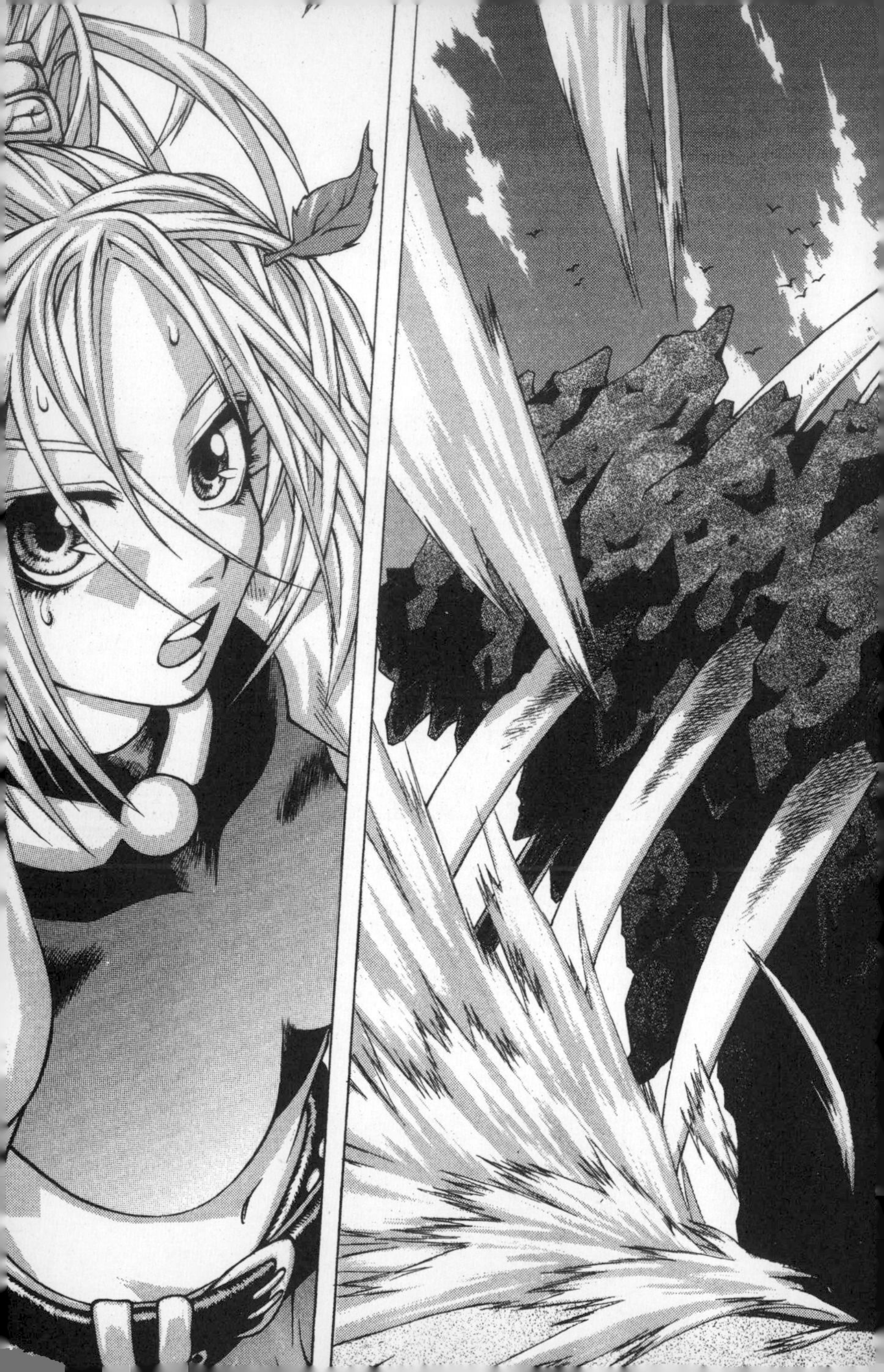

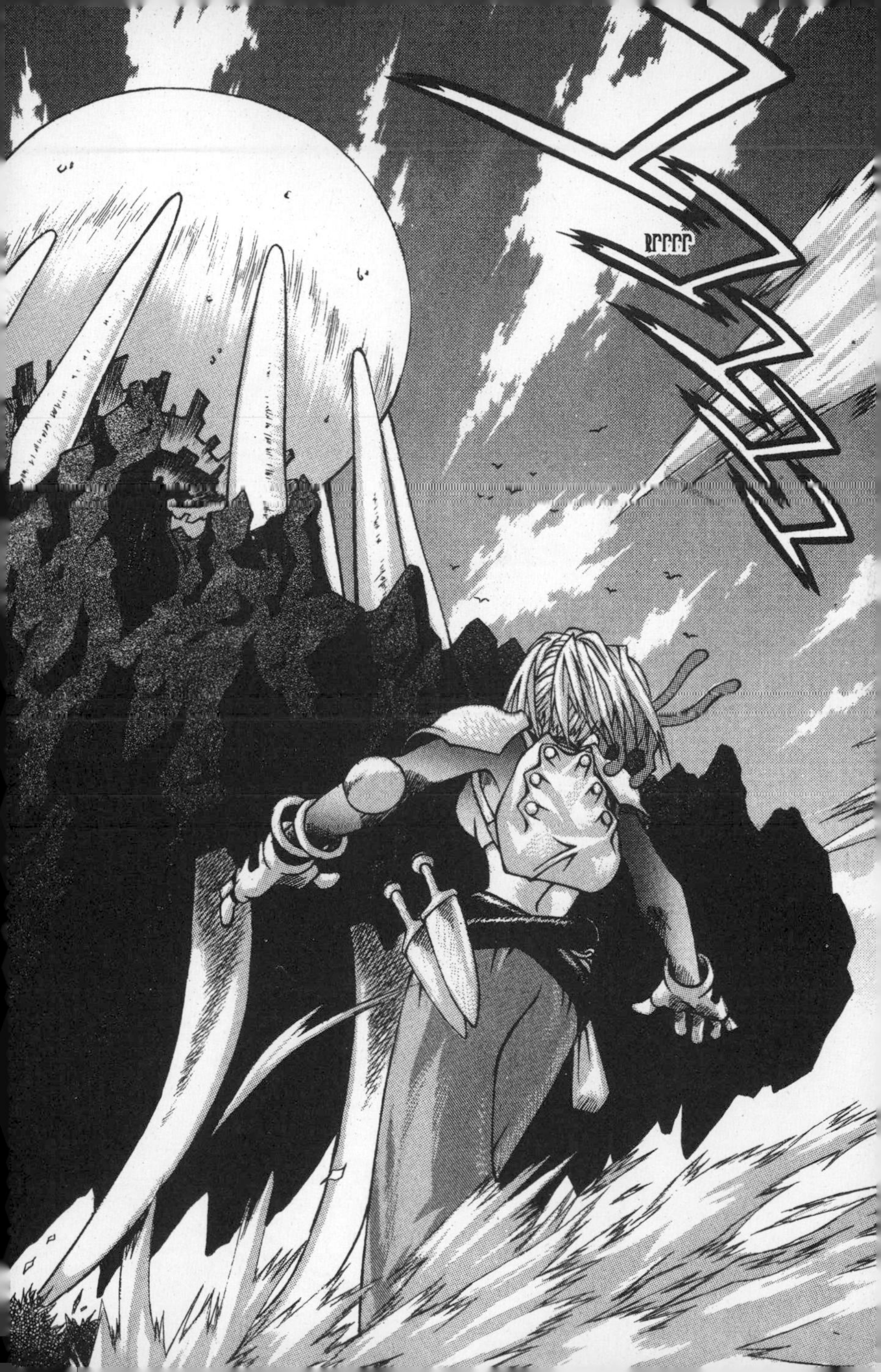
Rrrrr

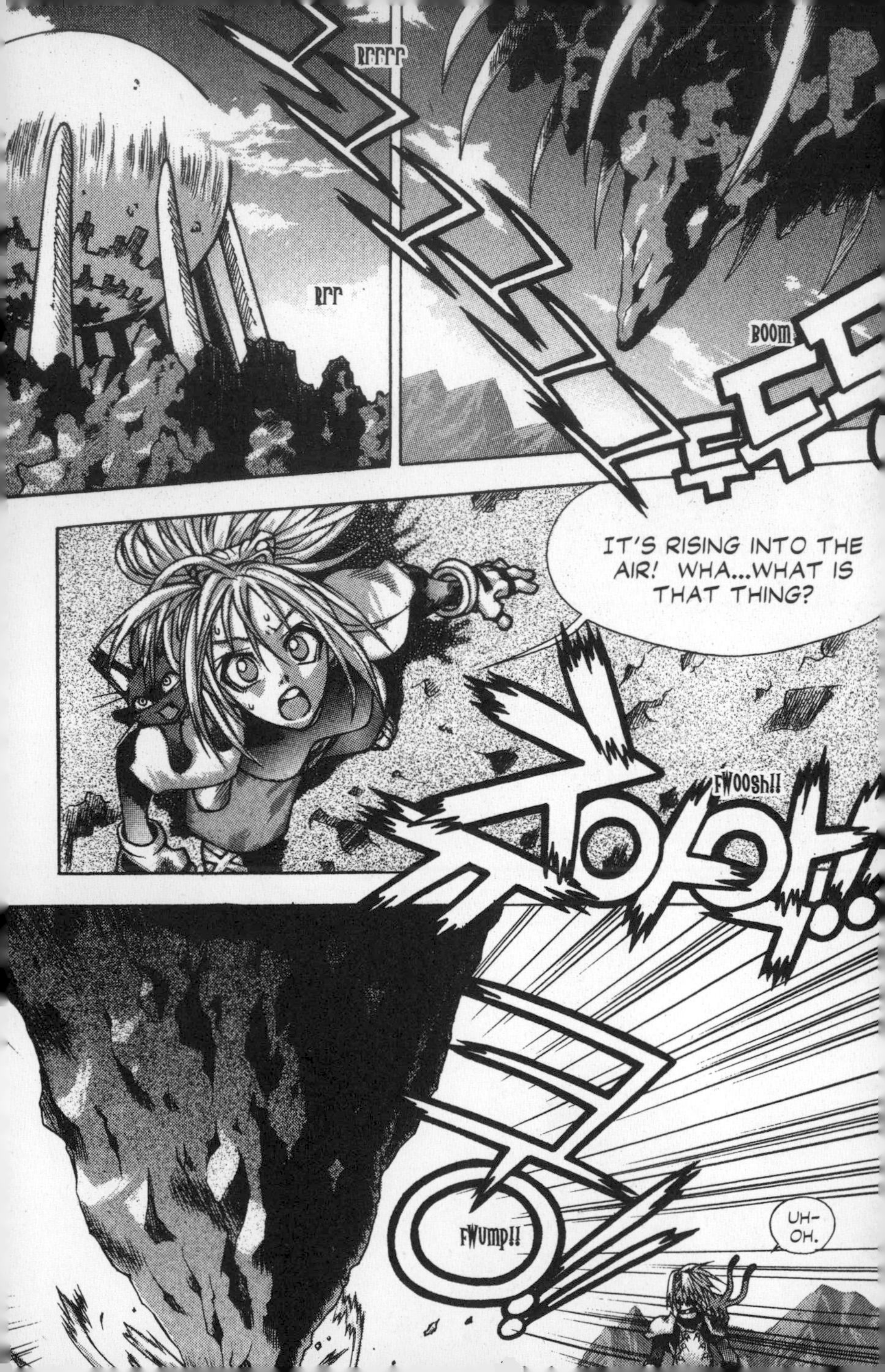
RRRRR
RRR
BOOM
IT'S RISING INTO THE AIR! WHA...WHAT IS THAT THING?
FWOOSH!!
FWUMP!!
UH-OH.

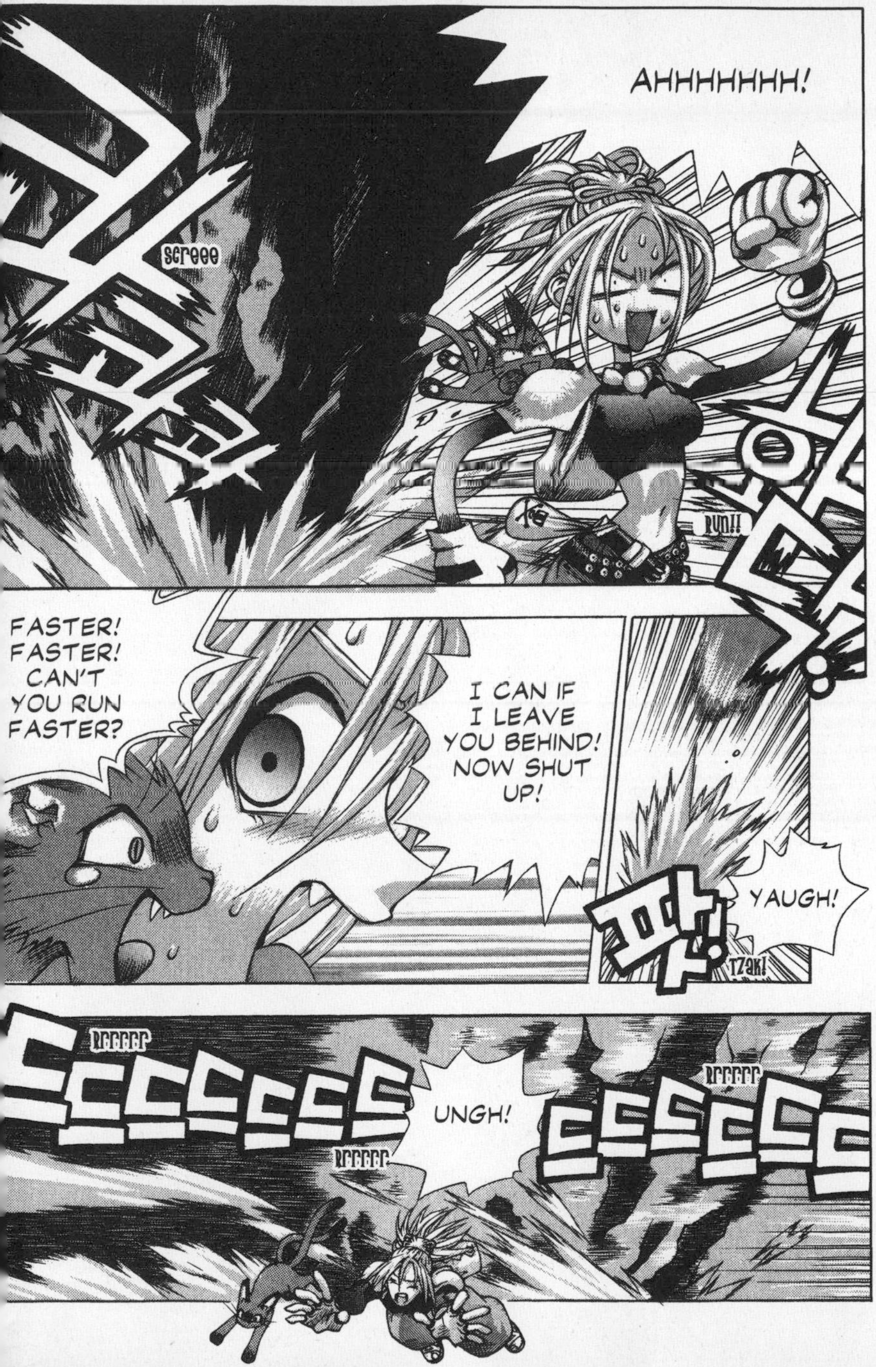
SCREEE
AHHHHHHH!
RUN!!
FASTER! FASTER! CAN'T YOU RUN FASTER?
I CAN IF I LEAVE YOU BEHIND! NOW SHUT UP!
YAUGH!
TZAK!
RRRRRR
RRRRRR
UNGH!
RRRRRR

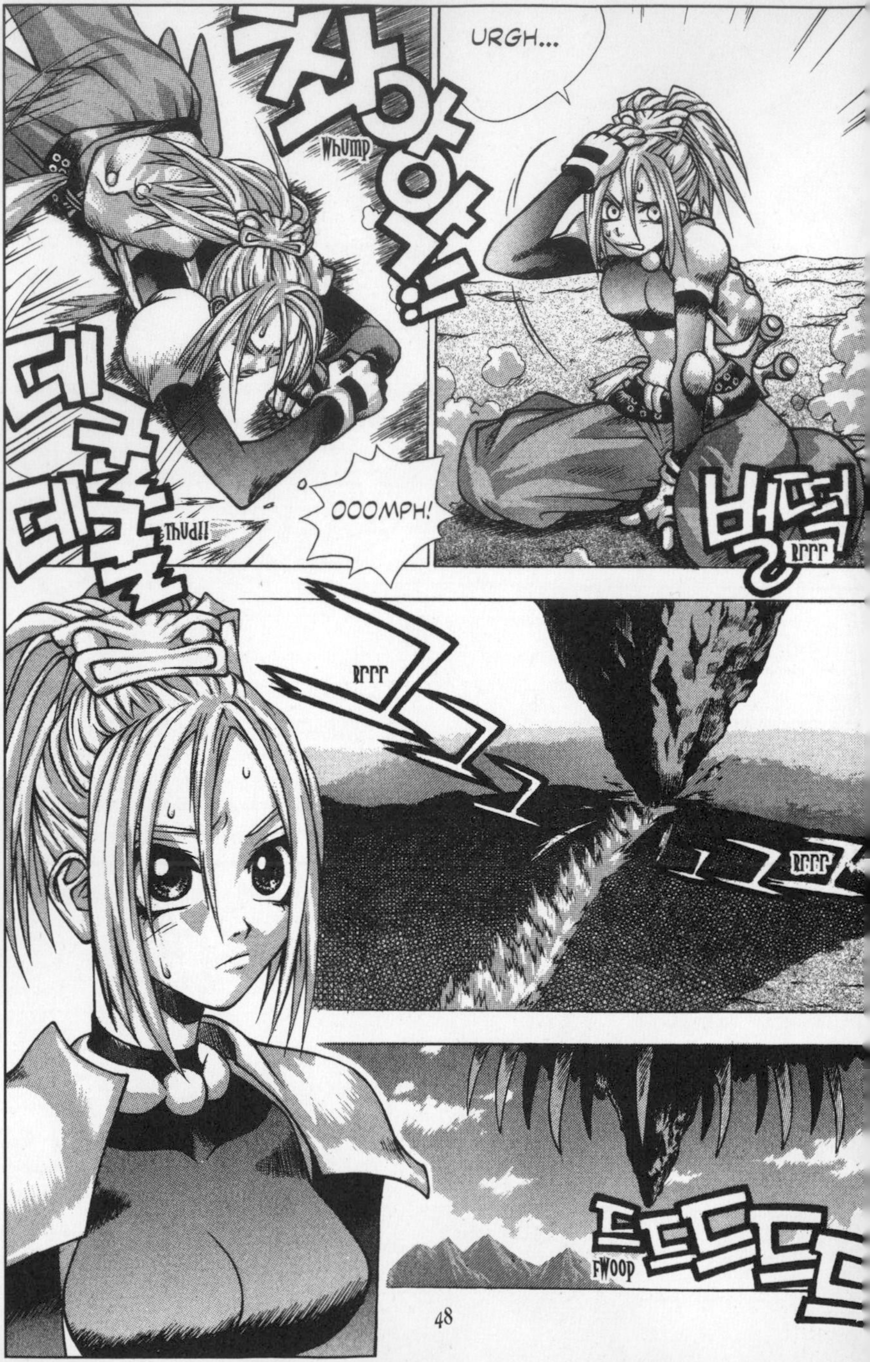

차앙앗!!
WHUMP
데굴데굴
THUD!!
OOOMPH!
URGH...
벌떡
RRRR
RRRR
RRRR
FWOOP

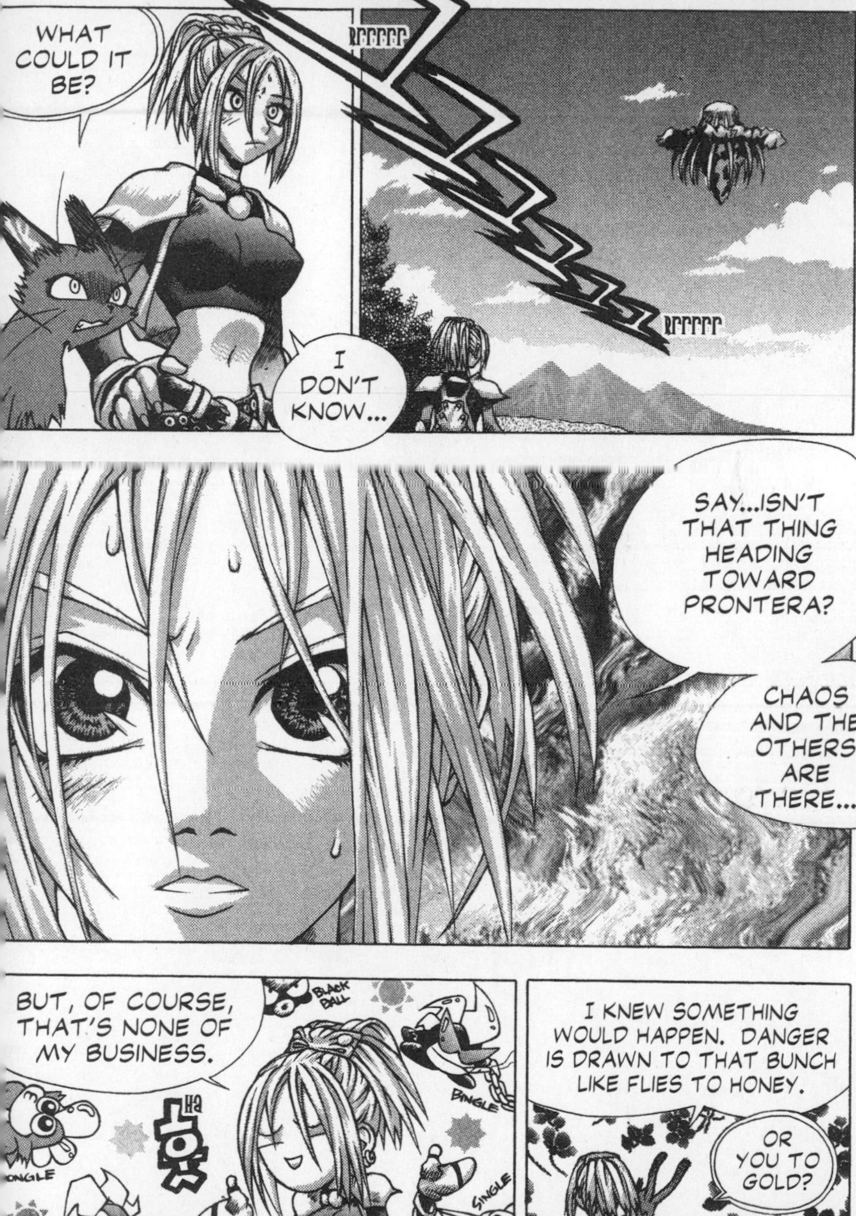
WHAT COULD IT BE?
I DON'T KNOW...
RRRRRR
RRRRRR
SAY...ISN'T THAT THING HEADING TOWARD PRONTERA?
CHAOS AND THE OTHERS ARE THERE...
BUT, OF COURSE, THAT'S NONE OF MY BUSINESS.
BLACK BALL
HA
BINGLE
ONGLE
SINGLE
DINGLE
I KNEW SOMETHING WOULD HAPPEN. DANGER IS DRAWN TO THAT BUNCH LIKE FLIES TO HONEY.
OR YOU TO GOLD?

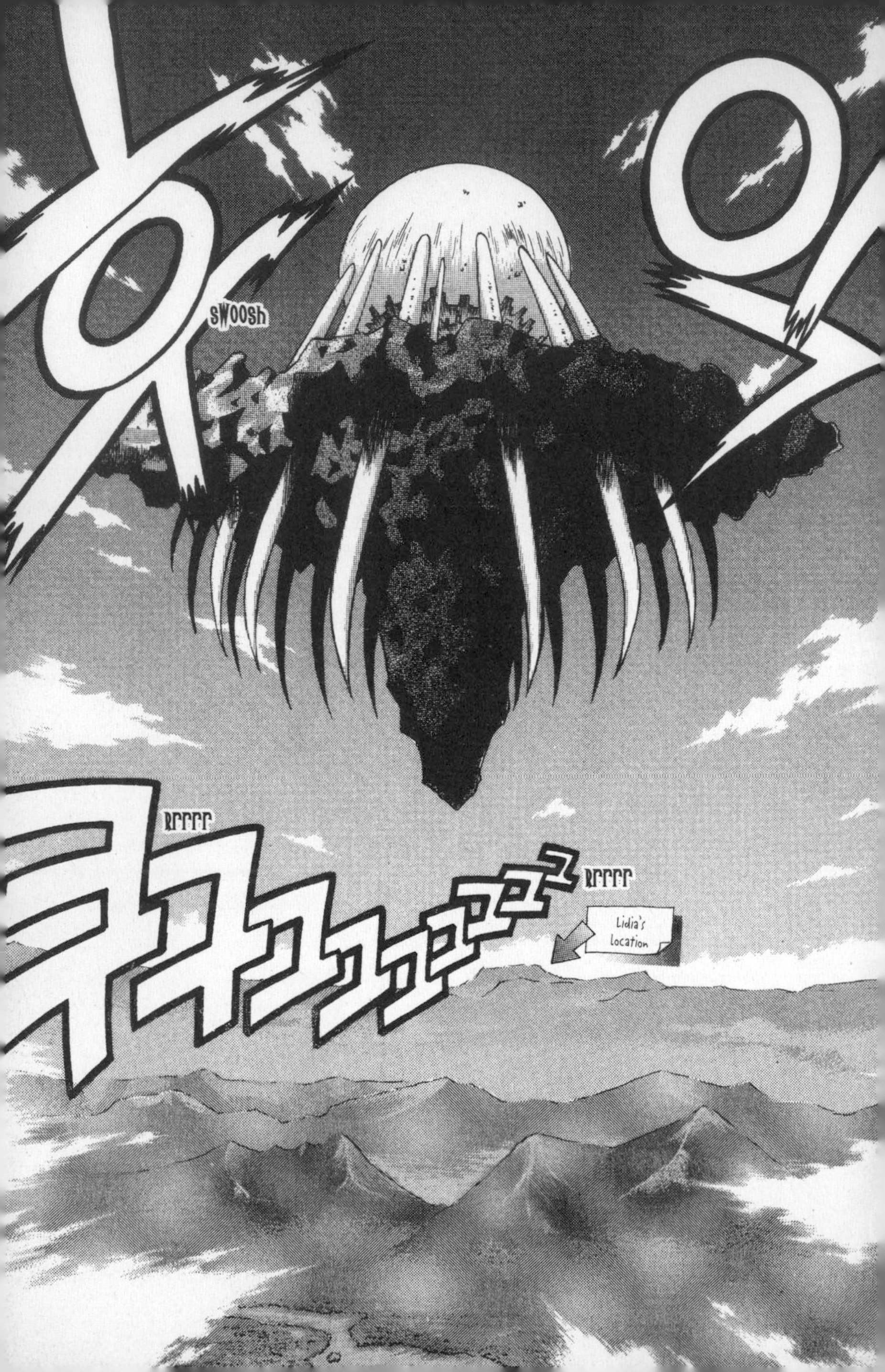
SWOOSH
RRRR
RRRR
Lidia's location

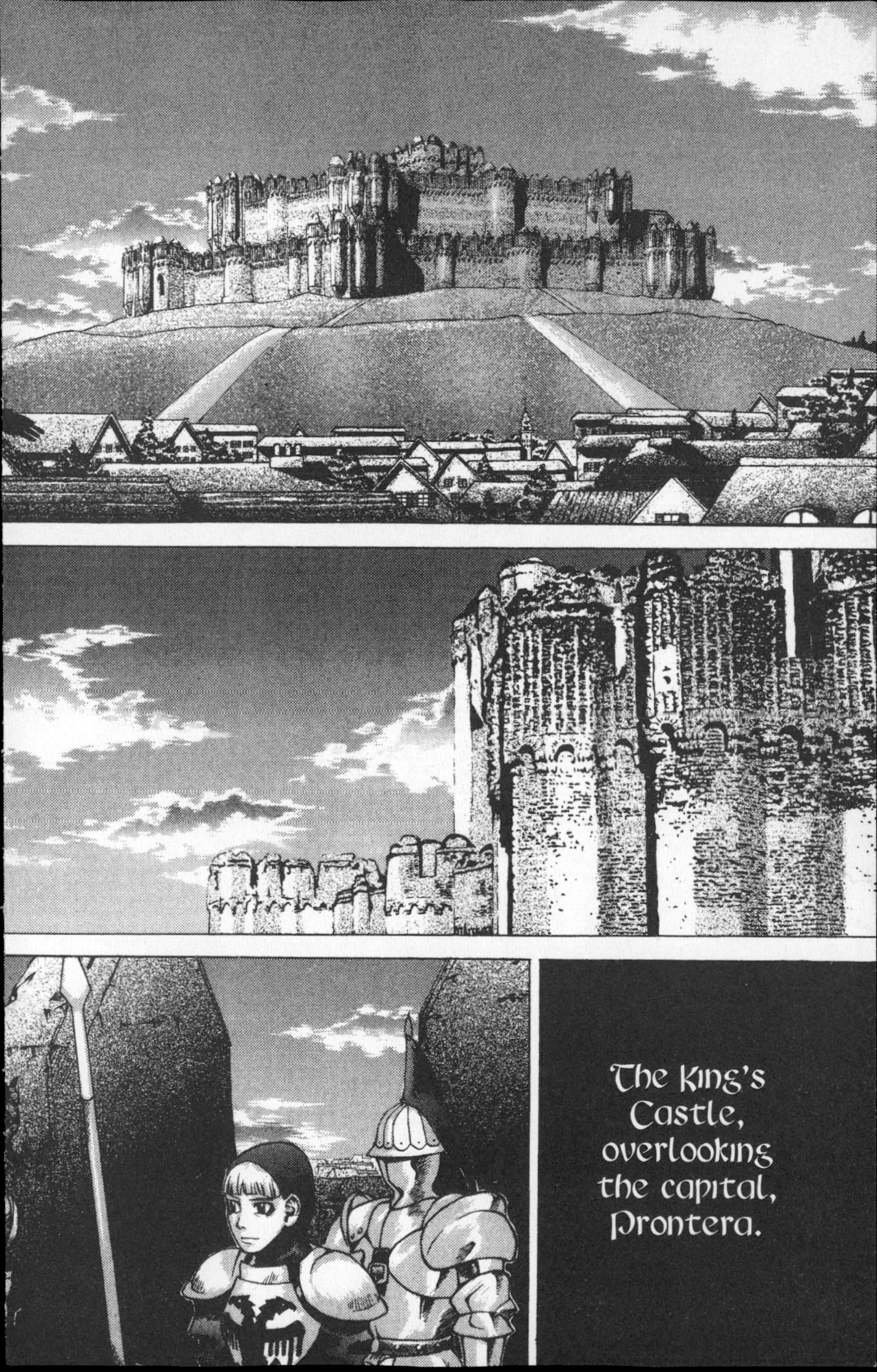
The King's Castle, overlooking the capital, Prontera.

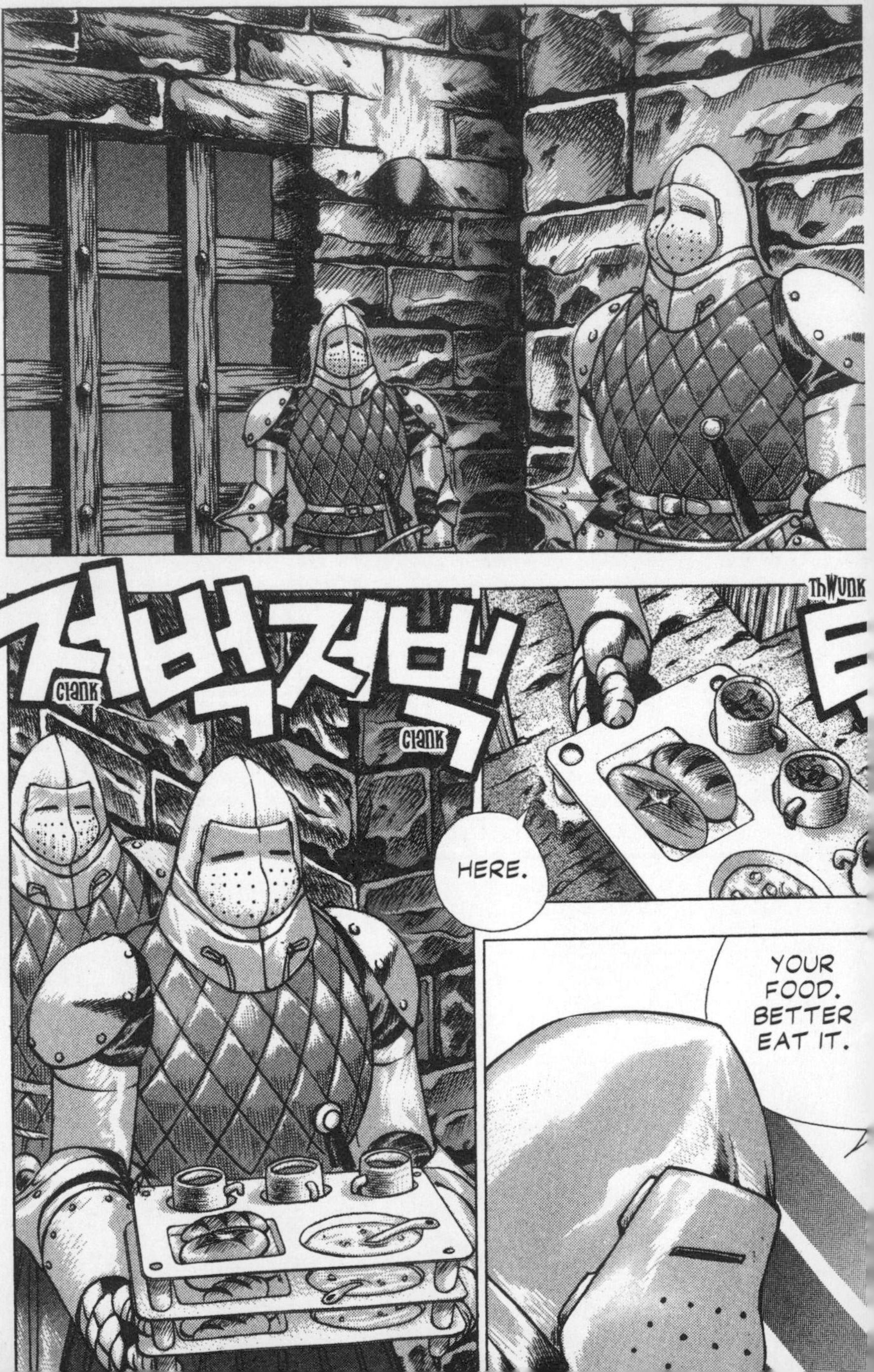
저벅
CLANK
저벅
CLANK
ThWUNK
HERE.
YOUR FOOD. BETTER EAT IT.

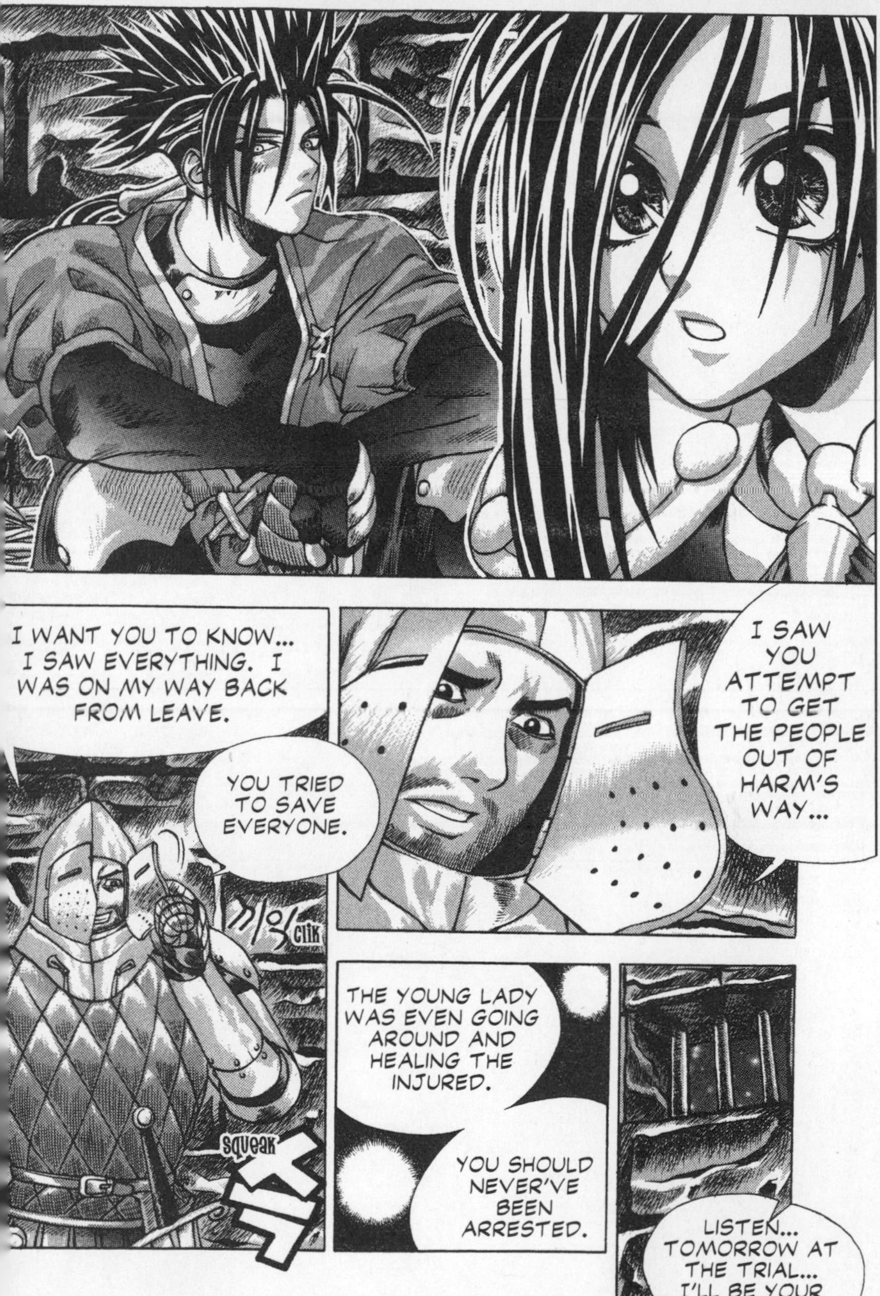
I WANT YOU TO KNOW... I SAW EVERYTHING. I WAS ON MY WAY BACK FROM LEAVE.
YOU TRIED TO SAVE EVERYONE.
clik
squeak
I SAW YOU ATTEMPT TO GET THE PEOPLE OUT OF HARM'S WAY...
THE YOUNG LADY WAS EVEN GOING AROUND AND HEALING THE INJURED.
YOU SHOULD NEVER'VE BEEN ARRESTED.
LISTEN... TOMORROW AT THE TRIAL... I'LL BE YOUR WITNESS.

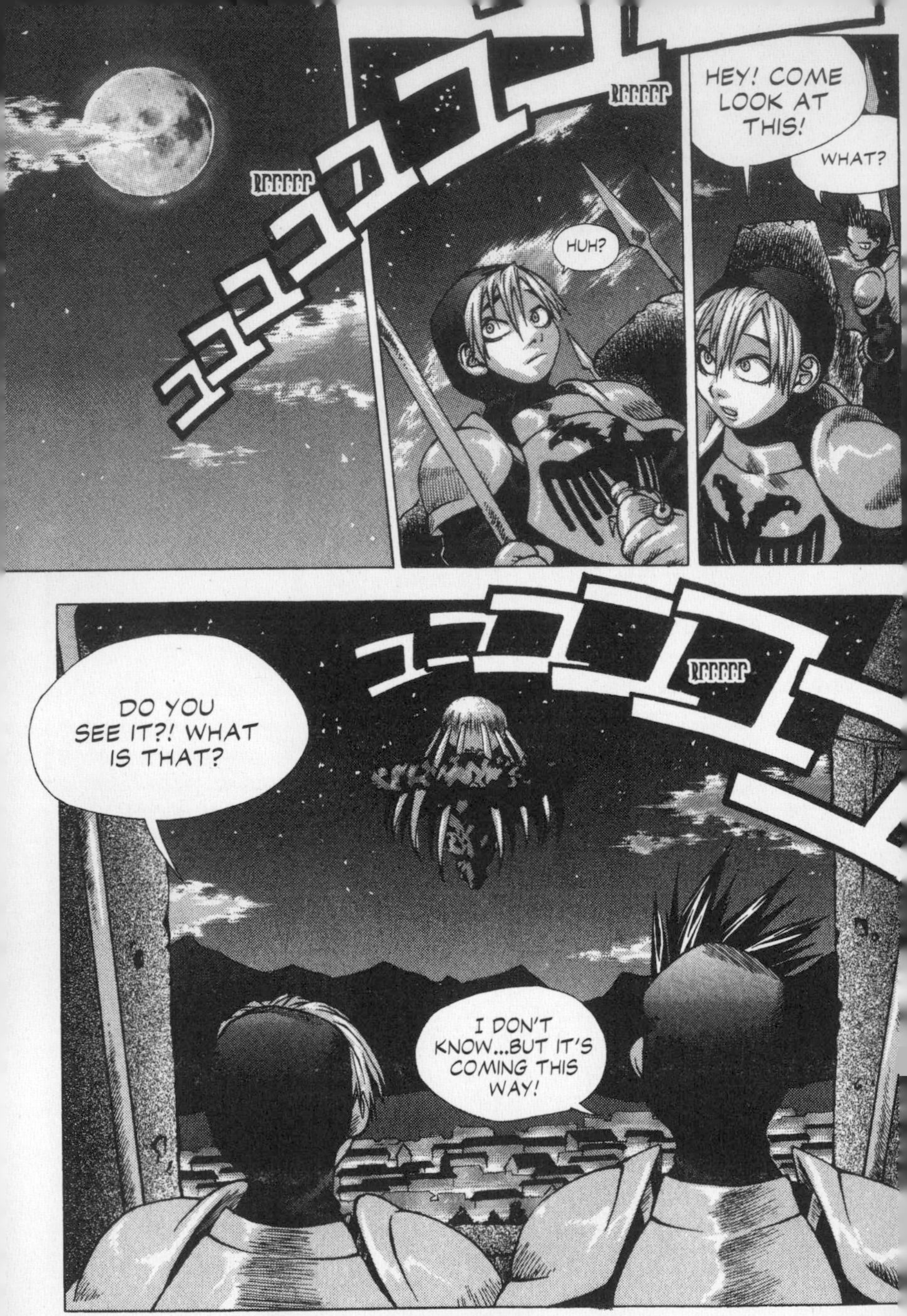
RRRRRR
RRRRRR
HUH?
HEY! COME LOOK AT THIS!
WHAT?
DO YOU SEE IT?! WHAT IS THAT?
RRRRRR
I DON'T KNOW...BUT IT'S COMING THIS WAY!

RAGNAROK
라그나로크
IN TO THE ABYSS

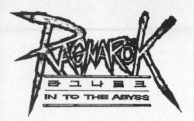

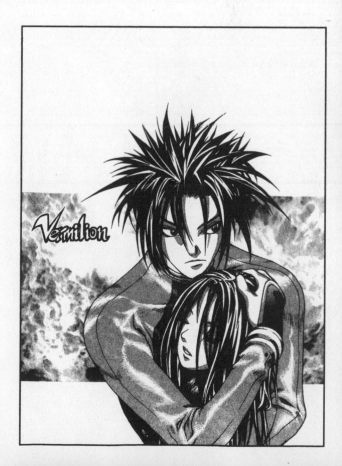

Vermilion

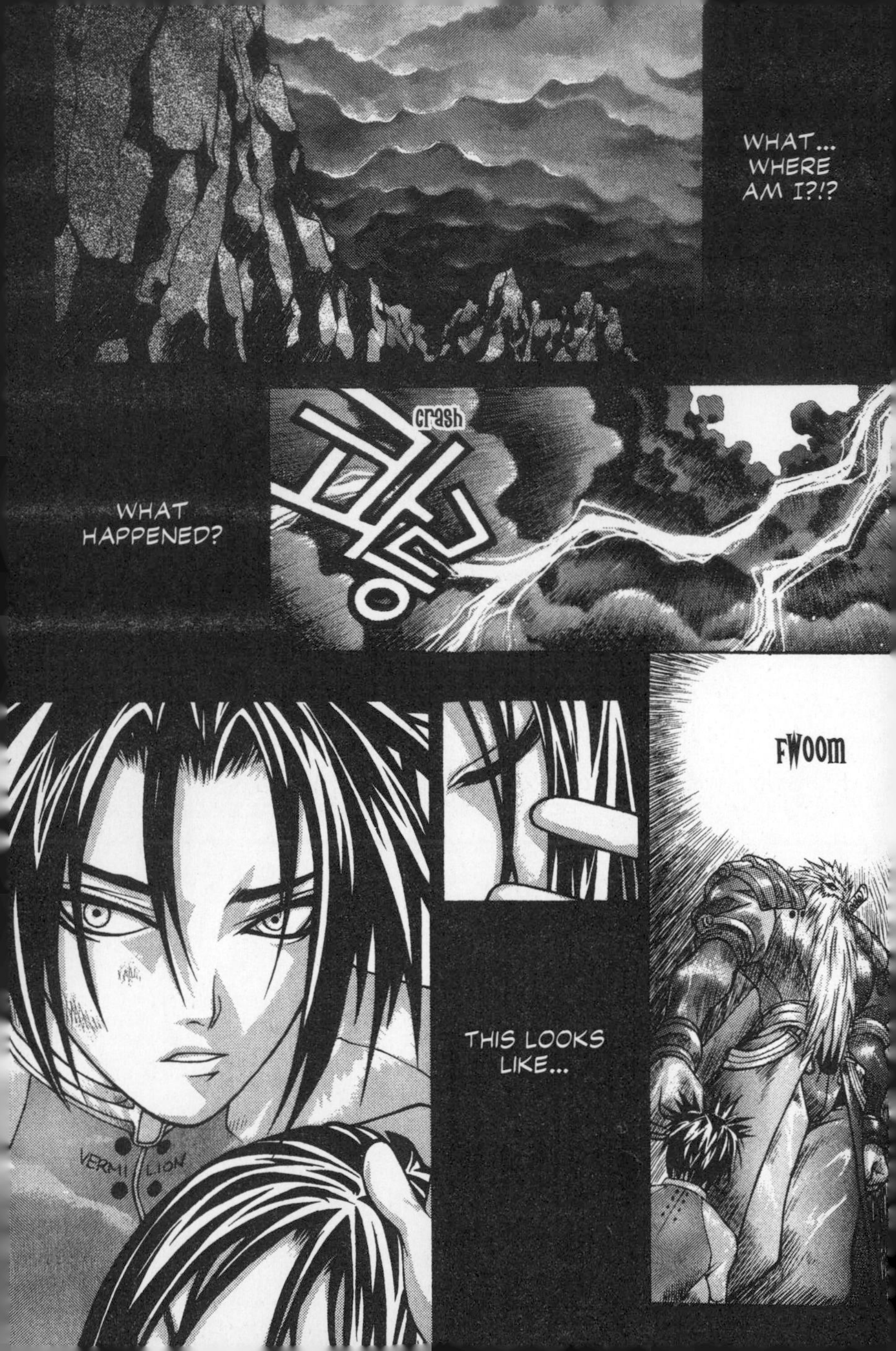
WHAT...
WHERE
AM I?!?
WHAT
HAPPENED?
crash
VERMILION
THIS LOOKS
LIKE...
FWOOM

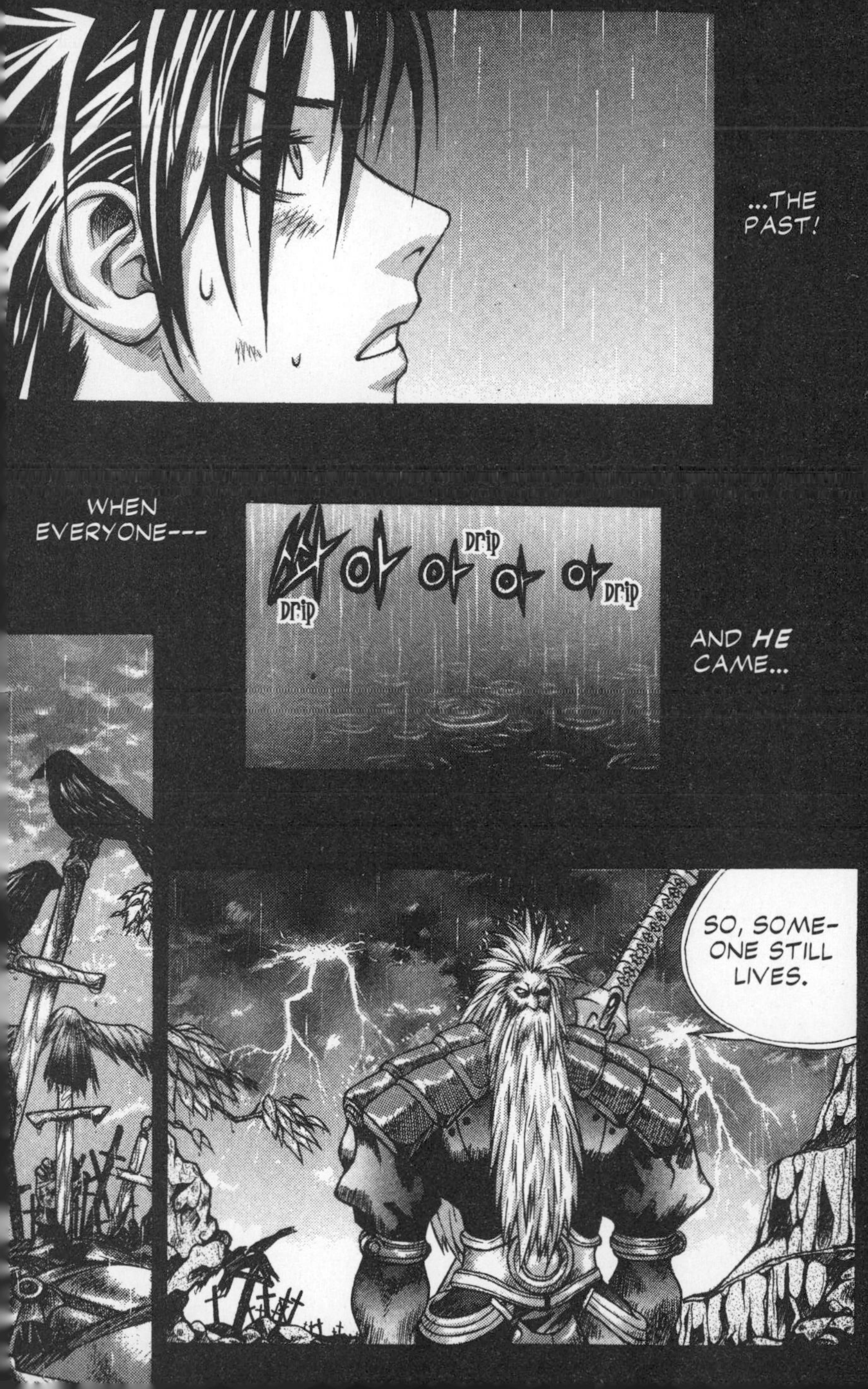
...THE PAST!
WHEN EVERYONE---
쏴아아아아
Drip
Drip
Drip
AND HE CAME...
SO, SOME-ONE STILL LIVES.

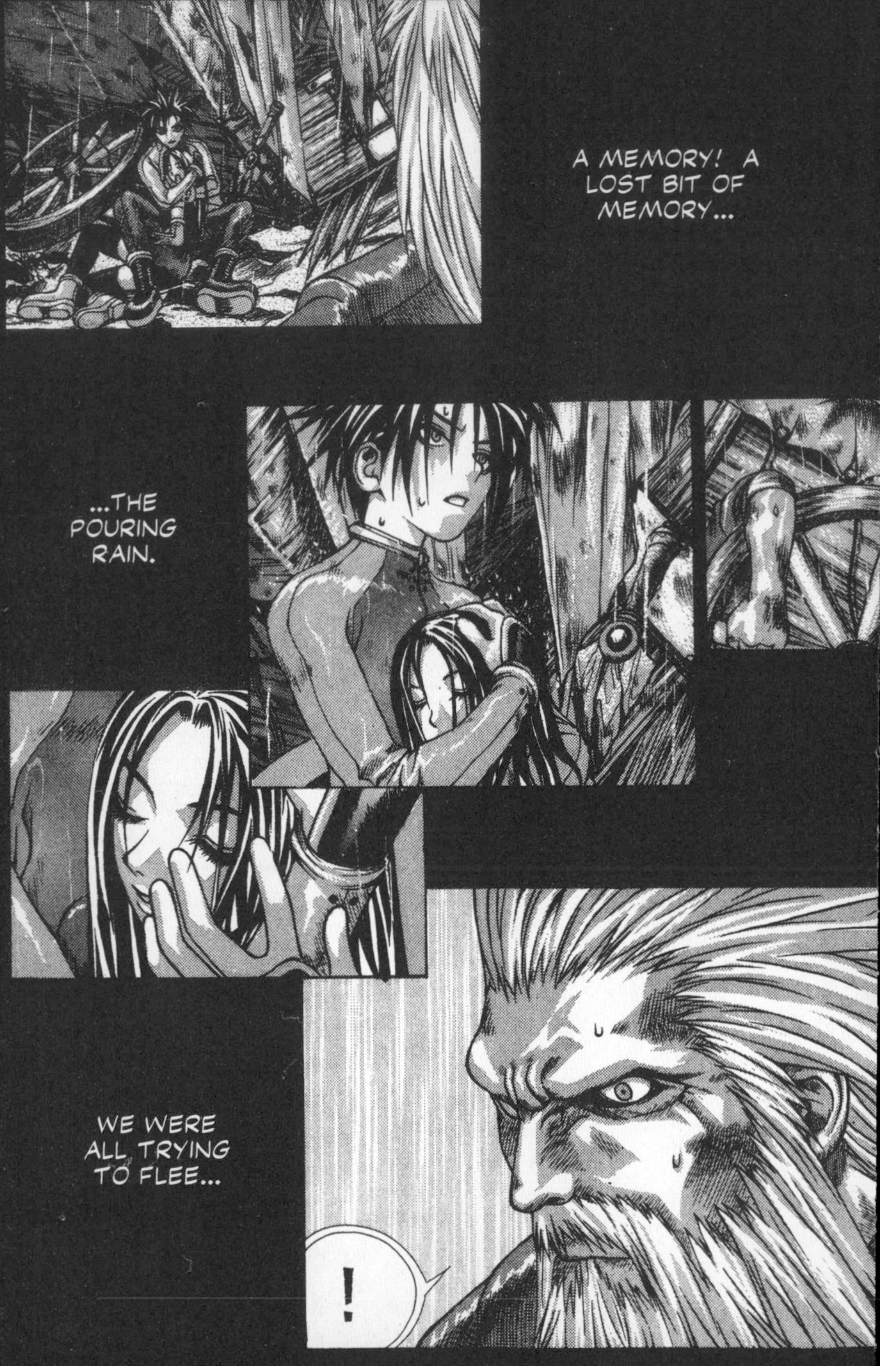
A MEMORY! A LOST BIT OF MEMORY...
...THE POURING RAIN.
WE WERE ALL TRYING TO FLEE...
!

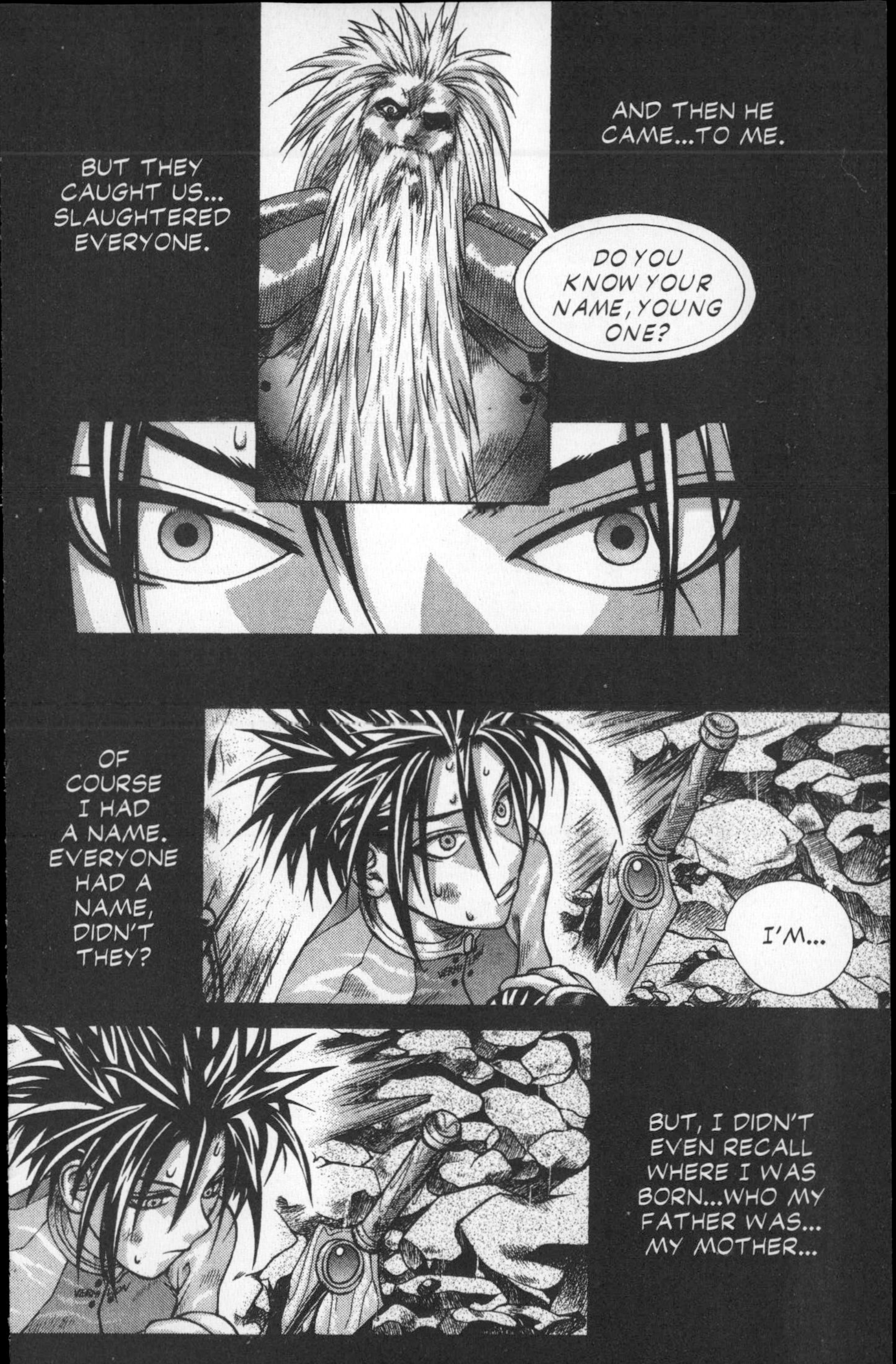
BUT THEY CAUGHT US... SLAUGHTERED EVERYONE.
AND THEN HE CAME...TO ME.
DO YOU KNOW YOUR NAME, YOUNG ONE?
OF COURSE I HAD A NAME. EVERYONE HAD A NAME, DIDN'T THEY?
I'M...
BUT, I DIDN'T EVEN RECALL WHERE I WAS BORN...WHO MY FATHER WAS... MY MOTHER...

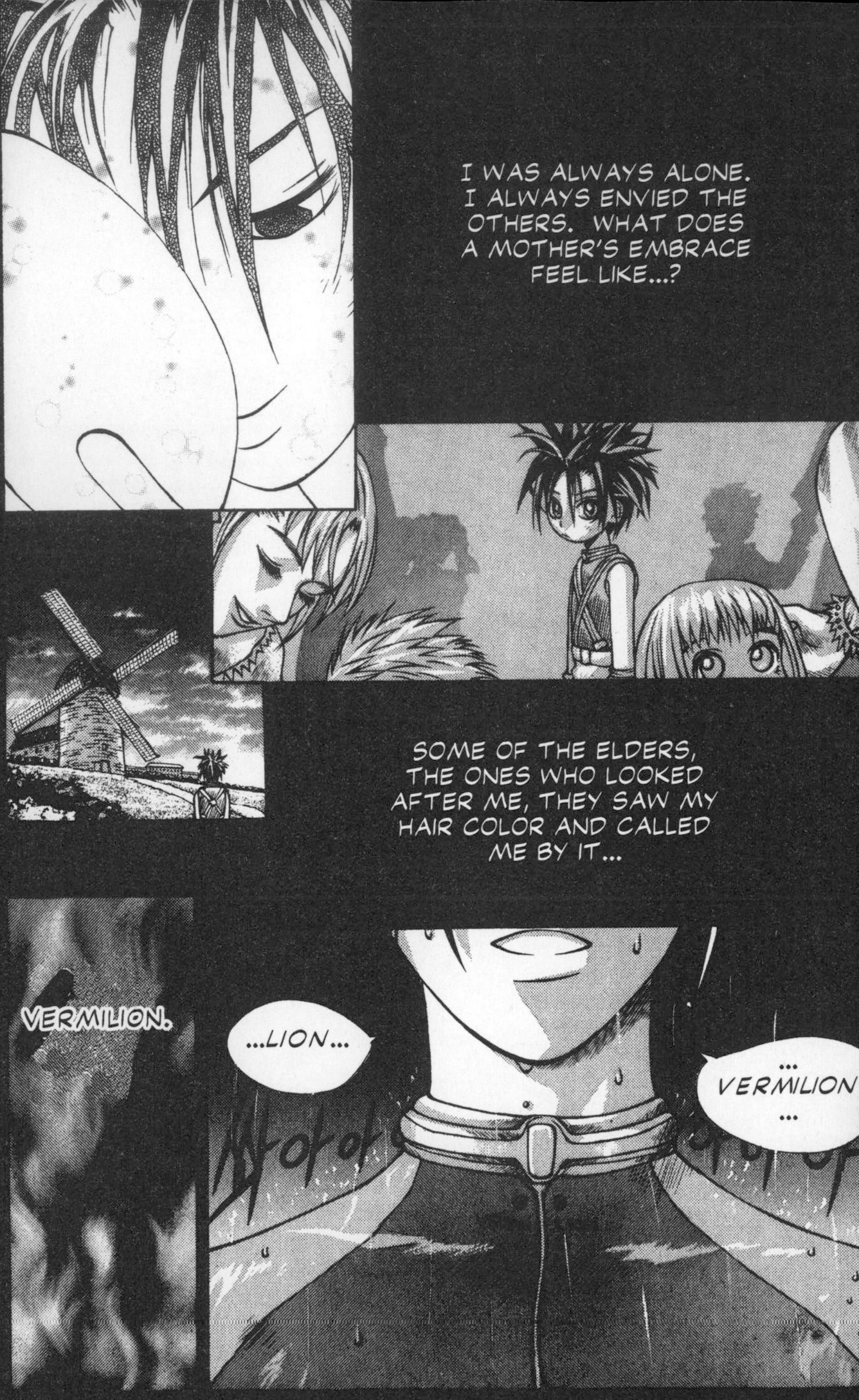
I WAS ALWAYS ALONE. I ALWAYS ENVIED THE OTHERS. WHAT DOES A MOTHER'S EMBRACE FEEL LIKE...?
SOME OF THE ELDERS, THE ONES WHO LOOKED AFTER ME, THEY SAW MY HAIR COLOR AND CALLED ME BY IT...
VERMILION.
...LION...
...VERMILION...

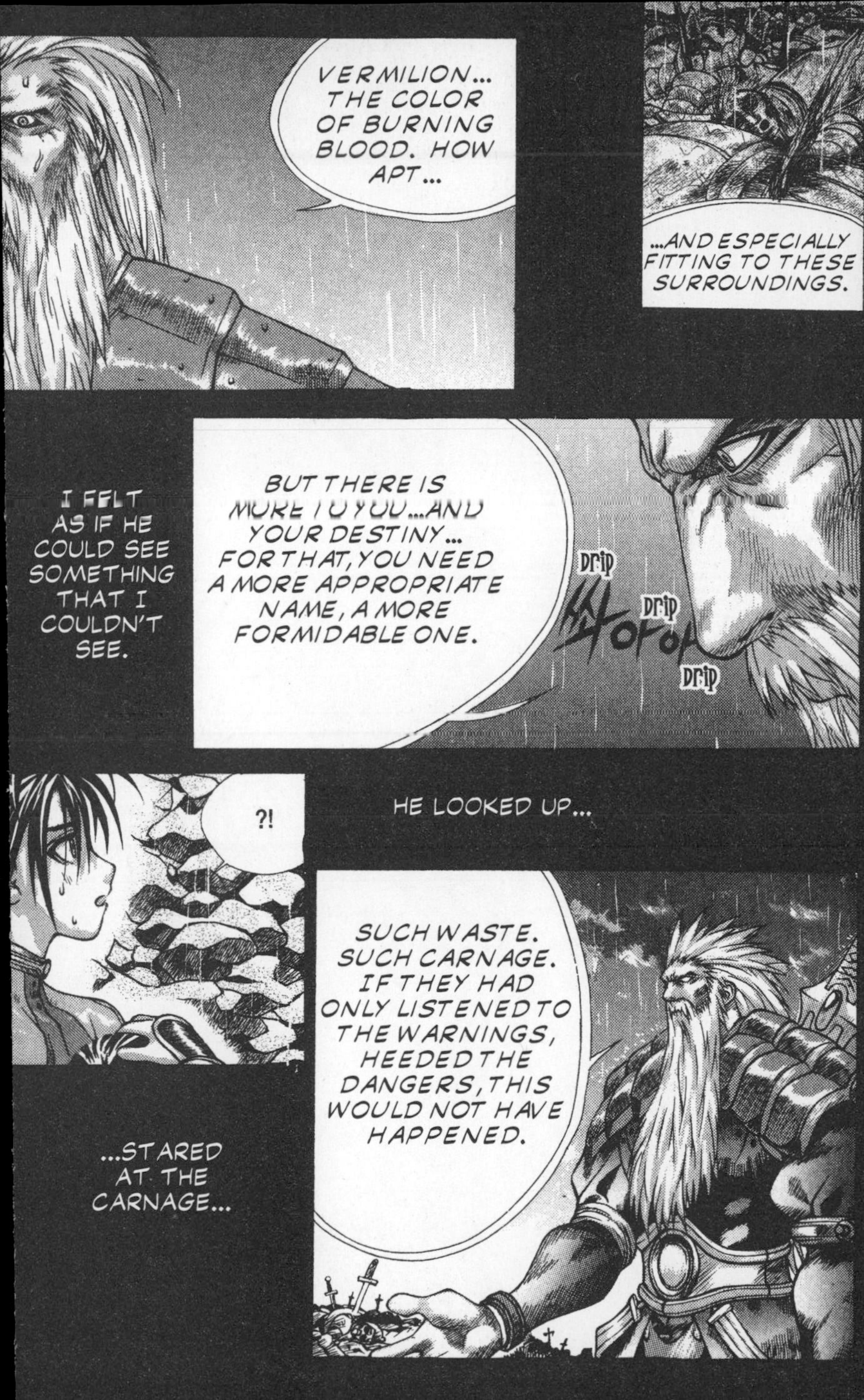
VERMILION... THE COLOR OF BURNING BLOOD. HOW APT...
...AND ESPECIALLY FITTING TO THESE SURROUNDINGS.
I FELT AS IF HE COULD SEE SOMETHING THAT I COULDN'T SEE.
BUT THERE IS MORE TO YOU...AND YOUR DESTINY... FOR THAT, YOU NEED A MORE APPROPRIATE NAME, A MORE FORMIDABLE ONE.
Drip
쏴아아
Drip
Drip
?!
HE LOOKED UP...
SUCH WASTE. SUCH CARNAGE. IF THEY HAD ONLY LISTENED TO THE WARNINGS, HEEDED THE DANGERS, THIS WOULD NOT HAVE HAPPENED.
...STARED AT THE CARNAGE...

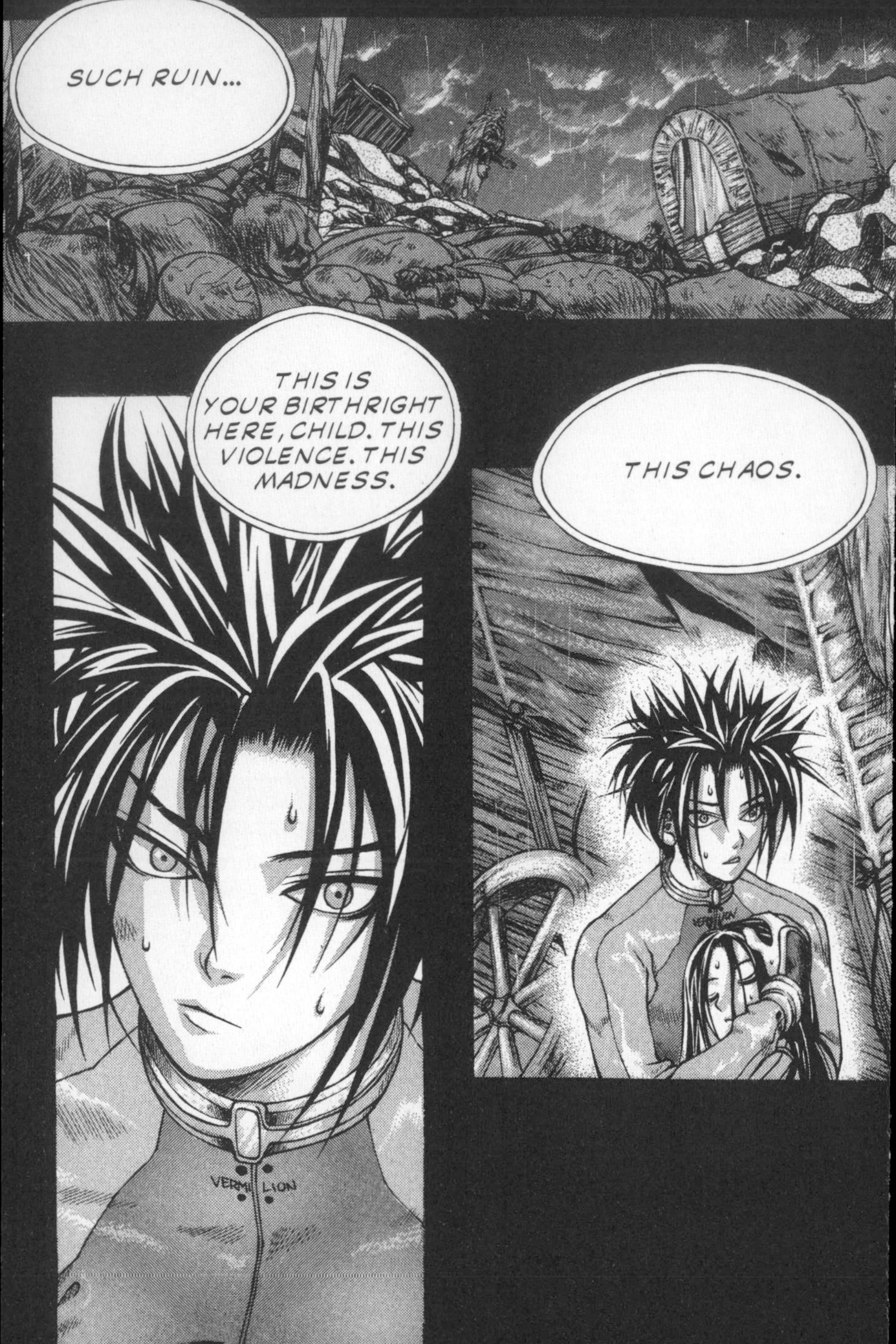
SUCH RUIN...
THIS IS YOUR BIRTHRIGHT HERE, CHILD. THIS VIOLENCE. THIS MADNESS.
VERMILION
THIS CHAOS.

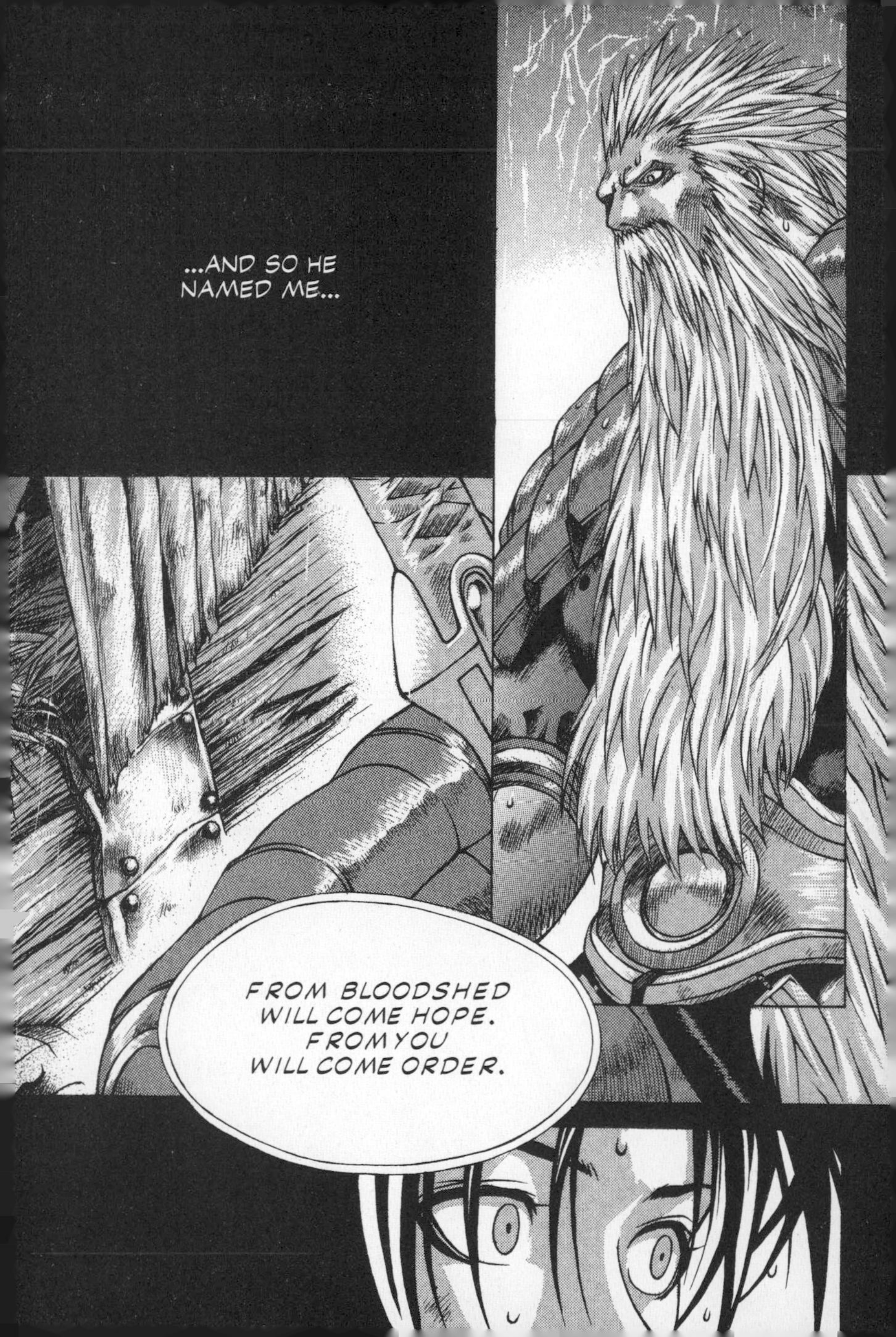
...AND SO HE NAMED ME...
FROM BLOODSHED WILL COME HOPE. FROM YOU WILL COME ORDER.

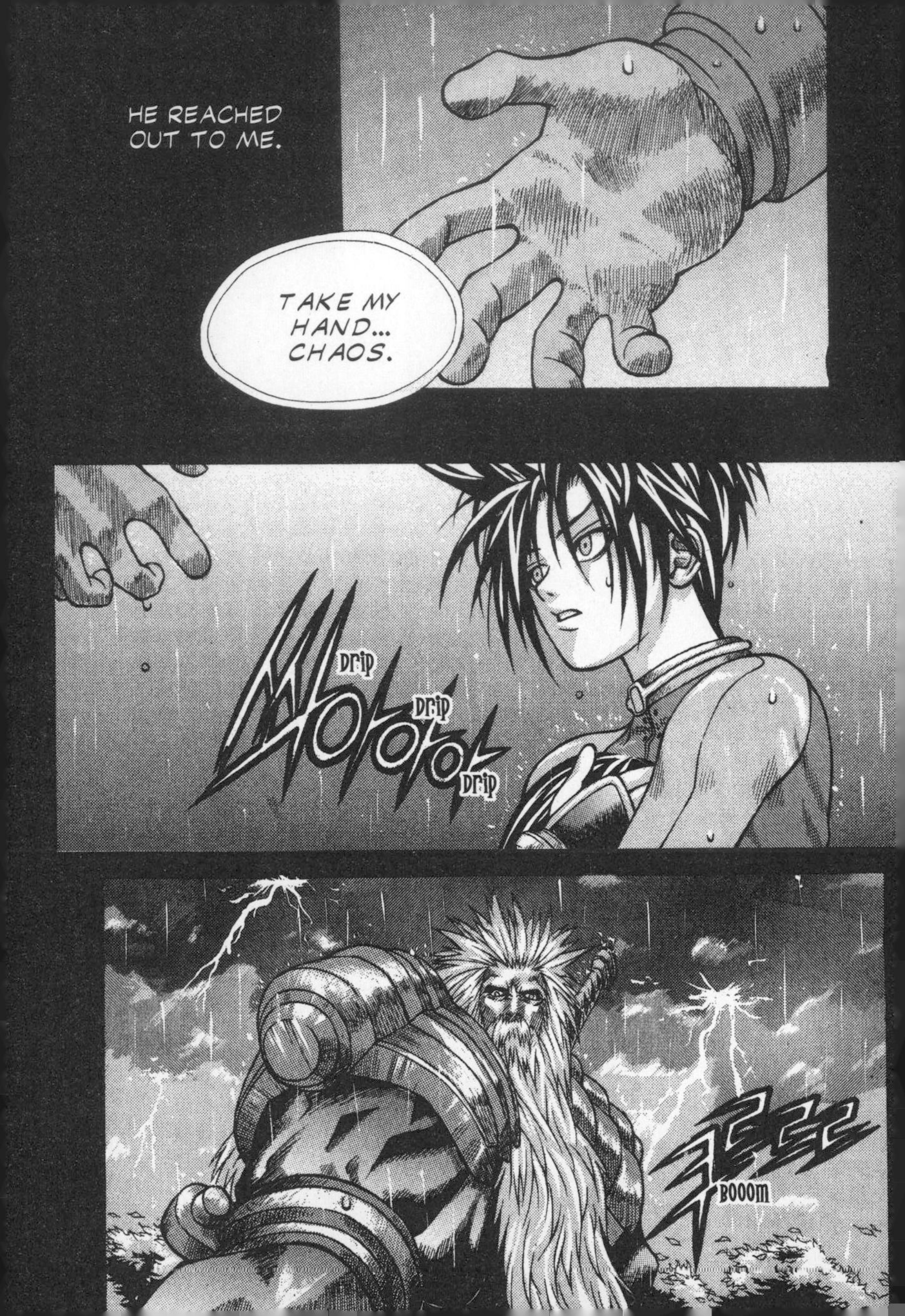
HE REACHED OUT TO ME.
TAKE MY HAND... CHAOS.
DRIP
DRIP
DRIP
BOOOM

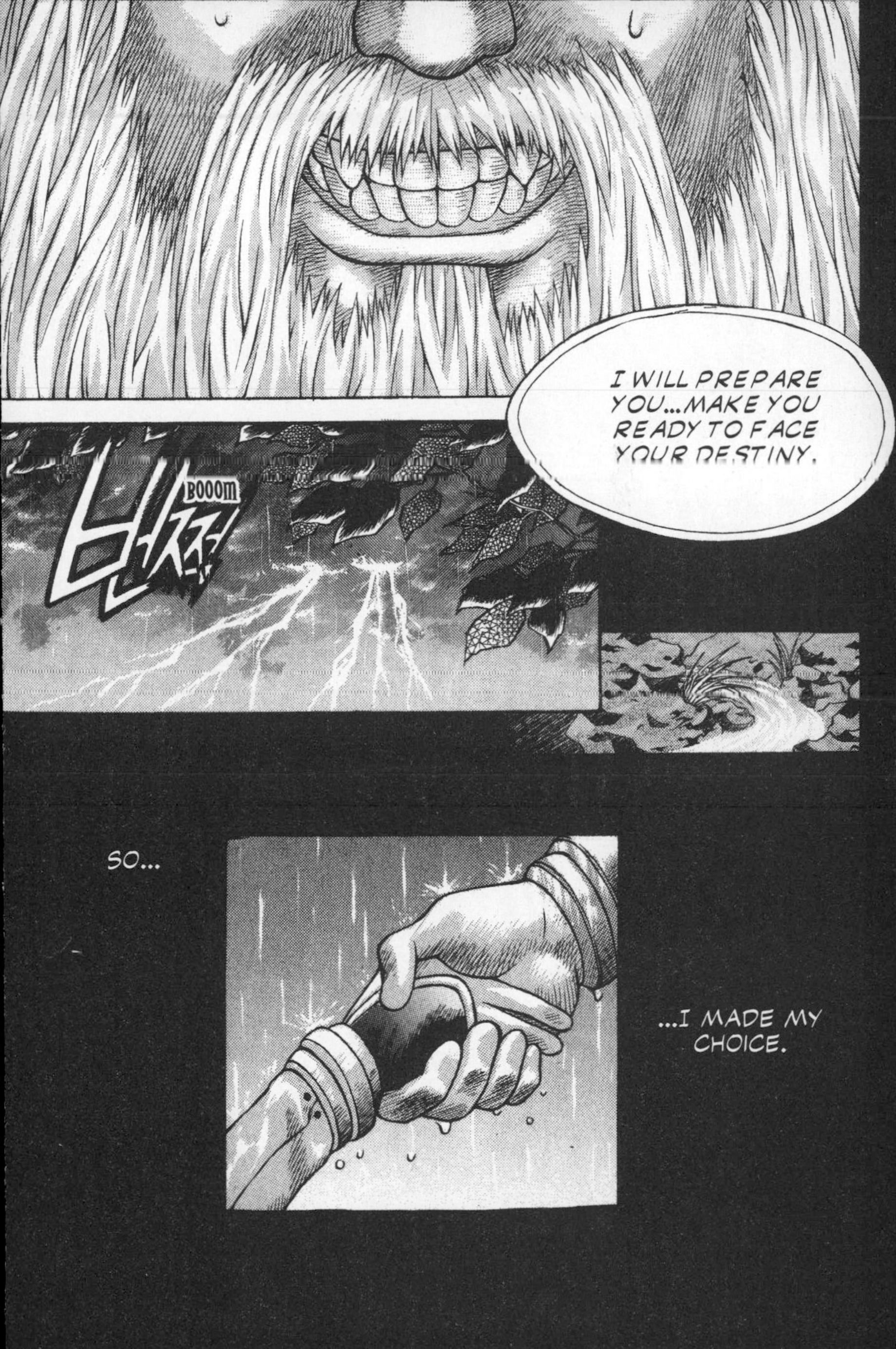
I WILL PREPARE YOU...MAKE YOU READY TO FACE YOUR DESTINY.
BOOOM
SO...
...I MADE MY CHOICE.

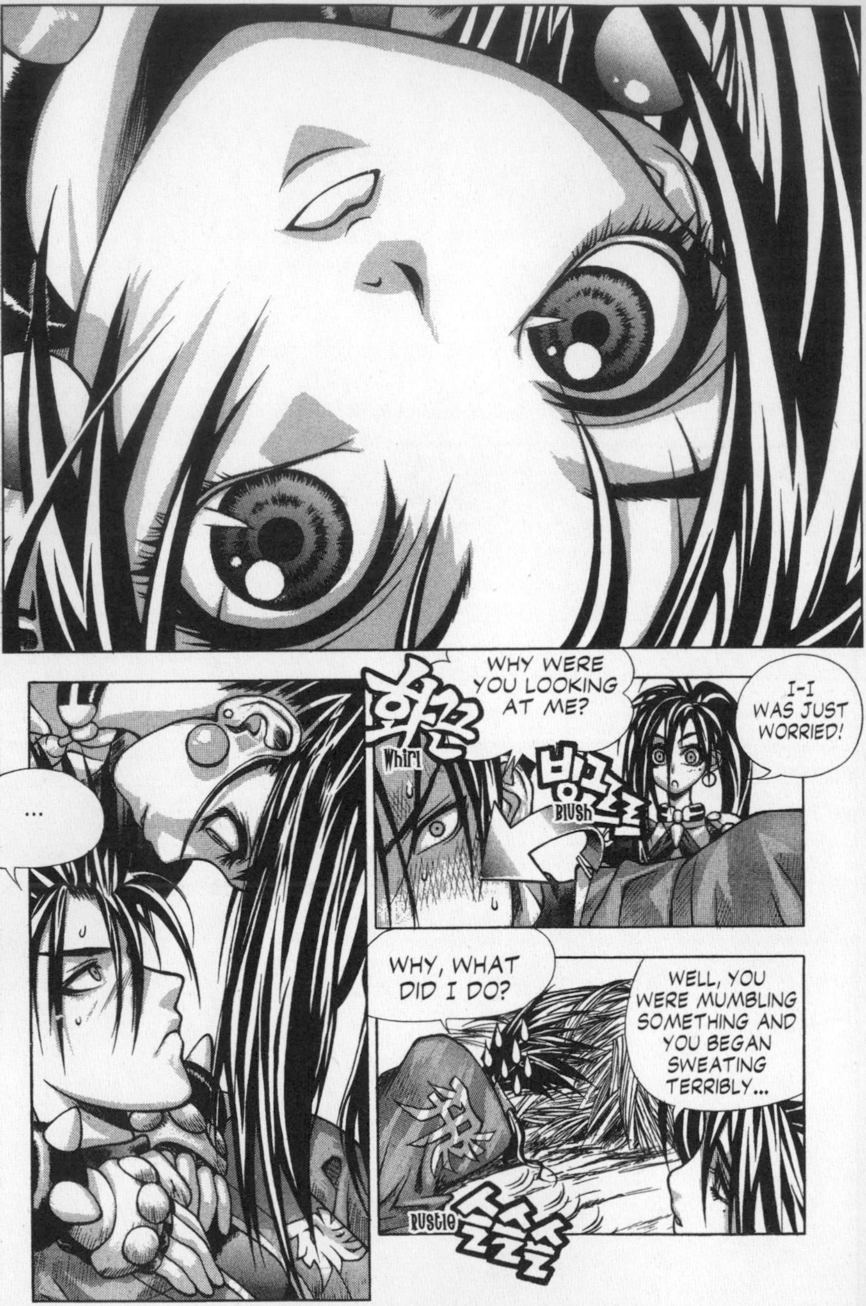
...
Whirl
WHY WERE YOU LOOKING AT ME?
Blush
I-I WAS JUST WORRIED!
WHY, WHAT DID I DO?
WELL, YOU WERE MUMBLING SOMETHING AND YOU BEGAN SWEATING TERRIBLY...
Rustle

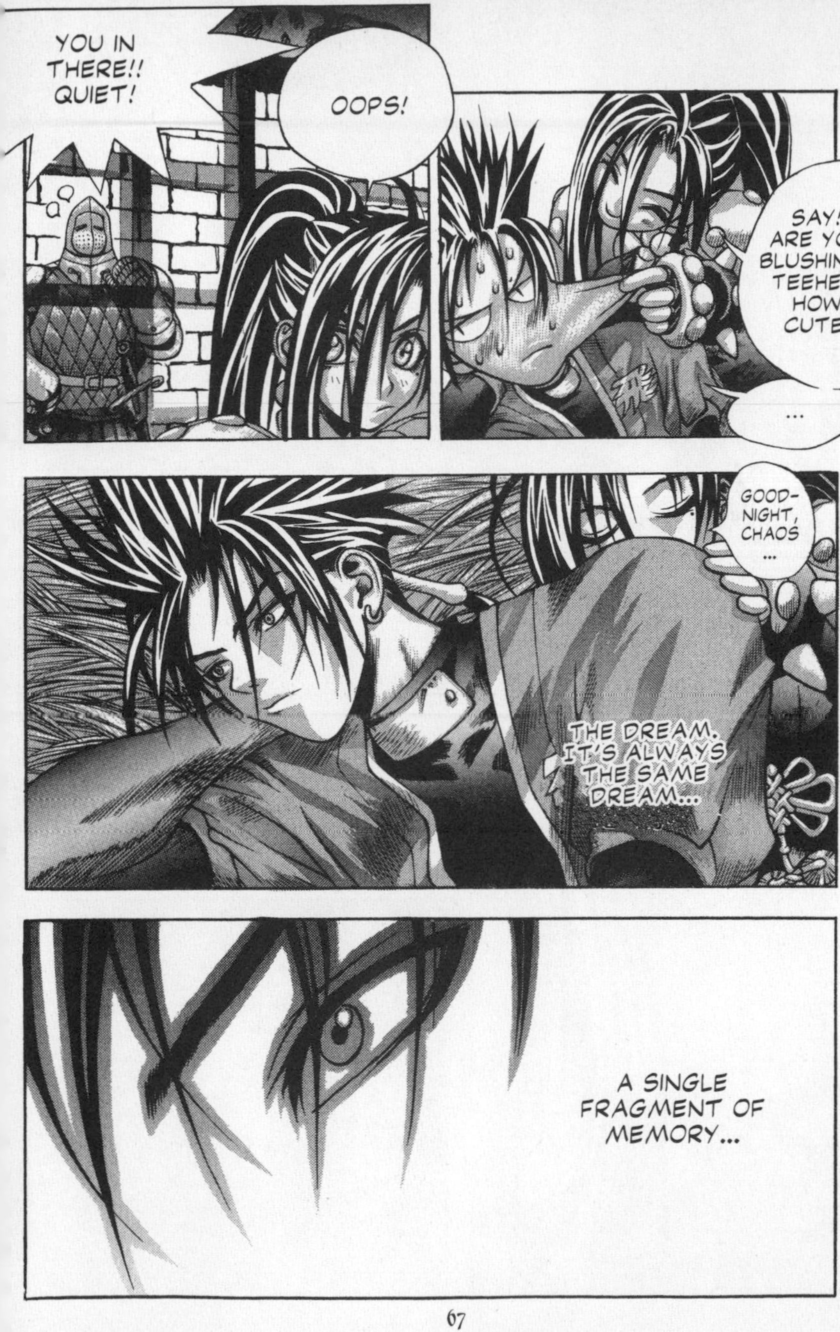
YOU IN THERE!! QUIET!
OOPS!
SAY! ARE YOU BLUSHING? TEEHEE! HOW CUTE!
...
GOOD-NIGHT, CHAOS ...
THE DREAM. IT'S ALWAYS THE SAME DREAM...
A SINGLE FRAGMENT OF MEMORY...

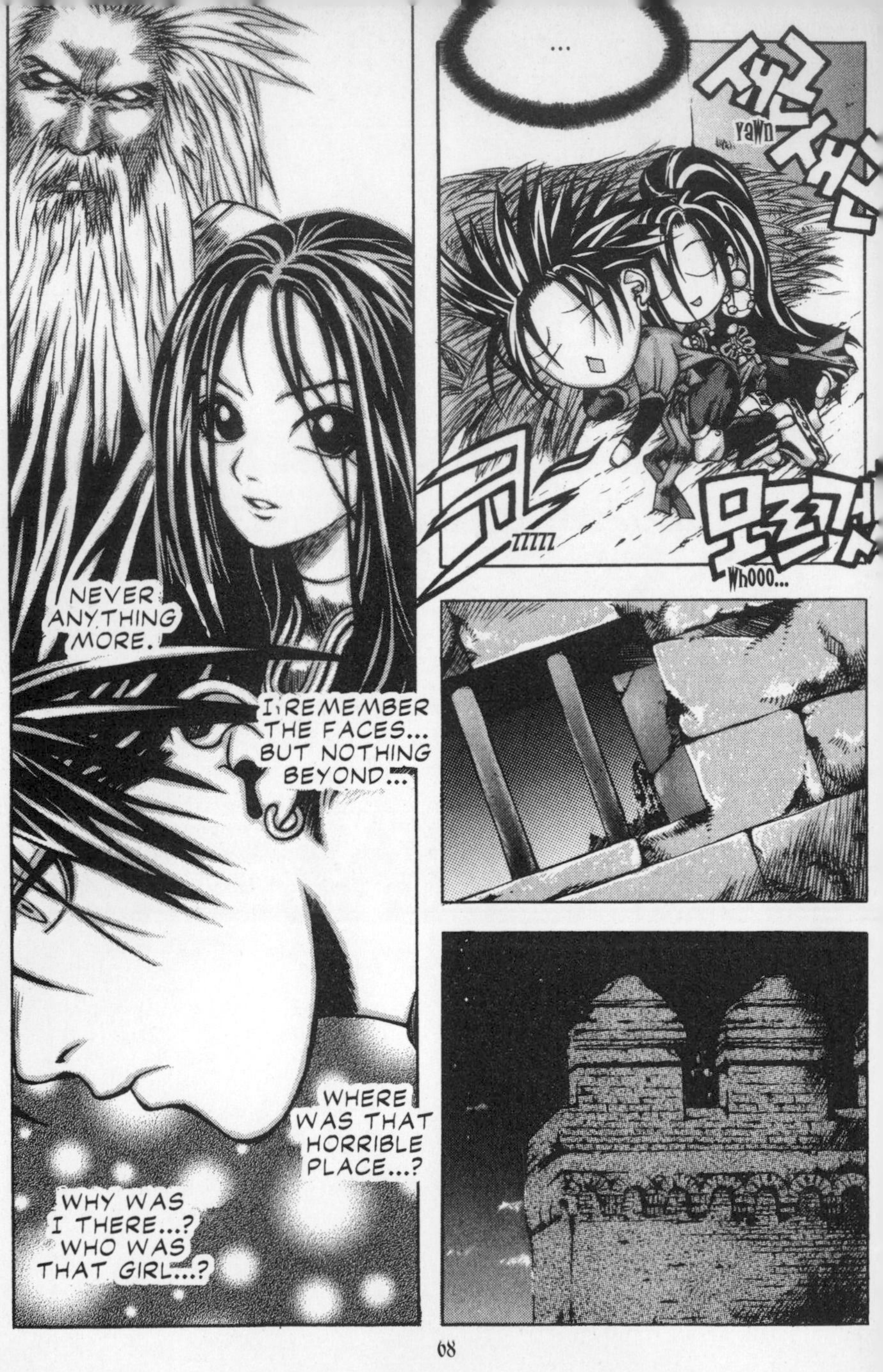
NEVER ANYTHING MORE.
I REMEMBER THE FACES... BUT NOTHING BEYOND...
WHERE WAS THAT HORRIBLE PLACE...?
WHY WAS I THERE...? WHO WAS THAT GIRL...?
...
yawn
zzzzz
Whooo...

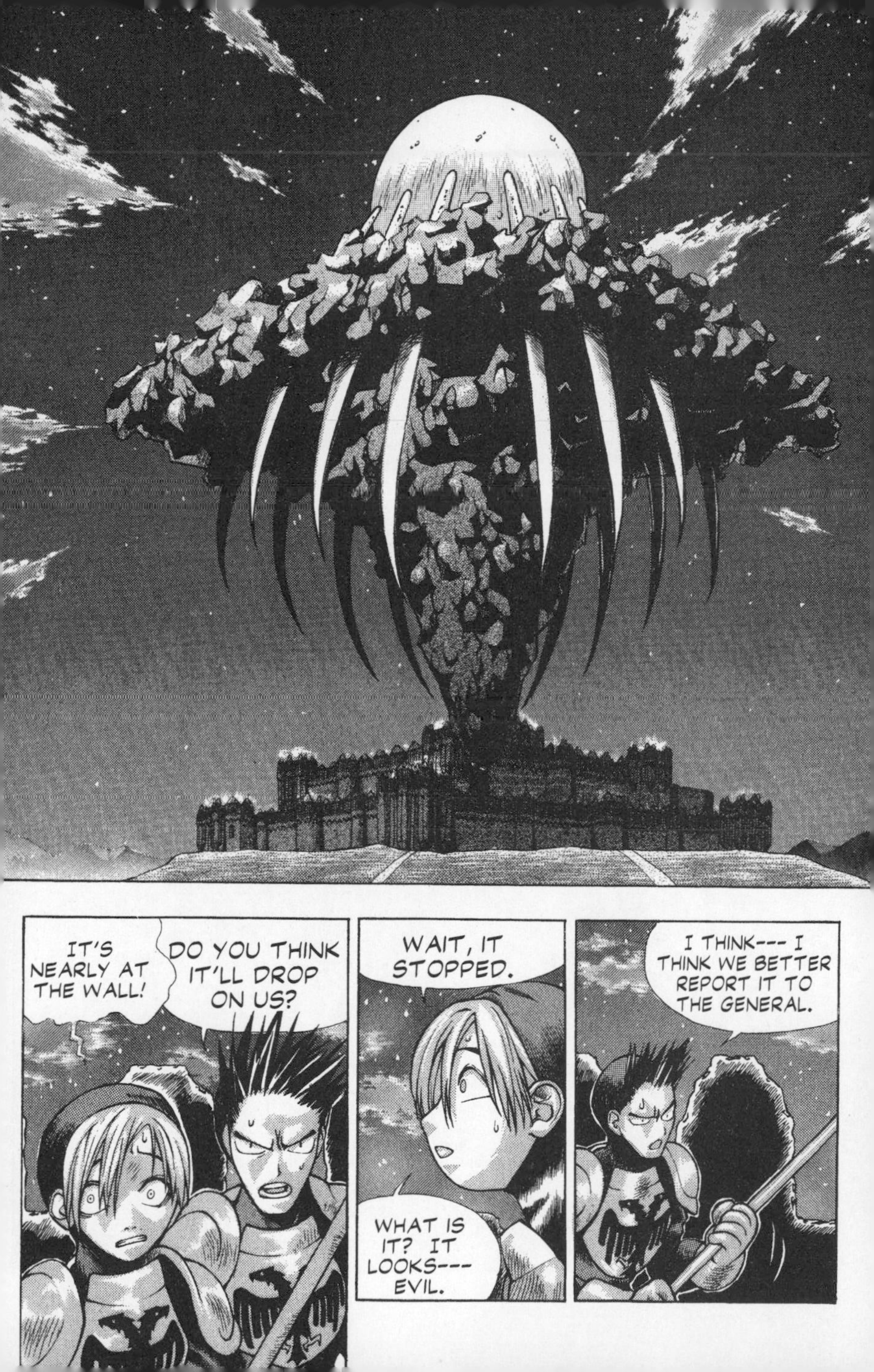
IT'S NEARLY AT THE WALL!
DO YOU THINK IT'LL DROP ON US?
WAIT, IT STOPPED.
WHAT IS IT? IT LOOKS--- EVIL.
I THINK--- I THINK WE BETTER REPORT IT TO THE GENERAL.

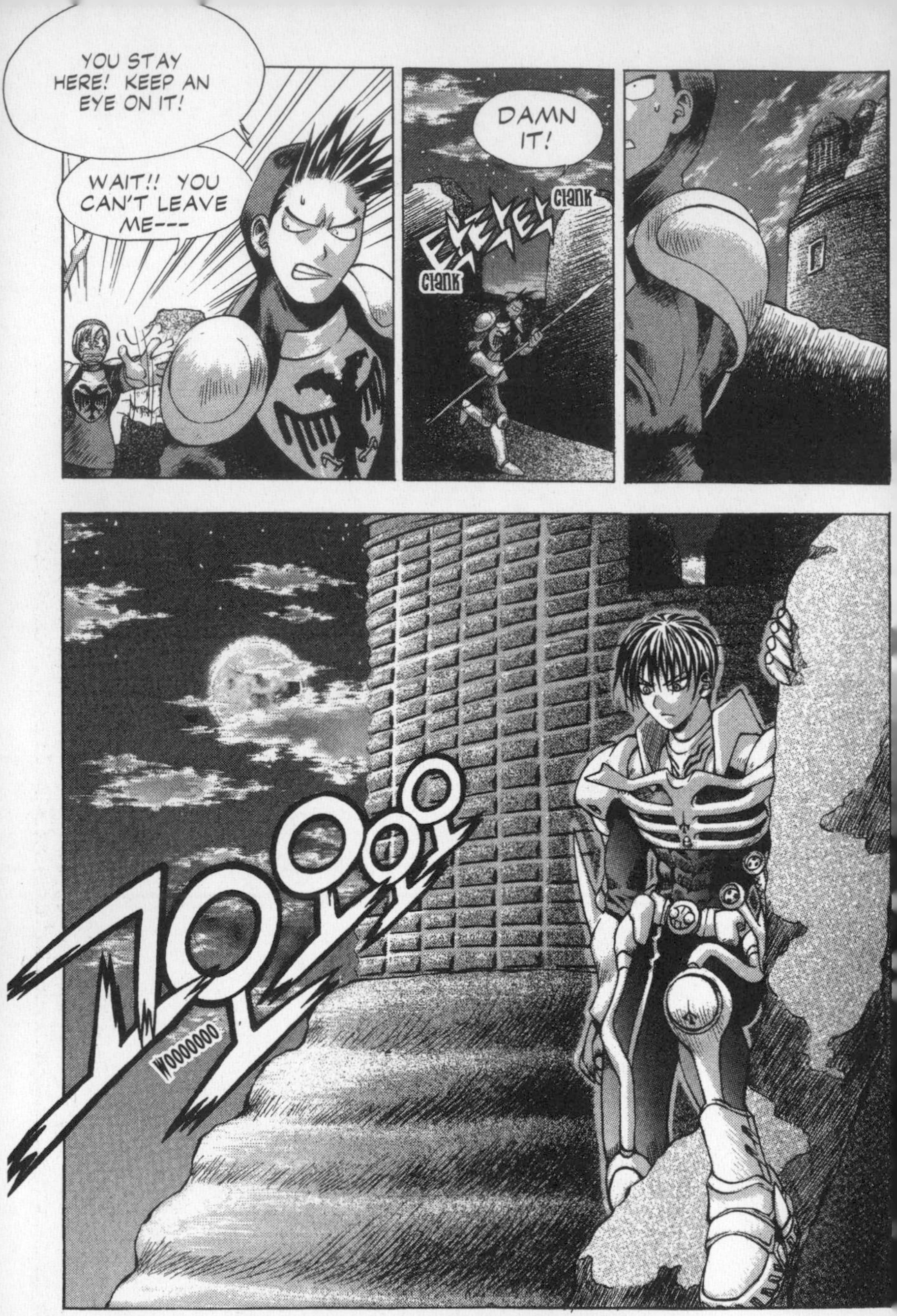
YOU STAY HERE! KEEP AN EYE ON IT!
WAIT!! YOU CAN'T LEAVE ME---
DAMN IT!
CLANK
CLANK
WOOOOOOO

RAGNAROK
라그나로크
IN TO THE ABYSS

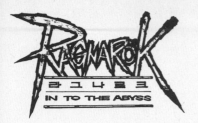

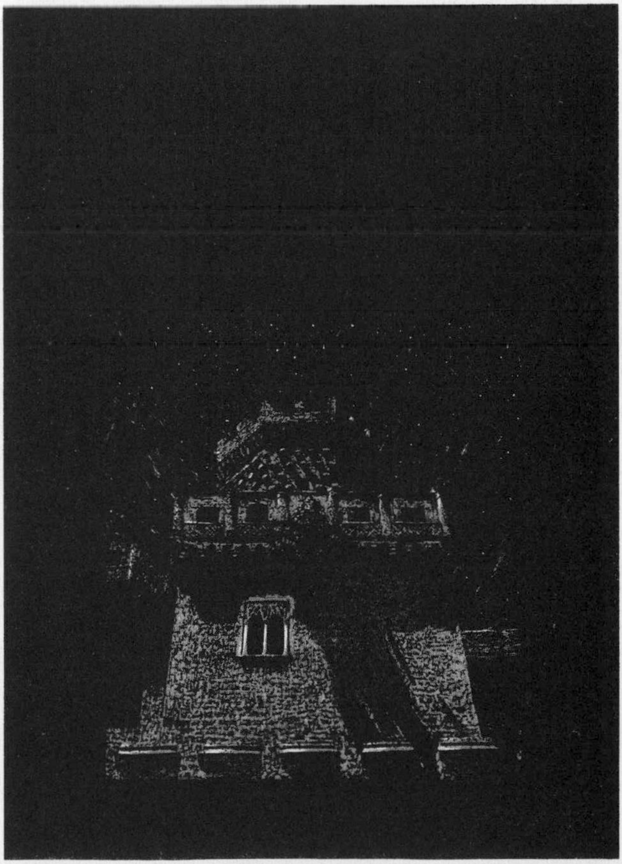

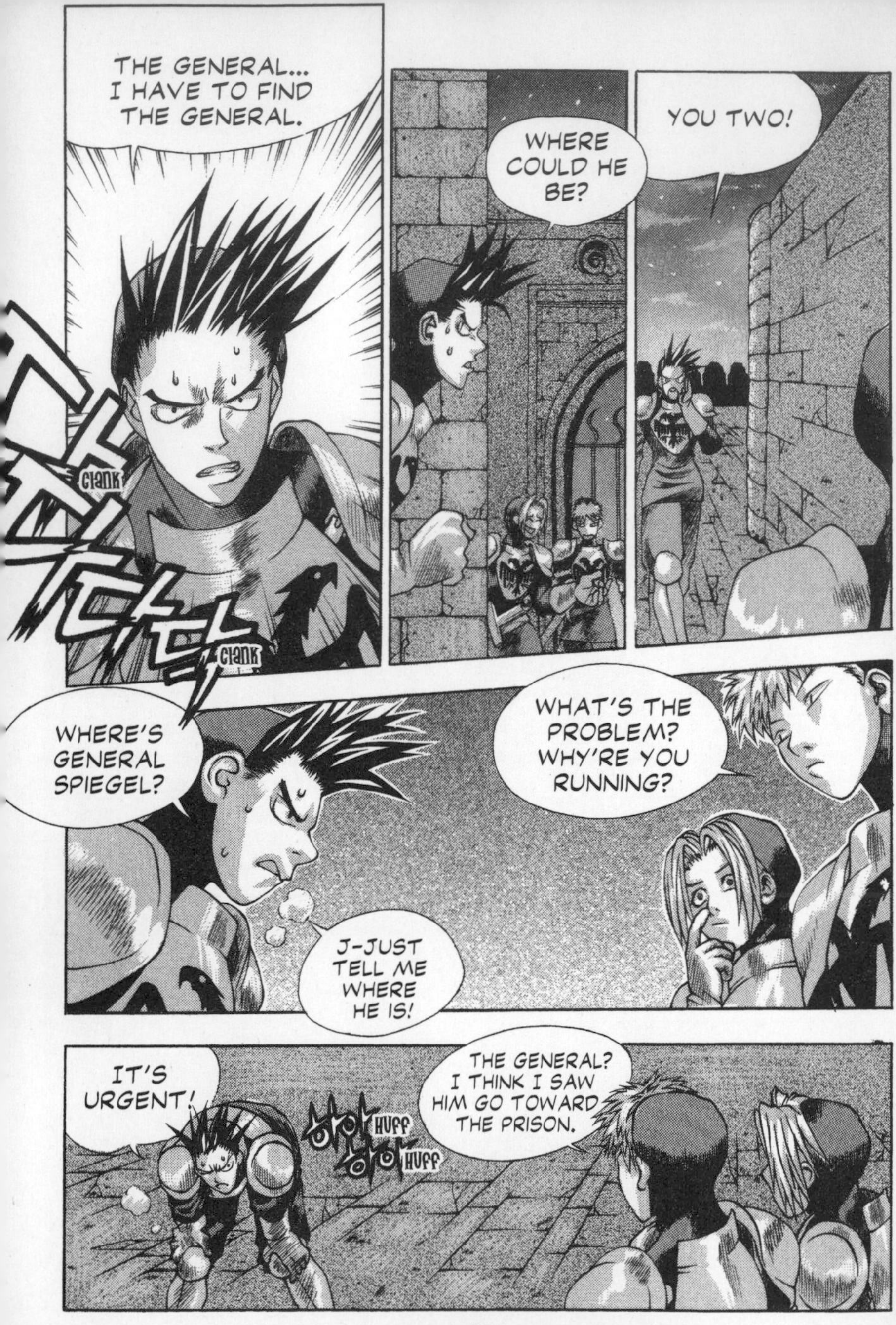
THE GENERAL... I HAVE TO FIND THE GENERAL.
CLANK
CLANK
WHERE COULD HE BE?
YOU TWO!
WHERE'S GENERAL SPIEGEL?
WHAT'S THE PROBLEM? WHY'RE YOU RUNNING?
J-JUST TELL ME WHERE HE IS!
IT'S URGENT!
HUFF
HUFF
THE GENERAL? I THINK I SAW HIM GO TOWARD THE PRISON.

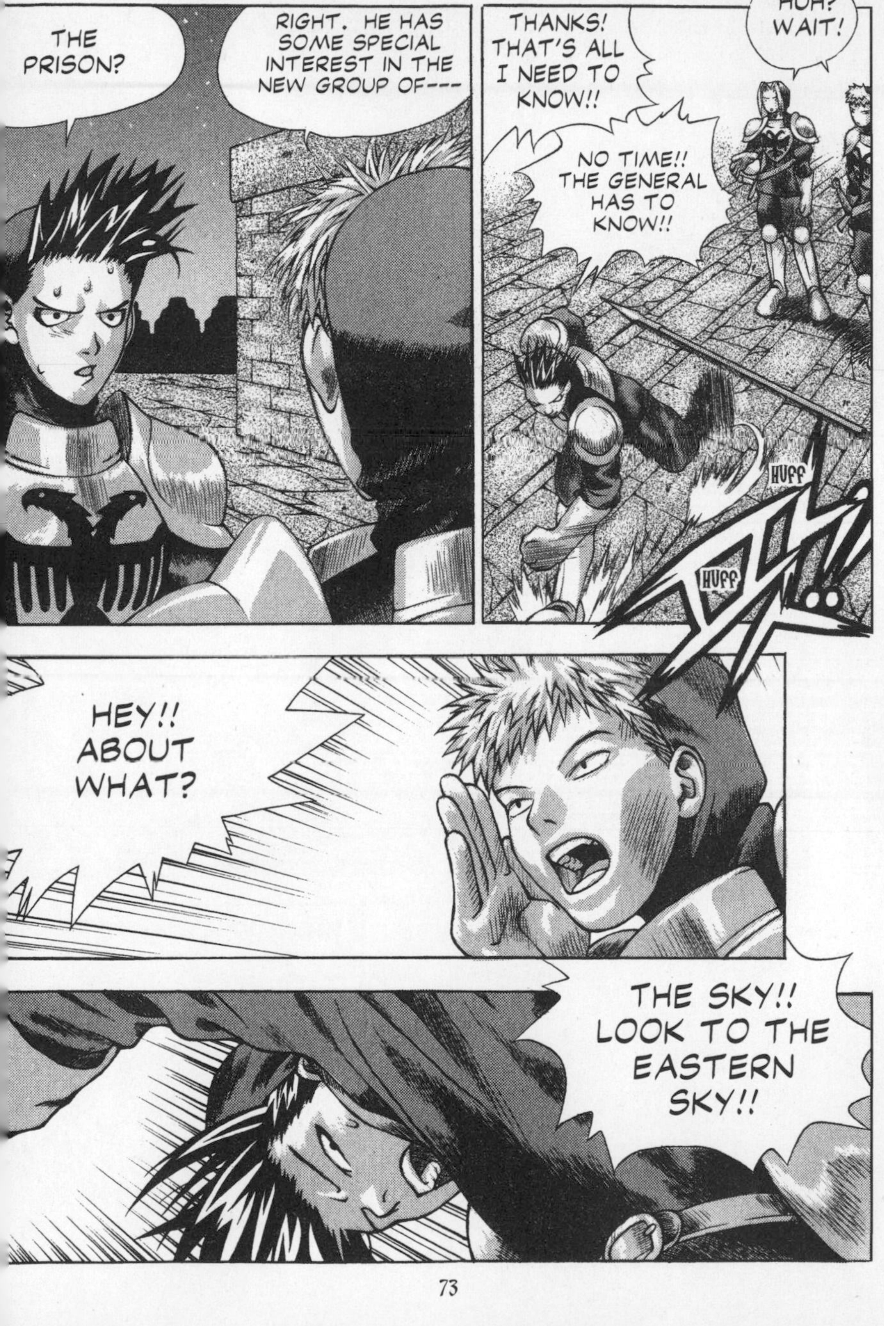
THE PRISON?
RIGHT. HE HAS SOME SPECIAL INTEREST IN THE NEW GROUP OF---
THANKS! THAT'S ALL I NEED TO KNOW!!
HUH? WAIT!
NO TIME!! THE GENERAL HAS TO KNOW!!
HUFF
HUFF
HEY!! ABOUT WHAT?
THE SKY!! LOOK TO THE EASTERN SKY!!

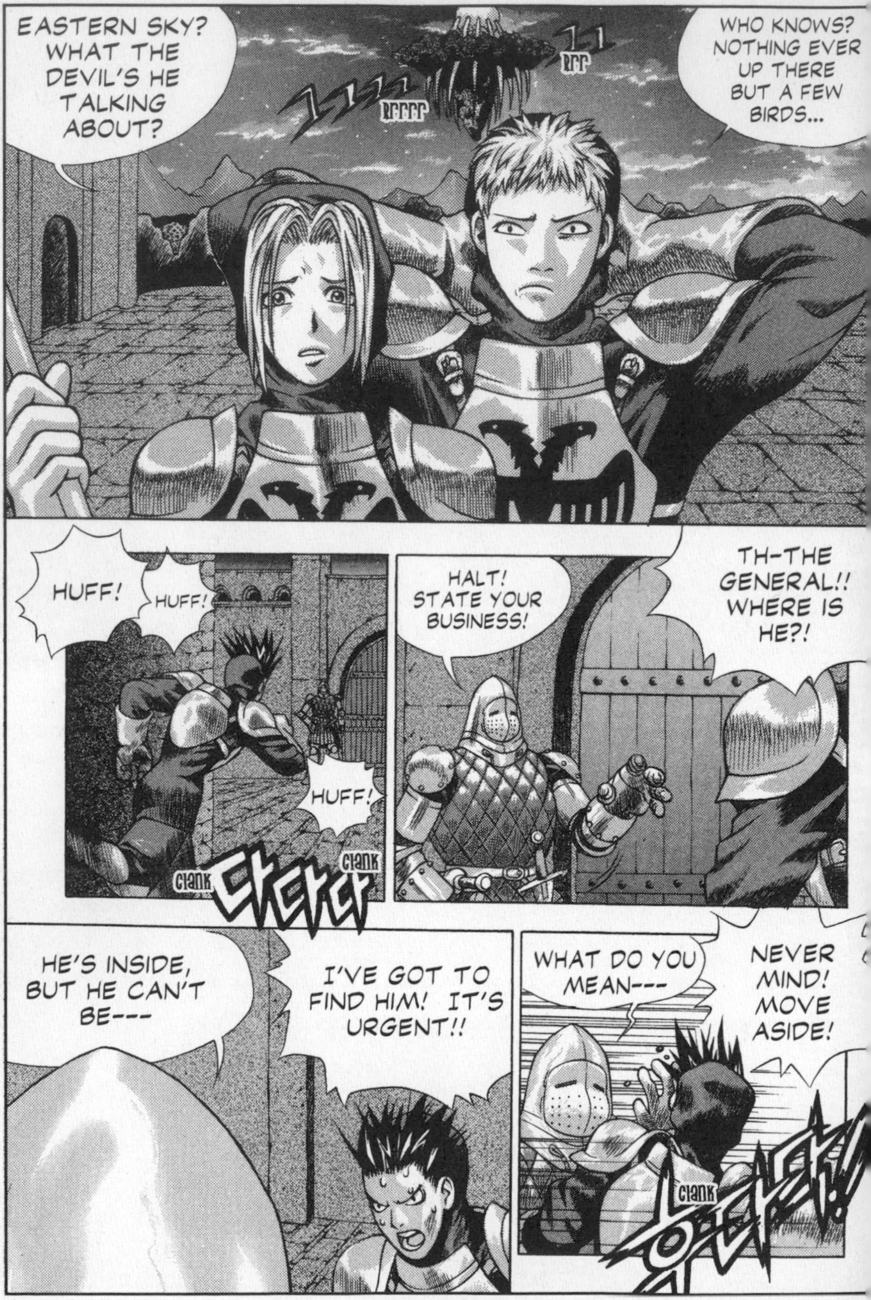

EASTERN SKY? WHAT THE DEVIL'S HE TALKING ABOUT?
WHO KNOWS? NOTHING EVER UP THERE BUT A FEW BIRDS...
HUFF!
HUFF!
HUFF!
CLANK
CLANK
HALT! STATE YOUR BUSINESS!
TH-THE GENERAL!! WHERE IS HE?!
HE'S INSIDE, BUT HE CAN'T BE---
I'VE GOT TO FIND HIM! IT'S URGENT!!
WHAT DO YOU MEAN---
NEVER MIND! MOVE ASIDE!
CLANK

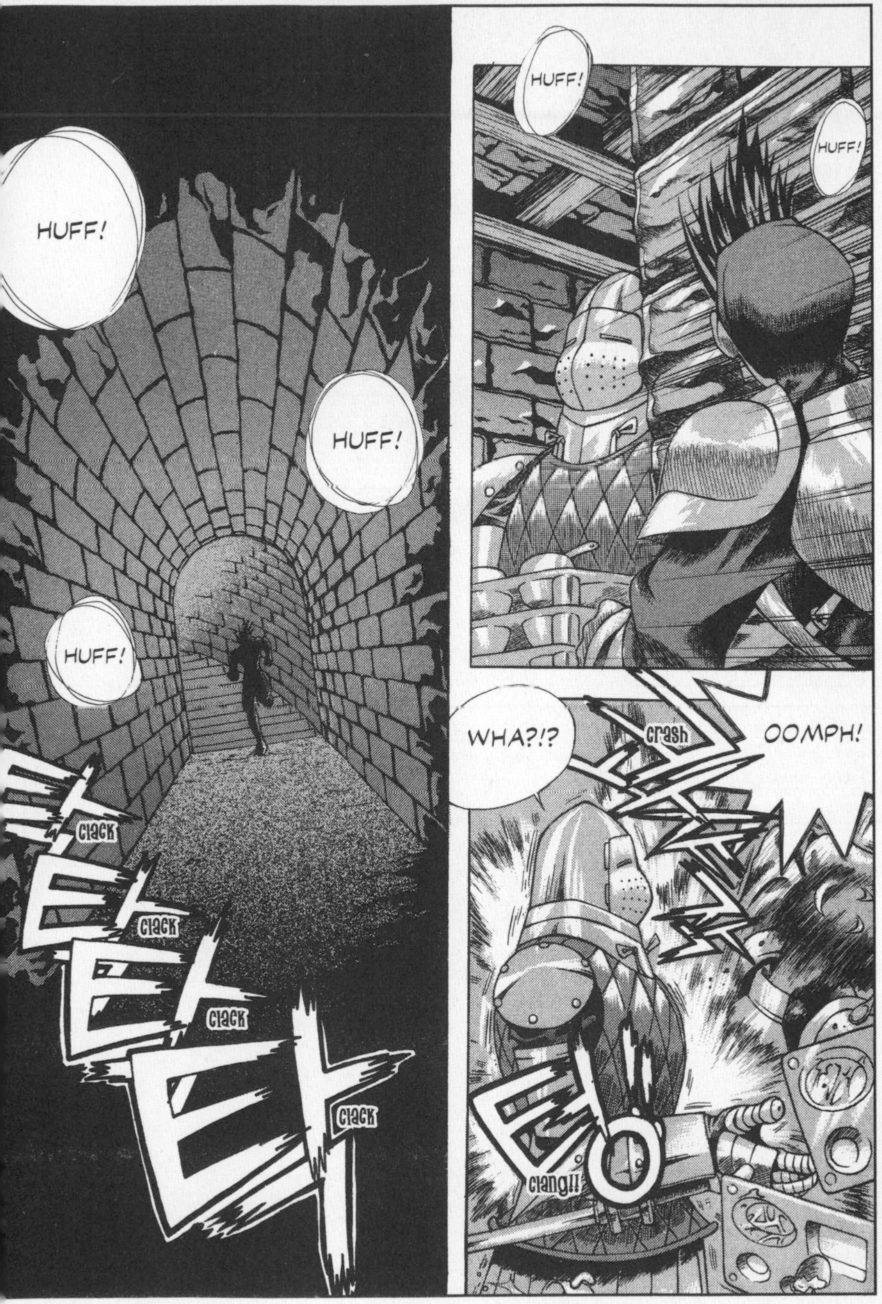
HUFF!
HUFF!
HUFF!
clack
clack
clack
clack
HUFF!
HUFF!
WHA?!?
crash
OOMPH!
clang!!

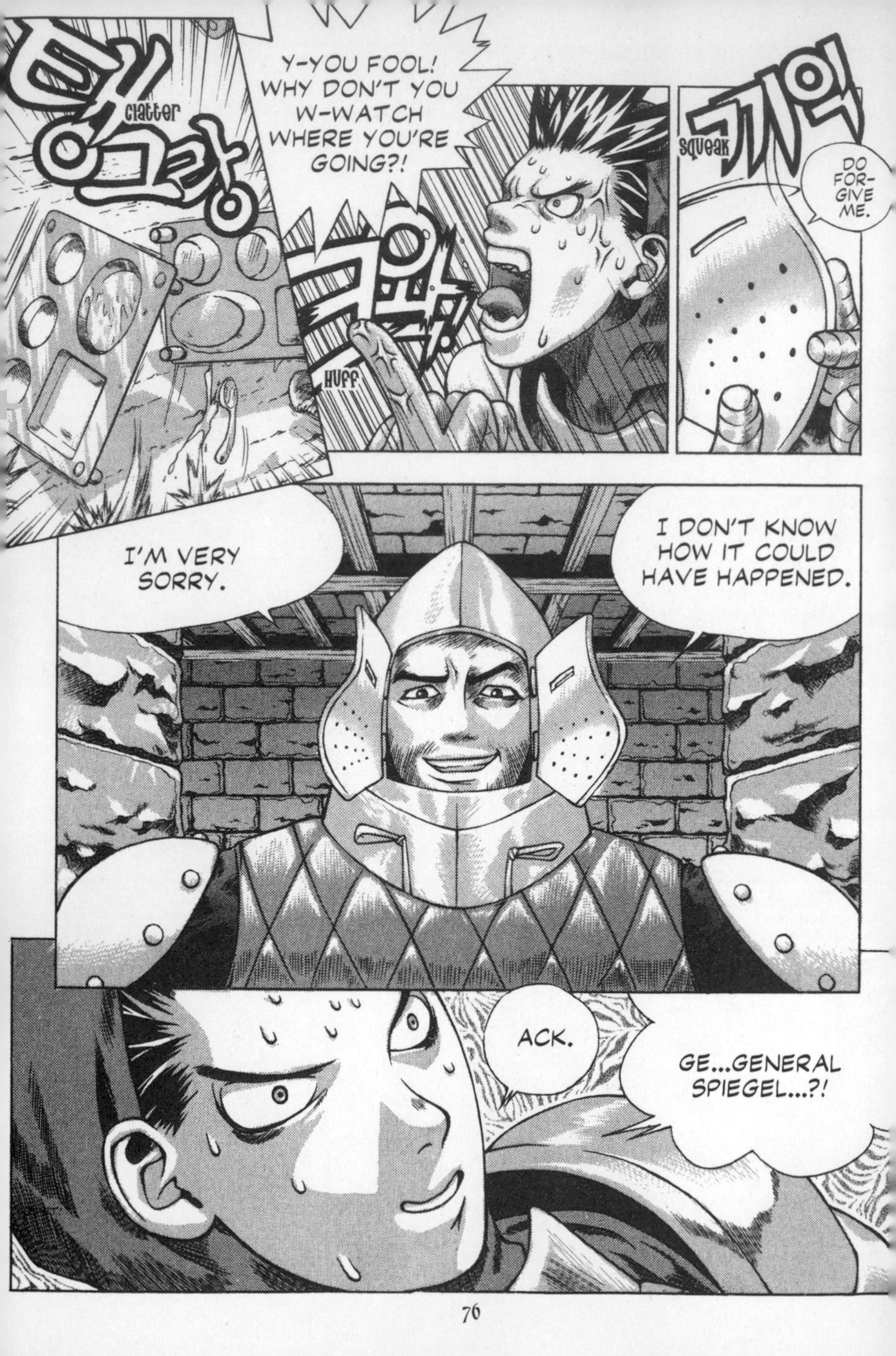

clatter
Y-YOU FOOL! WHY DON'T YOU W-WATCH WHERE YOU'RE GOING?!
HUFF
끼익
squeak
DO FOR-GIVE ME.
I'M VERY SORRY.
I DON'T KNOW HOW IT COULD HAVE HAPPENED.
ACK.
GE...GENERAL SPIEGEL...?!

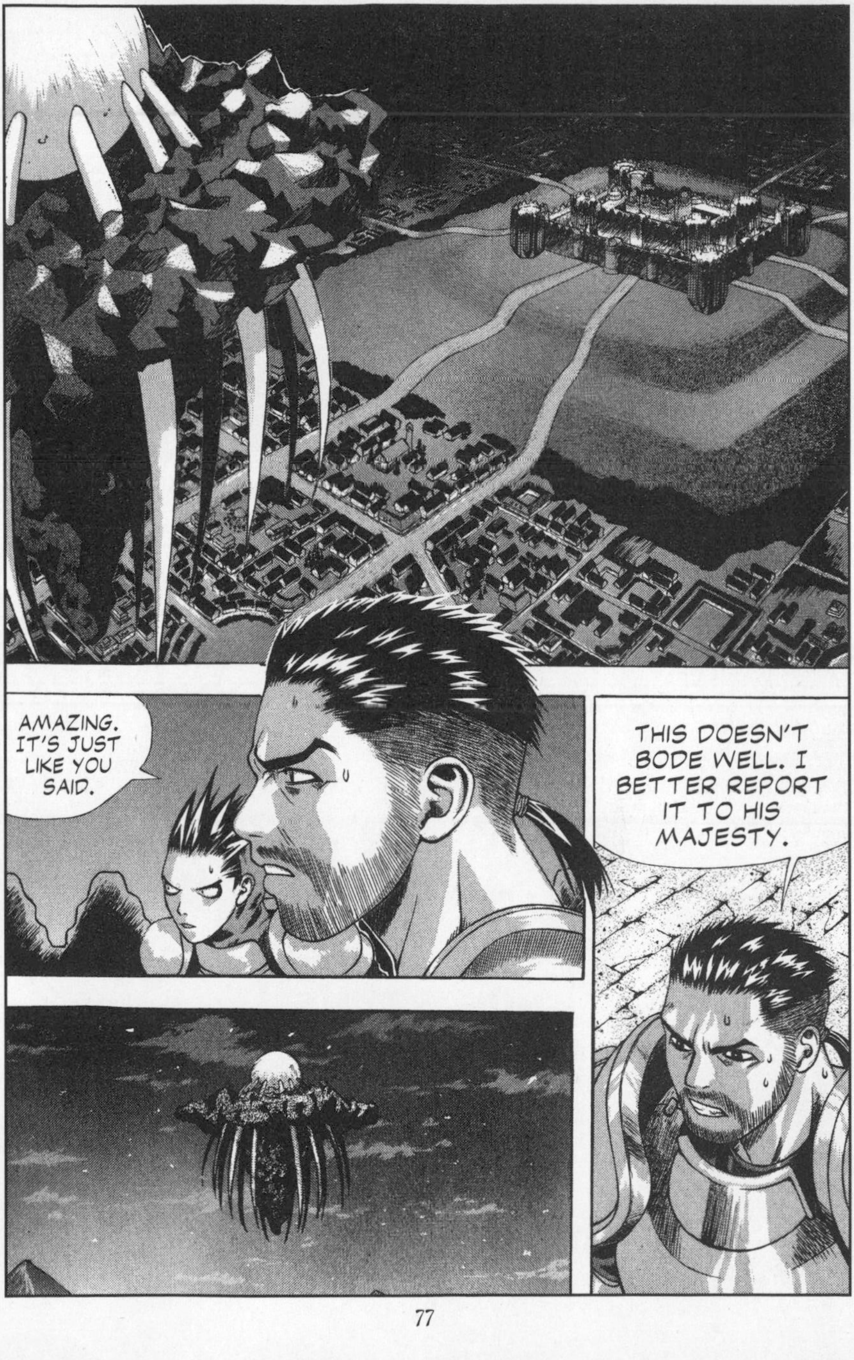
AMAZING. IT'S JUST LIKE YOU SAID.
THIS DOESN'T BODE WELL. I BETTER REPORT IT TO HIS MAJESTY.

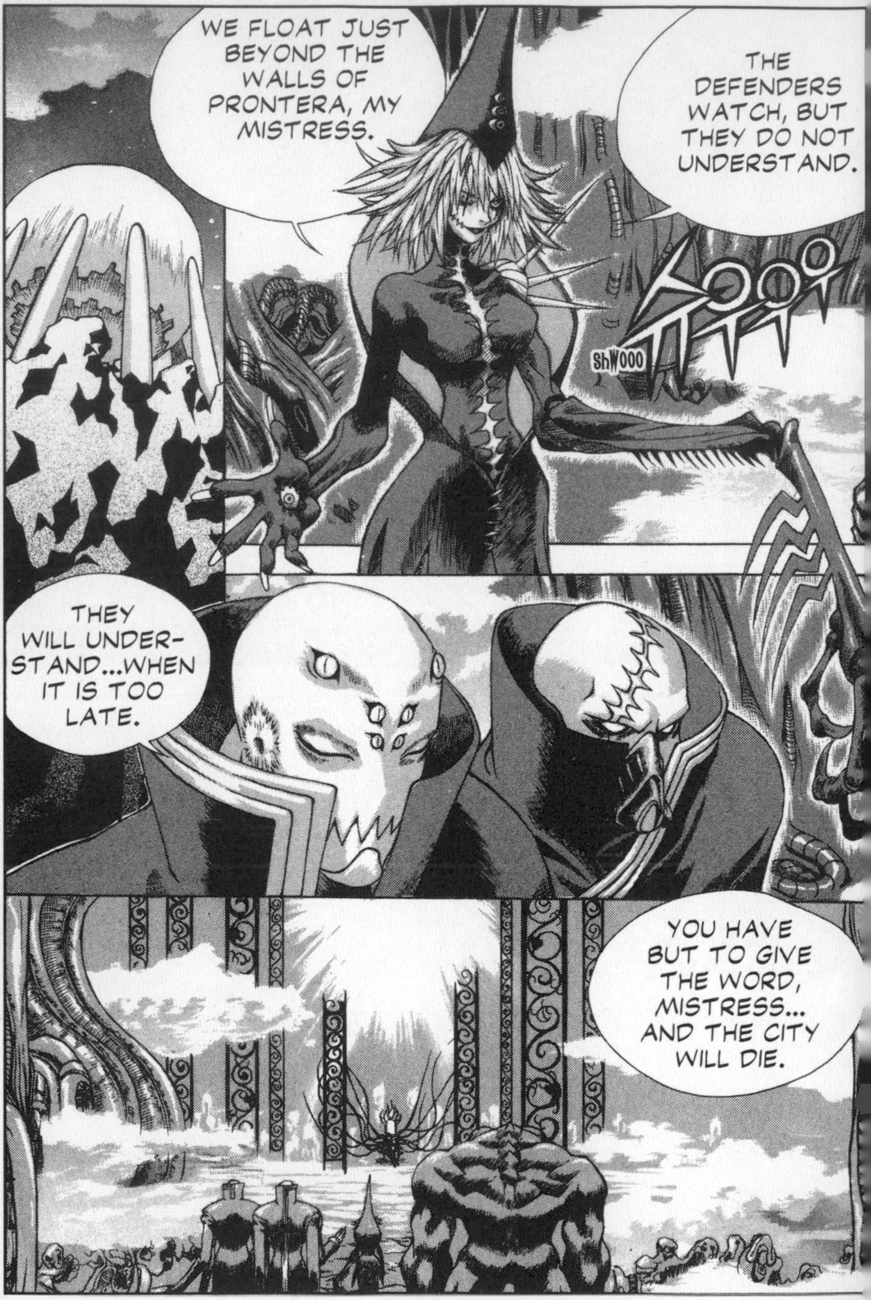
WE FLOAT JUST BEYOND THE WALLS OF PRONTERA, MY MISTRESS.
THE DEFENDERS WATCH, BUT THEY DO NOT UNDERSTAND.
KOOO
ShWOOO
THEY WILL UNDER-STAND...WHEN IT IS TOO LATE.
YOU HAVE BUT TO GIVE THE WORD, MISTRESS... AND THE CITY WILL DIE.

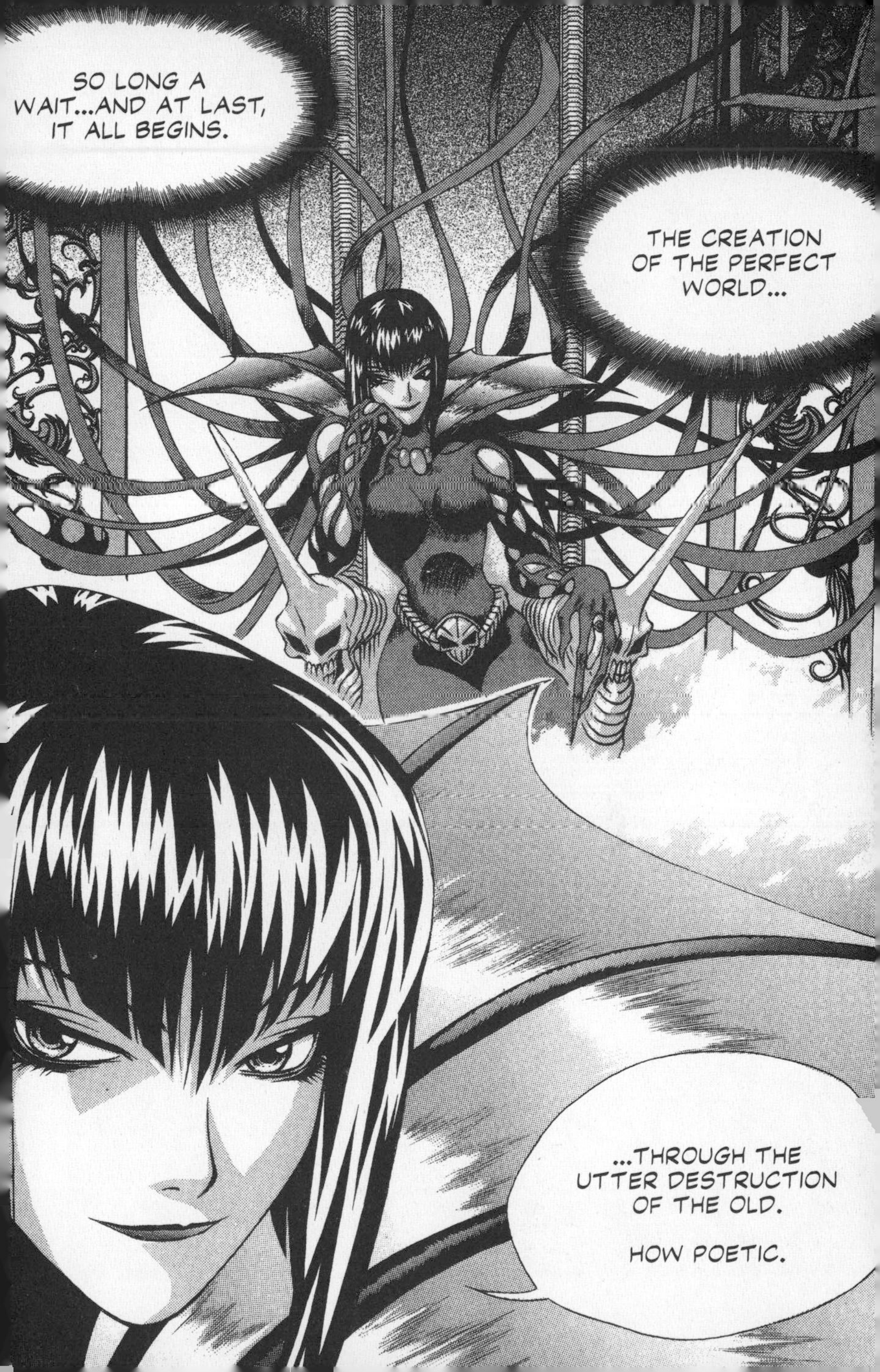
SO LONG A WAIT...AND AT LAST, IT ALL BEGINS.
THE CREATION OF THE PERFECT WORLD...
...THROUGH THE UTTER DESTRUCTION OF THE OLD.
HOW POETIC.

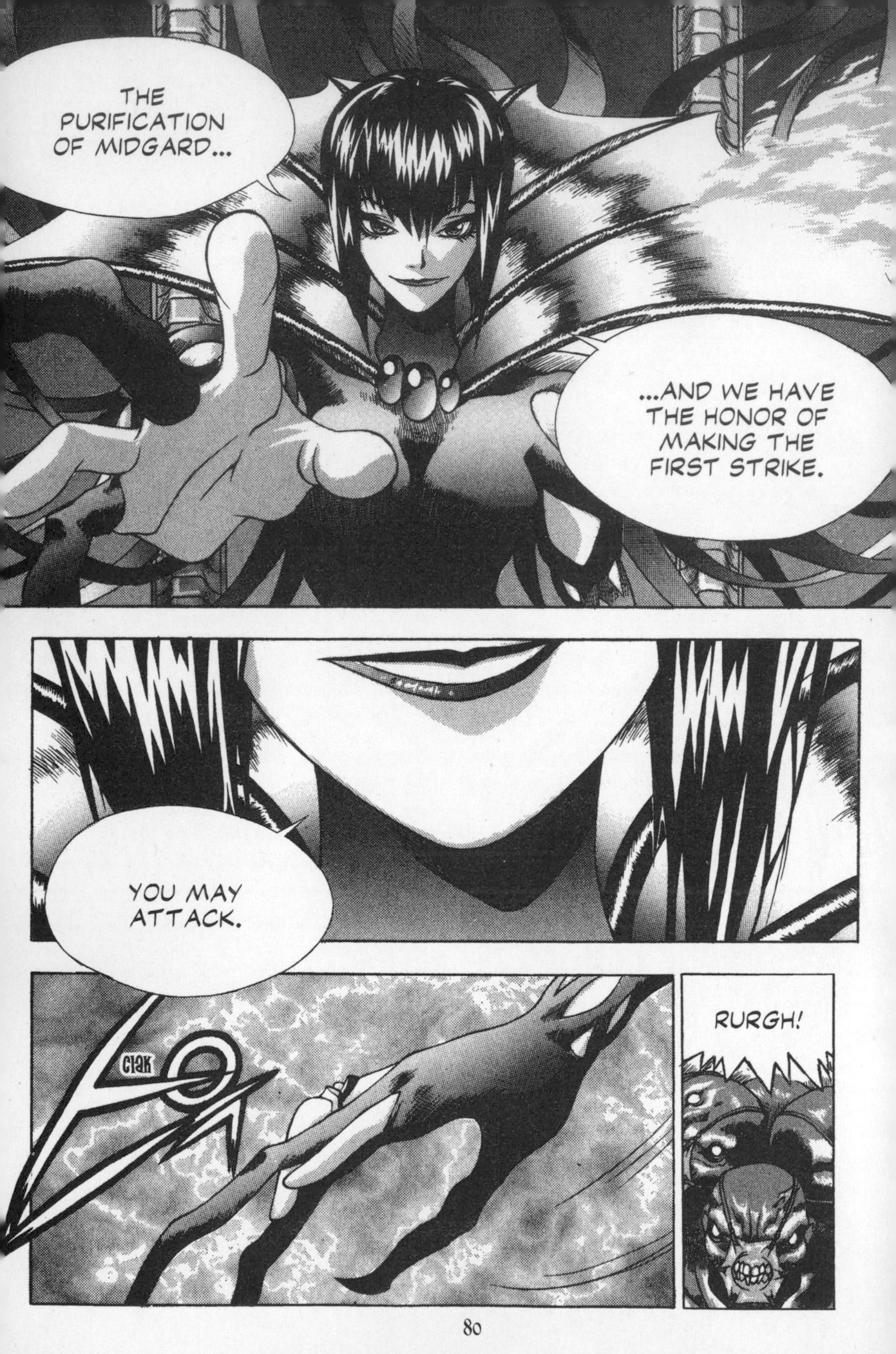
THE PURIFICATION OF MIDGARD...
...AND WE HAVE THE HONOR OF MAKING THE FIRST STRIKE.
YOU MAY ATTACK.
CLAK
RURGH!

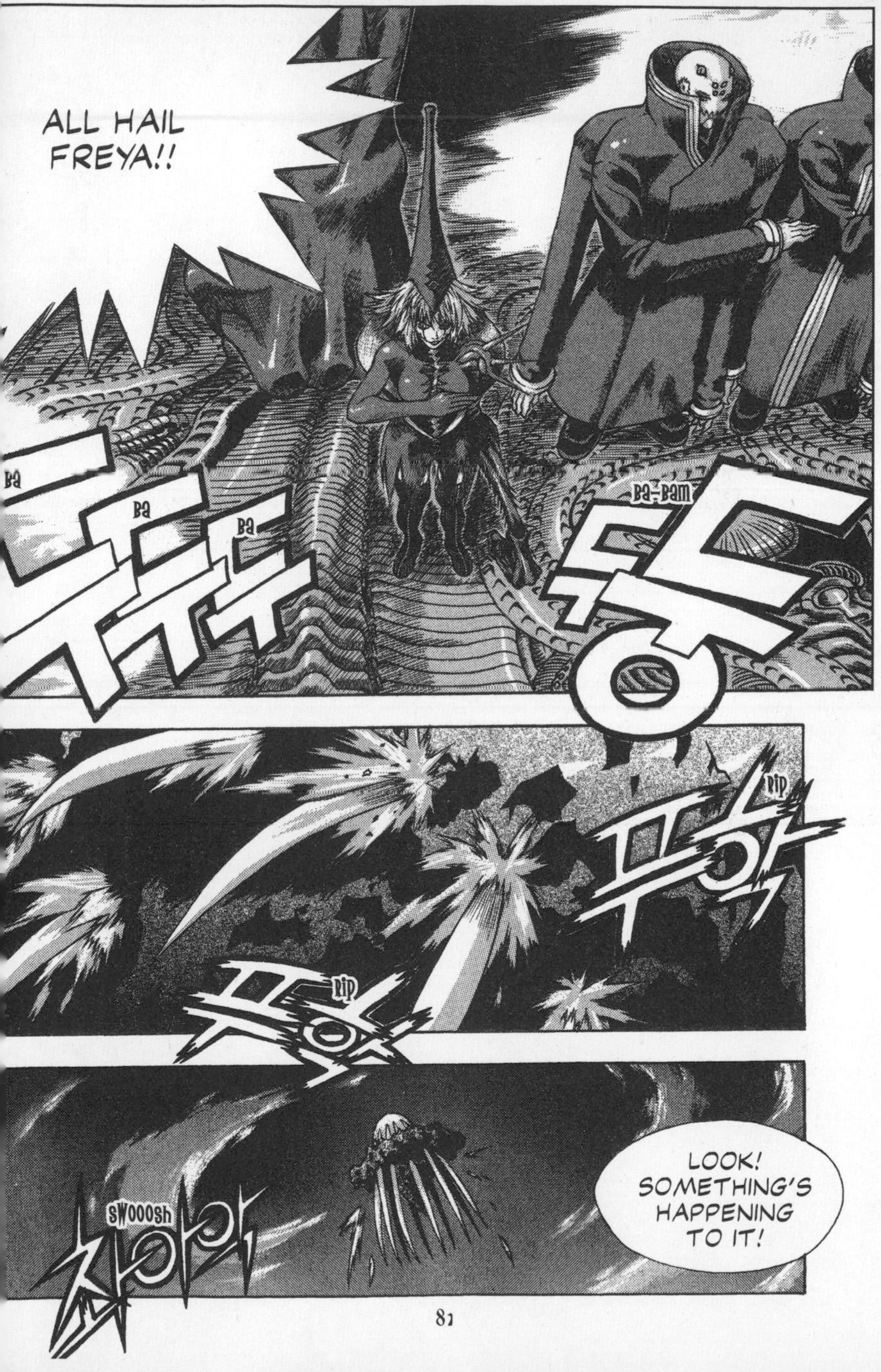
ALL HAIL FREYA!!
BA
BA
BA
BA-BAM
RIP
RIP
SWOOOSH
LOOK! SOMETHING'S HAPPENING TO IT!

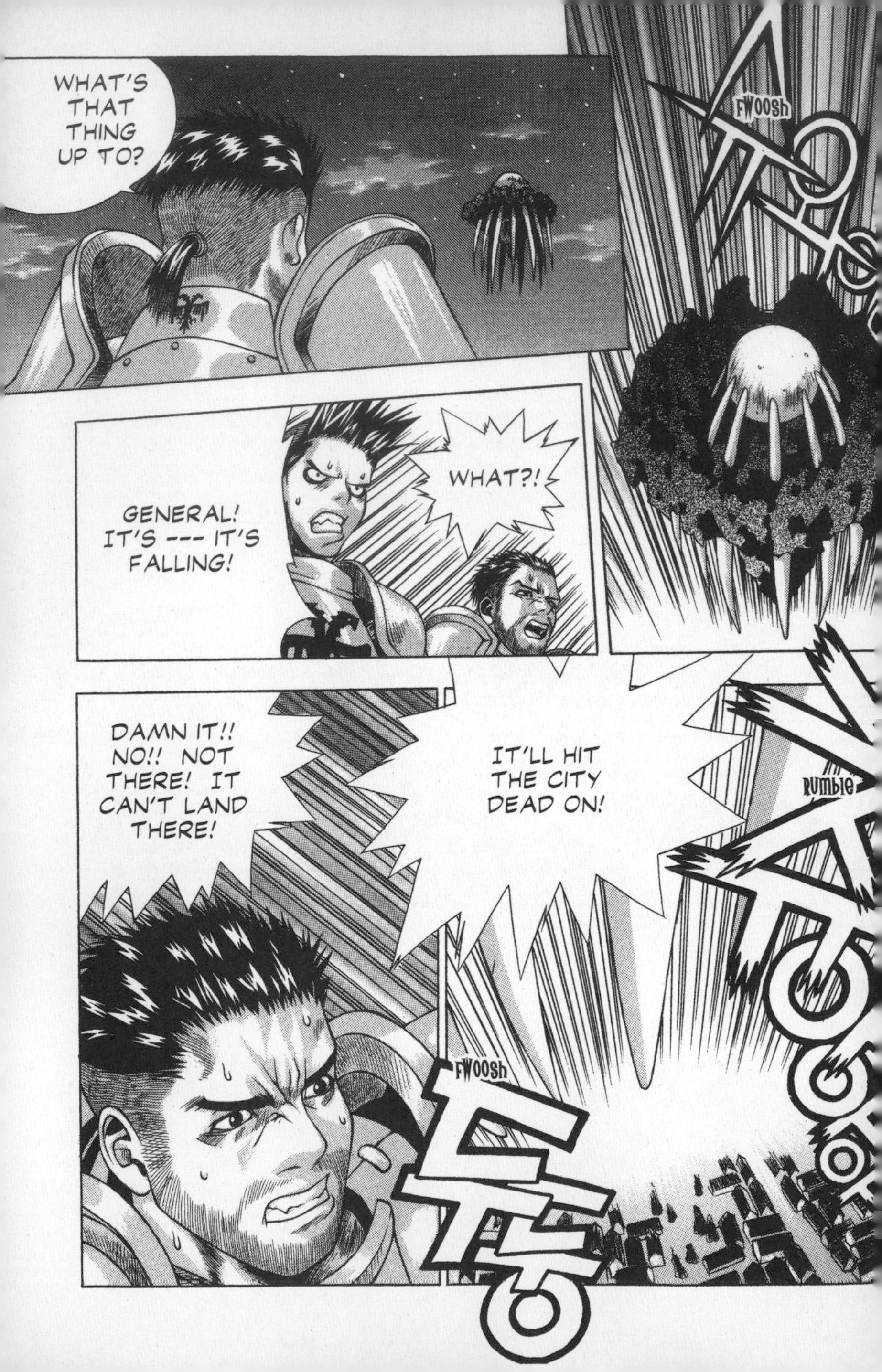
WHAT'S THAT THING UP TO?
FWOOSH
GENERAL! IT'S --- IT'S FALLING!
WHAT?!
DAMN IT!! NO!! NOT THERE! IT CAN'T LAND THERE!
IT'LL HIT THE CITY DEAD ON!
RUMBLE
FWOOSH

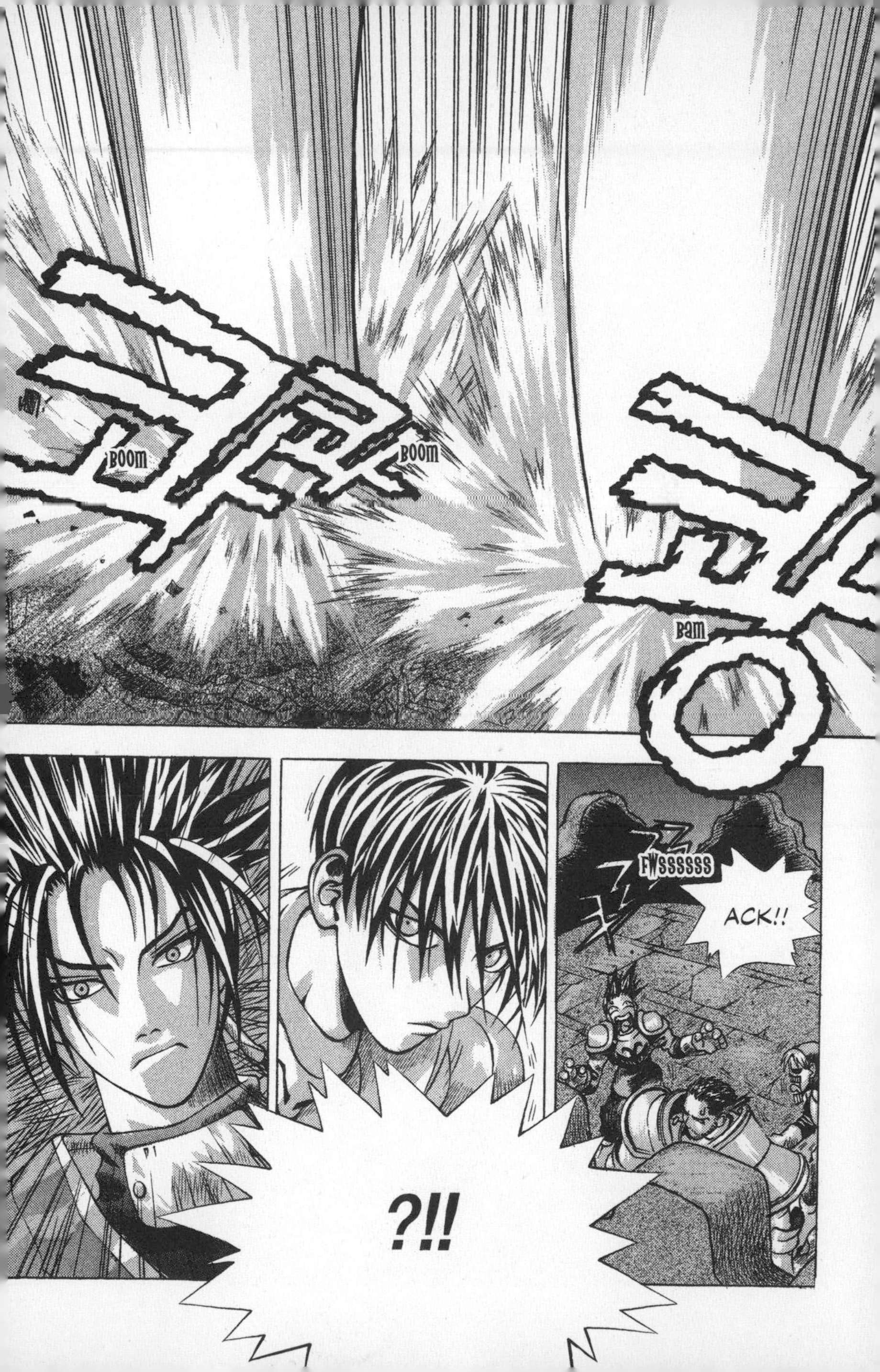
BOOM
BOOM
BAM
FWSSSSSS
ACK!!
?!!

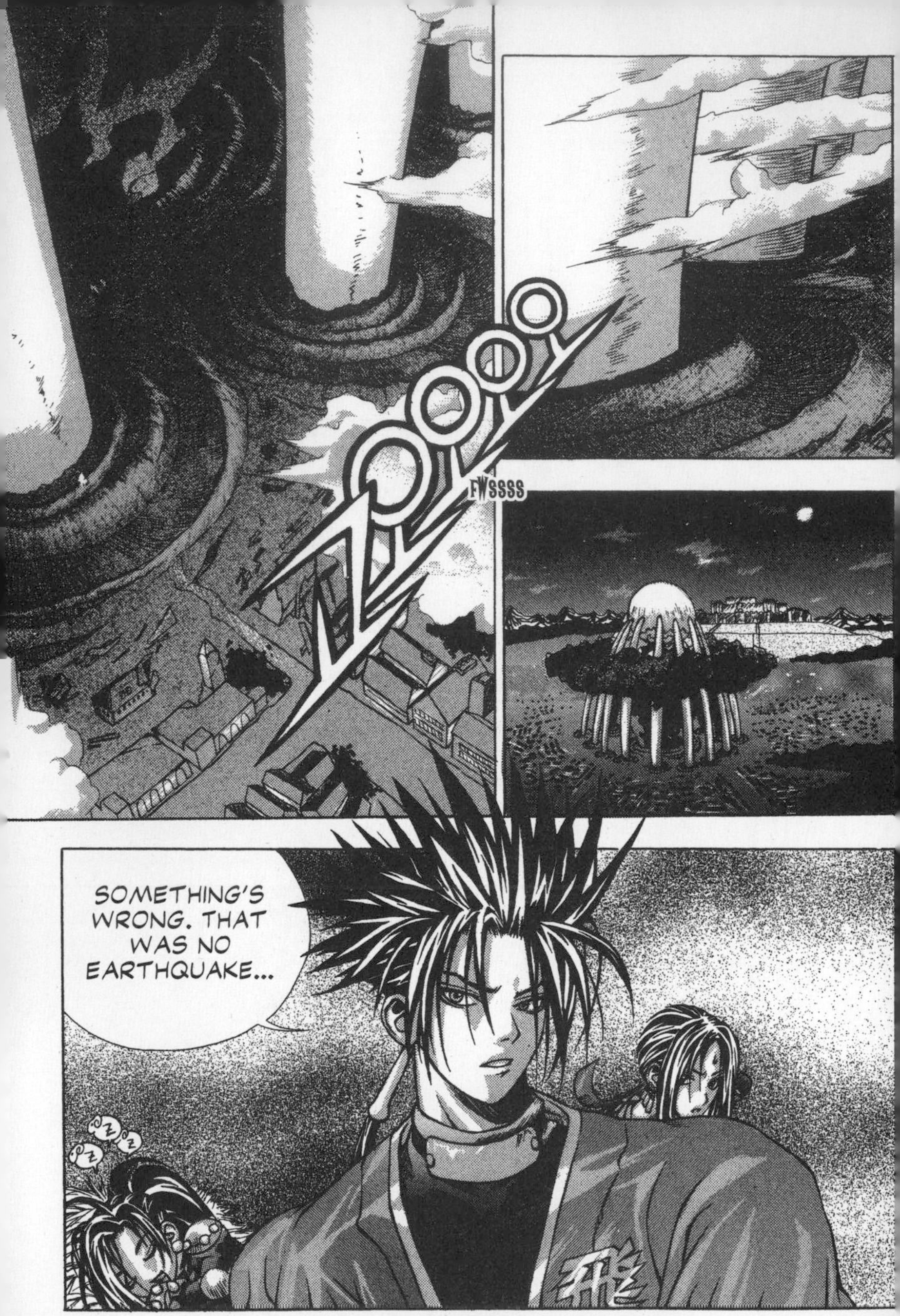
ZOOOOOM
FWSSSS
SOMETHING'S WRONG. THAT WAS NO EARTHQUAKE...

RAGNAROK
라그나로크
IN TO THE ABYSS

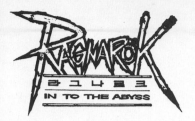

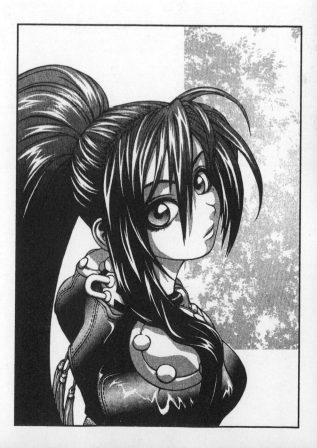

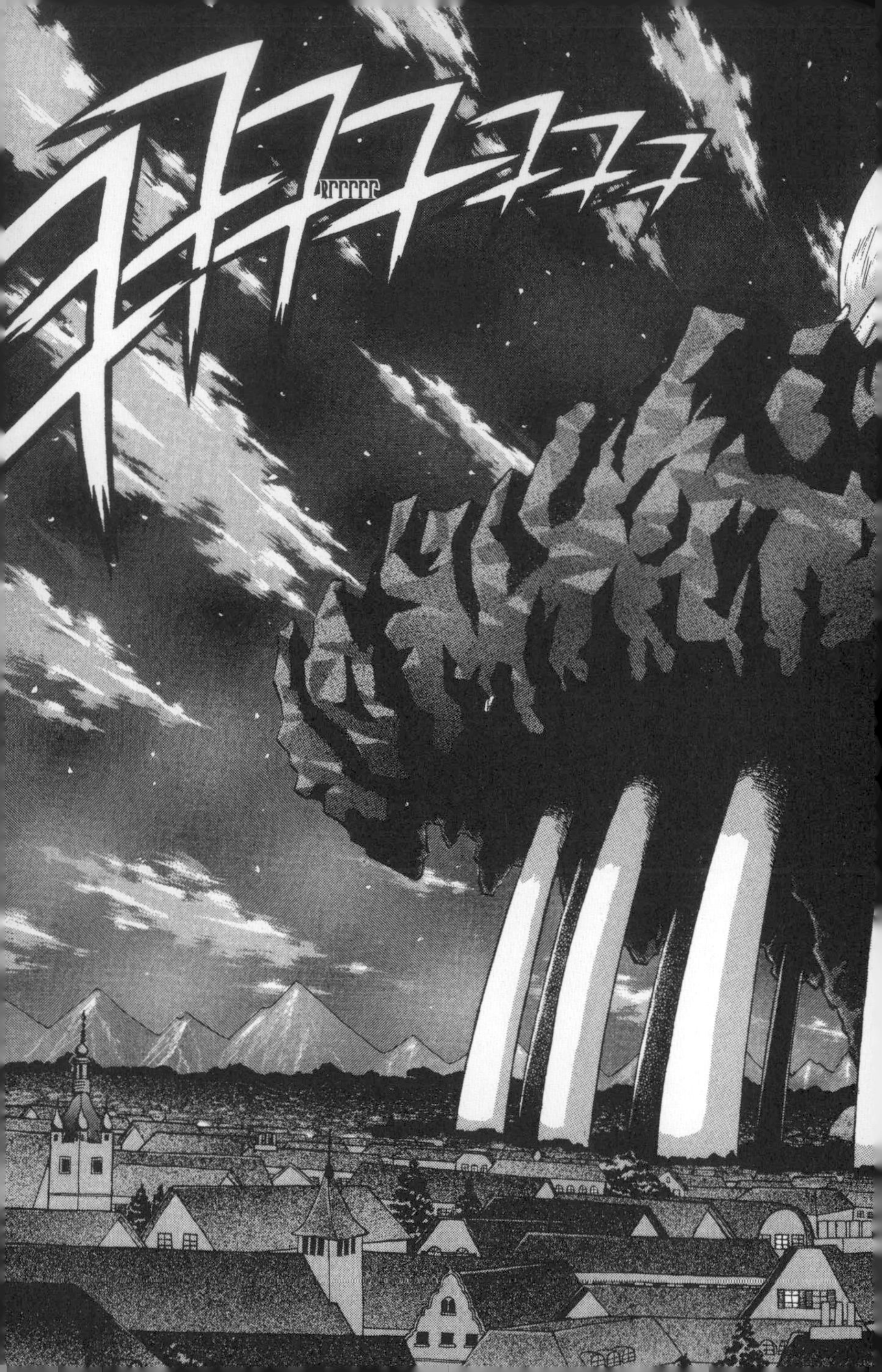
Rrrrrr

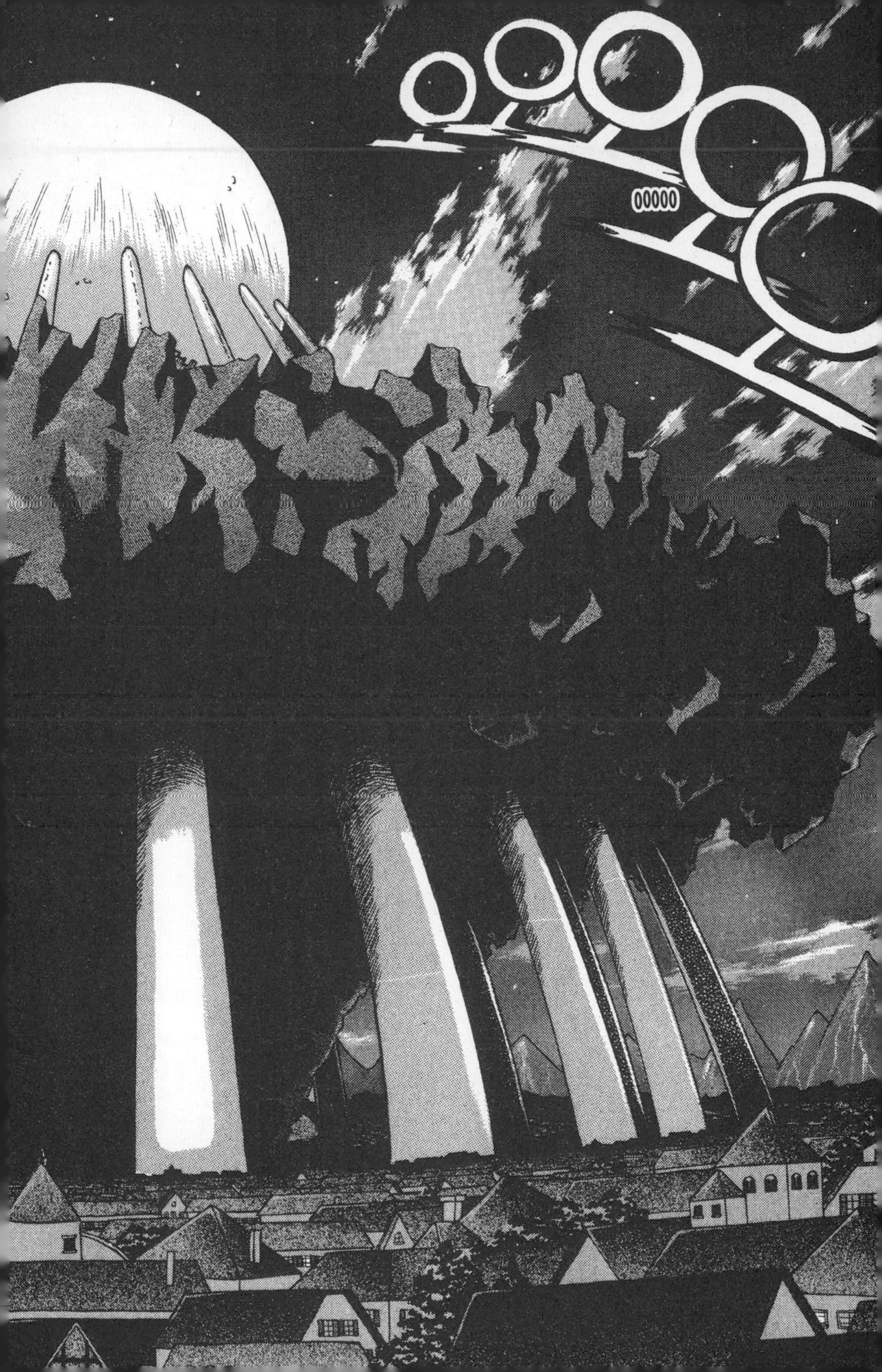
OOOOO

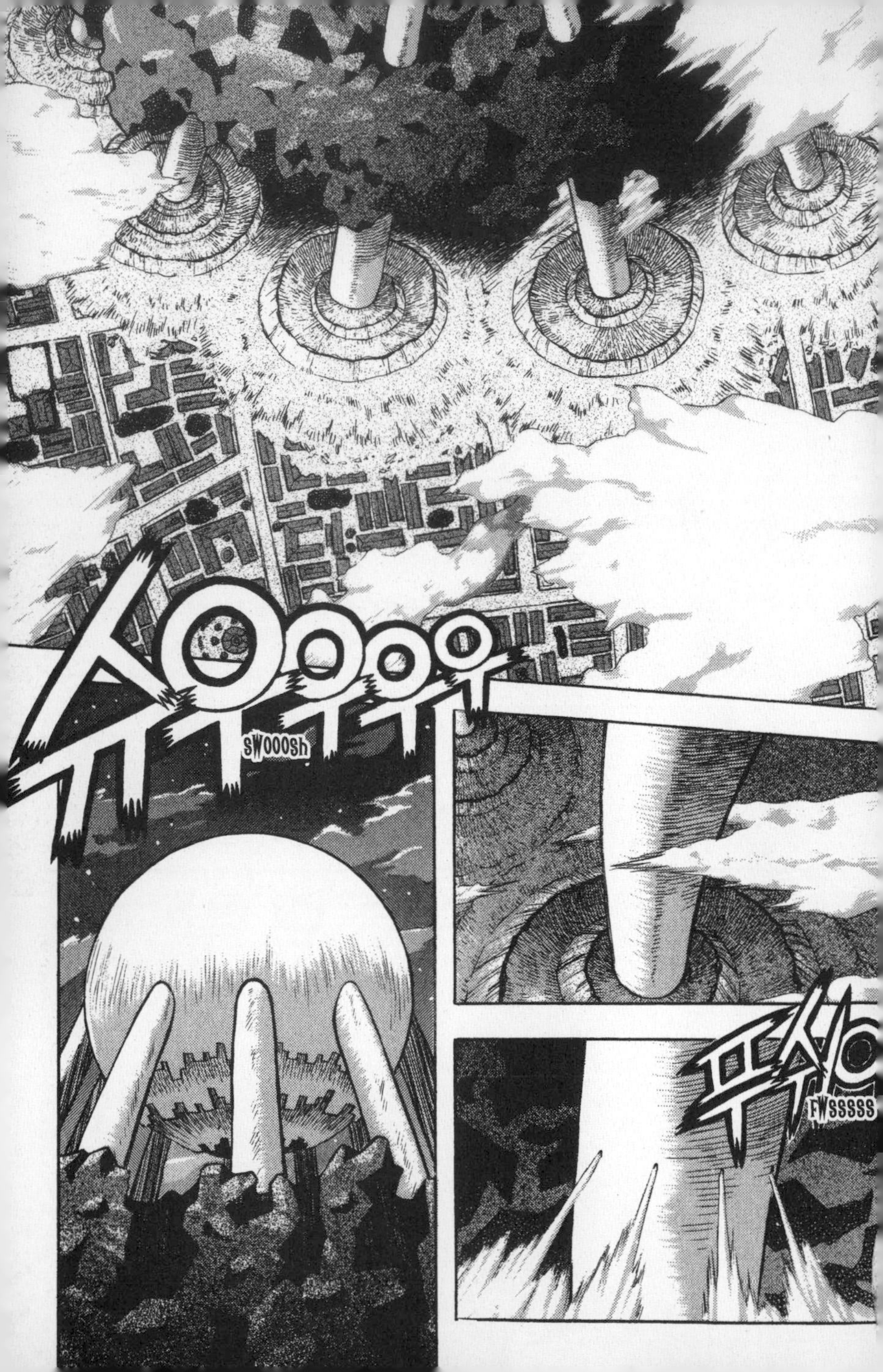
SWOOOSh
FWSSSSS

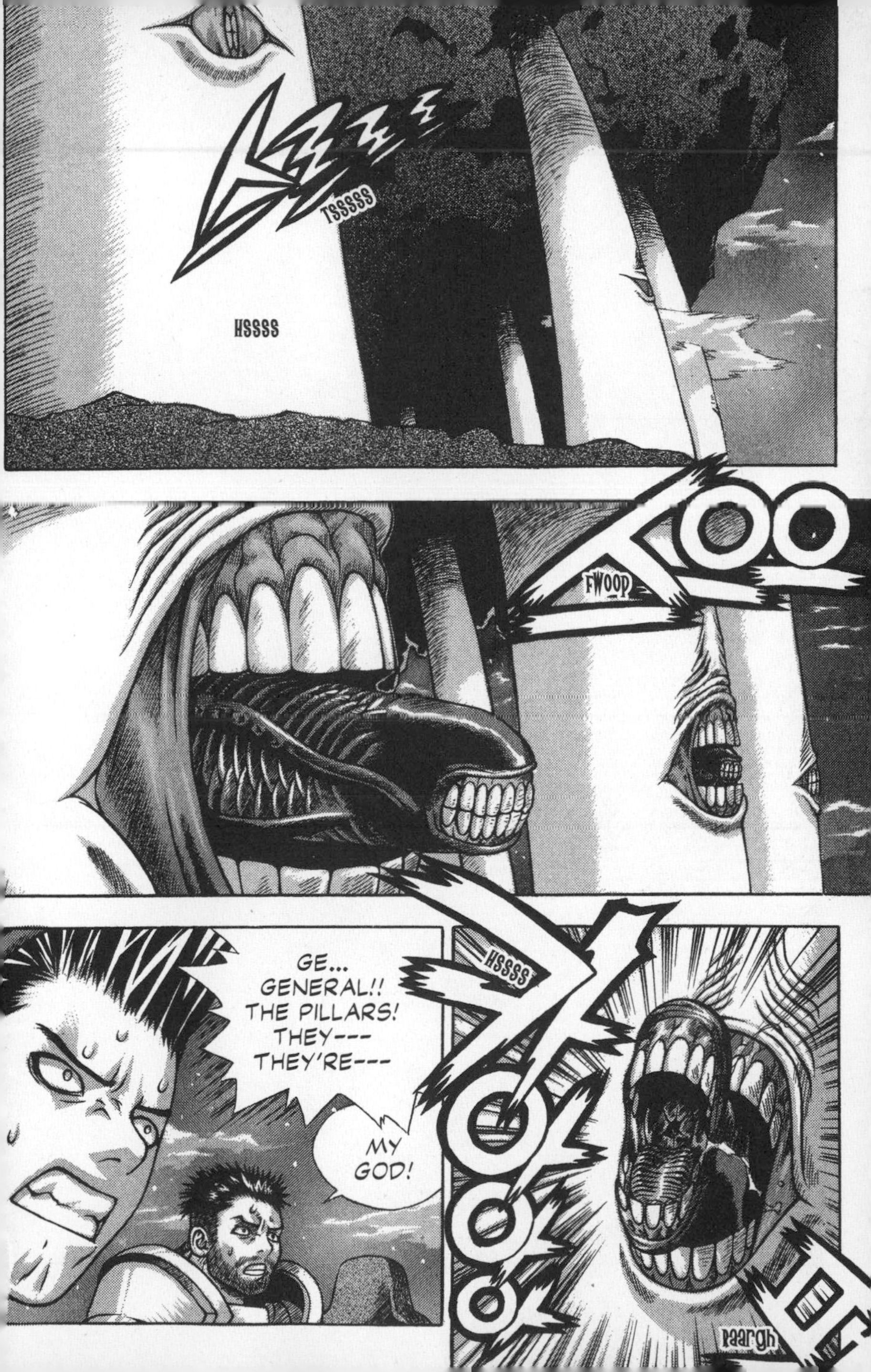
TSSSSS
HSSSS
FWOOP
GE... GENERAL!! THE PILLARS! THEY--- THEY'RE---
MY GOD!
HSSSS
RAARGH

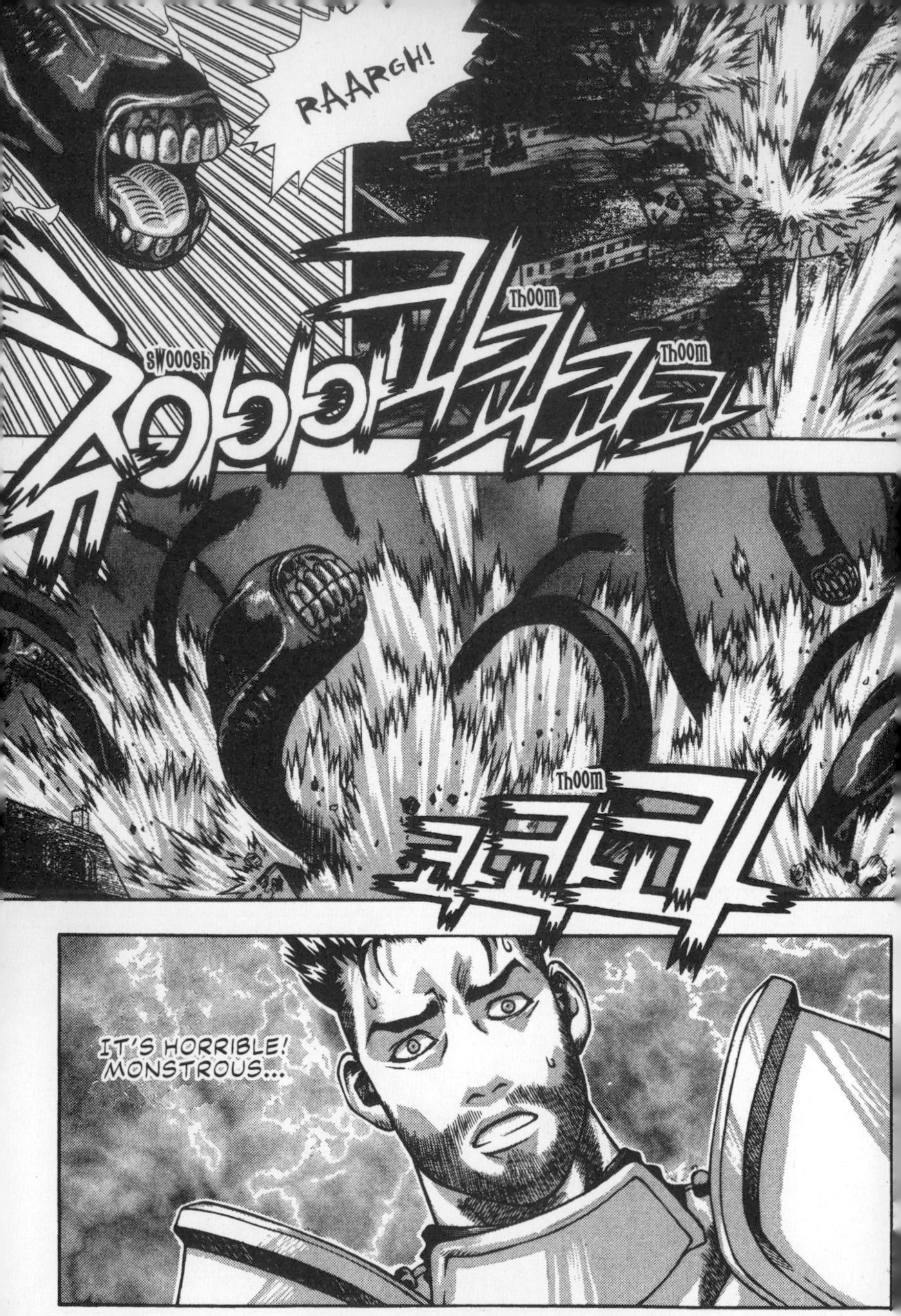
RAARGH!
SWOOOSH
THOOM
THOOM
THOOM
IT'S HORRIBLE! MONSTROUS...

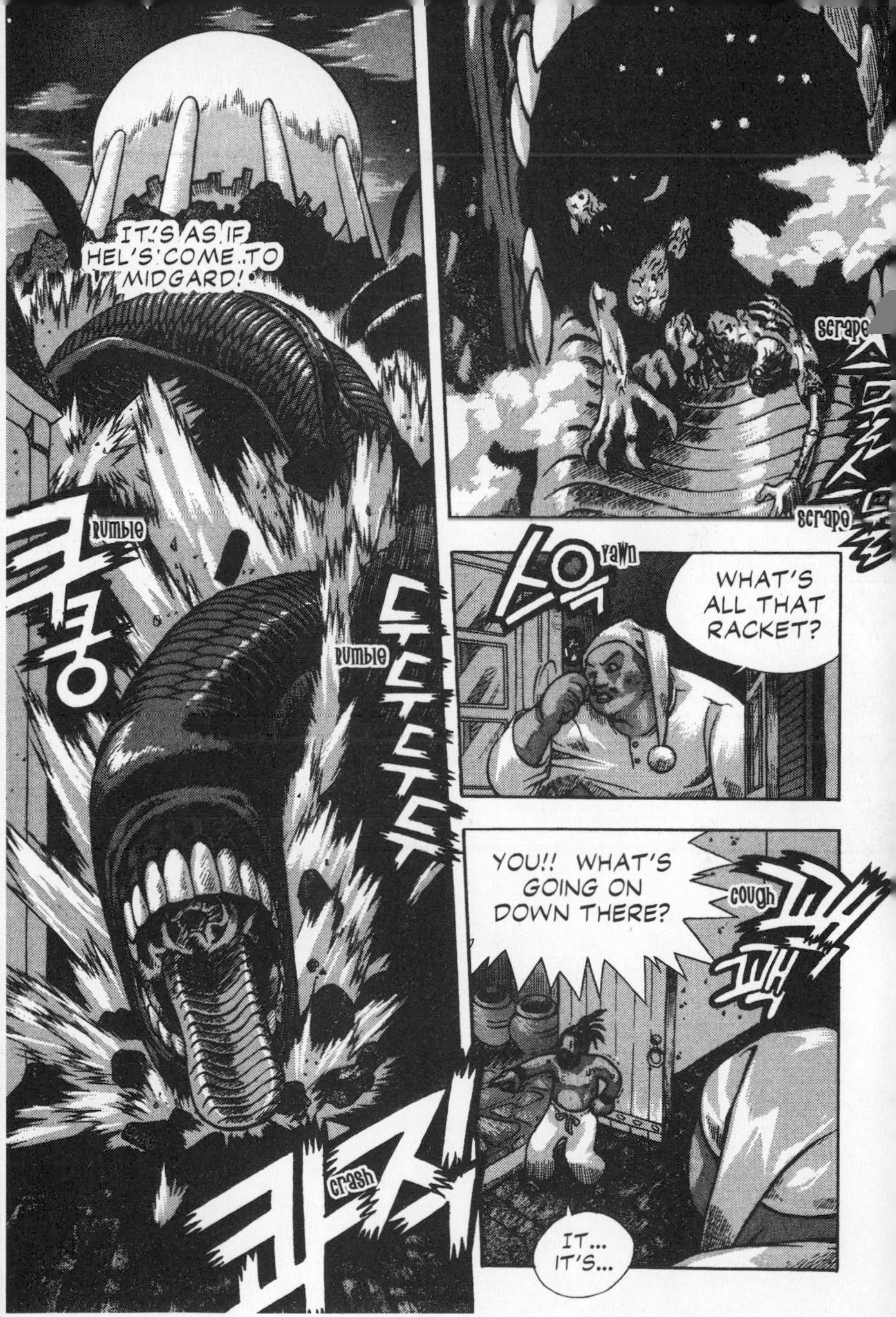
IT'S AS IF HEL'S COME TO MIDGARD!
RUMBLE
RUMBLE
CRASH
SCRAPE
SCRAPE
YAWN
WHAT'S ALL THAT RACKET?
YOU!! WHAT'S GOING ON DOWN THERE?
COUGH
IT... IT'S...

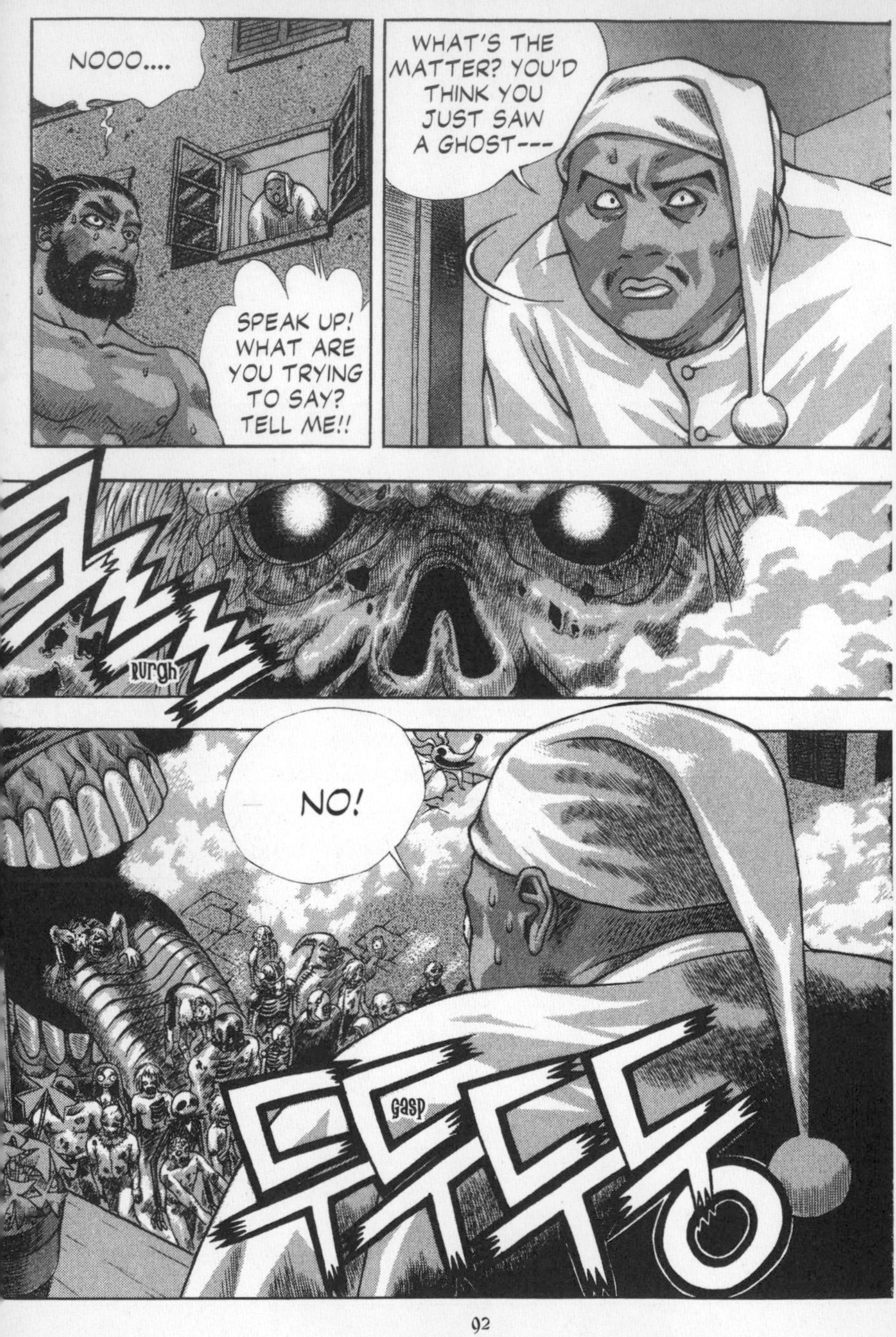
NOOO....
SPEAK UP! WHAT ARE YOU TRYING TO SAY? TELL ME!!
WHAT'S THE MATTER? YOU'D THINK YOU JUST SAW A GHOST---
RURGH
NO!
GASP

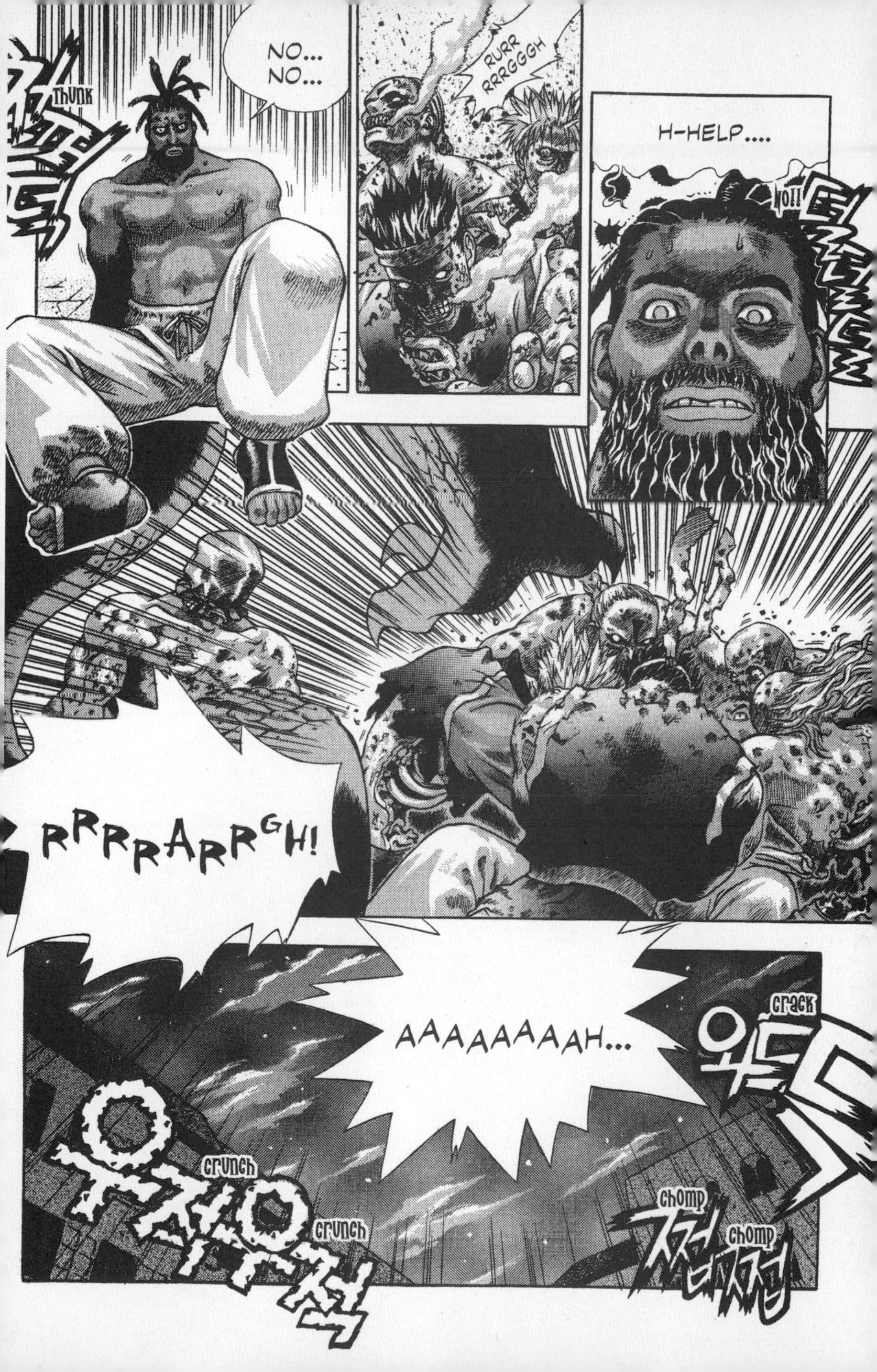
THUNK
NO... NO...
RURR RRRGGGH
H-HELP....
NO!!
RRRRARRGH!
AAAAAAAAH...
crack
crunch
crunch
chomp
chomp

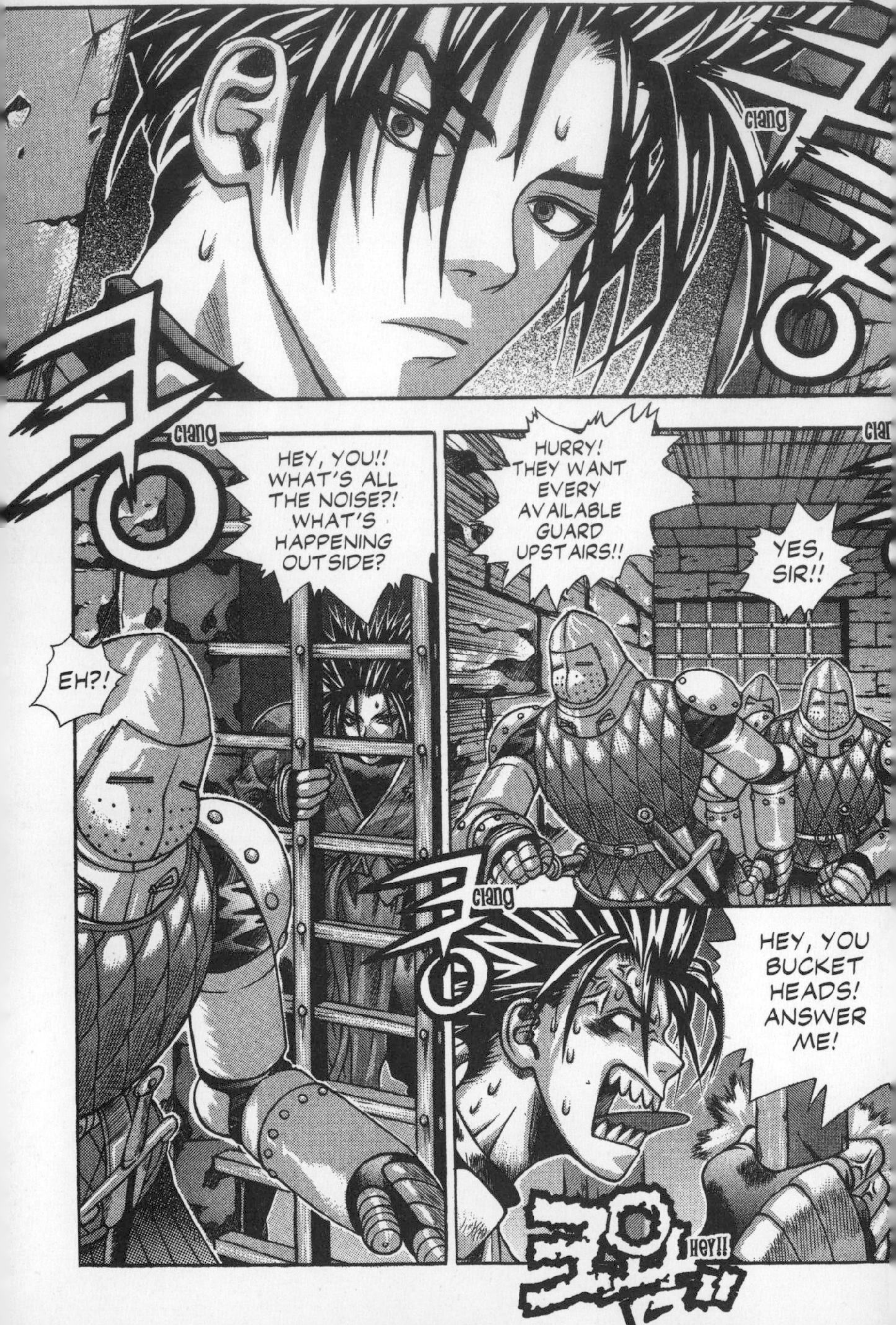
clang
clang
HEY, YOU!! WHAT'S ALL THE NOISE?! WHAT'S HAPPENING OUTSIDE?
HURRY! THEY WANT EVERY AVAILABLE GUARD UPSTAIRS!!
YES, SIR!!
EH?!
clang
HEY, YOU BUCKET HEADS! ANSWER ME!
HEY!!

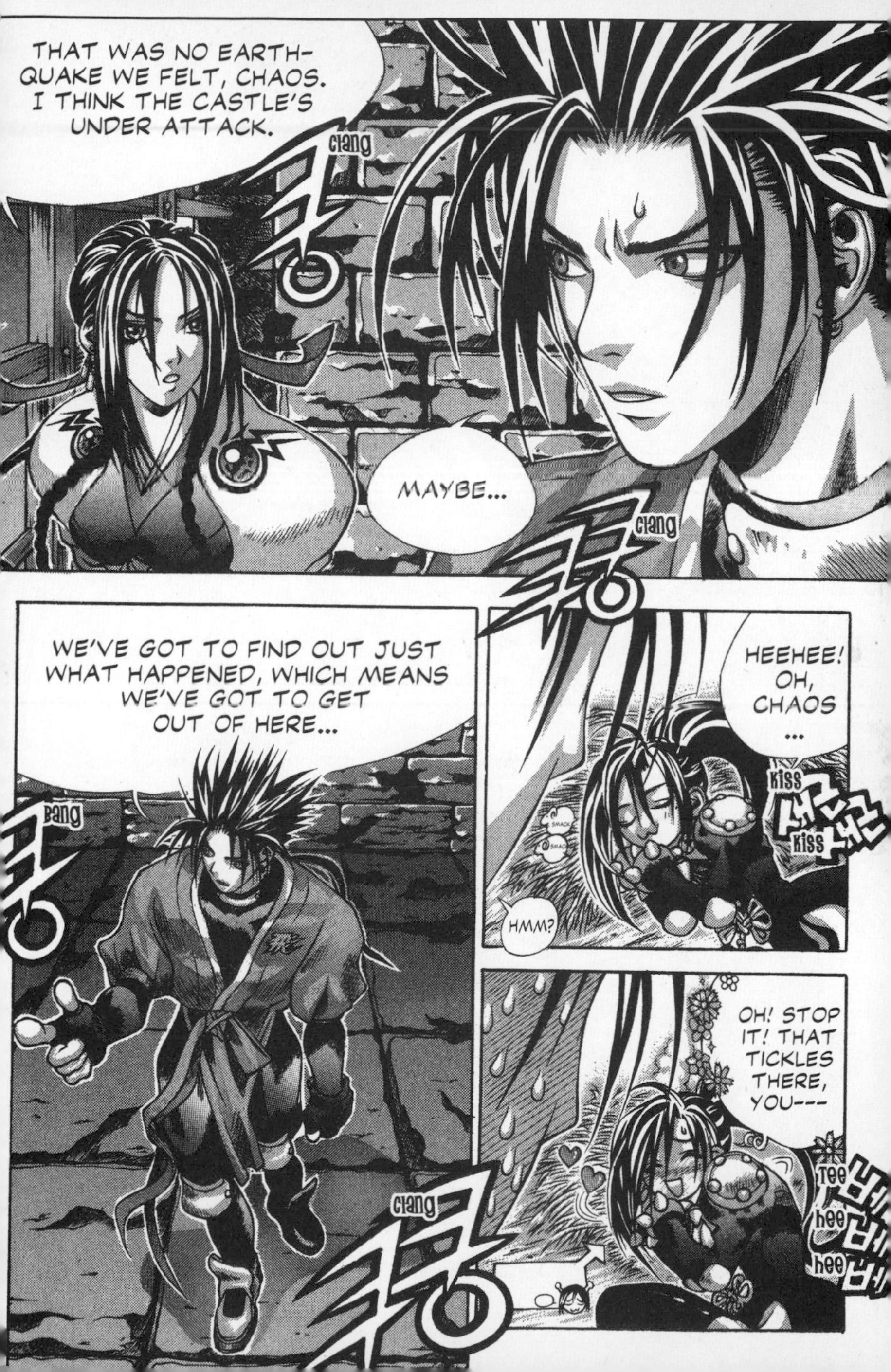
THAT WAS NO EARTH-QUAKE WE FELT, CHAOS. I THINK THE CASTLE'S UNDER ATTACK.
Clang
MAYBE...
Clang
WE'VE GOT TO FIND OUT JUST WHAT HAPPENED, WHICH MEANS WE'VE GOT TO GET OUT OF HERE...
Bang
Clang
HEEHEE! OH, CHAOS ...
Kiss
Kiss
HMM?
OH! STOP IT! THAT TICKLES THERE, YOU---
Tee
hee
hee

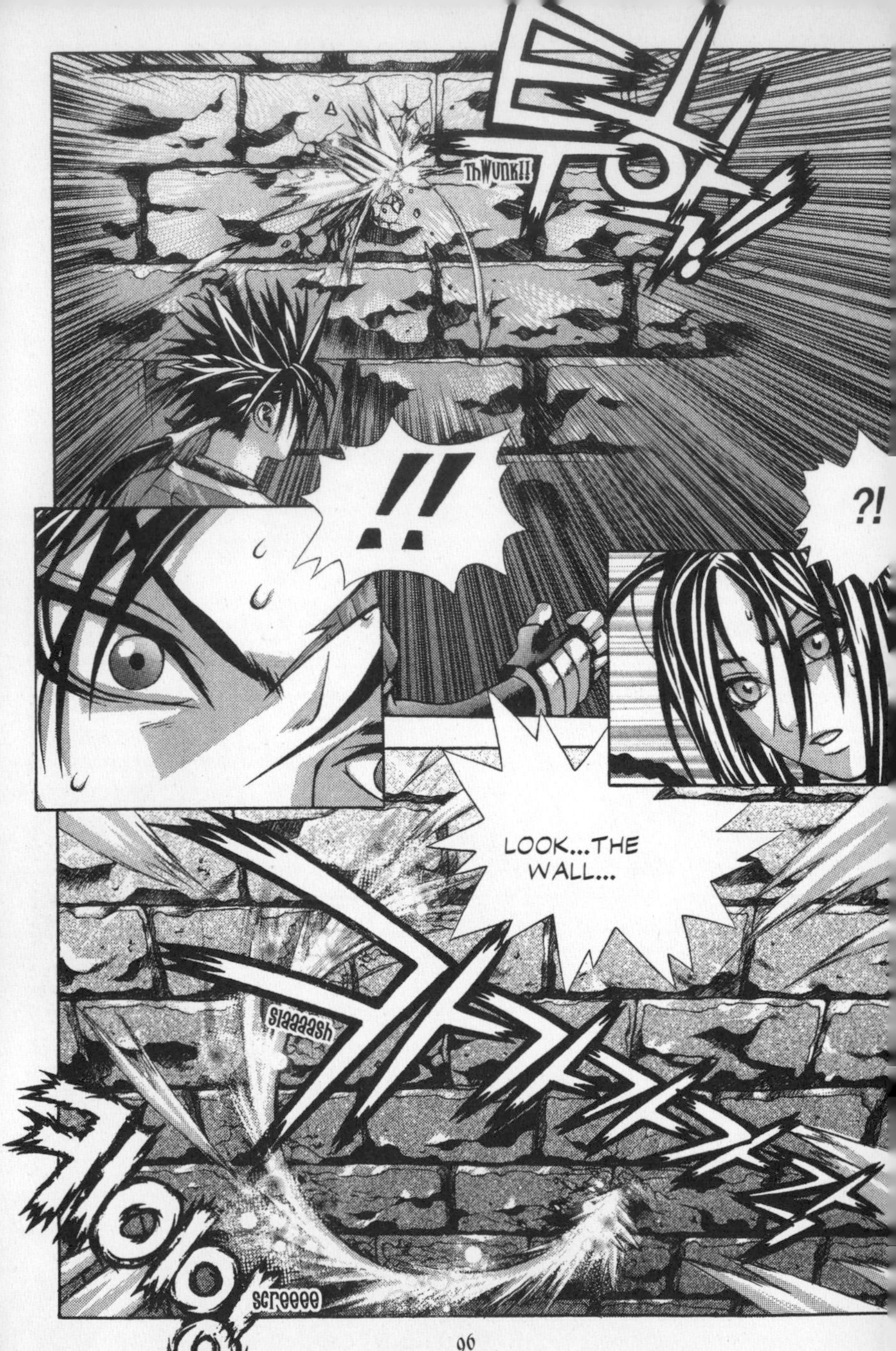
ThWUNK!!
!!
?!
LOOK...THE WALL...
slaaaash
screeee

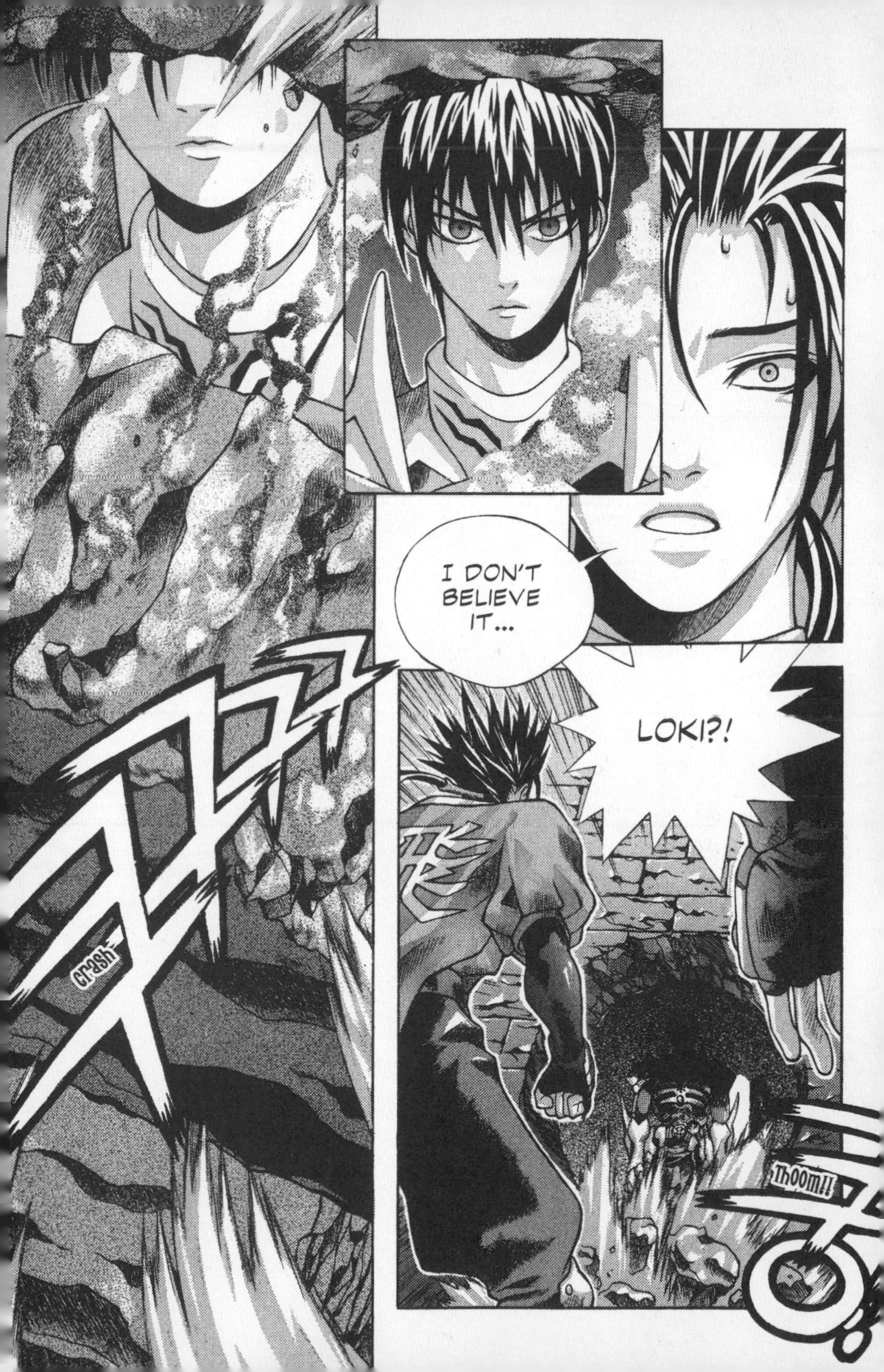
I DON'T BELIEVE IT...
LOKI?!
crash
THOOM!!

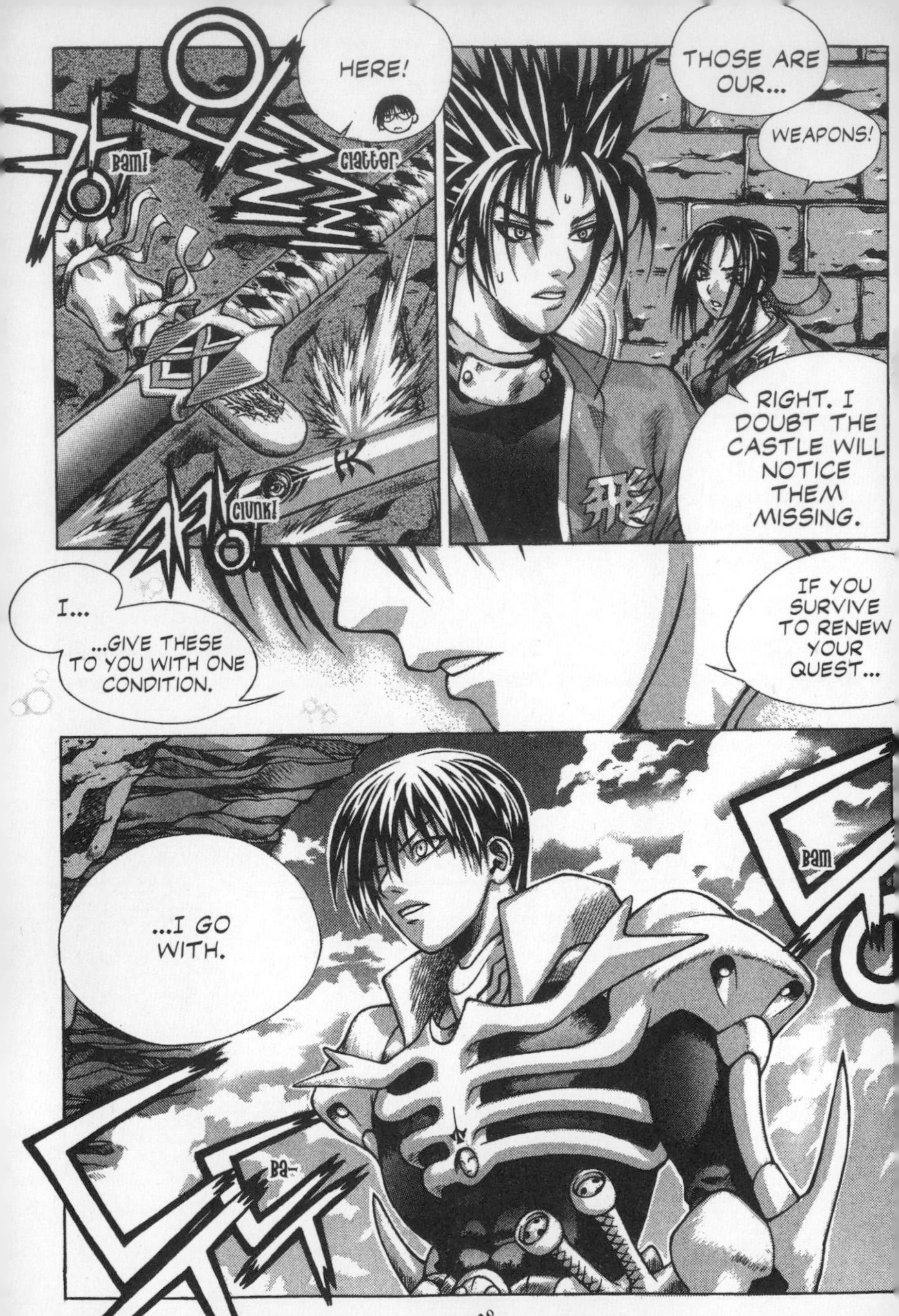

BAM!
HERE!
CLATTER
CLUNK!
THOSE ARE OUR...
WEAPONS!
RIGHT. I DOUBT THE CASTLE WILL NOTICE THEM MISSING.
I...
...GIVE THESE TO YOU WITH ONE CONDITION.
IF YOU SURVIVE TO RENEW YOUR QUEST...
...I GO WITH.
BAM
BA-

RAGNAROK
라그나로크
IN TO THE ABYSS

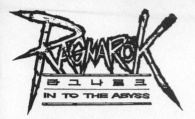

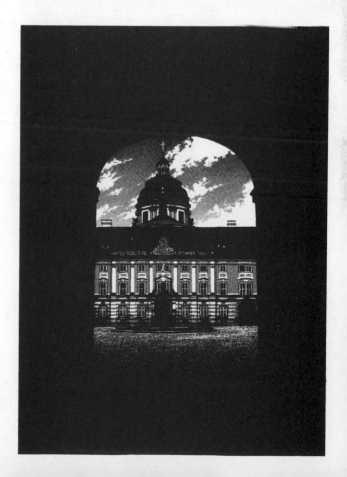

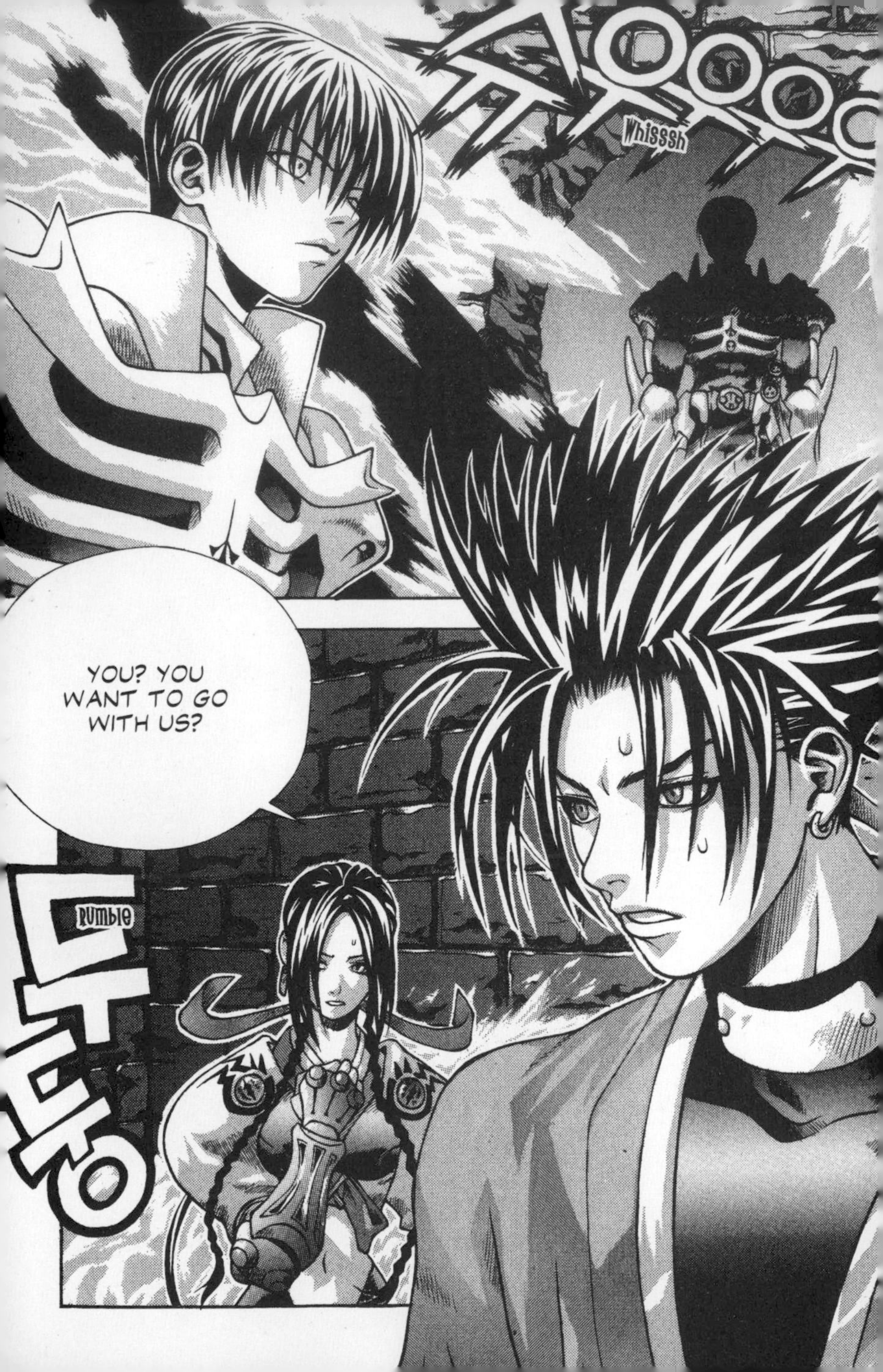
Whisssh
YOU? YOU WANT TO GO WITH US?
Rumble

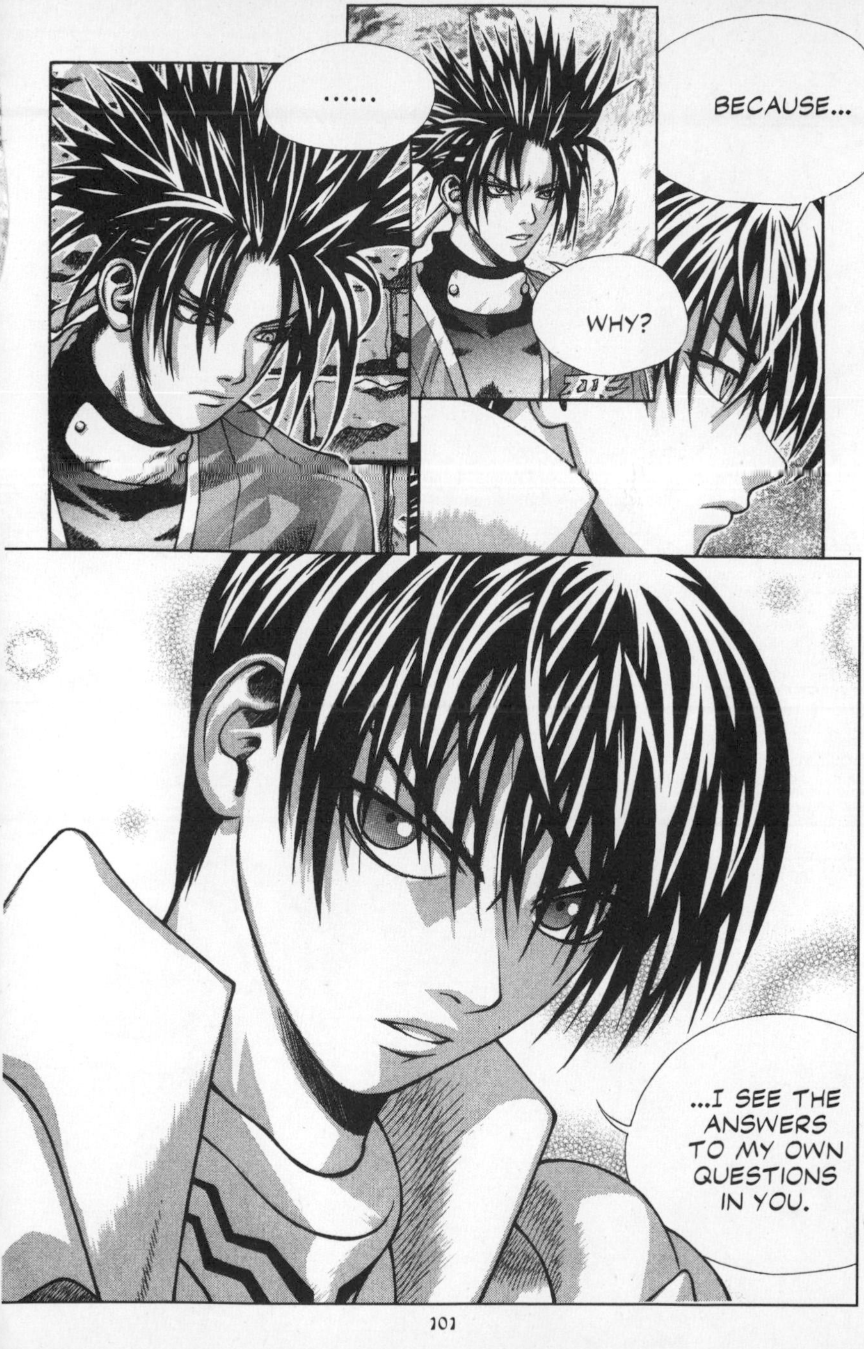
......
WHY?
BECAUSE...
...I SEE THE ANSWERS TO MY OWN QUESTIONS IN YOU.

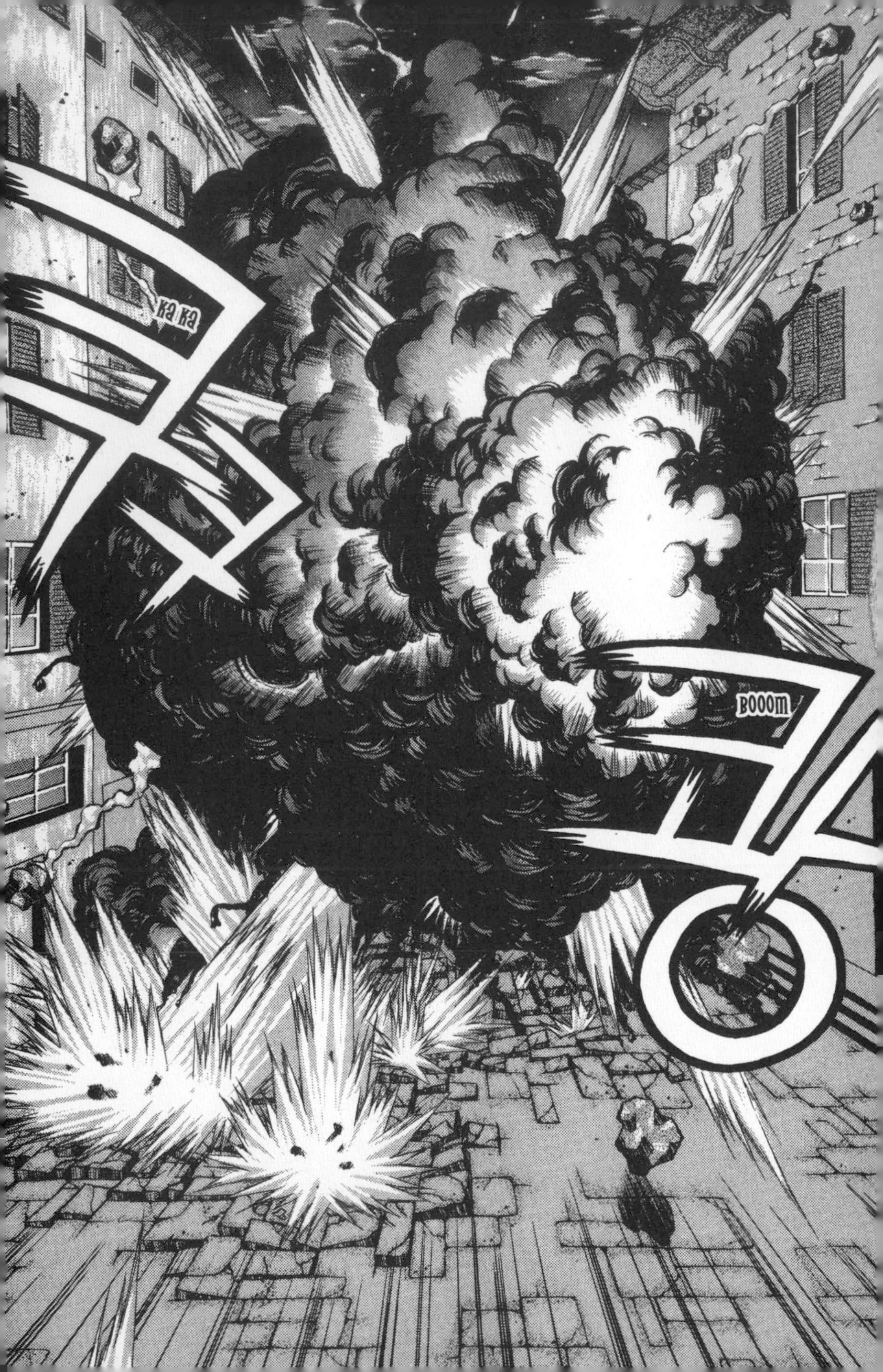
KA KA
BOOOM

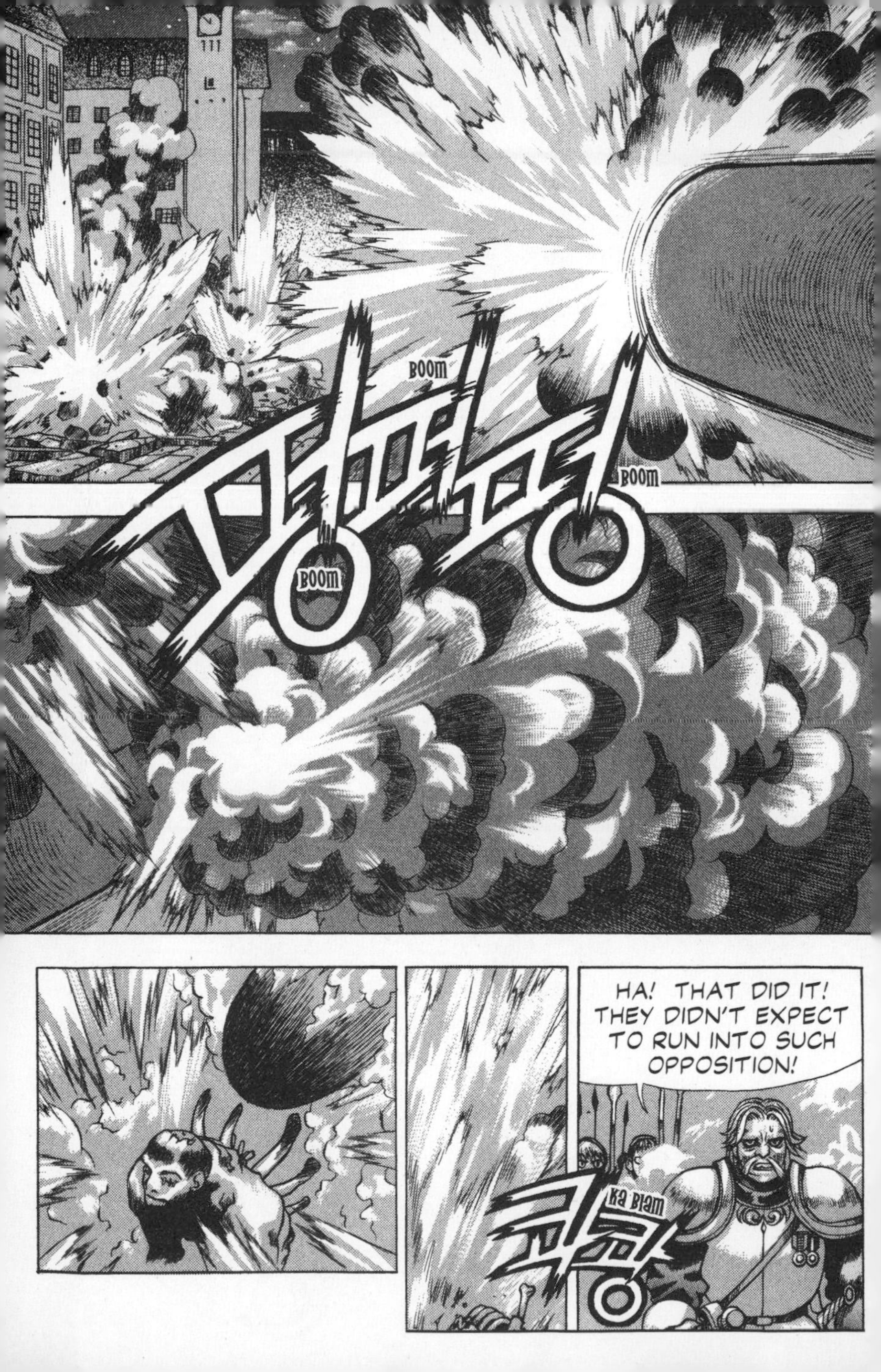
BOOM
BOOM
BOOM
HA! THAT DID IT! THEY DIDN'T EXPECT TO RUN INTO SUCH OPPOSITION!
KA BLAM

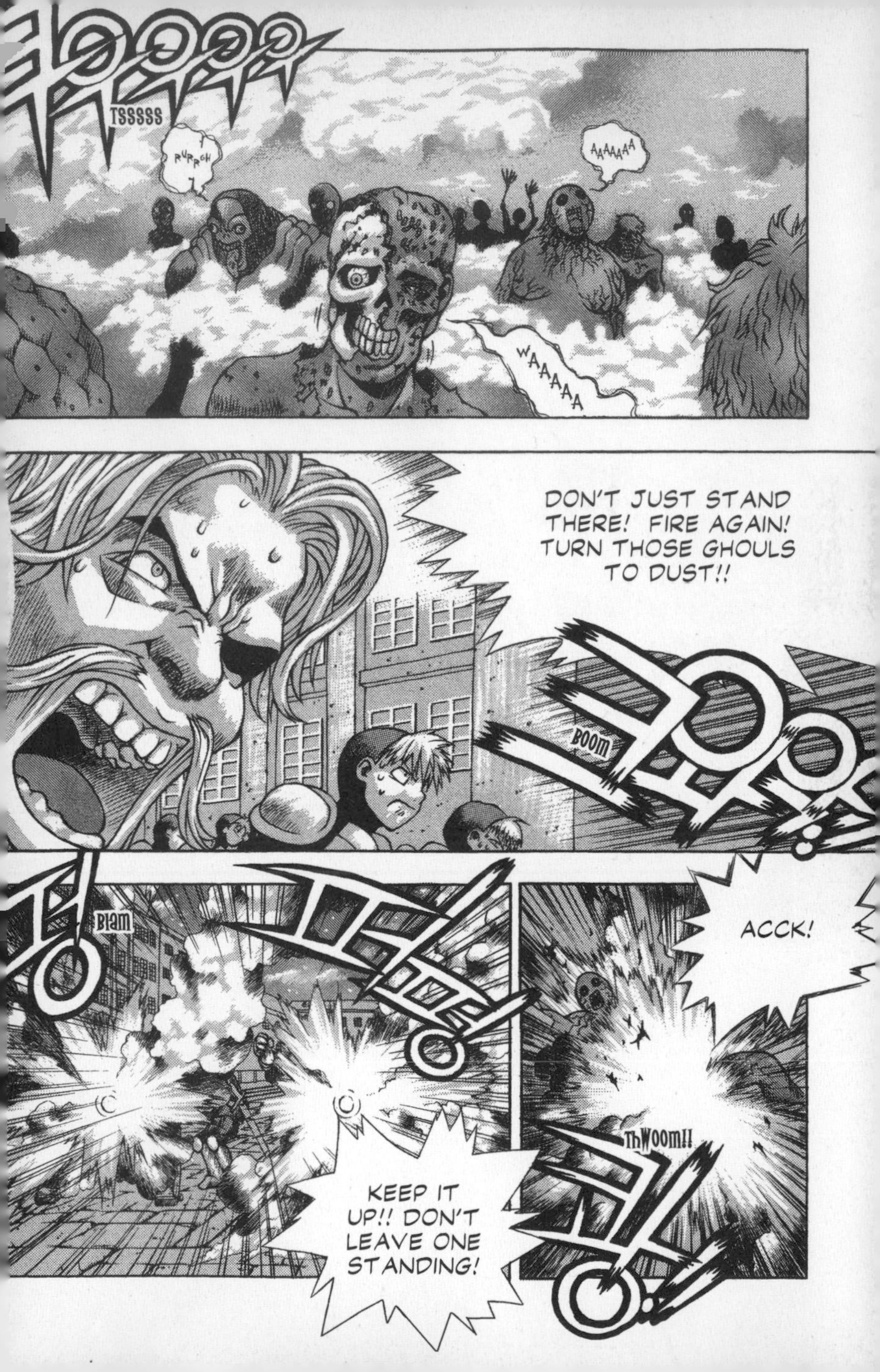
TSSSSS
RURRGH
AAAAAAA
WAAAAAA
DON'T JUST STAND THERE! FIRE AGAIN! TURN THOSE GHOULS TO DUST!!
BOOM
Blam
KEEP IT UP!! DON'T LEAVE ONE STANDING!
ACCK!
ThWoom!!

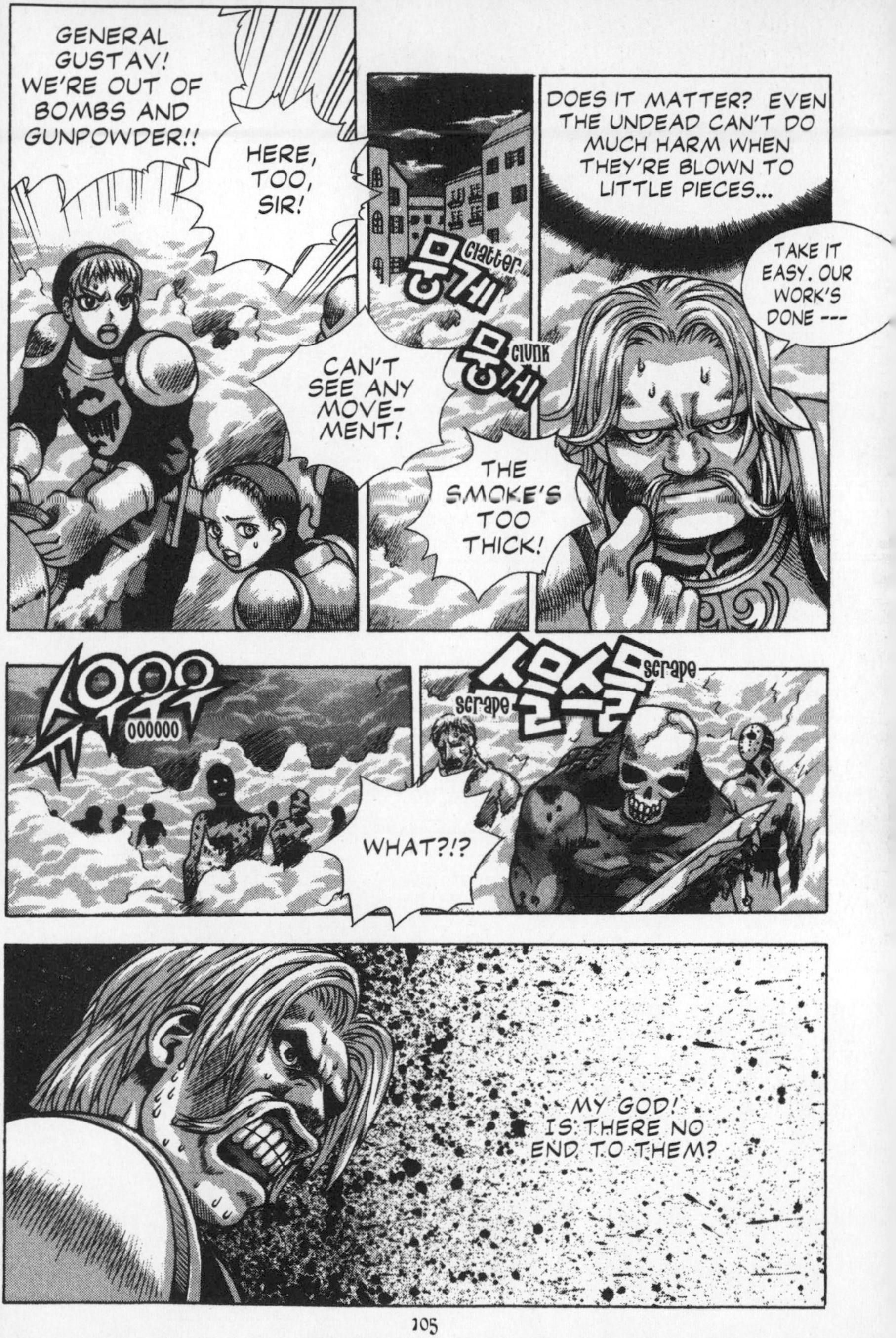
GENERAL GUSTAV! WE'RE OUT OF BOMBS AND GUNPOWDER!!
HERE, TOO, SIR!
clatter
clunk
CAN'T SEE ANY MOVE-MENT!
THE SMOKE'S TOO THICK!
DOES IT MATTER? EVEN THE UNDEAD CAN'T DO MUCH HARM WHEN THEY'RE BLOWN TO LITTLE PIECES...
TAKE IT EASY. OUR WORK'S DONE ---
oooooo
scrape
scrape
WHAT?!?
MY GOD! IS THERE NO END TO THEM?

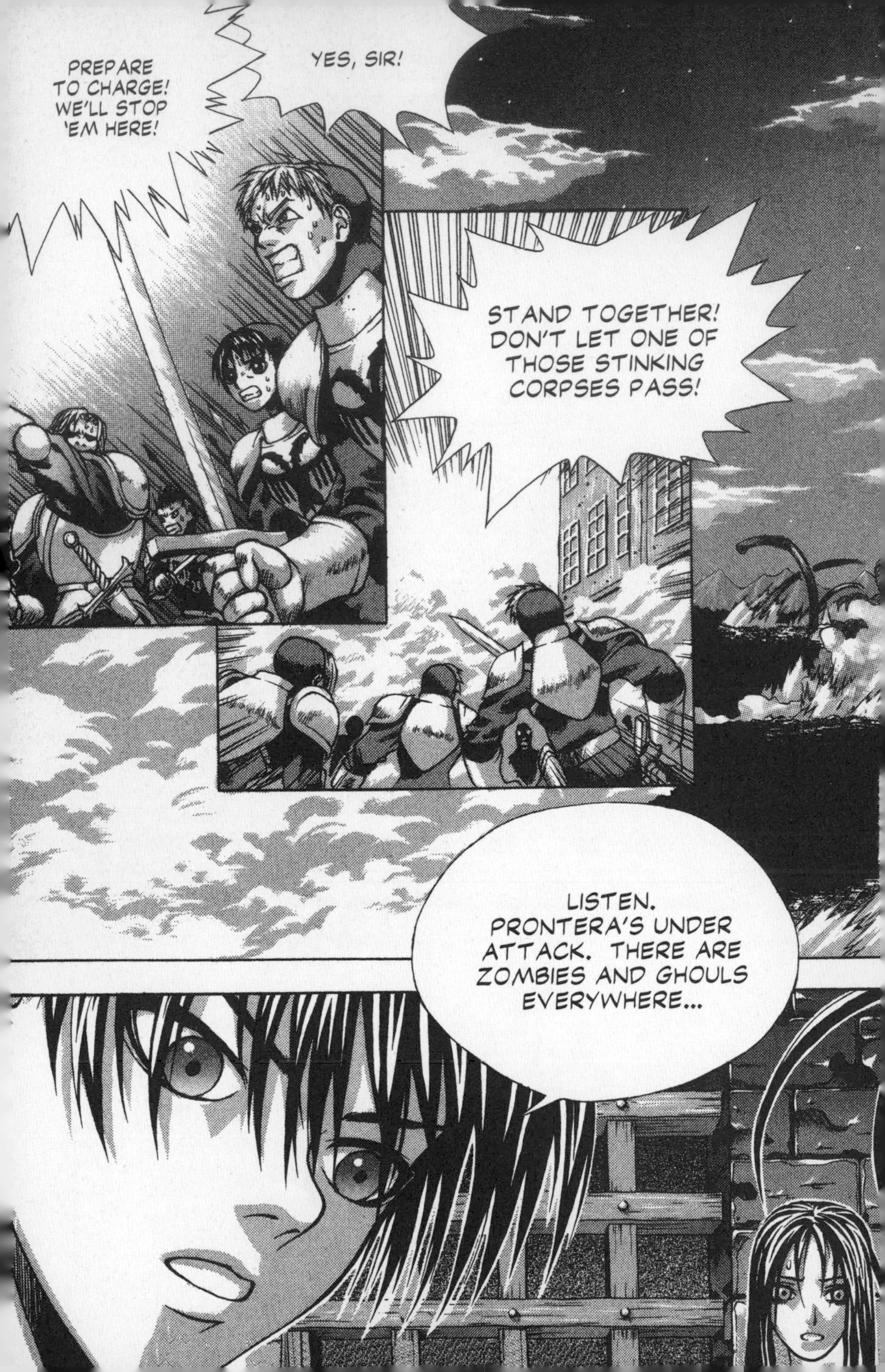
PREPARE TO CHARGE! WE'LL STOP 'EM HERE!
YES, SIR!
STAND TOGETHER! DON'T LET ONE OF THOSE STINKING CORPSES PASS!
LISTEN. PRONTERA'S UNDER ATTACK. THERE ARE ZOMBIES AND GHOULS EVERYWHERE...

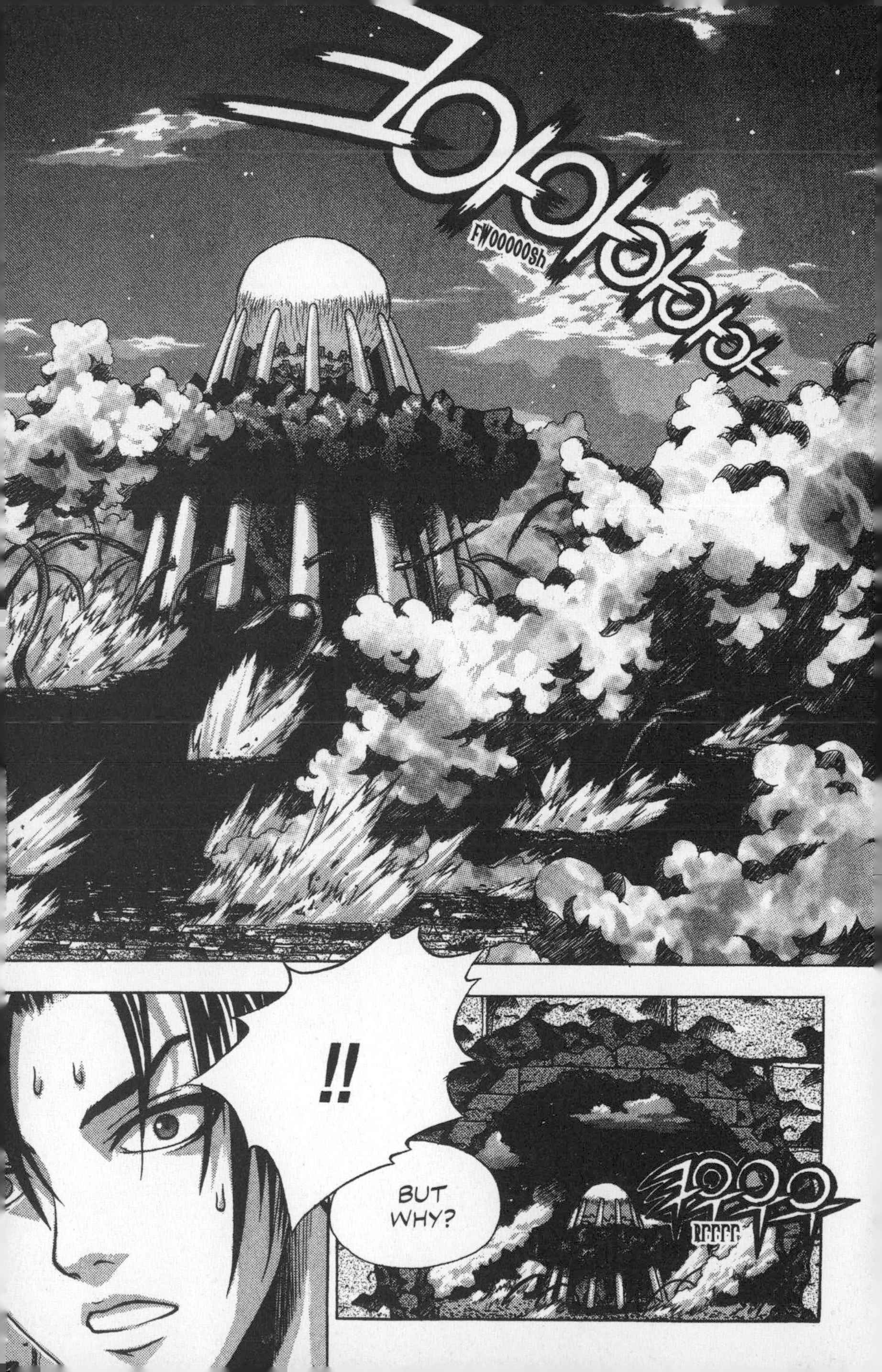
FWOOOOOSH
!!
BUT WHY?
RRRRR

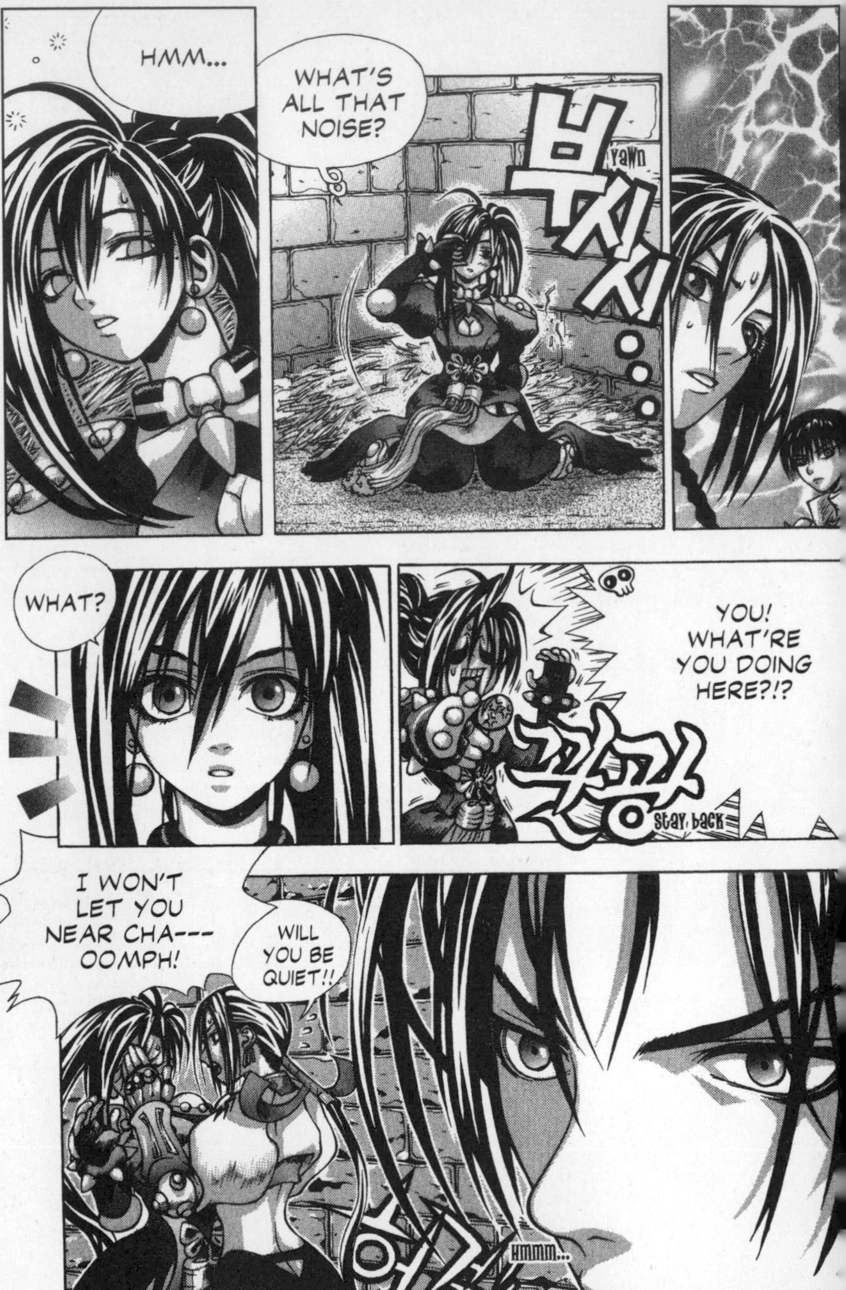
HMM...
WHAT'S ALL THAT NOISE?
YAWN
WHAT?
YOU! WHAT'RE YOU DOING HERE?!?
STAY BACK
I WON'T LET YOU NEAR CHA--- OOMPH!
WILL YOU BE QUIET!!
HMMM...

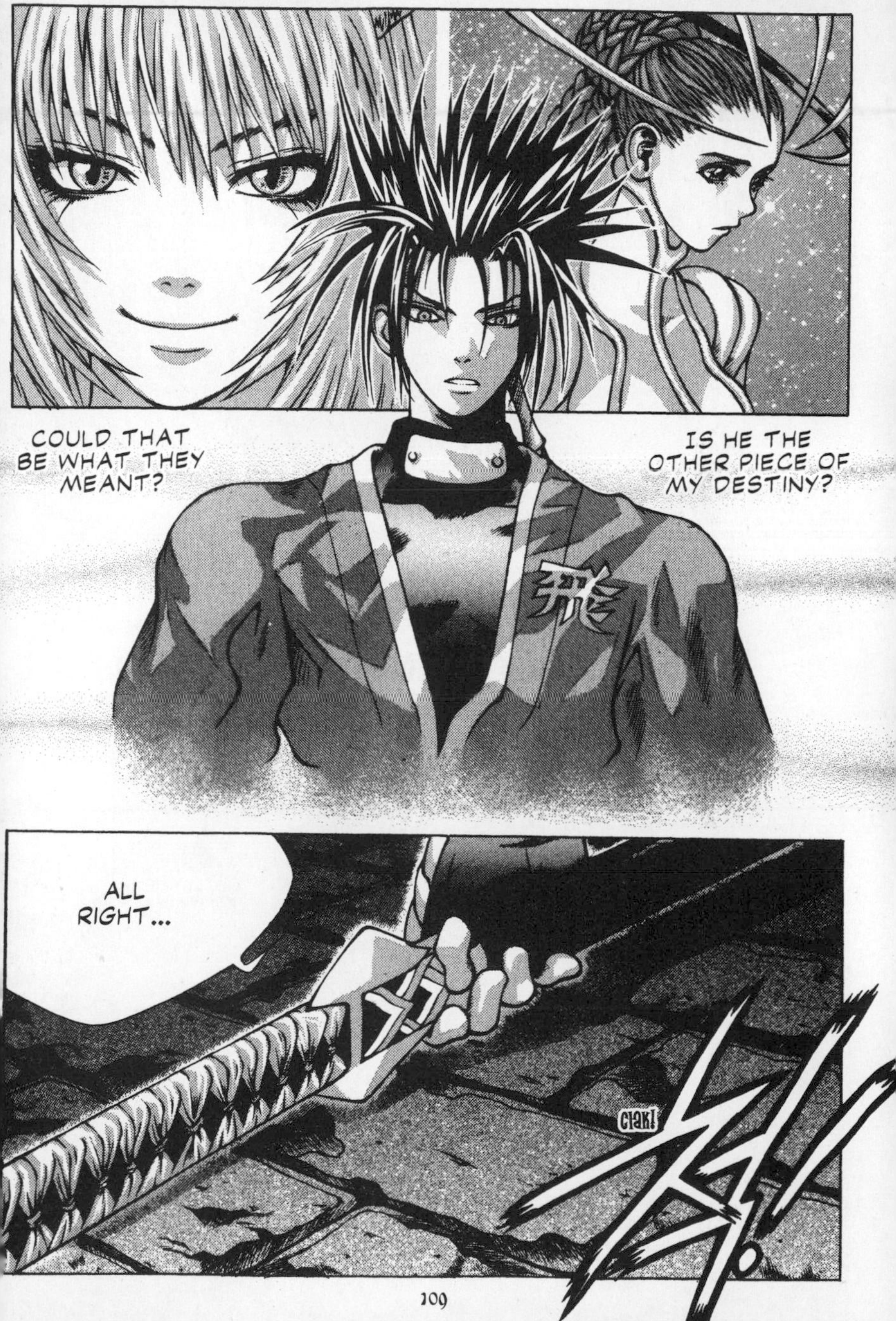
COULD THAT BE WHAT THEY MEANT?
IS HE THE OTHER PIECE OF MY DESTINY?
ALL RIGHT...
CLAK!

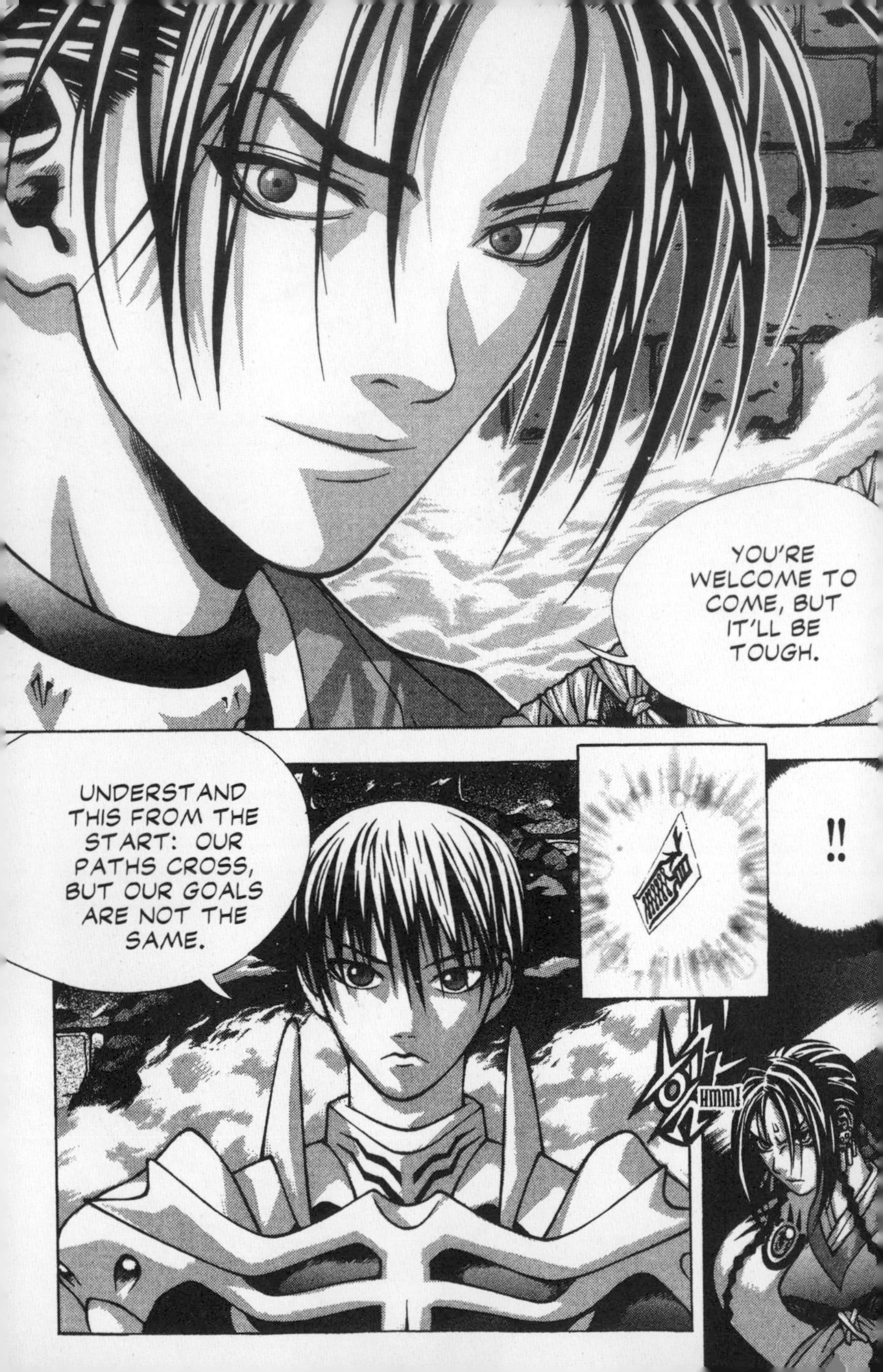
YOU'RE WELCOME TO COME, BUT IT'LL BE TOUGH.
!!
UNDERSTAND THIS FROM THE START: OUR PATHS CROSS, BUT OUR GOALS ARE NOT THE SAME.
HMM!

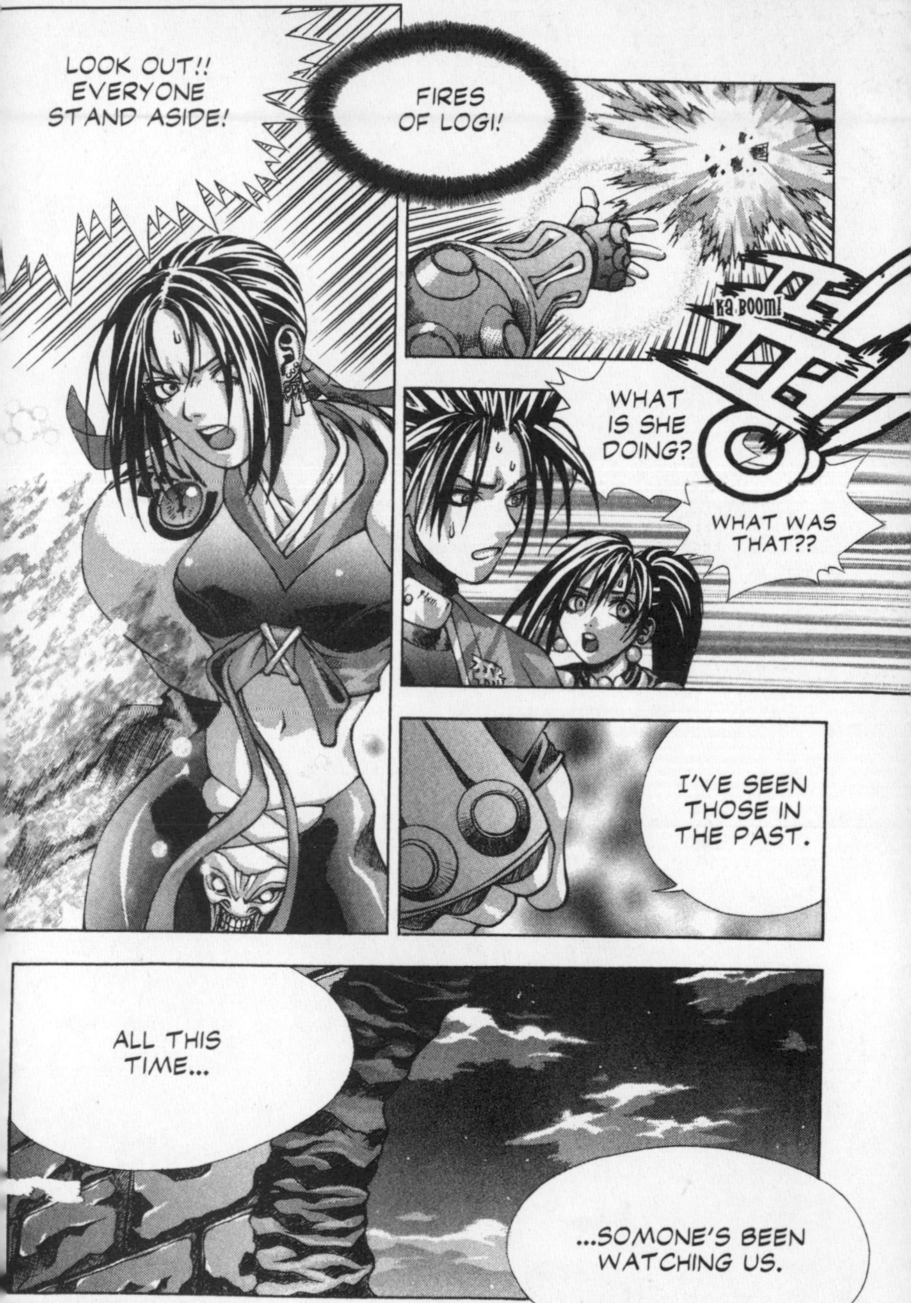
LOOK OUT!! EVERYONE STAND ASIDE!
FIRES OF LOGI!
KA BOOM!
WHAT IS SHE DOING?
WHAT WAS THAT??
I'VE SEEN THOSE IN THE PAST.
ALL THIS TIME...
...SOMONE'S BEEN WATCHING US.

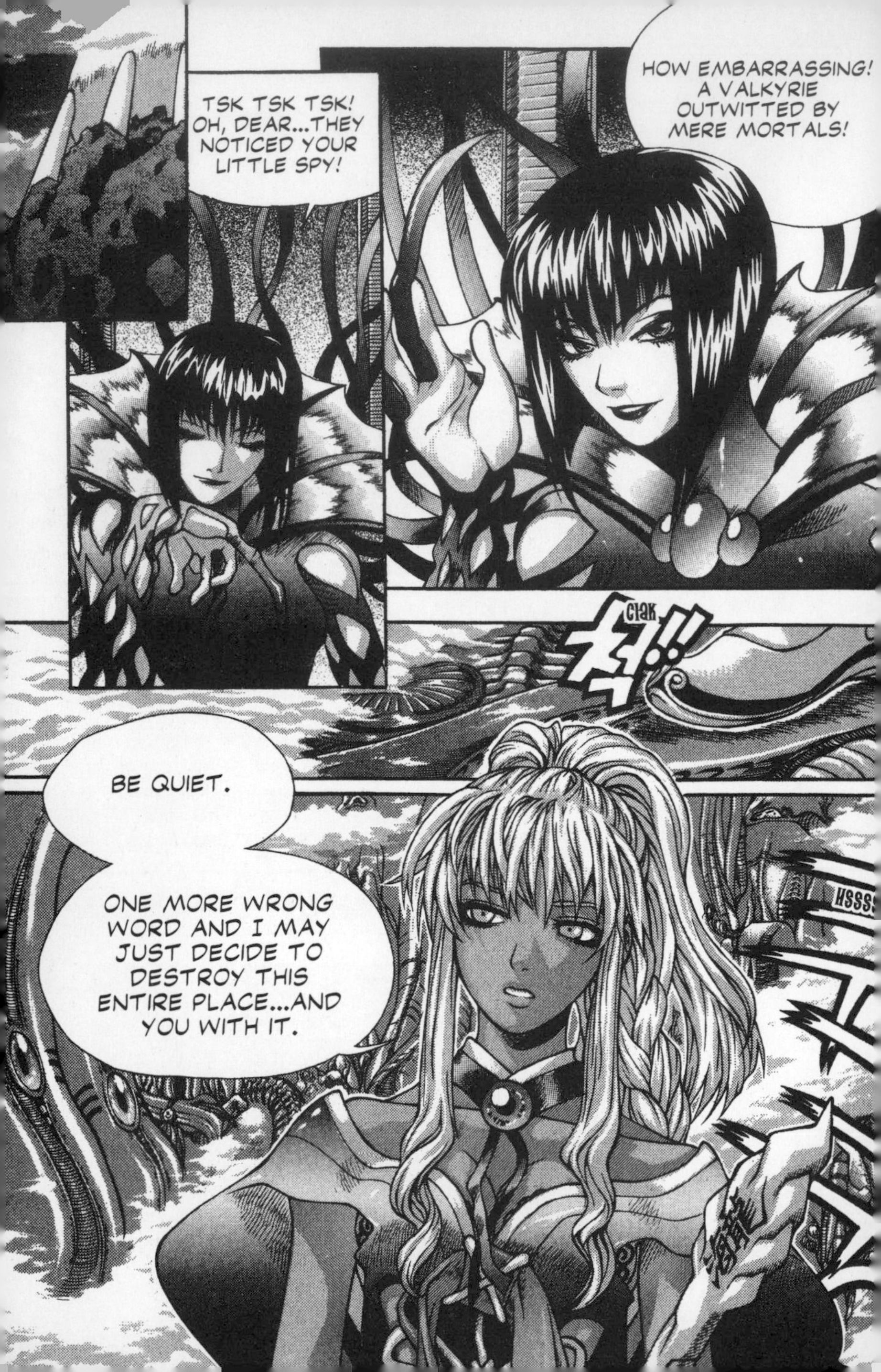
TSK TSK TSK! OH, DEAR...THEY NOTICED YOUR LITTLE SPY!
HOW EMBARRASSING! A VALKYRIE OUTWITTED BY MERE MORTALS!
CLAK
BE QUIET.
ONE MORE WRONG WORD AND I MAY JUST DECIDE TO DESTROY THIS ENTIRE PLACE...AND YOU WITH IT.
HSSSS

RAGNAROK
라그나로크
IN TO THE ABYSS

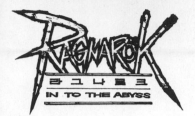

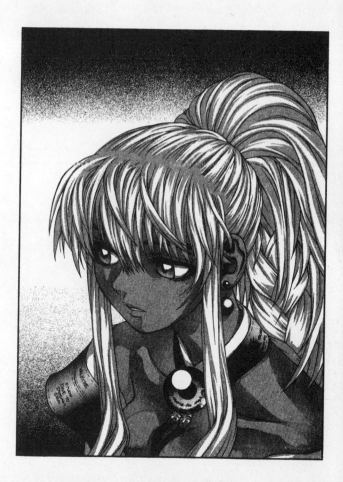

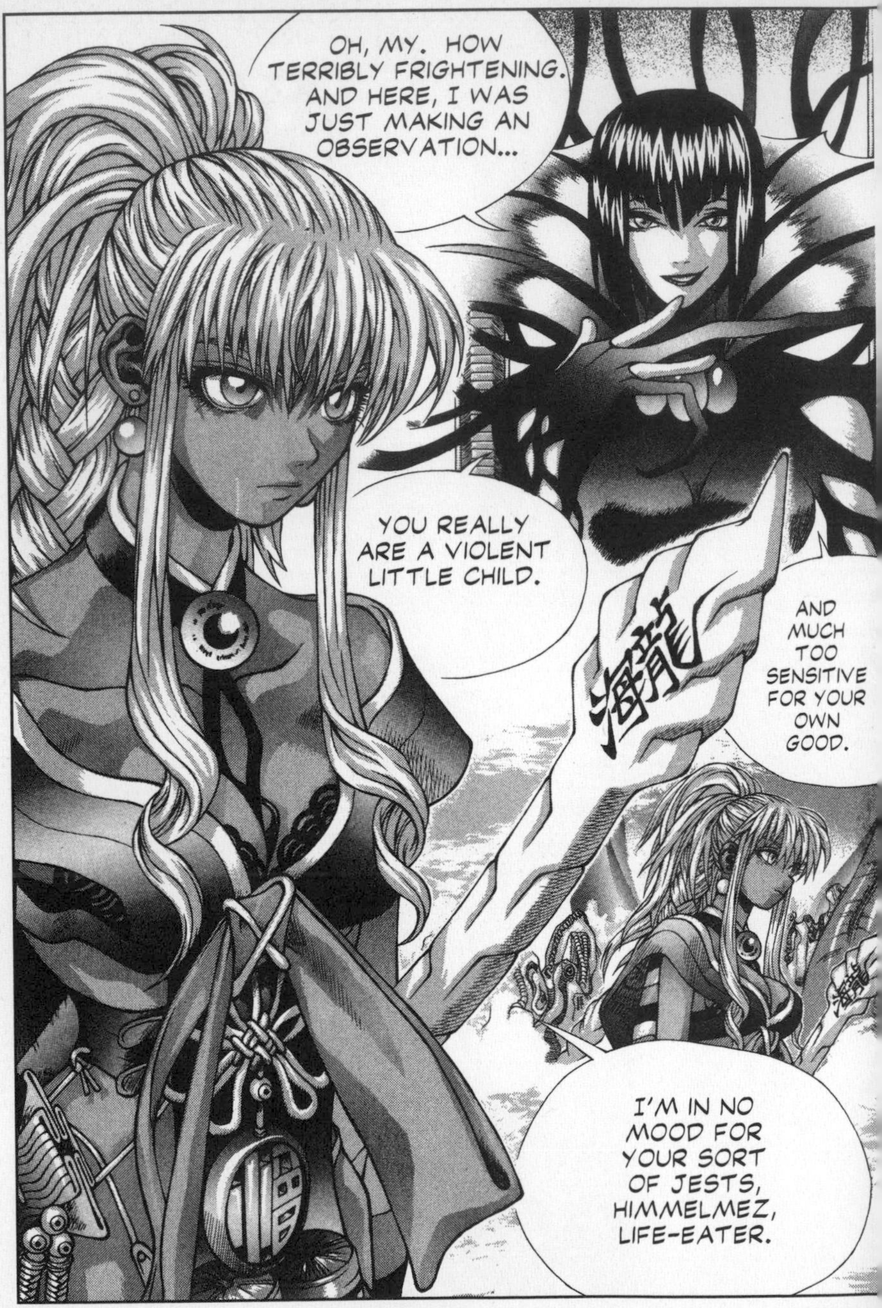
OH, MY. HOW TERRIBLY FRIGHTENING. AND HERE, I WAS JUST MAKING AN OBSERVATION...
YOU REALLY ARE A VIOLENT LITTLE CHILD.
海龍
AND MUCH TOO SENSITIVE FOR YOUR OWN GOOD.
I'M IN NO MOOD FOR YOUR SORT OF JESTS, HIMMELMEZ, LIFE-EATER.

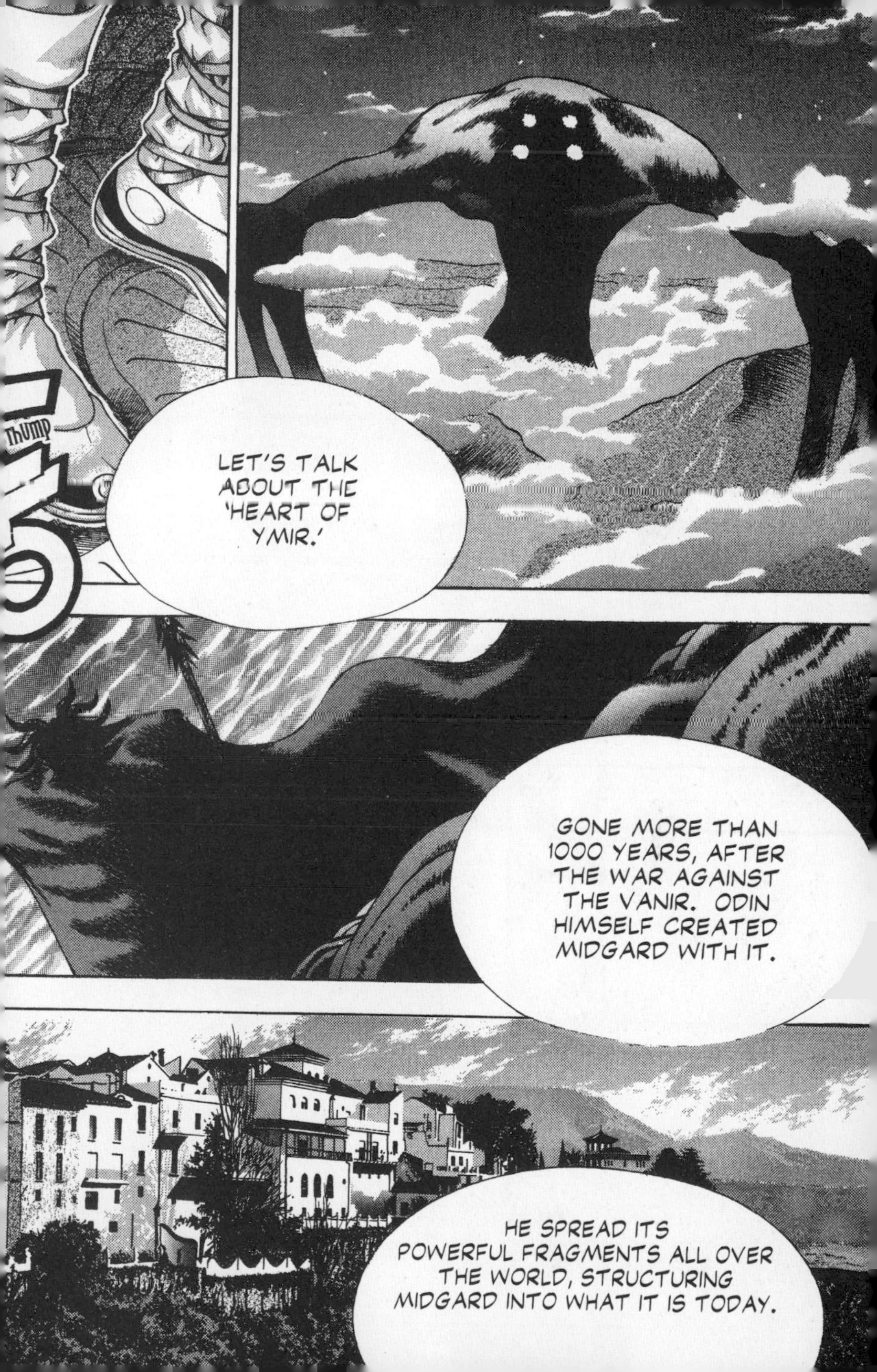
THUMP
LET'S TALK ABOUT THE 'HEART OF YMIR.'
GONE MORE THAN 1000 YEARS, AFTER THE WAR AGAINST THE VANIR. ODIN HIMSELF CREATED MIDGARD WITH IT.
HE SPREAD ITS POWERFUL FRAGMENTS ALL OVER THE WORLD, STRUCTURING MIDGARD INTO WHAT IT IS TODAY.

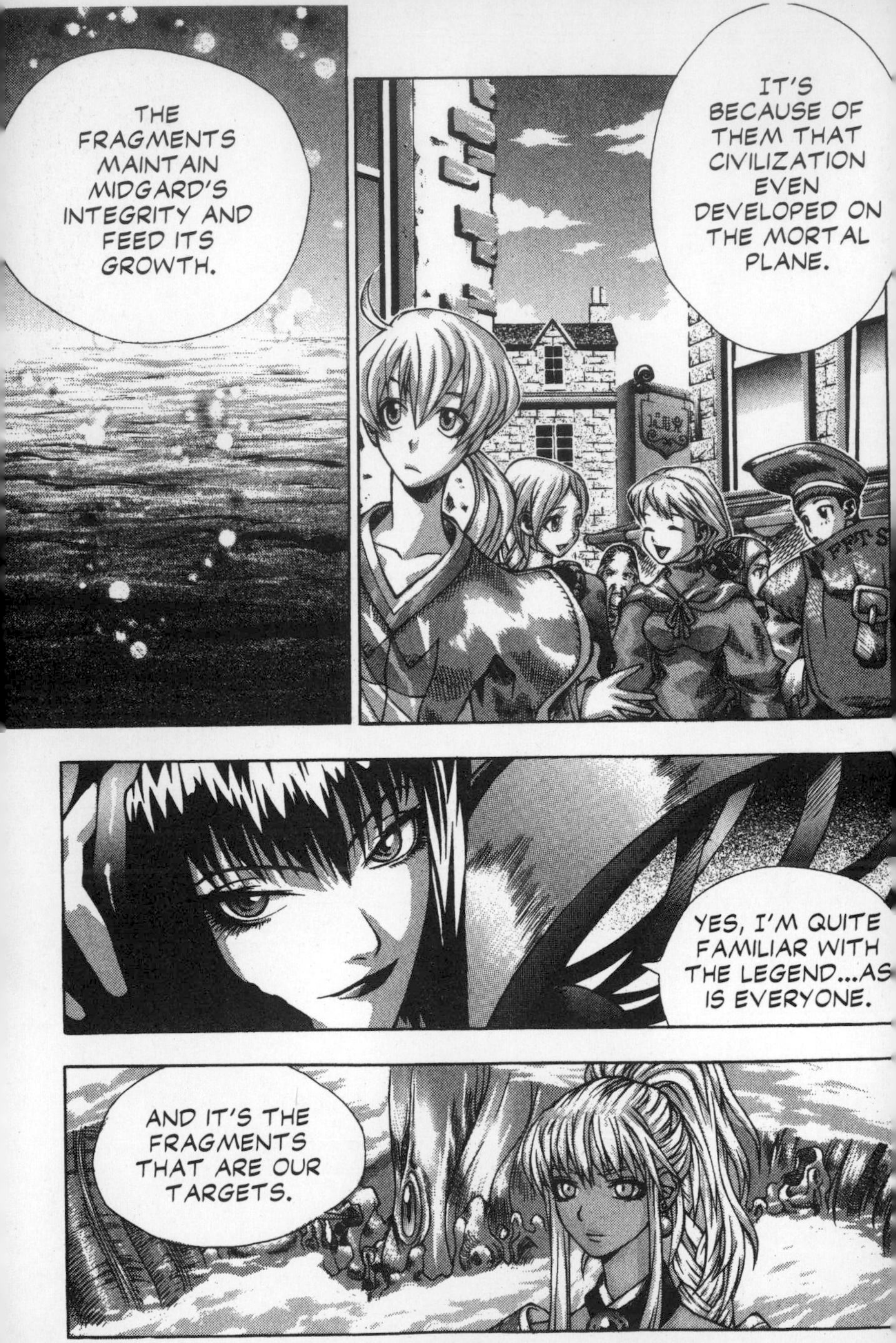
THE FRAGMENTS MAINTAIN MIDGARD'S INTEGRITY AND FEED ITS GROWTH.
IT'S BECAUSE OF THEM THAT CIVILIZATION EVEN DEVELOPED ON THE MORTAL PLANE.
YES, I'M QUITE FAMILIAR WITH THE LEGEND...AS IS EVERYONE.
AND IT'S THE FRAGMENTS THAT ARE OUR TARGETS.

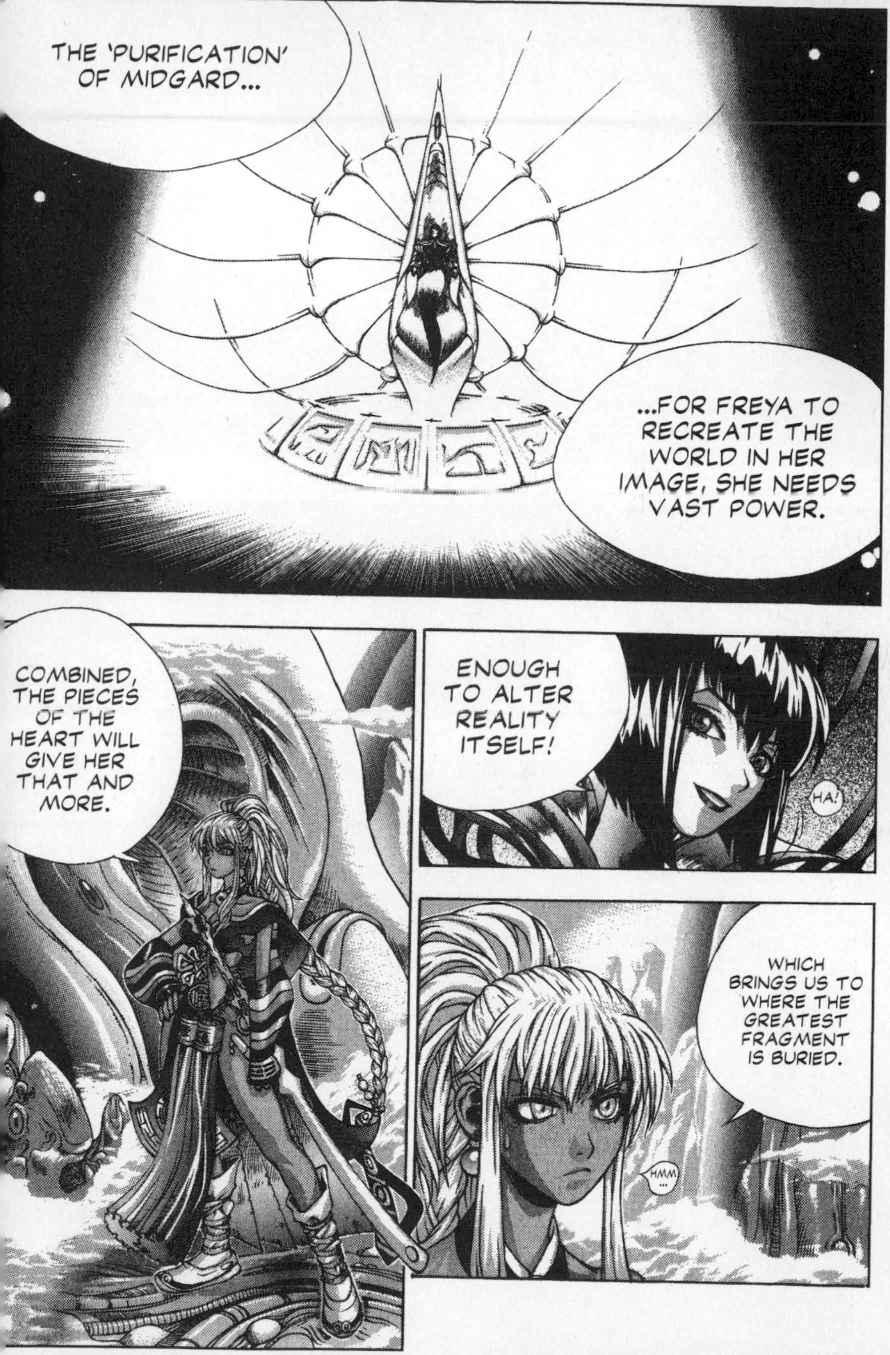
THE 'PURIFICATION' OF MIDGARD...
...FOR FREYA TO RECREATE THE WORLD IN HER IMAGE, SHE NEEDS VAST POWER.
COMBINED, THE PIECES OF THE HEART WILL GIVE HER THAT AND MORE.
ENOUGH TO ALTER REALITY ITSELF!
HA!
WHICH BRINGS US TO WHERE THE GREATEST FRAGMENT IS BURIED.
HMM ...

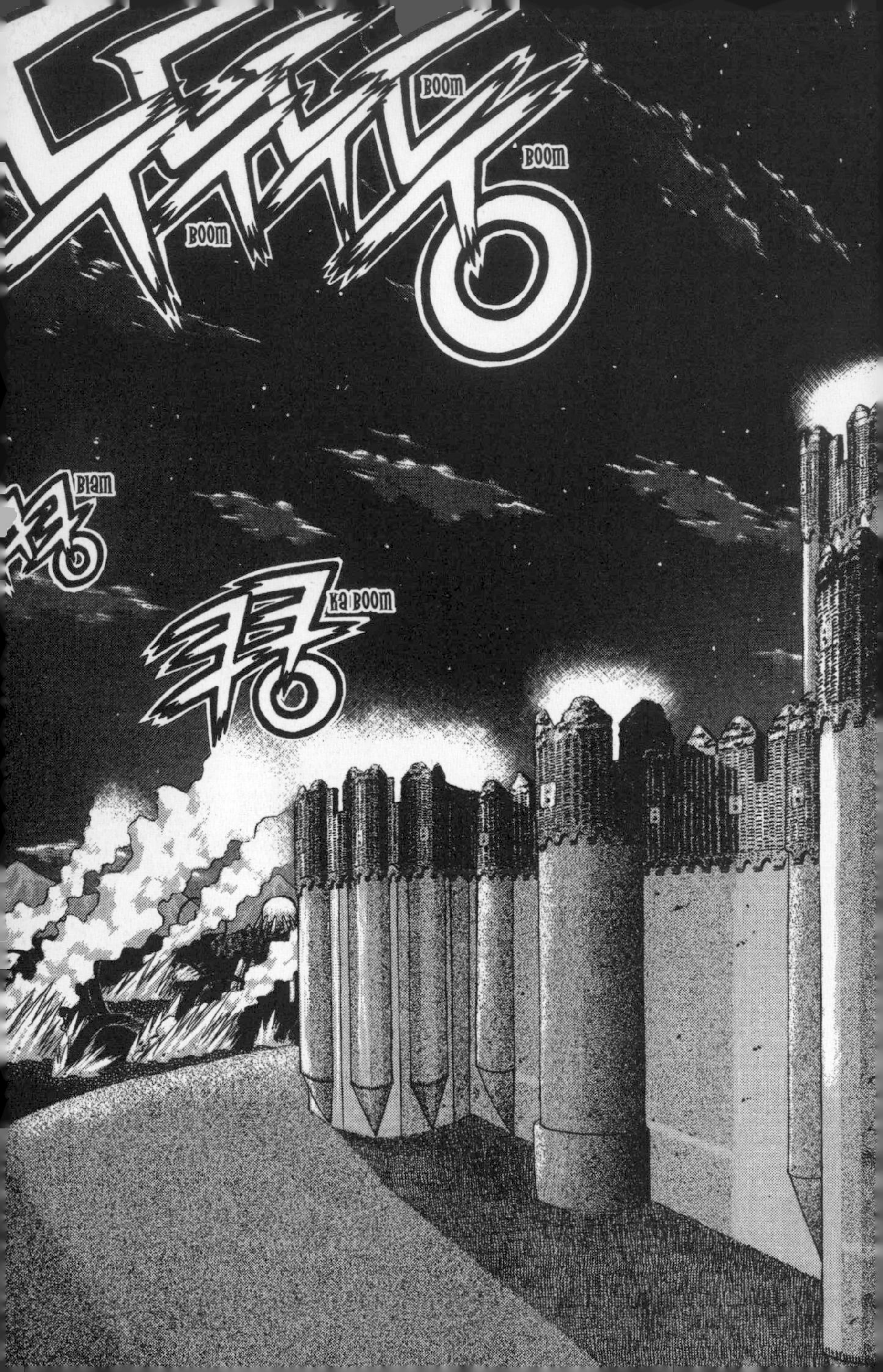
BOOM
BOOM
BOOM
BLAM
KA BOOM

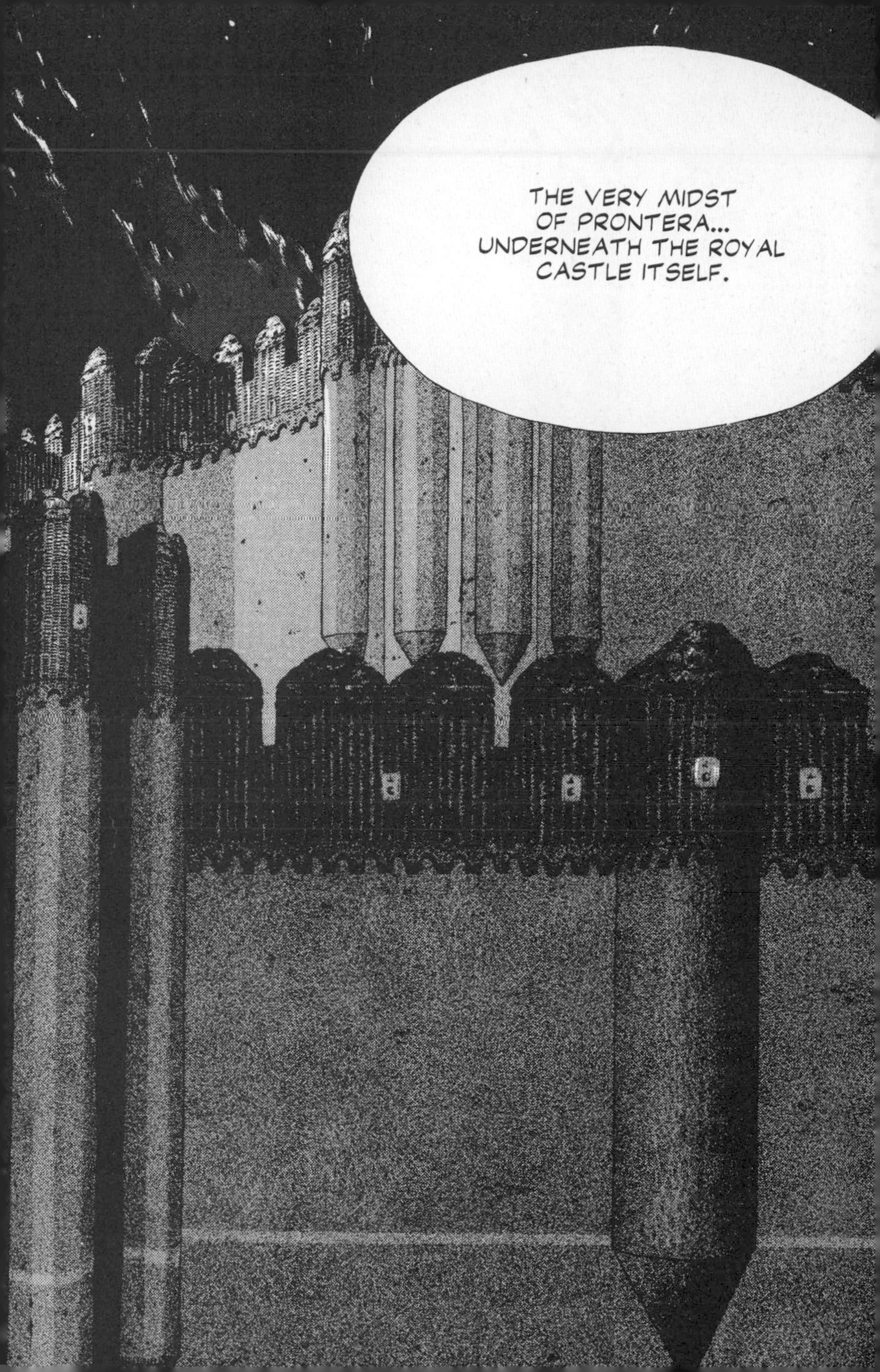
THE VERY MIDST OF PRONTERA... UNDERNEATH THE ROYAL CASTLE ITSELF.

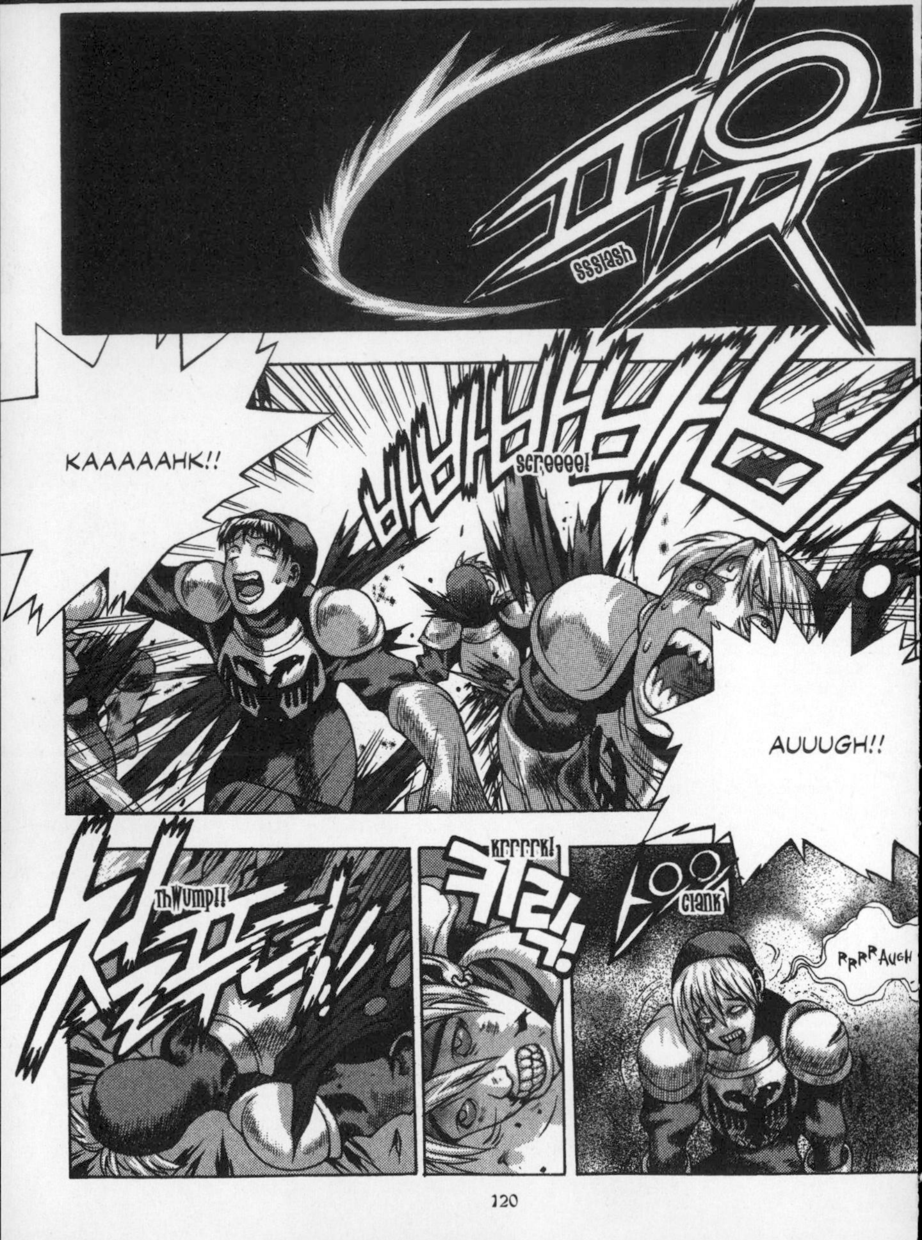
SSSLASH
KAAAAAHK!!
screeee!
AUUUGH!!
ThWump!!
Krrrrk!
clank
RRRRAUGH

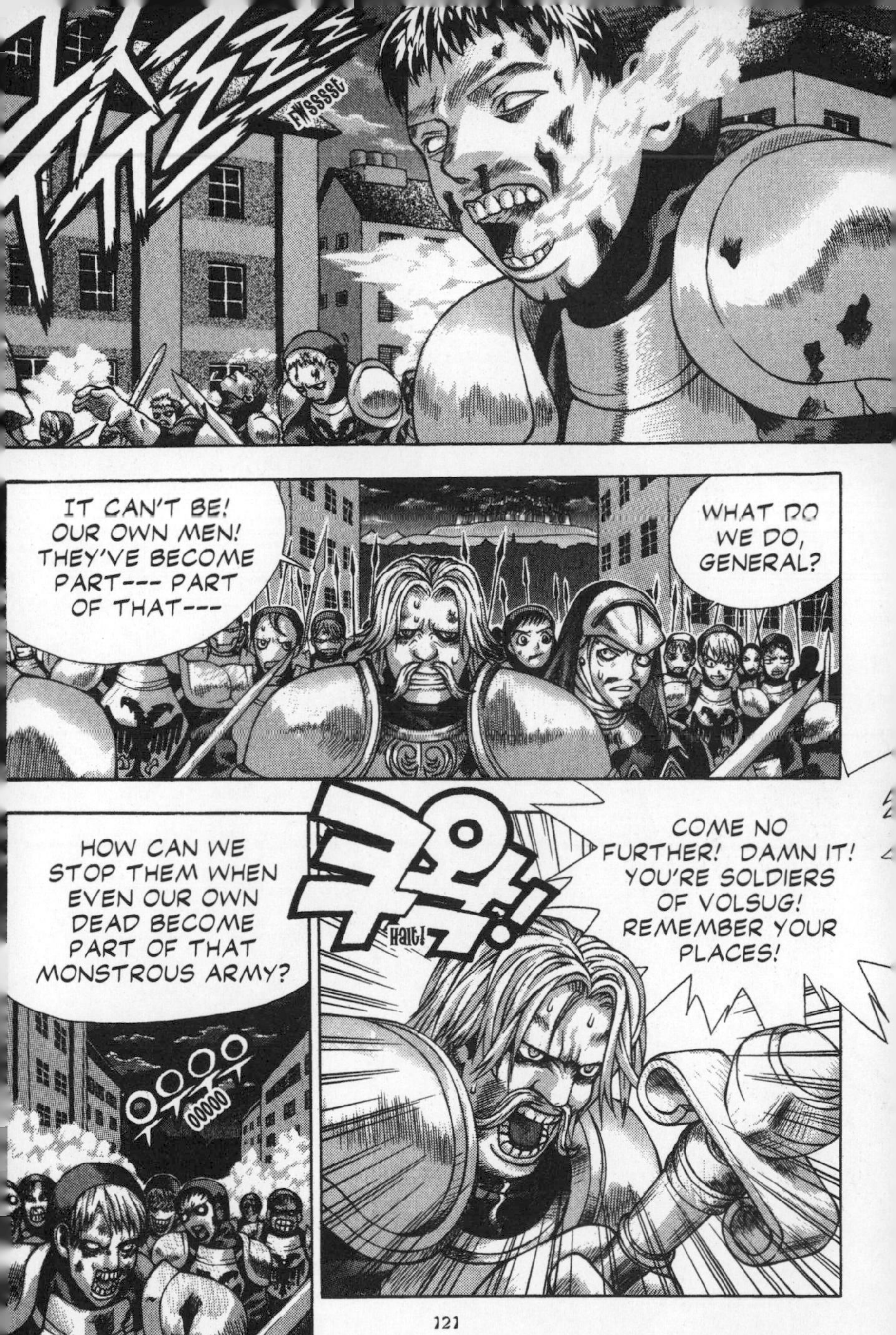
FWSSSSt
IT CAN'T BE! OUR OWN MEN! THEY'VE BECOME PART--- PART OF THAT---
WHAT DO WE DO, GENERAL?
HOW CAN WE STOP THEM WHEN EVEN OUR OWN DEAD BECOME PART OF THAT MONSTROUS ARMY?
Halt!
COME NO FURTHER! DAMN IT! YOU'RE SOLDIERS OF VOLSUG! REMEMBER YOUR PLACES!

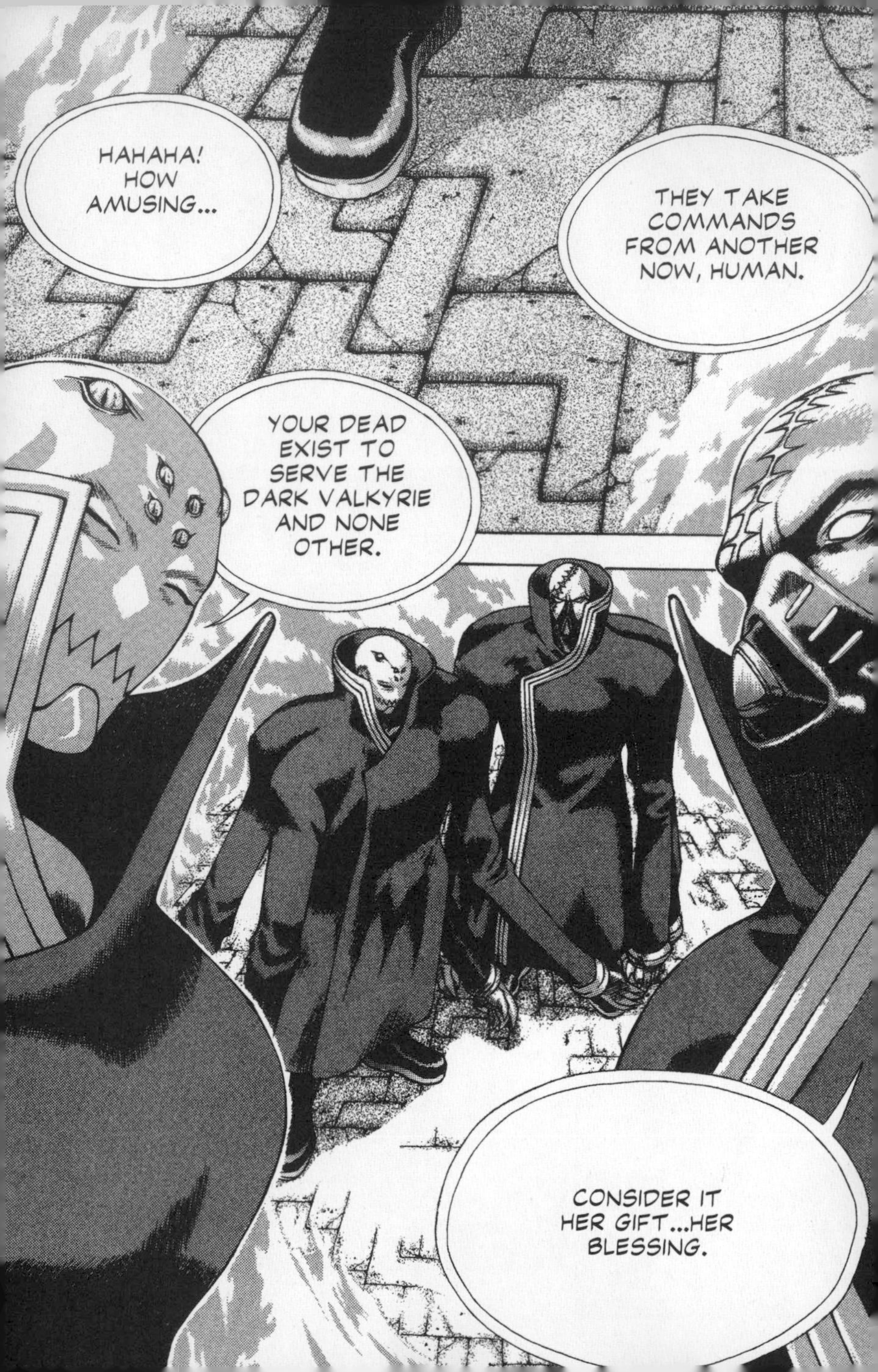
HAHAHA! HOW AMUSING...
THEY TAKE COMMANDS FROM ANOTHER NOW, HUMAN.
YOUR DEAD EXIST TO SERVE THE DARK VALKYRIE AND NONE OTHER.
CONSIDER IT HER GIFT...HER BLESSING.

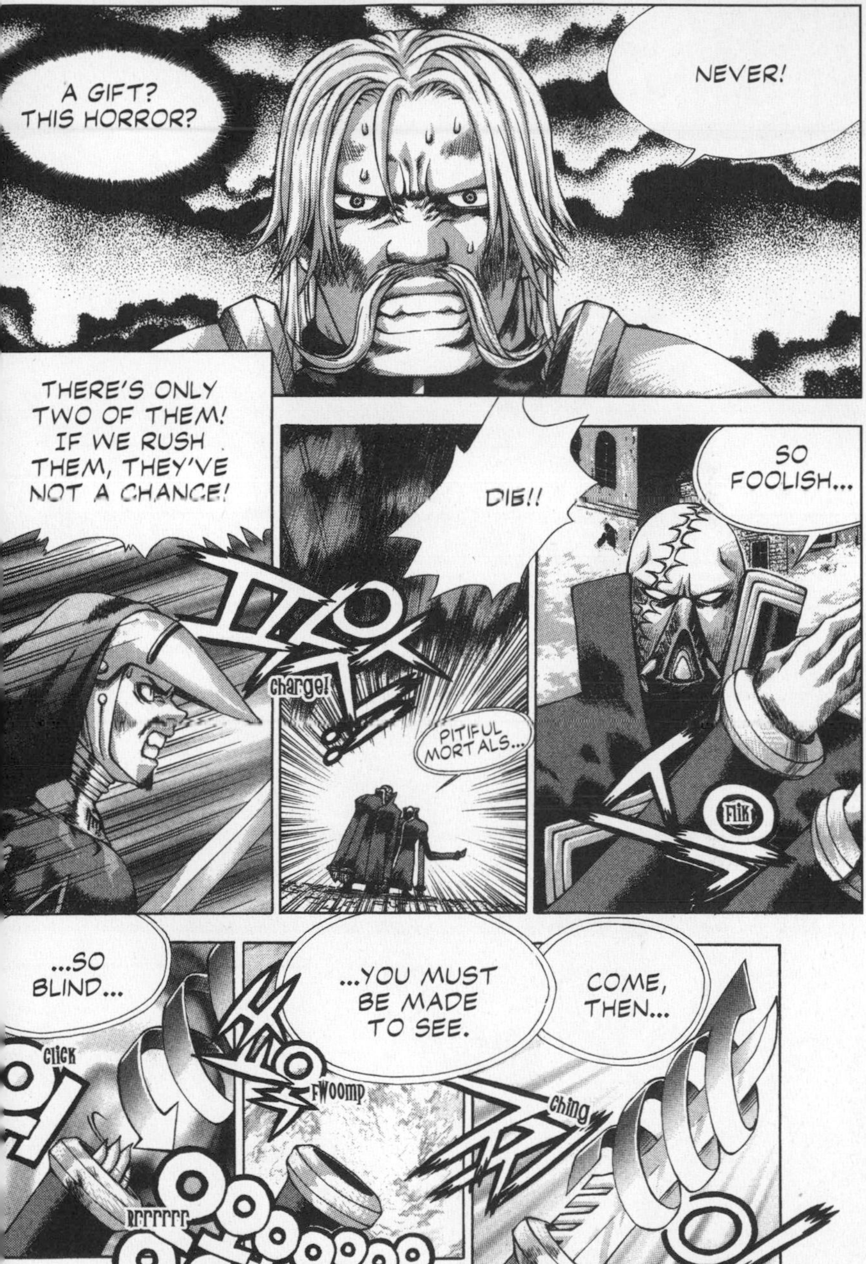
A GIFT? THIS HORROR?
NEVER!
THERE'S ONLY TWO OF THEM! IF WE RUSH THEM, THEY'VE NOT A CHANCE!
DIE!!
Charge!
PITIFUL MORTALS...
SO FOOLISH...
Flik
...SO BLIND...
Click
Rrrrrrr
...YOU MUST BE MADE TO SEE.
FWOOMP
COME, THEN...
Ching

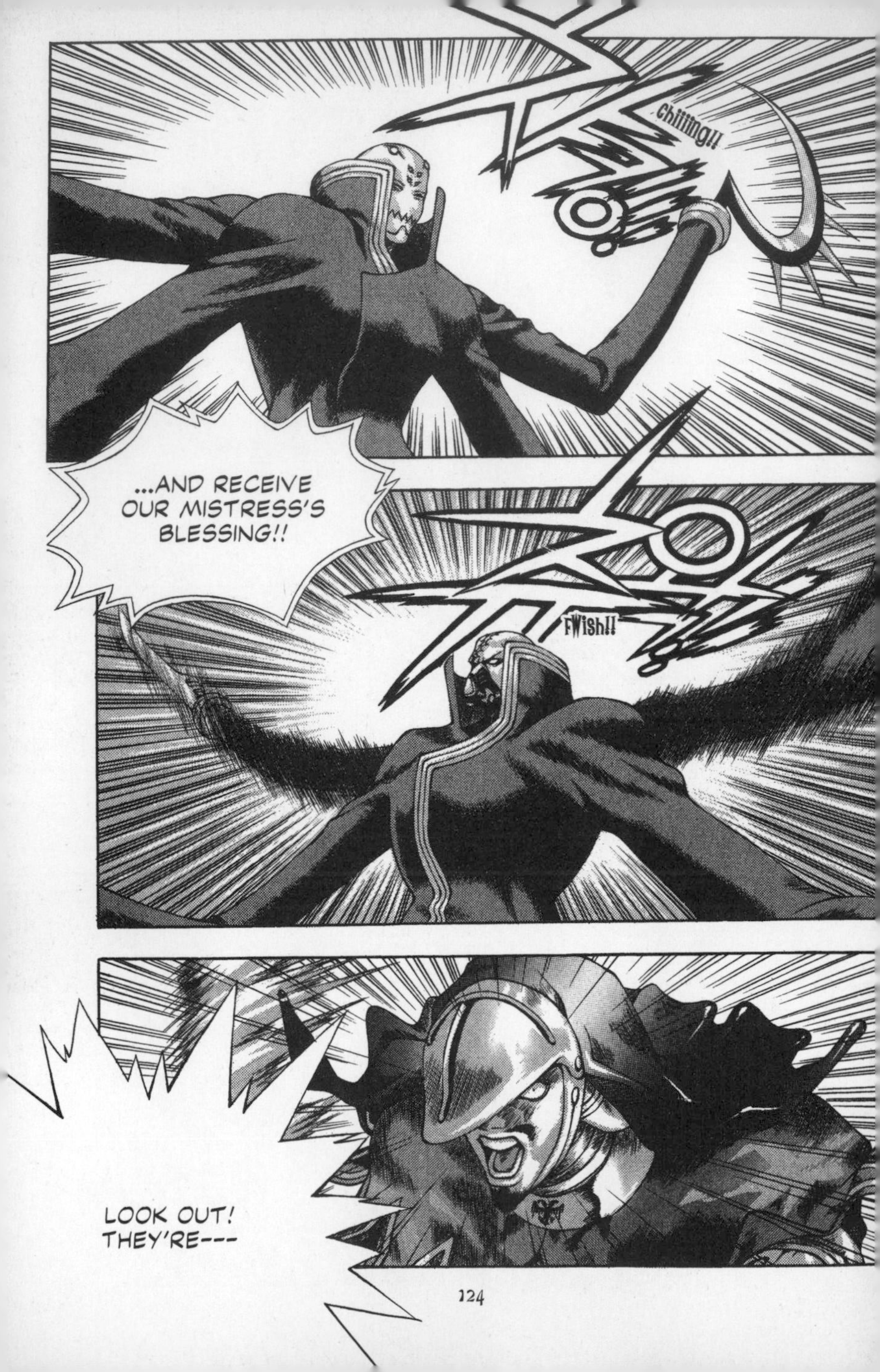
Chiiing!!
...AND RECEIVE OUR MISTRESS'S BLESSING!!
FWish!!
LOOK OUT! THEY'RE---

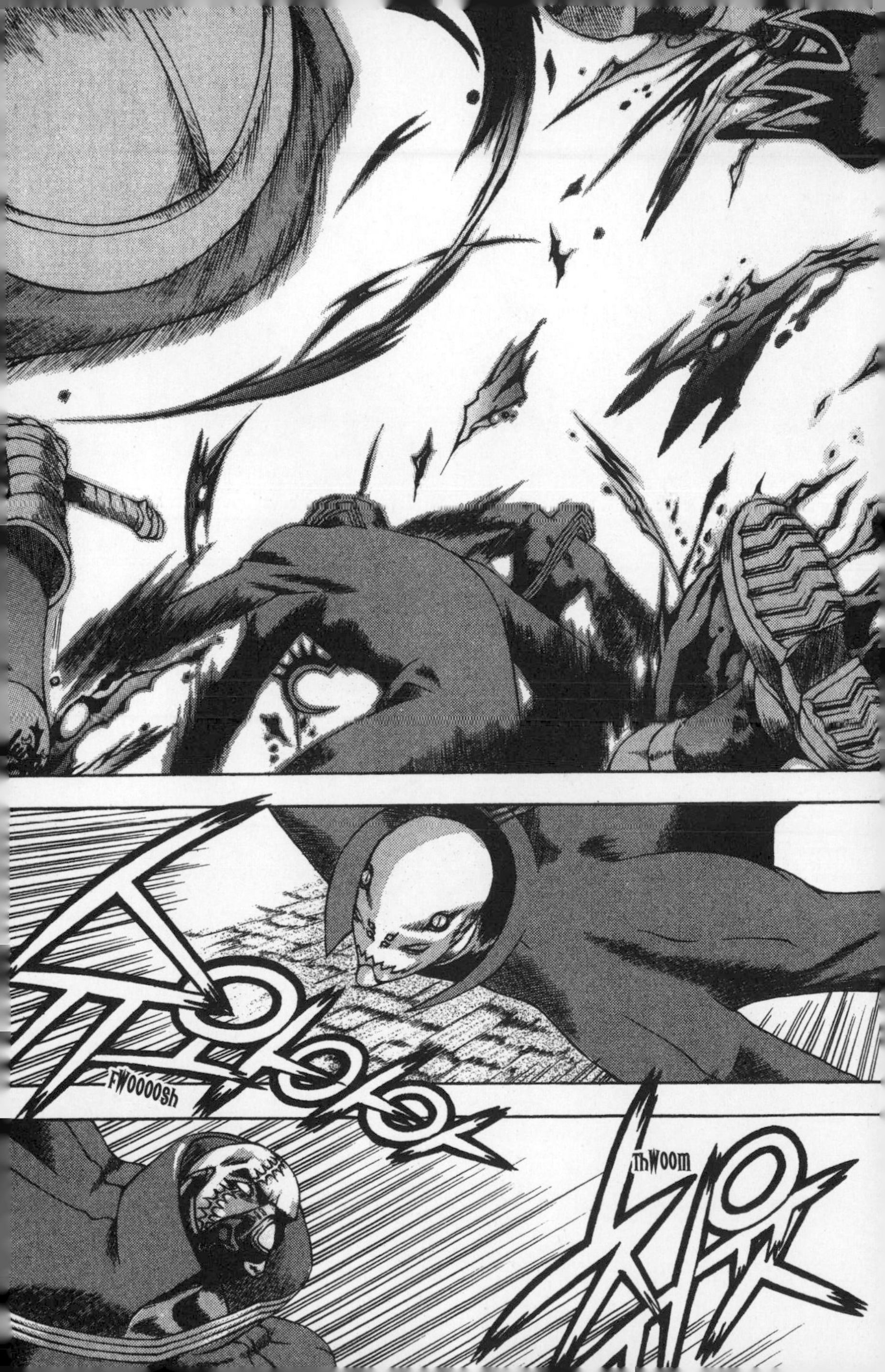
FWOOOOSh
ThWoom

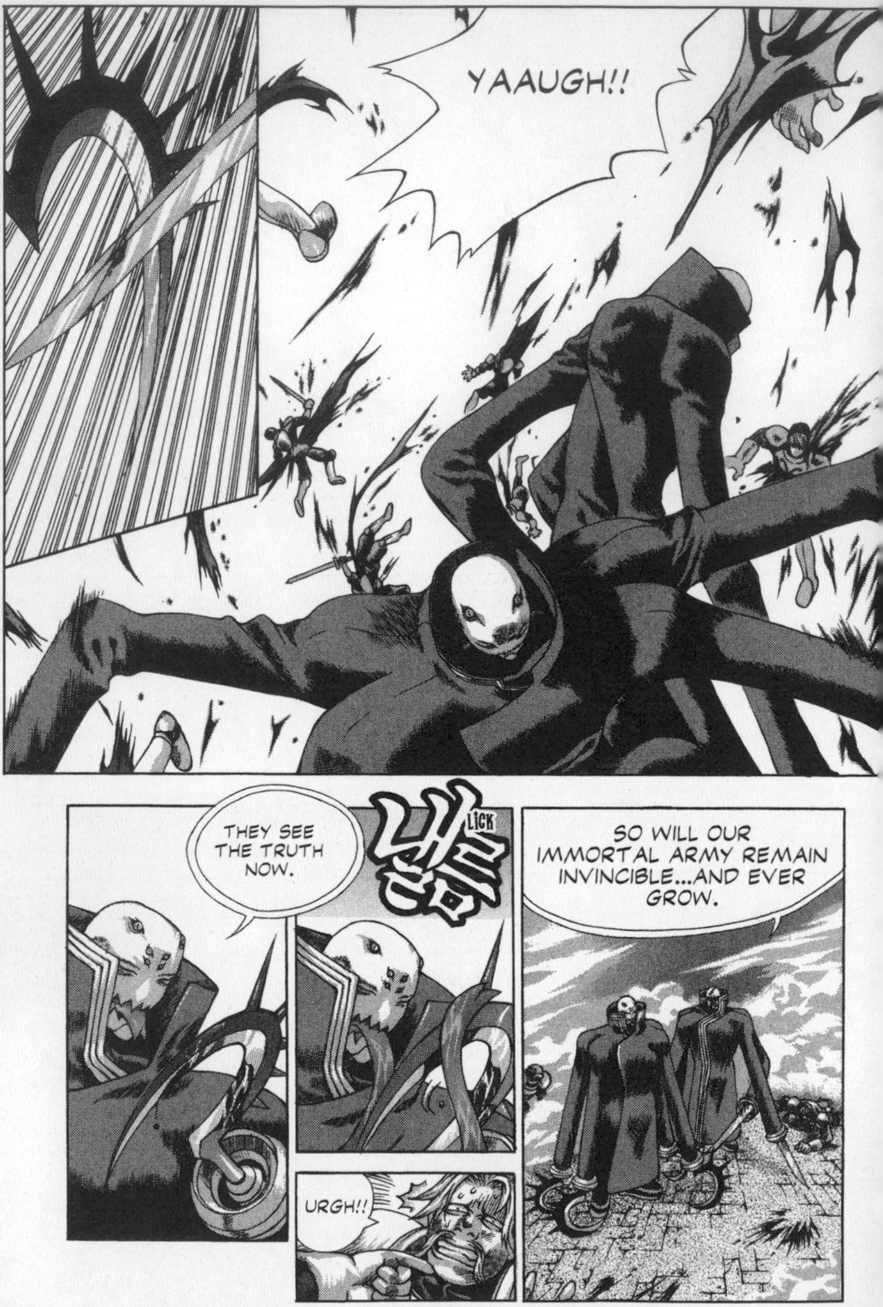
YAAUGH!!
THEY SEE THE TRUTH NOW.
낼름
LICK
URGH!!
SO WILL OUR IMMORTAL ARMY REMAIN INVINCIBLE...AND EVER GROW.

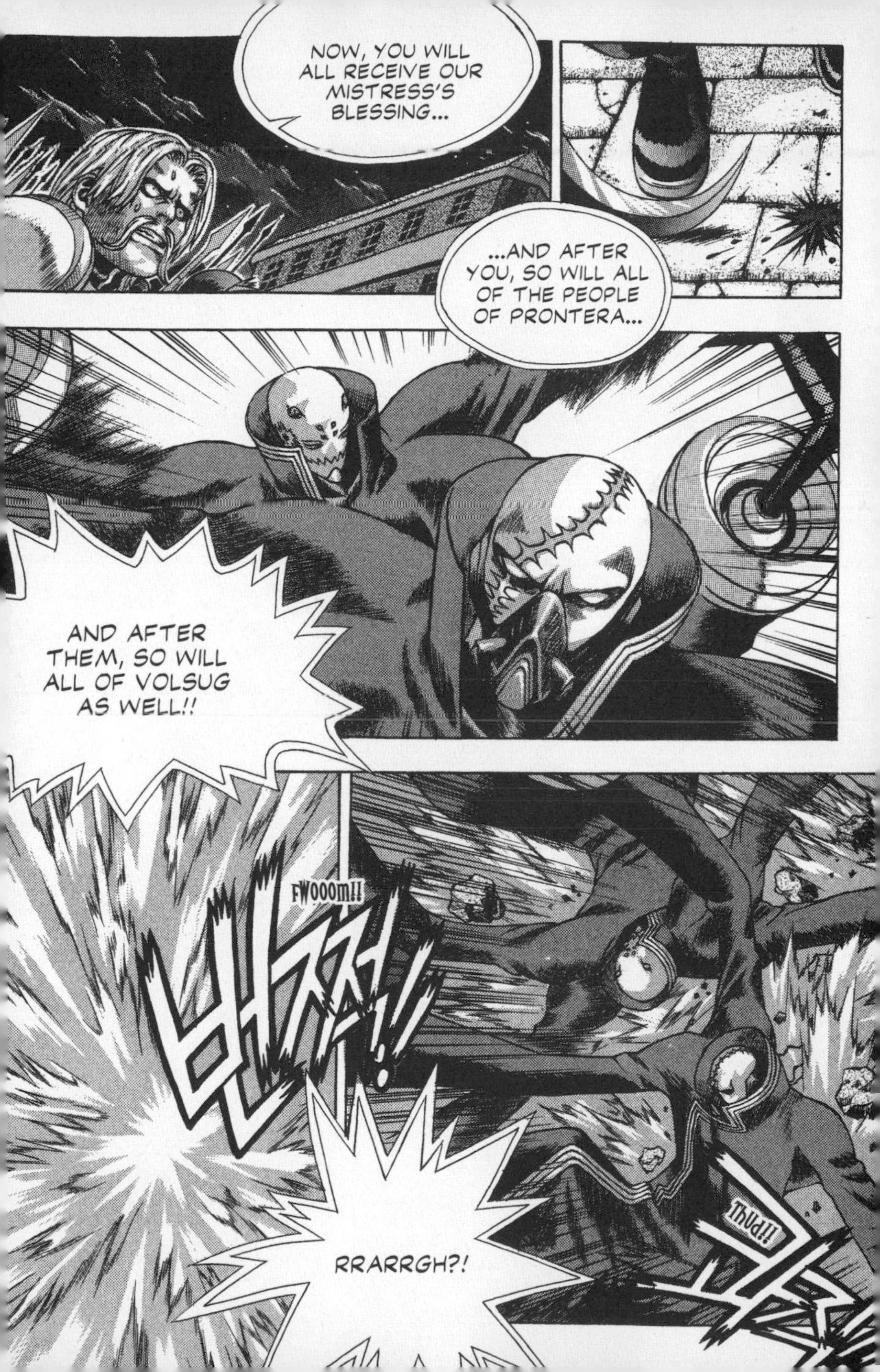
NOW, YOU WILL ALL RECEIVE OUR MISTRESS'S BLESSING...
...AND AFTER YOU, SO WILL ALL OF THE PEOPLE OF PRONTERA...
AND AFTER THEM, SO WILL ALL OF VOLSUG AS WELL!!
FWOOOM!!
RRARRGH?!
THUD!!

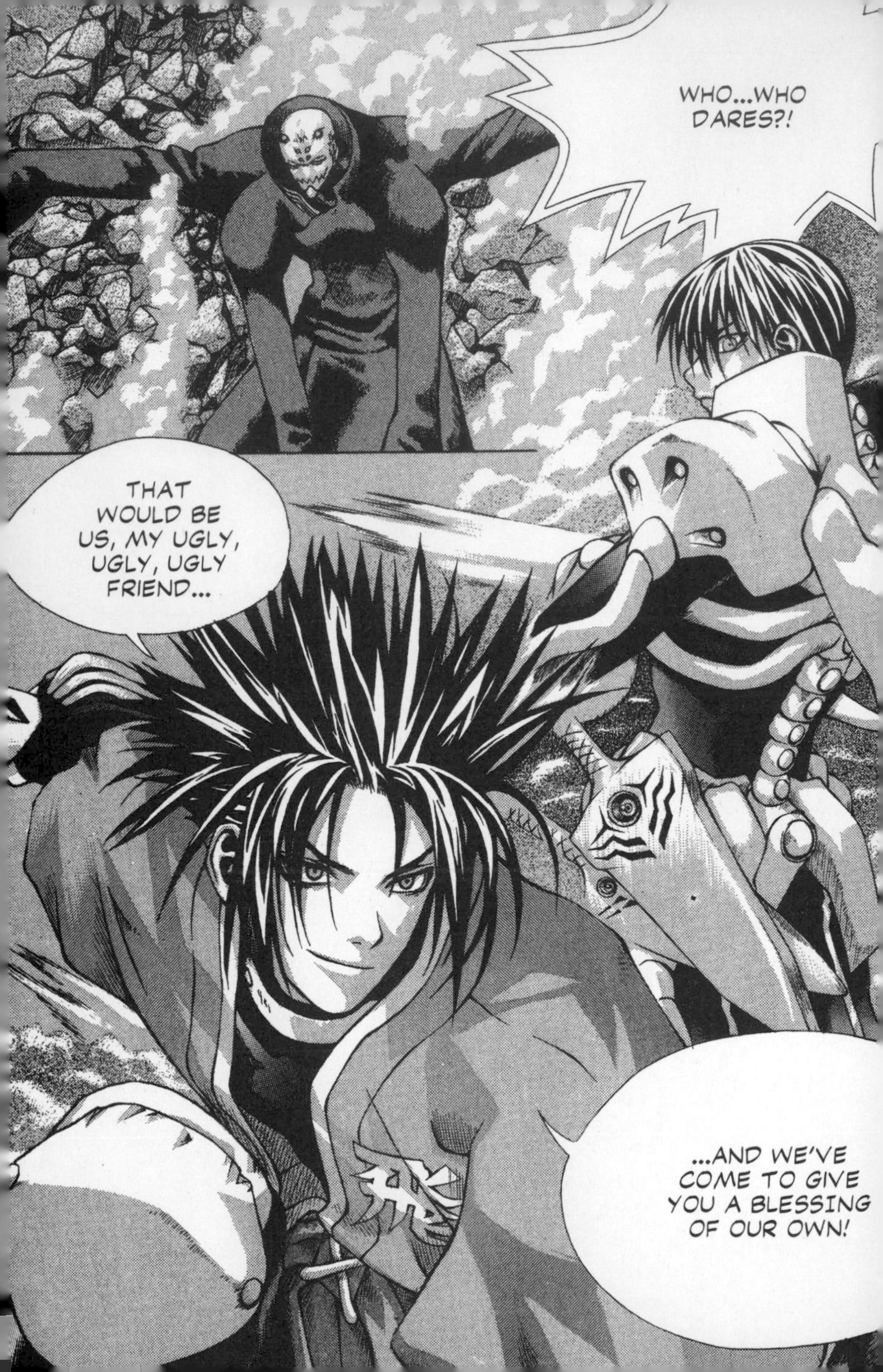
WHO...WHO DARES?!
THAT WOULD BE US, MY UGLY, UGLY, UGLY FRIEND...
...AND WE'VE COME TO GIVE YOU A BLESSING OF OUR OWN!

RAGNAROK
라그나로크
IN TO THE ABYSS

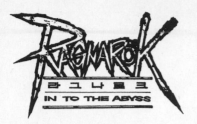

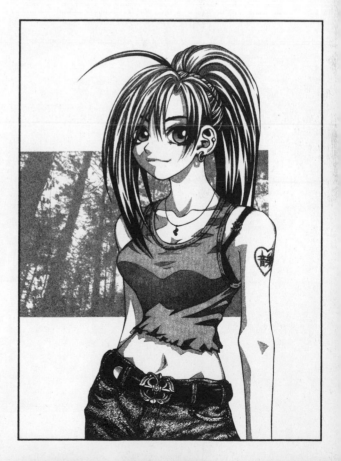

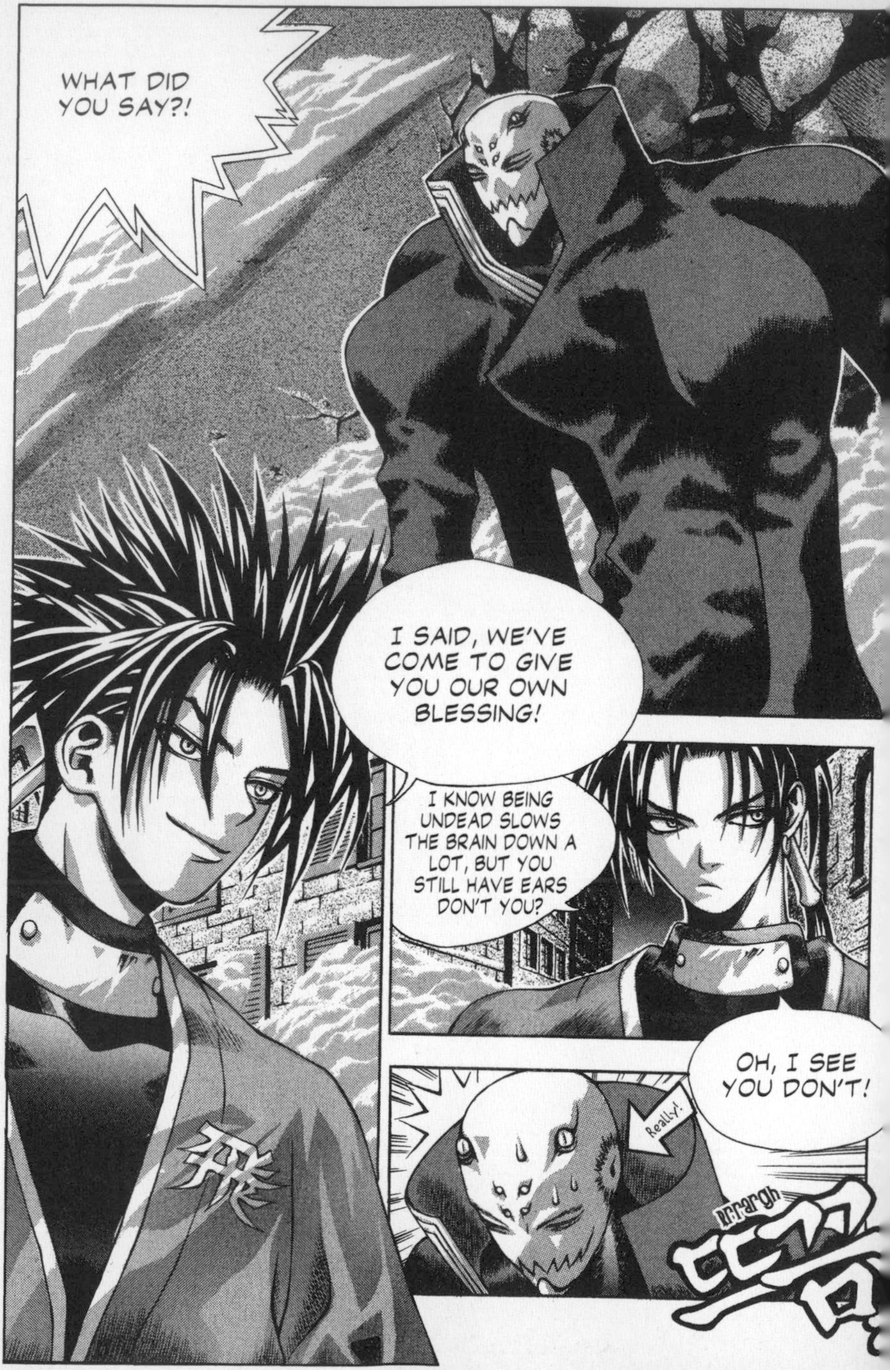
WHAT DID YOU SAY?!
I SAID, WE'VE COME TO GIVE YOU OUR OWN BLESSING!
I KNOW BEING UNDEAD SLOWS THE BRAIN DOWN A LOT, BUT YOU STILL HAVE EARS DON'T YOU?
OH, I SEE YOU DON'T!
Really!
Rrrargh

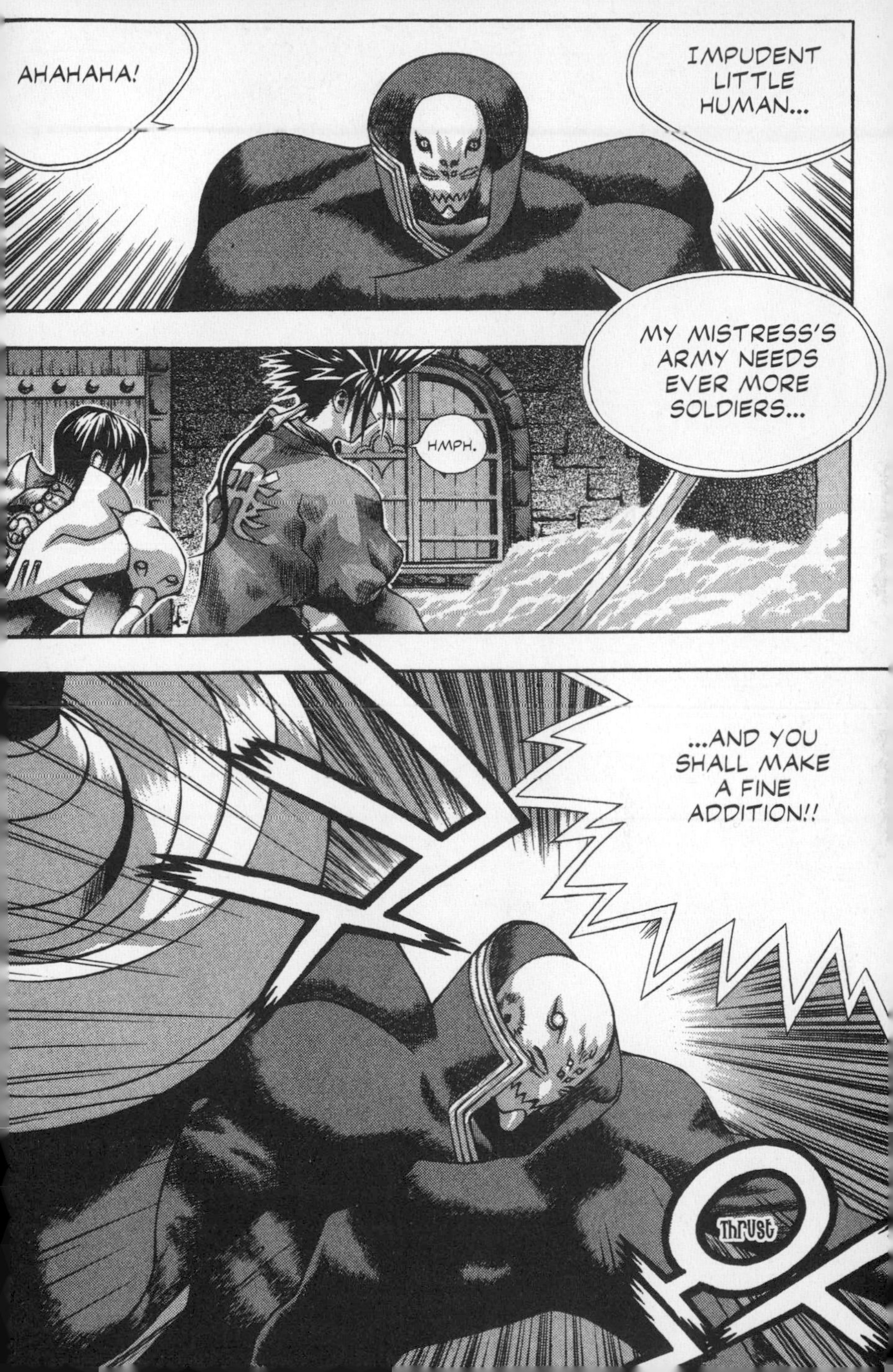
AHAHAHA!
IMPUDENT LITTLE HUMAN...
MY MISTRESS'S ARMY NEEDS EVER MORE SOLDIERS...
HMPH.
...AND YOU SHALL MAKE A FINE ADDITION!!
THRUST

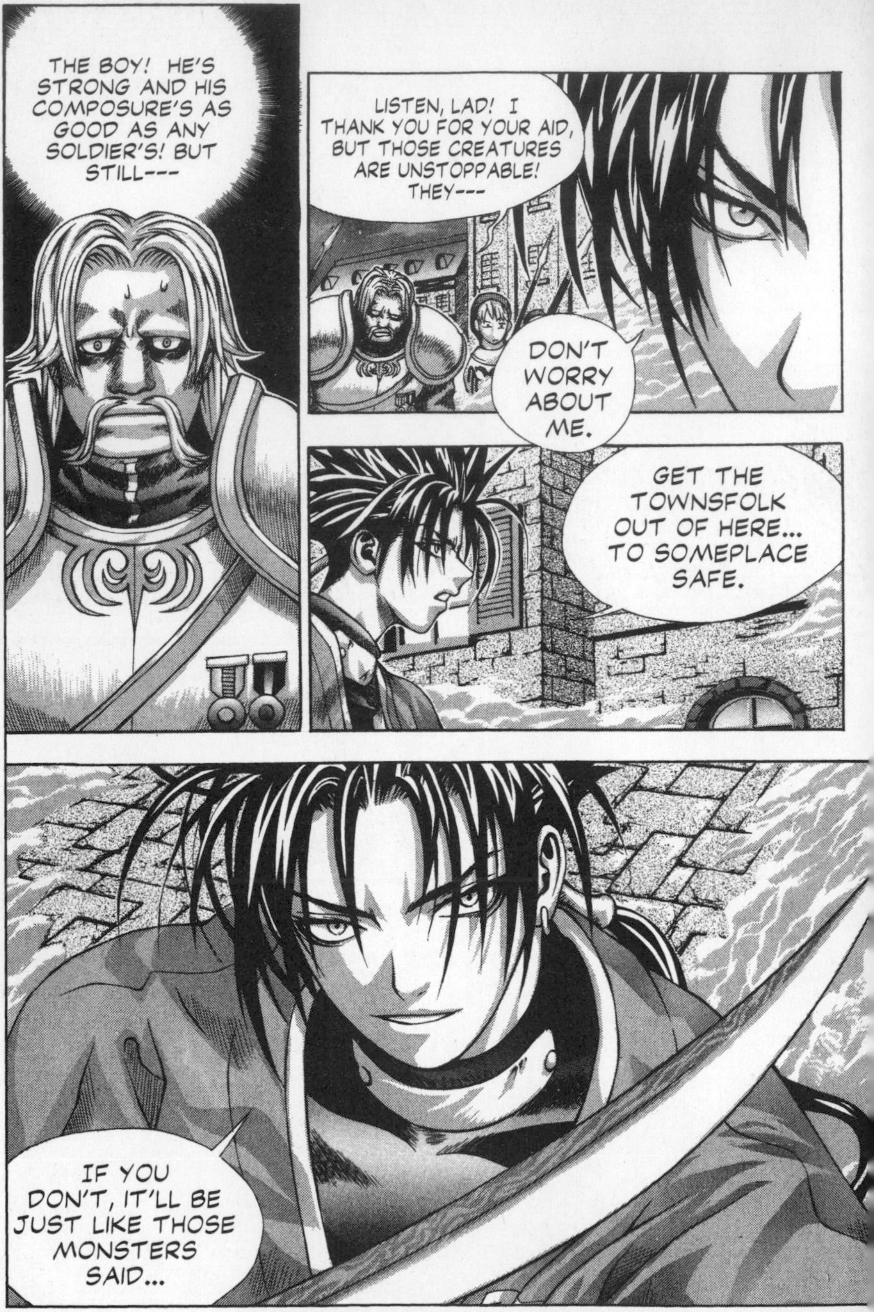
THE BOY! HE'S STRONG AND HIS COMPOSURE'S AS GOOD AS ANY SOLDIER'S! BUT STILL---
LISTEN, LAD! I THANK YOU FOR YOUR AID, BUT THOSE CREATURES ARE UNSTOPPABLE! THEY---
DON'T WORRY ABOUT ME.
GET THE TOWNSFOLK OUT OF HERE... TO SOMEPLACE SAFE.
IF YOU DON'T, IT'LL BE JUST LIKE THOSE MONSTERS SAID...

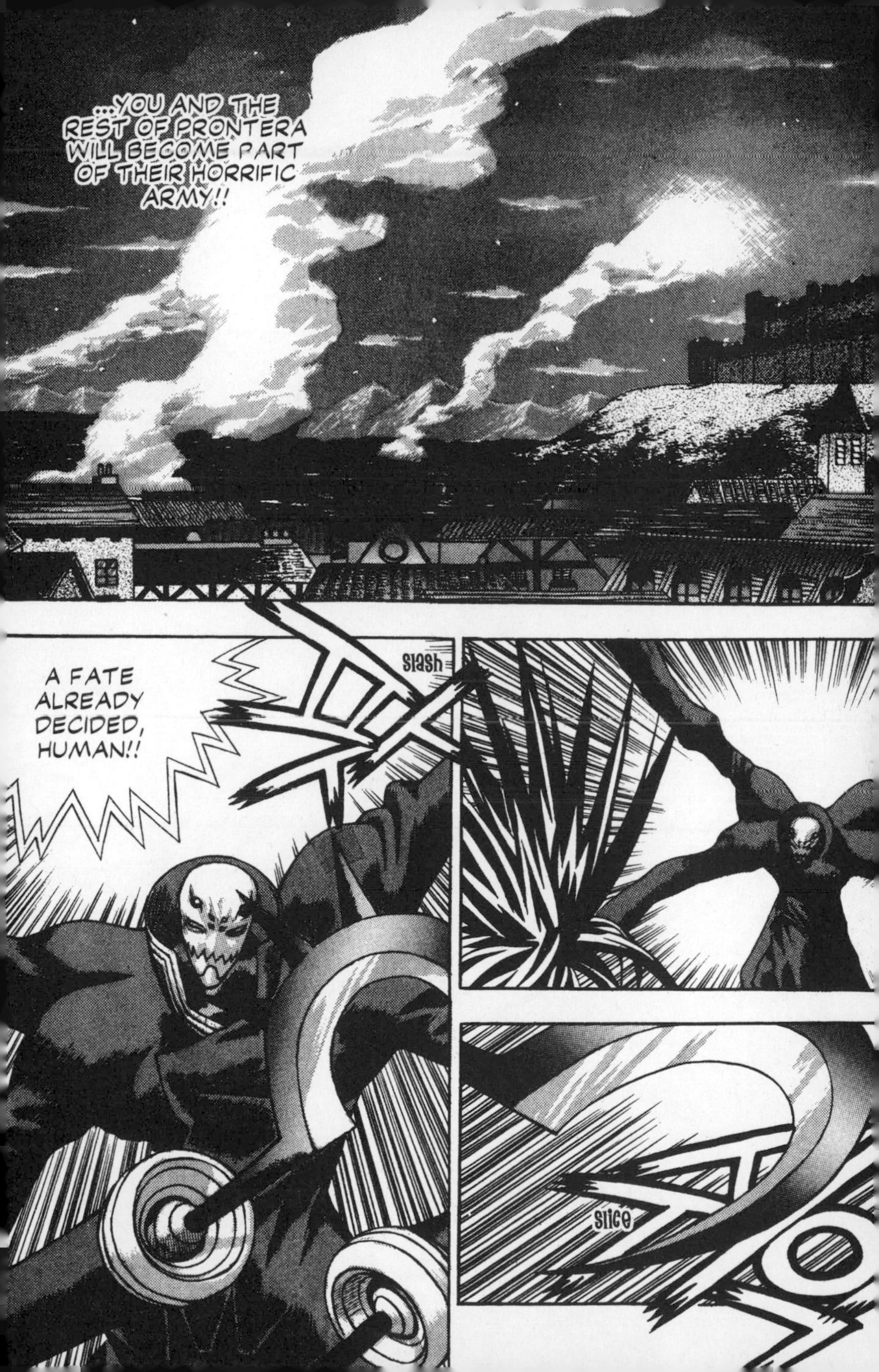
...YOU AND THE REST OF PRONTERA WILL BECOME PART OF THEIR HORRIFIC ARMY!!
A FATE ALREADY DECIDED, HUMAN!!
SLASH
SLICE

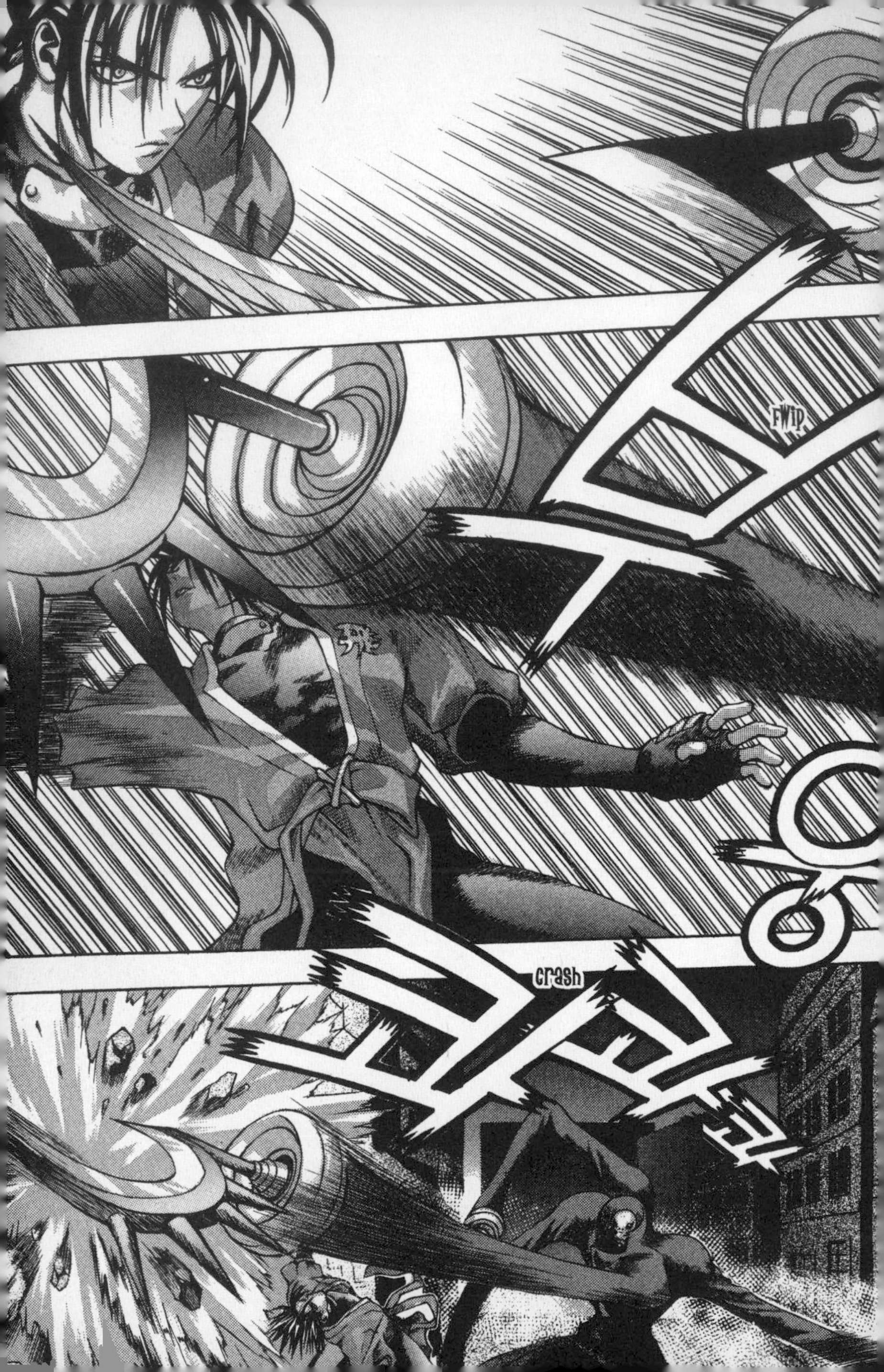
FWIP
crash

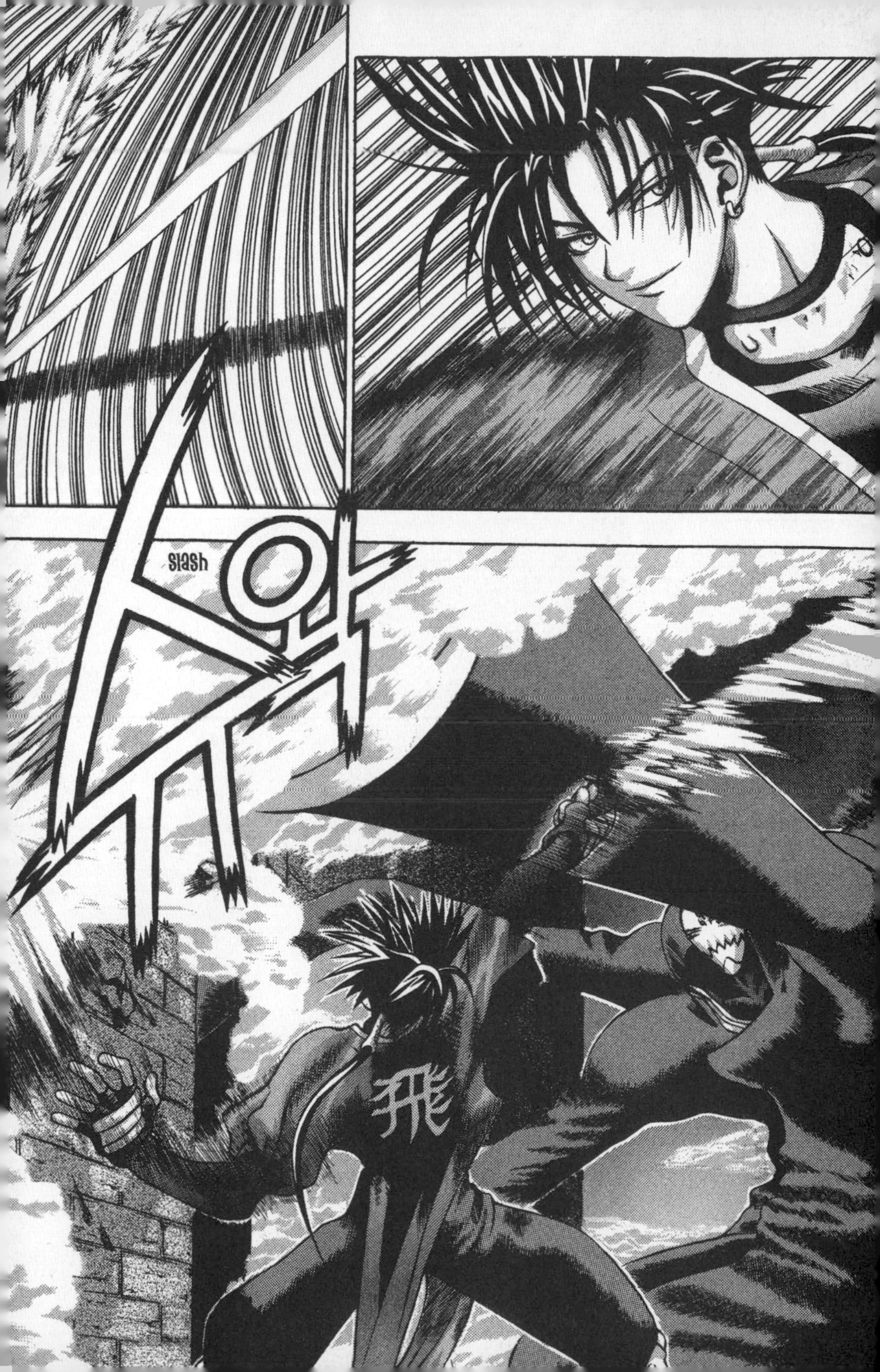
slash

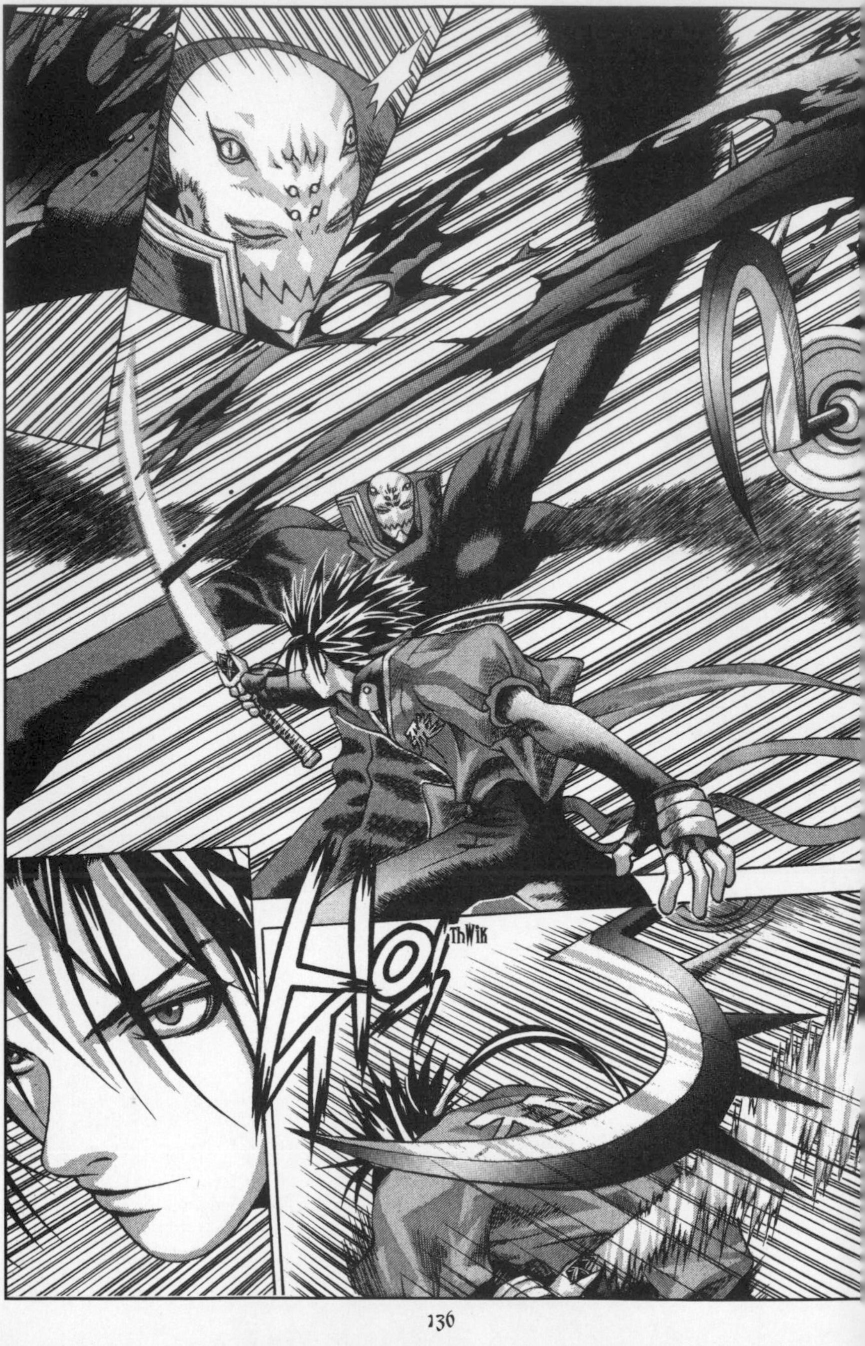
ThWiK

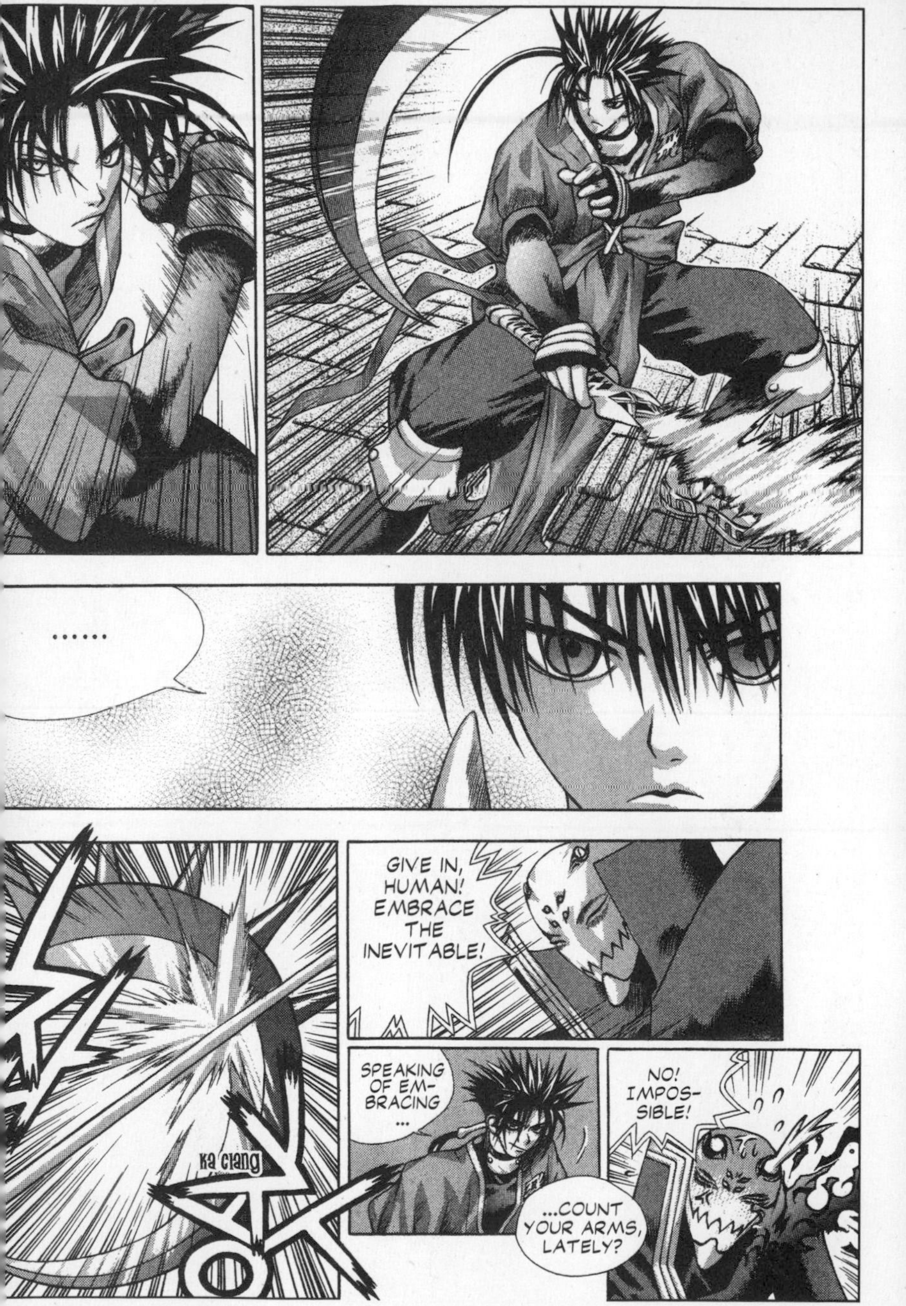
......
KA CLANG
GIVE IN, HUMAN! EMBRACE THE INEVITABLE!
SPEAKING OF EM-BRACING ...
...COUNT YOUR ARMS, LATELY?
NO! IMPOS-SIBLE!

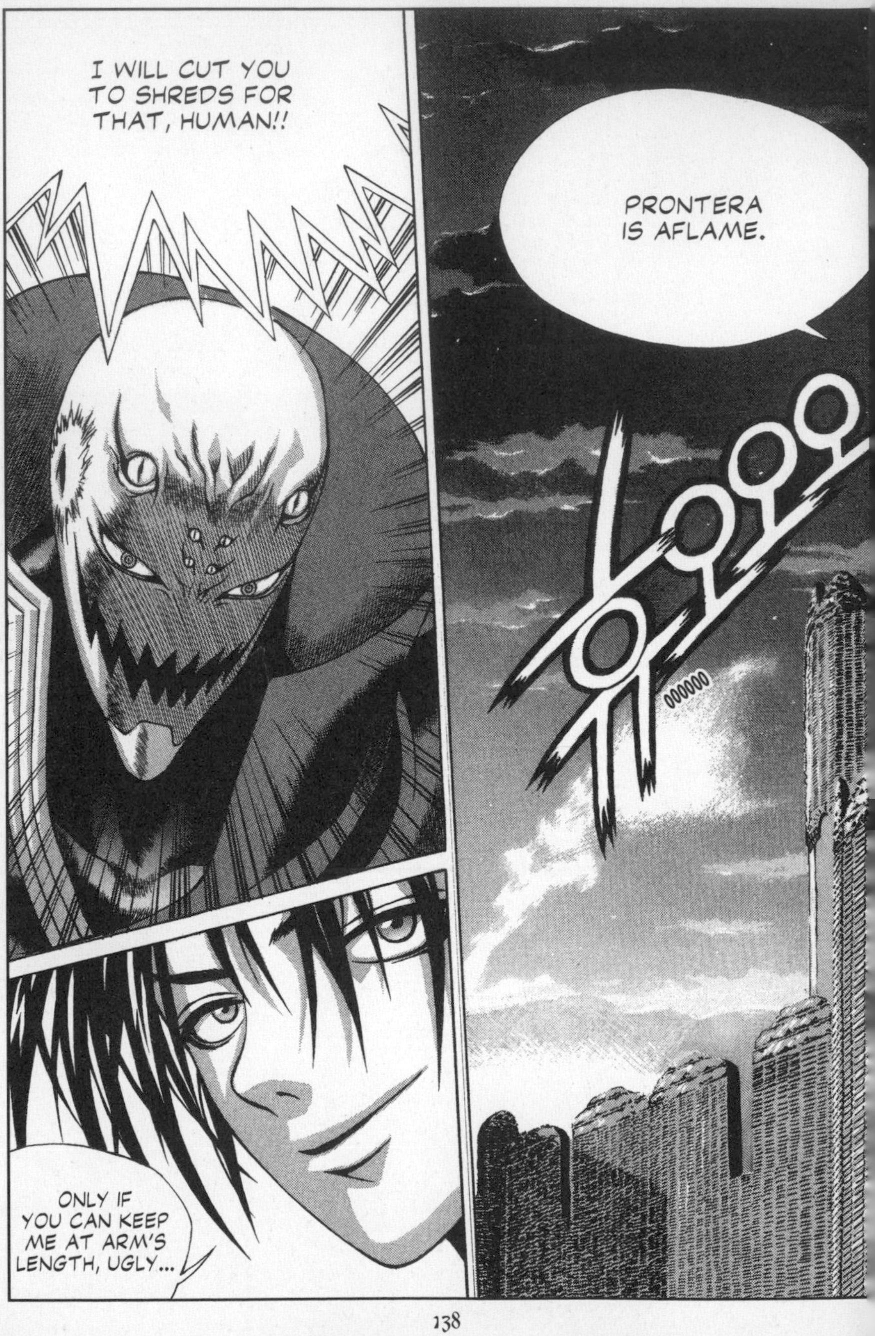
I WILL CUT YOU TO SHREDS FOR THAT, HUMAN!!
ONLY IF YOU CAN KEEP ME AT ARM'S LENGTH, UGLY...
PRONTERA IS AFLAME.

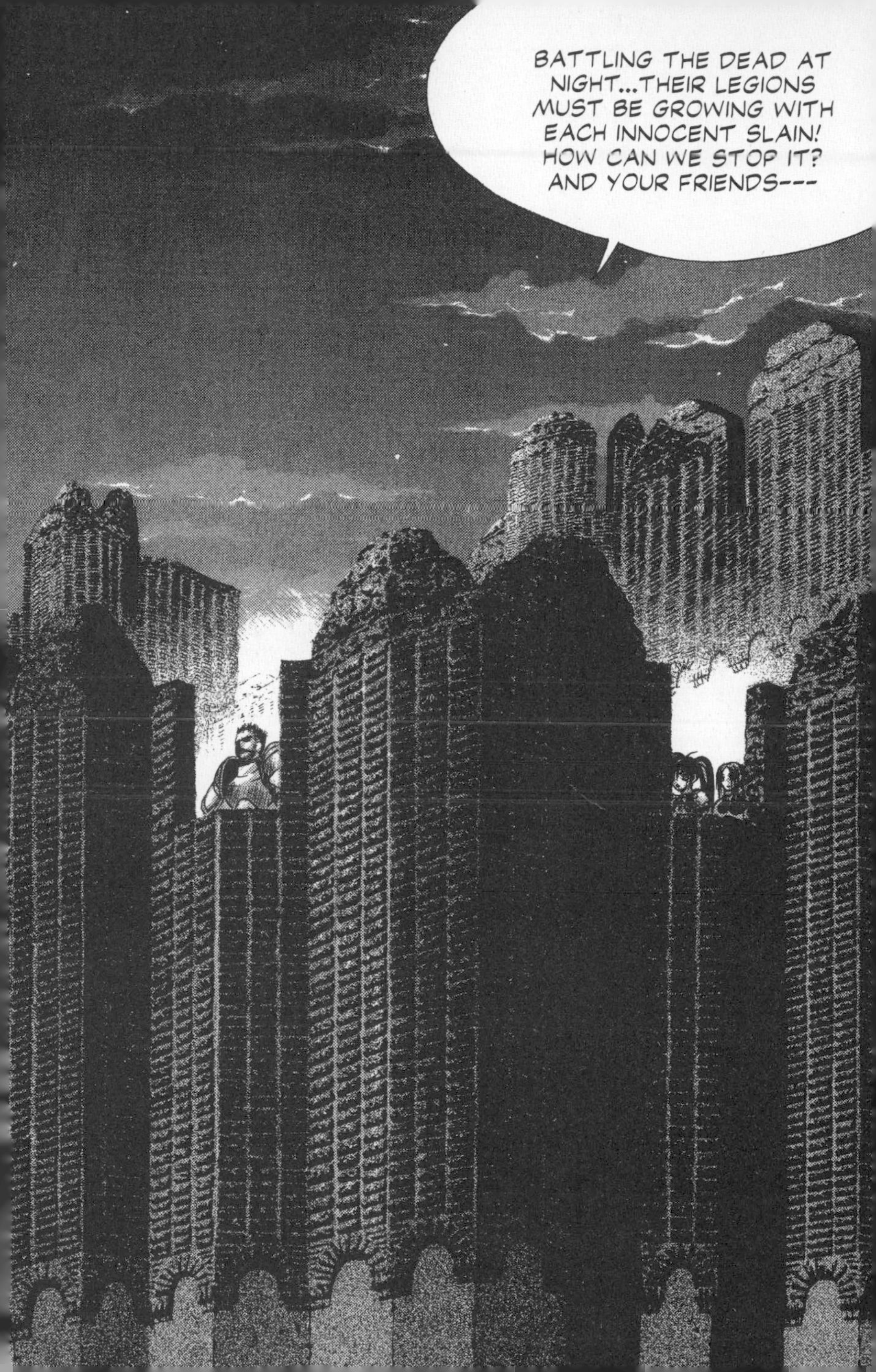
BATTLING THE DEAD AT NIGHT...THEIR LEGIONS MUST BE GROWING WITH EACH INNOCENT SLAIN! HOW CAN WE STOP IT? AND YOUR FRIENDS---

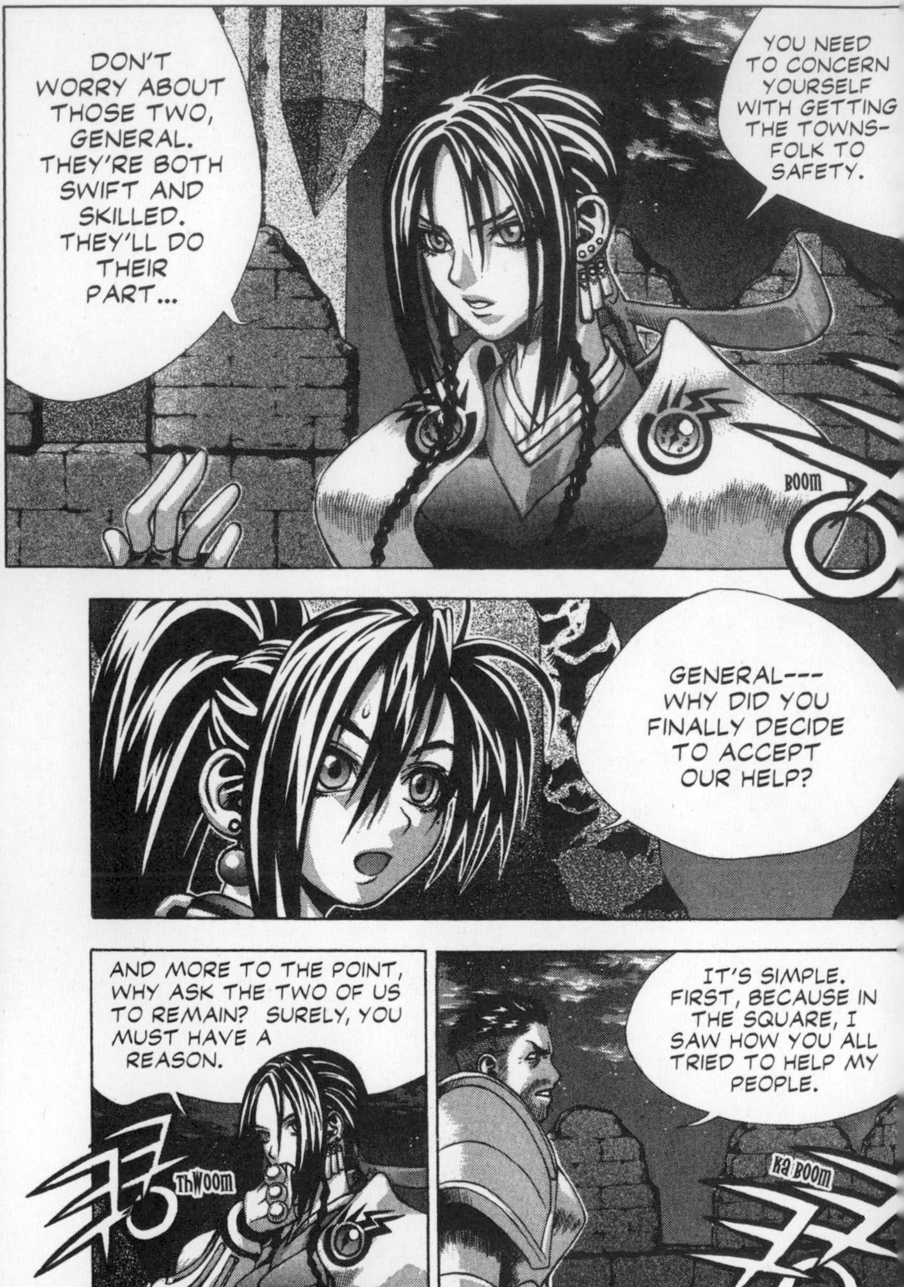
DON'T WORRY ABOUT THOSE TWO, GENERAL. THEY'RE BOTH SWIFT AND SKILLED. THEY'LL DO THEIR PART...
YOU NEED TO CONCERN YOURSELF WITH GETTING THE TOWNS-FOLK TO SAFETY.
BOOM
GENERAL--- WHY DID YOU FINALLY DECIDE TO ACCEPT OUR HELP?
AND MORE TO THE POINT, WHY ASK THE TWO OF US TO REMAIN? SURELY, YOU MUST HAVE A REASON.
ThWoom
IT'S SIMPLE. FIRST, BECAUSE IN THE SQUARE, I SAW HOW YOU ALL TRIED TO HELP MY PEOPLE.
Ka Boom

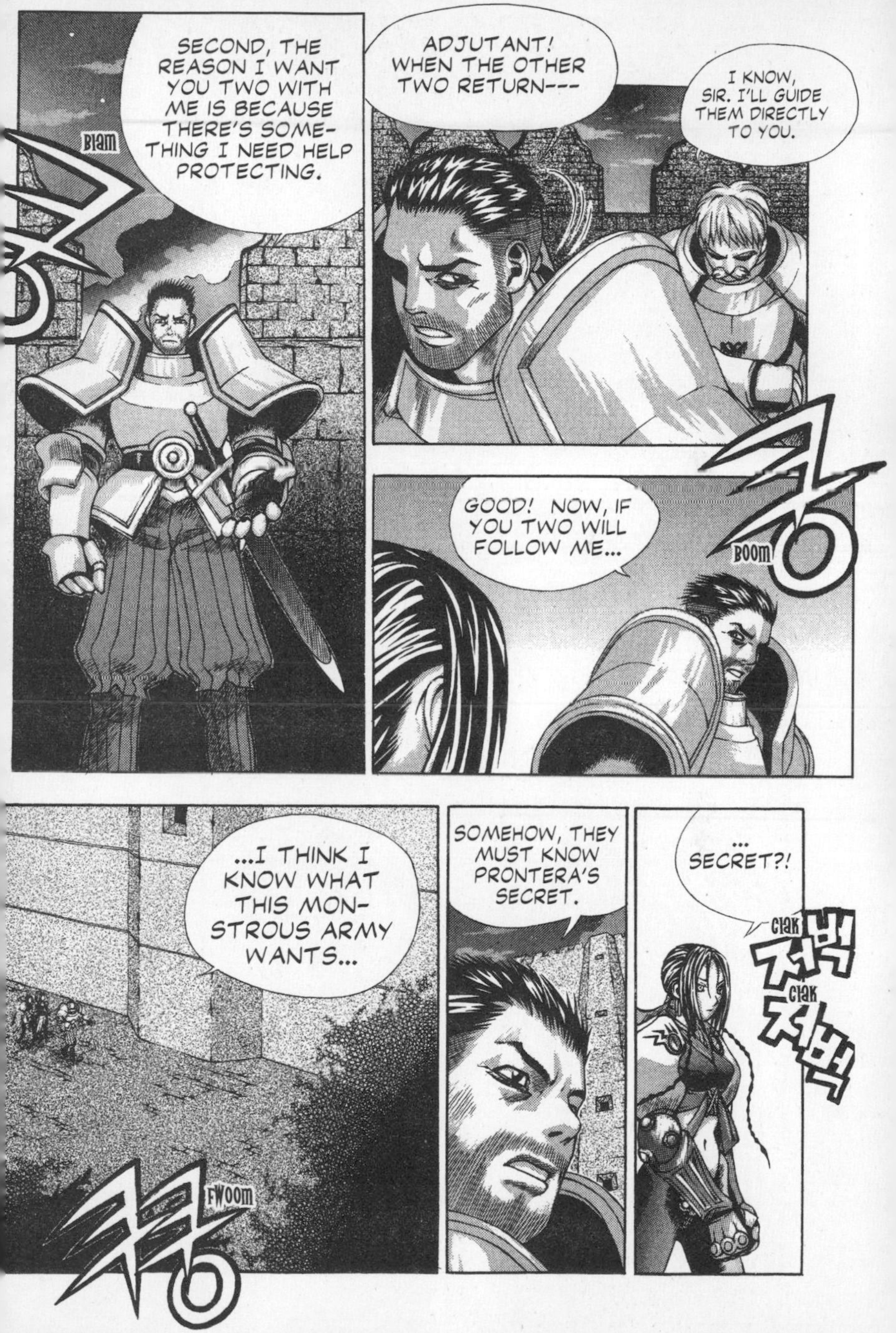
SECOND, THE REASON I WANT YOU TWO WITH ME IS BECAUSE THERE'S SOME-THING I NEED HELP PROTECTING.
BLAM
ADJUTANT! WHEN THE OTHER TWO RETURN---
I KNOW, SIR. I'LL GUIDE THEM DIRECTLY TO YOU.
GOOD! NOW, IF YOU TWO WILL FOLLOW ME...
BOOM
...I THINK I KNOW WHAT THIS MON-STROUS ARMY WANTS...
FWOOM
SOMEHOW, THEY MUST KNOW PRONTERA'S SECRET.
... SECRET?!
CLAK
CLAK

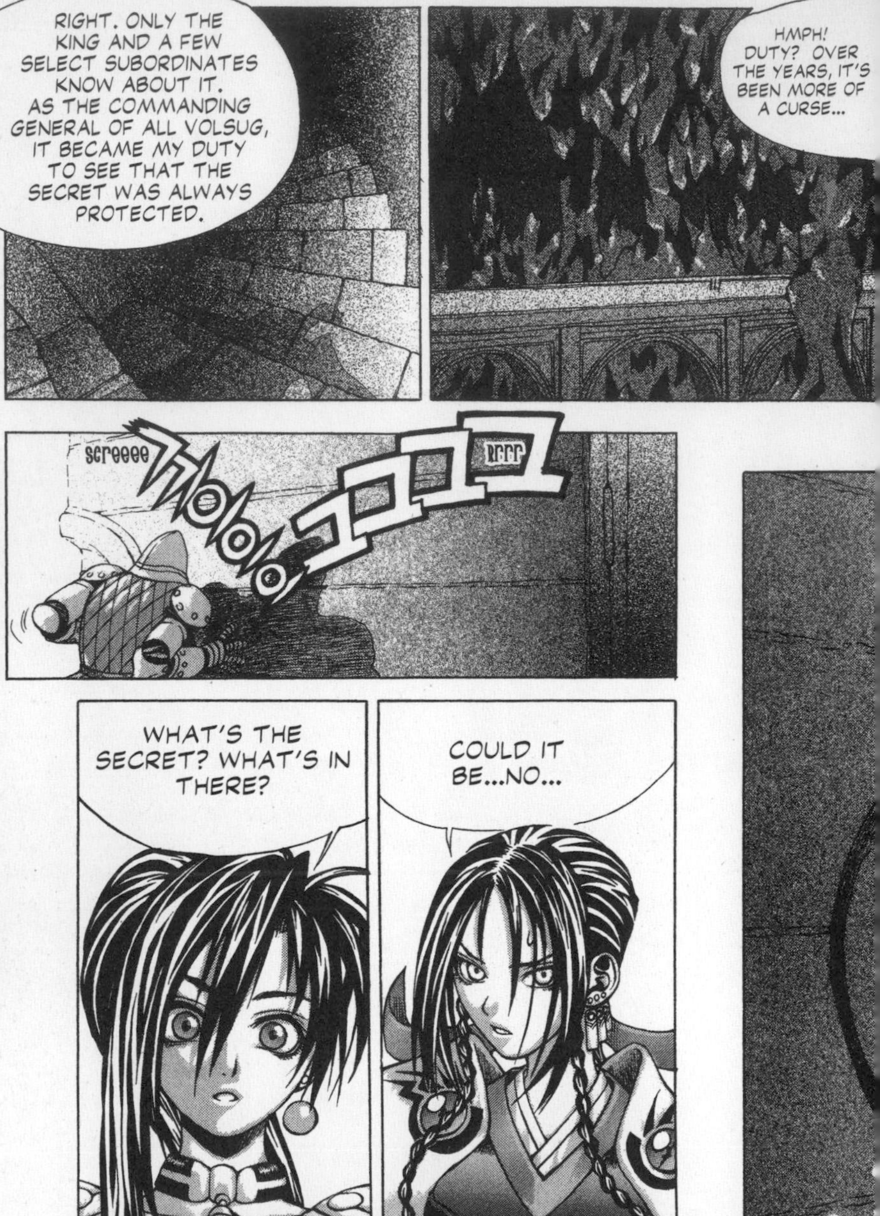
RIGHT. ONLY THE KING AND A FEW SELECT SUBORDINATES KNOW ABOUT IT. AS THE COMMANDING GENERAL OF ALL VOLSUG, IT BECAME MY DUTY TO SEE THAT THE SECRET WAS ALWAYS PROTECTED.
HMPH! DUTY? OVER THE YEARS, IT'S BEEN MORE OF A CURSE...
screeee
rrrr
WHAT'S THE SECRET? WHAT'S IN THERE?
COULD IT BE...NO...

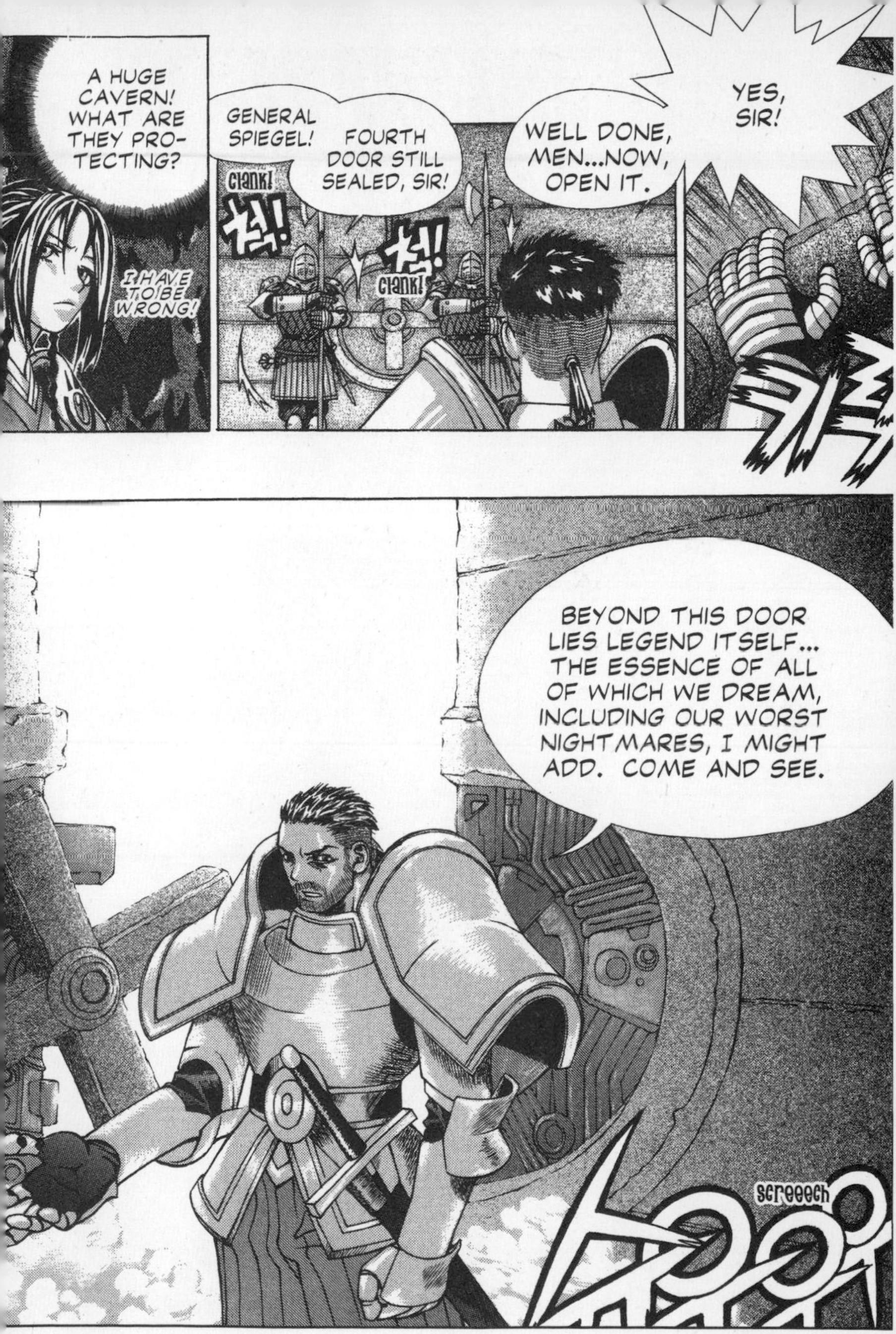
A HUGE CAVERN! WHAT ARE THEY PROTECTING?
I HAVE TO BE WRONG!
GENERAL SPIEGEL!
FOURTH DOOR STILL SEALED, SIR!
CLANK!
CLANK!
WELL DONE, MEN...NOW, OPEN IT.
YES, SIR!
BEYOND THIS DOOR LIES LEGEND ITSELF... THE ESSENCE OF ALL OF WHICH WE DREAM, INCLUDING OUR WORST NIGHTMARES, I MIGHT ADD. COME AND SEE.
SCREEECH

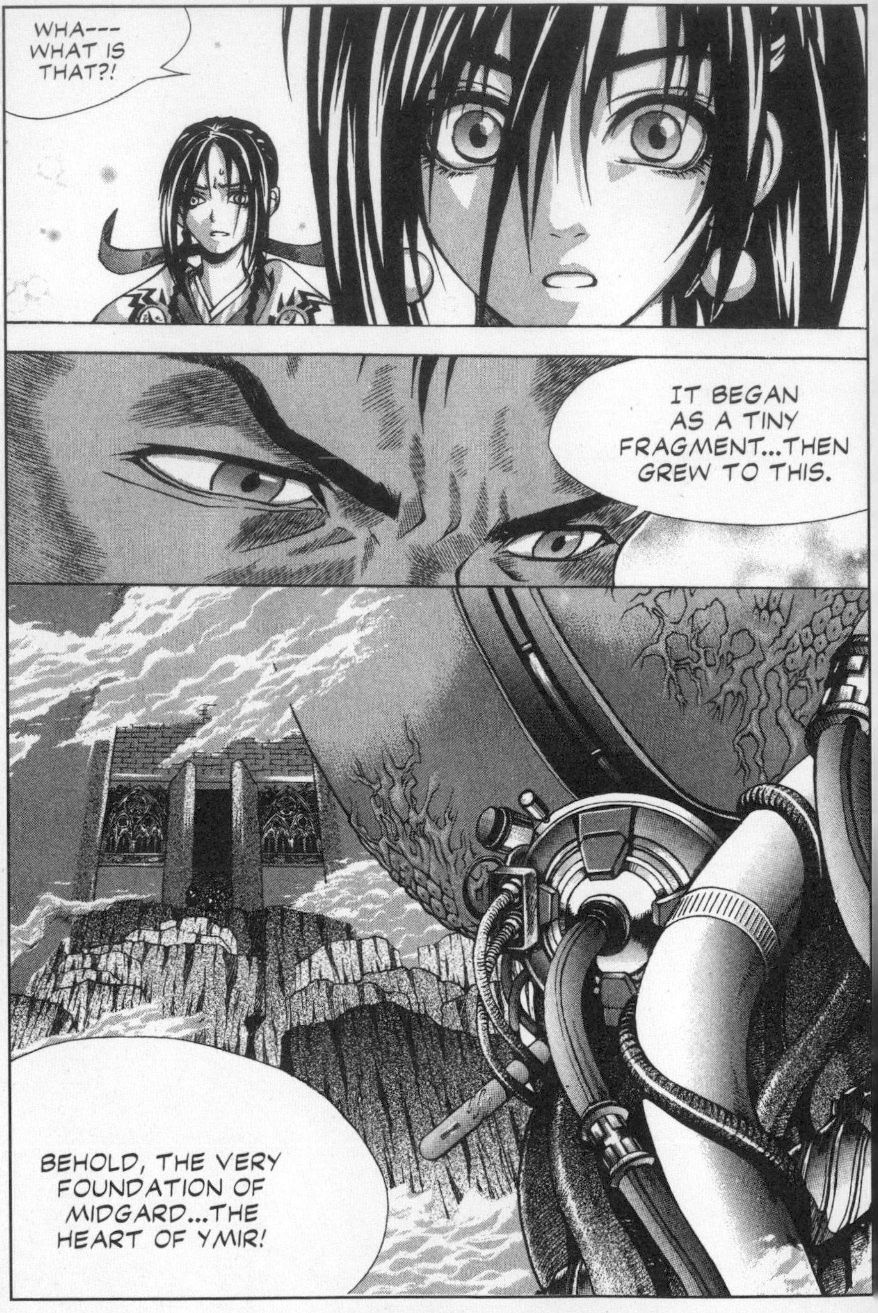
WHA--- WHAT IS THAT?!
IT BEGAN AS A TINY FRAGMENT...THEN GREW TO THIS.
BEHOLD, THE VERY FOUNDATION OF MIDGARD...THE HEART OF YMIR!

RAGNAROK
라그나로크
IN TO THE ABYSS

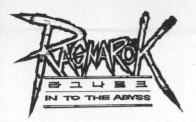

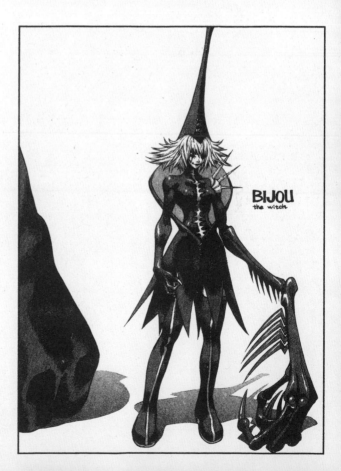

BIJOU
the witch

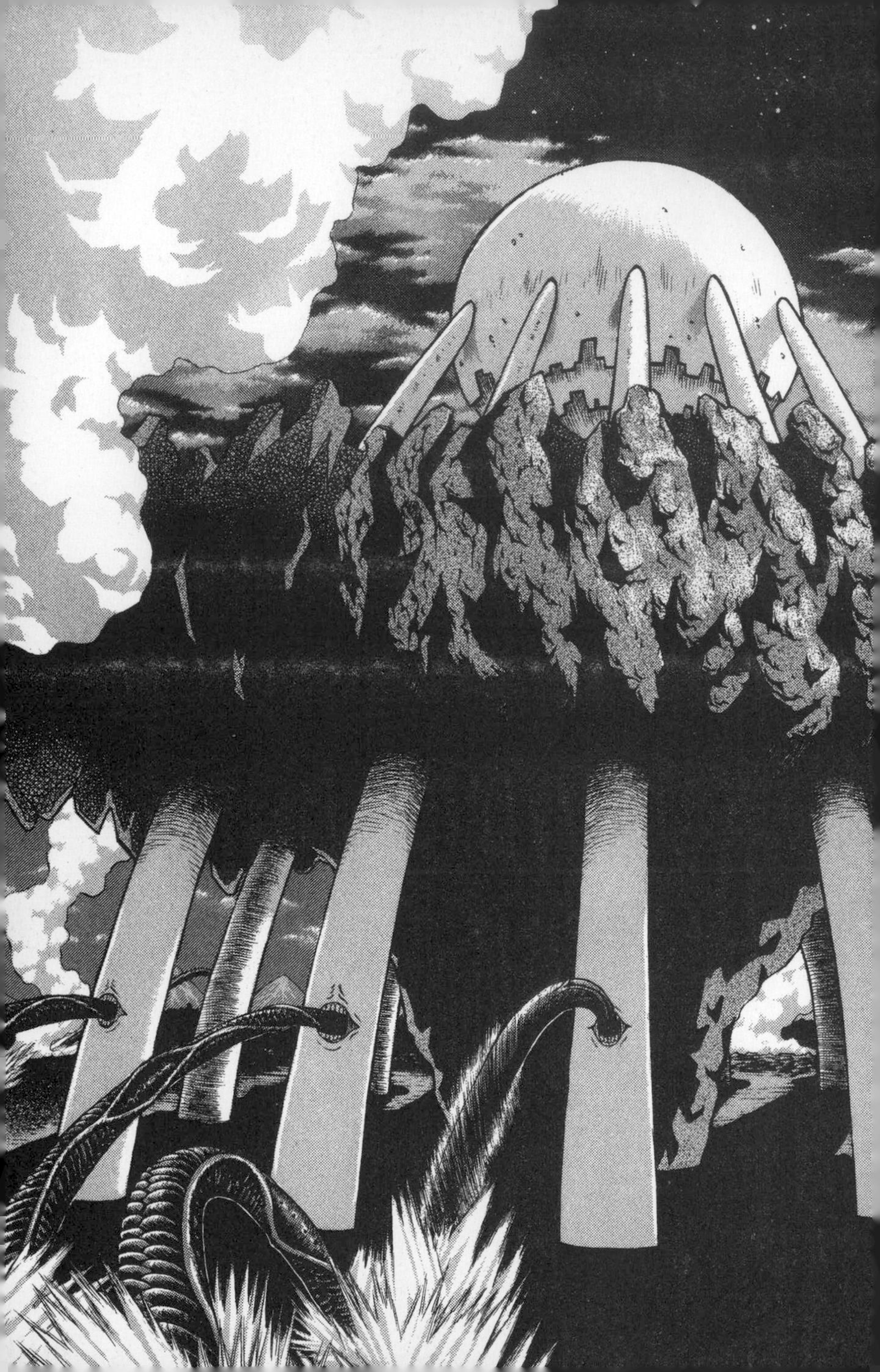

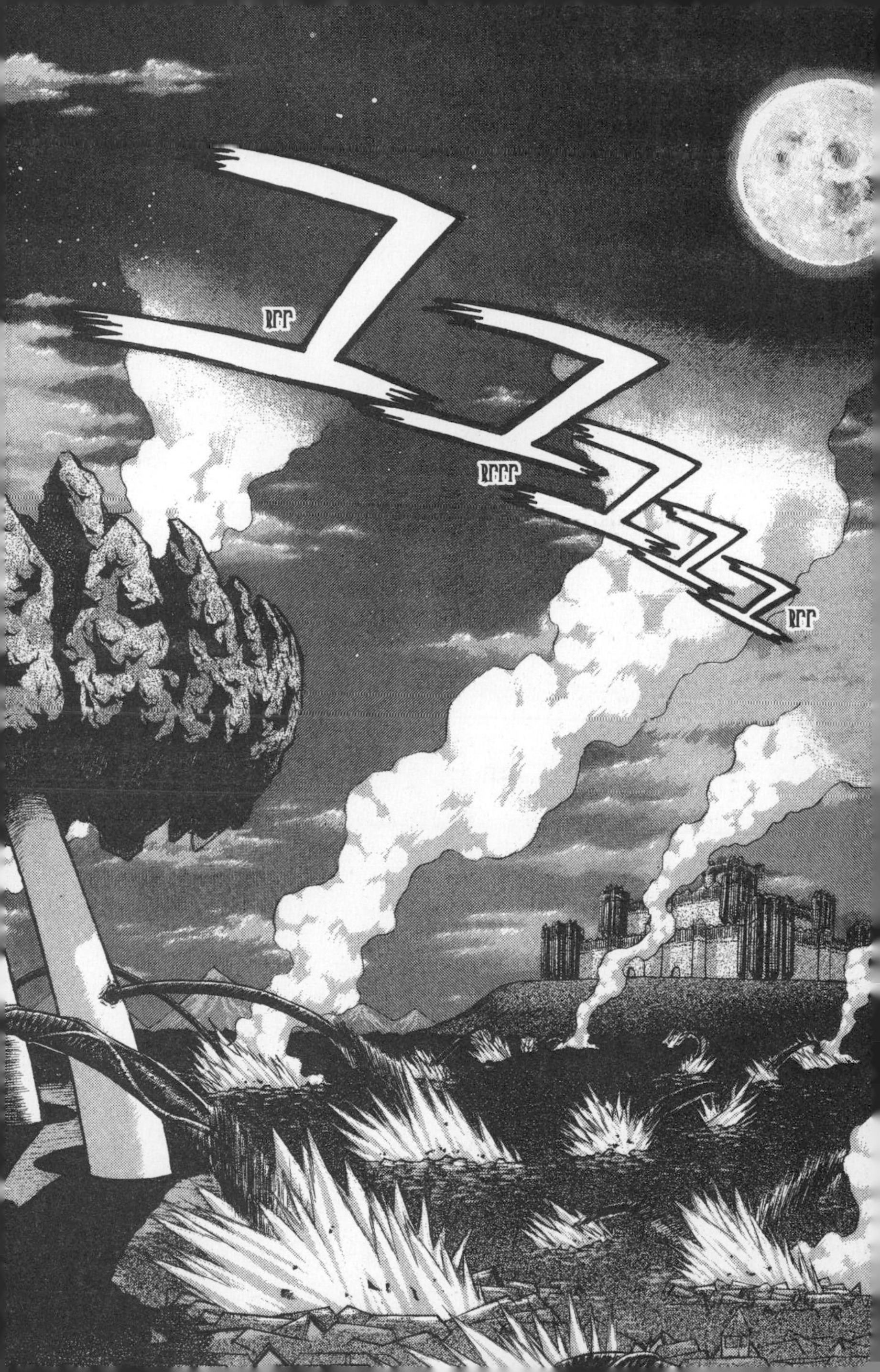
RrR
RRRR
RRR

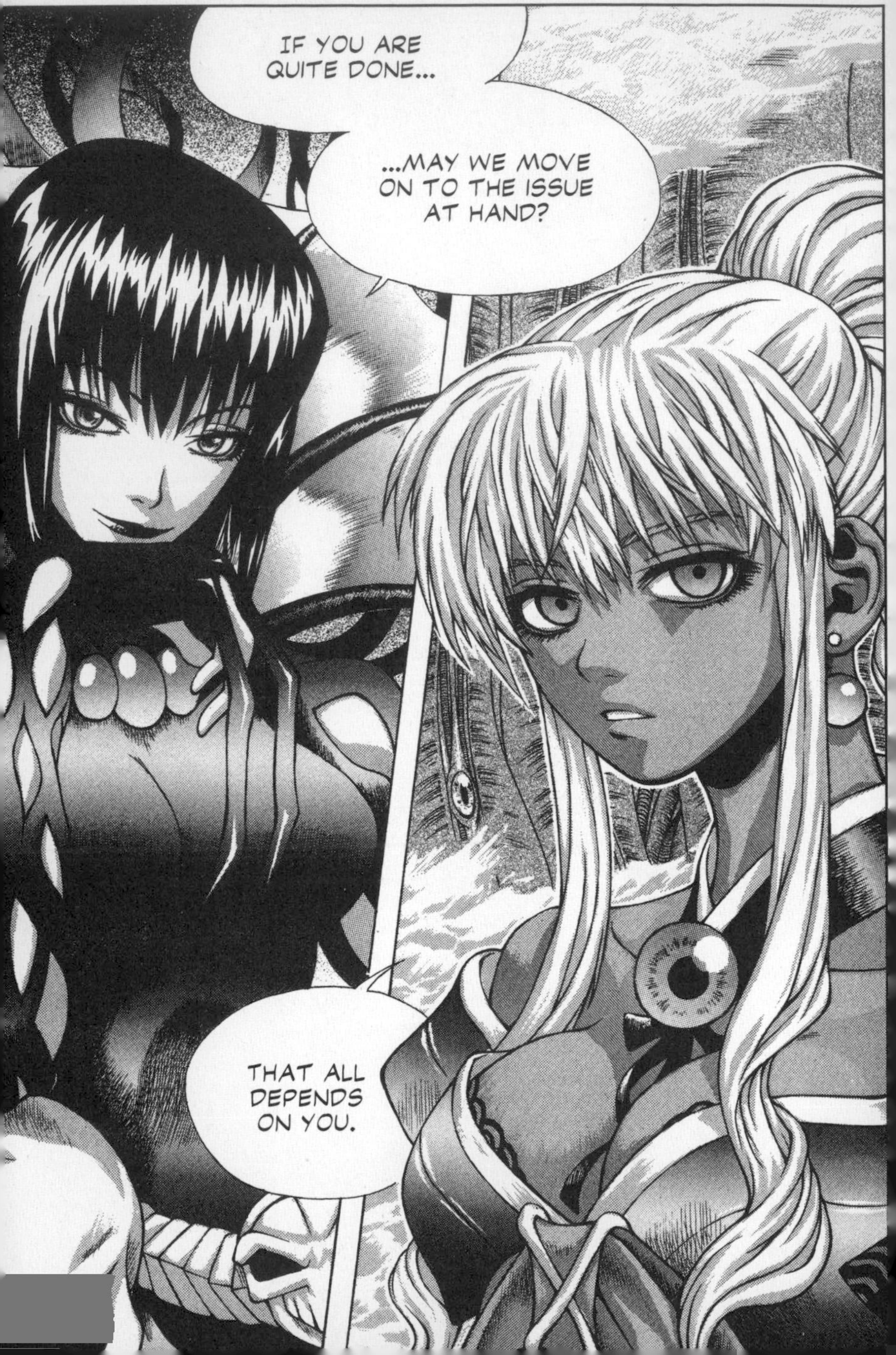
IF YOU ARE QUITE DONE...
...MAY WE MOVE ON TO THE ISSUE AT HAND?
THAT ALL DEPENDS ON YOU.

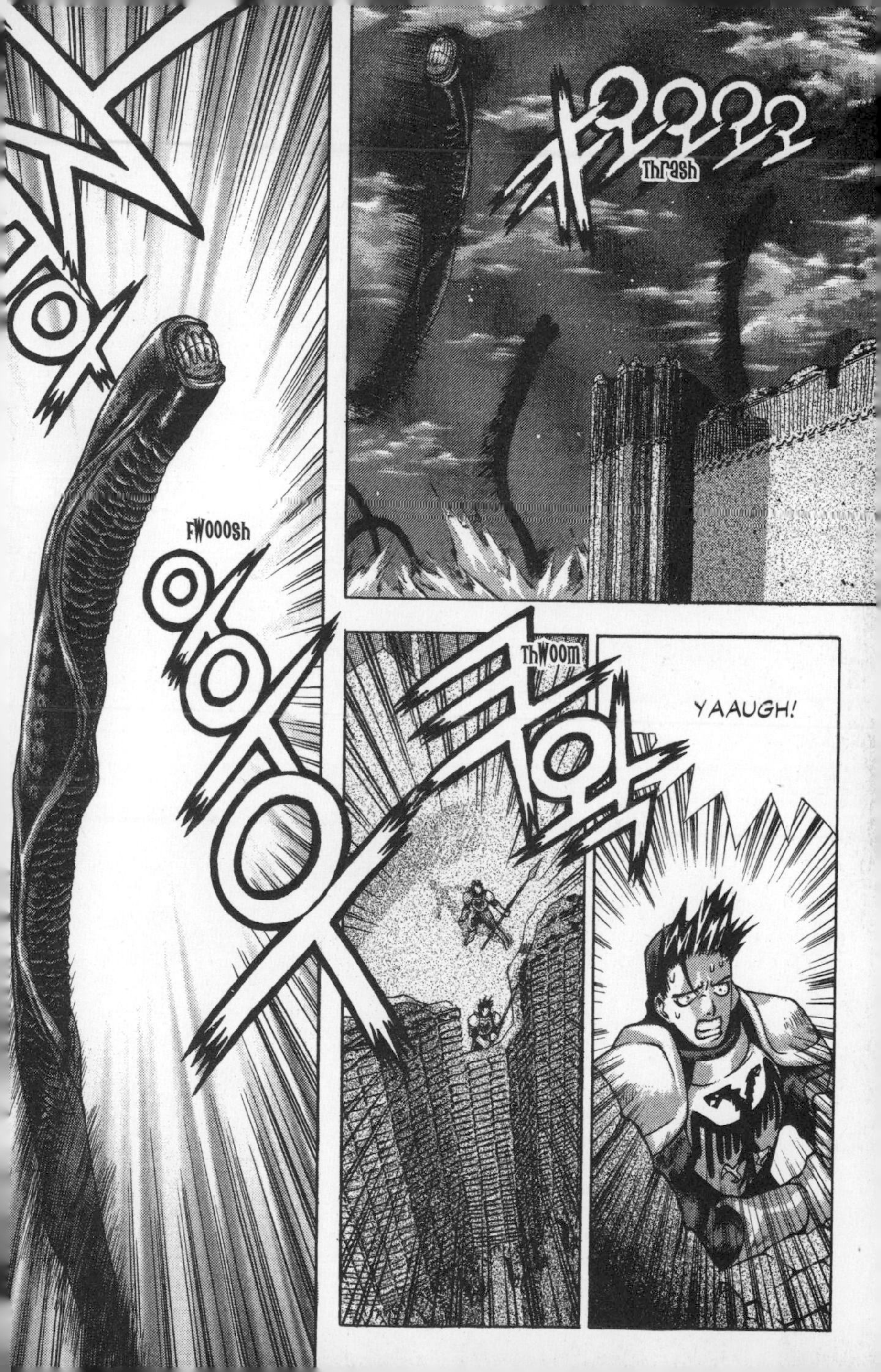
FWOOOSH
THRASH
THWOOM
YAAUGH!

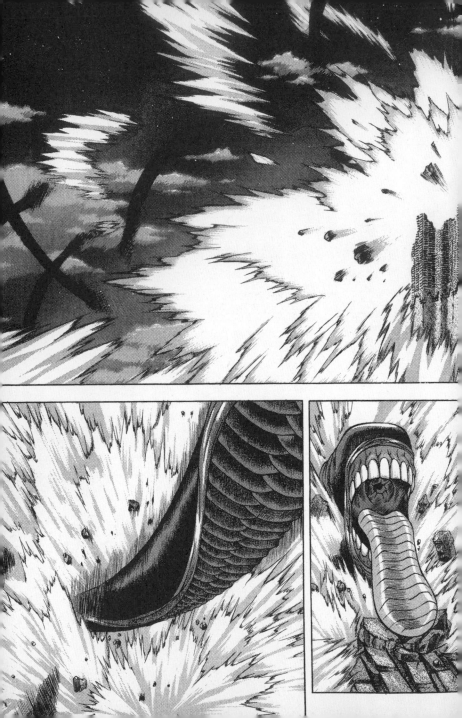

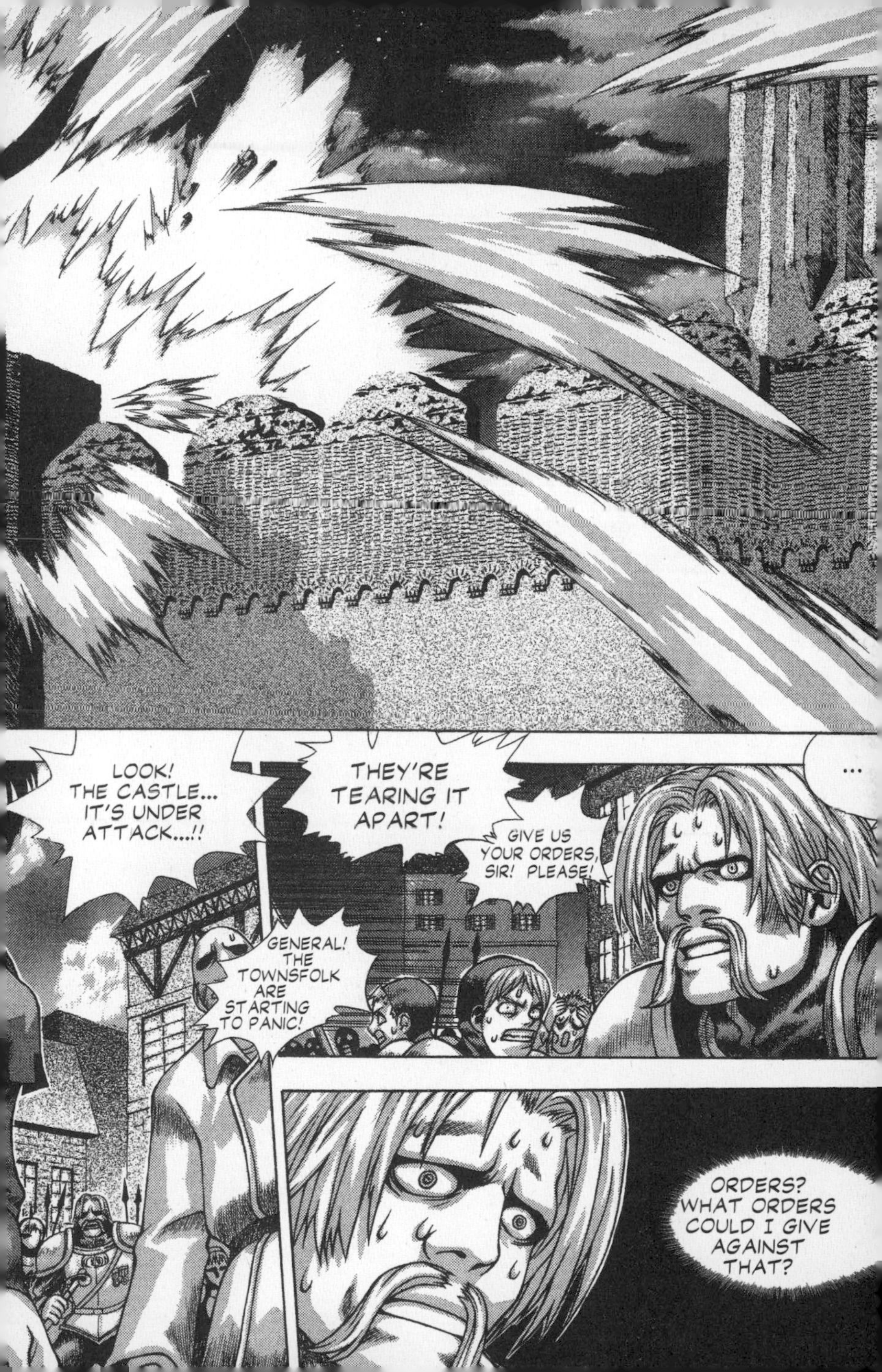
LOOK! THE CASTLE... IT'S UNDER ATTACK...!!
THEY'RE TEARING IT APART!
...
GIVE US YOUR ORDERS, SIR! PLEASE!
GENERAL! THE TOWNSFOLK ARE STARTING TO PANIC!
ORDERS? WHAT ORDERS COULD I GIVE AGAINST THAT?

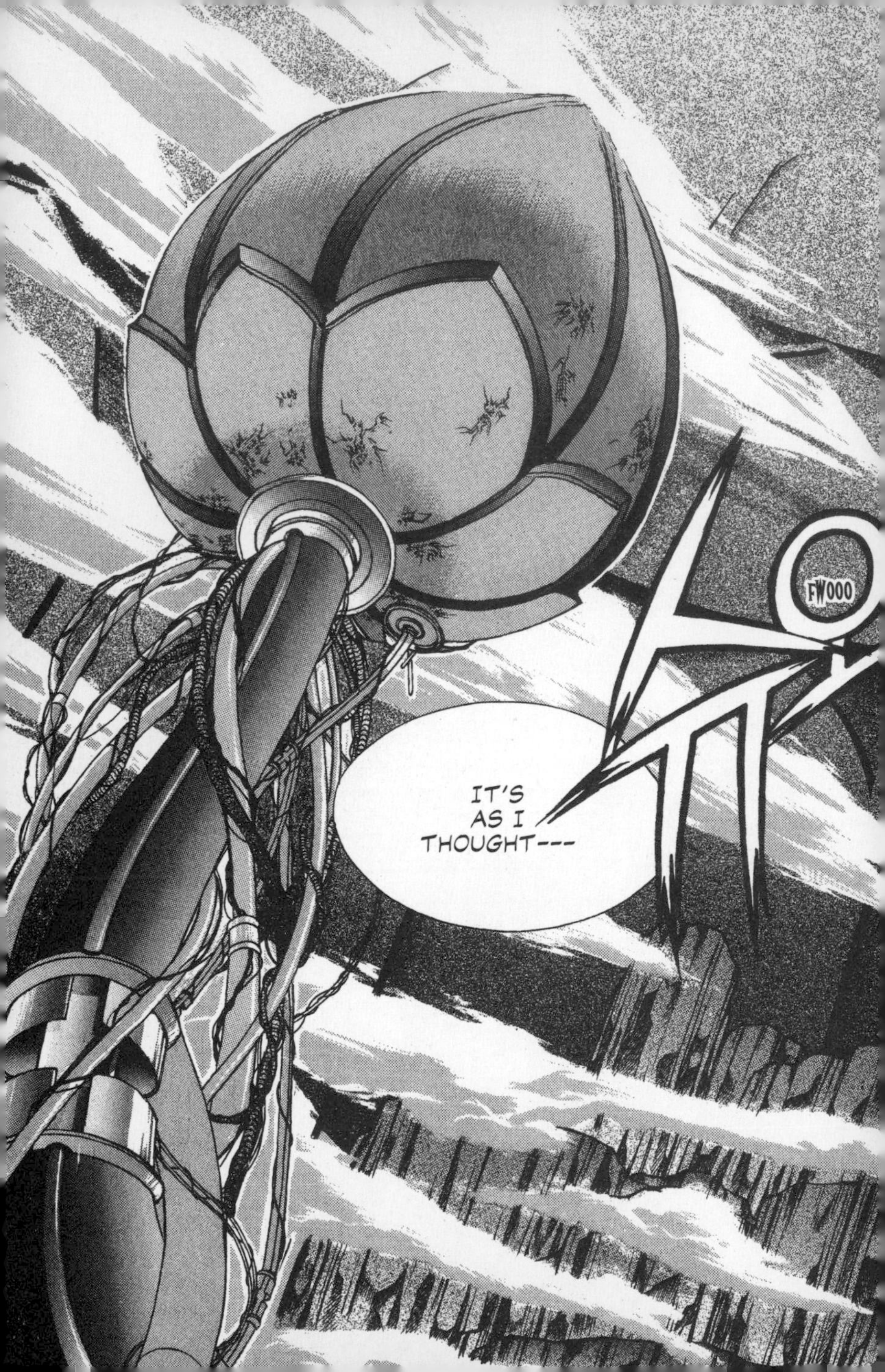
FWOOO
IT'S AS I THOUGHT---

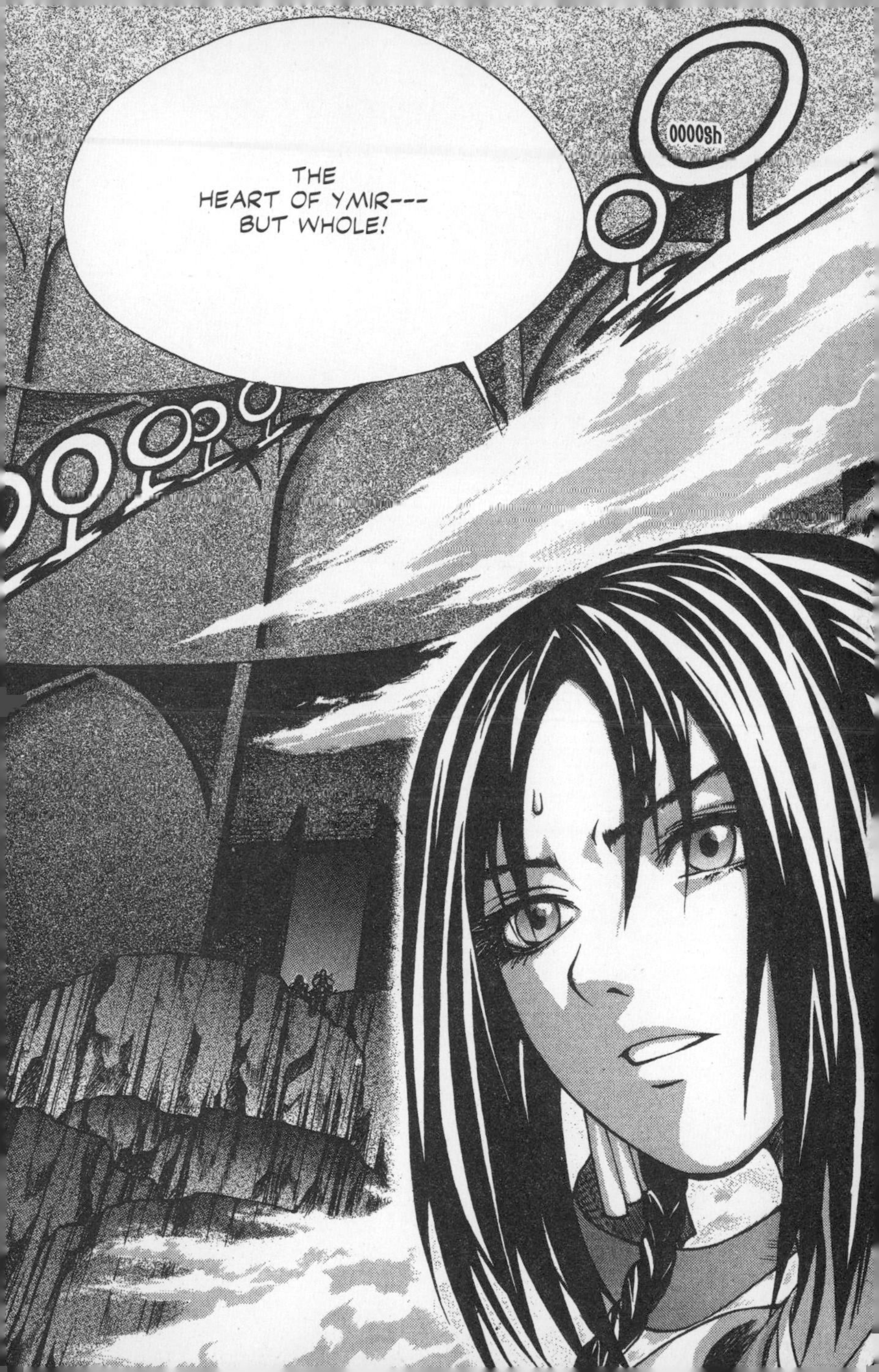
THE HEART OF YMIR--- BUT WHOLE!
OOOOSH

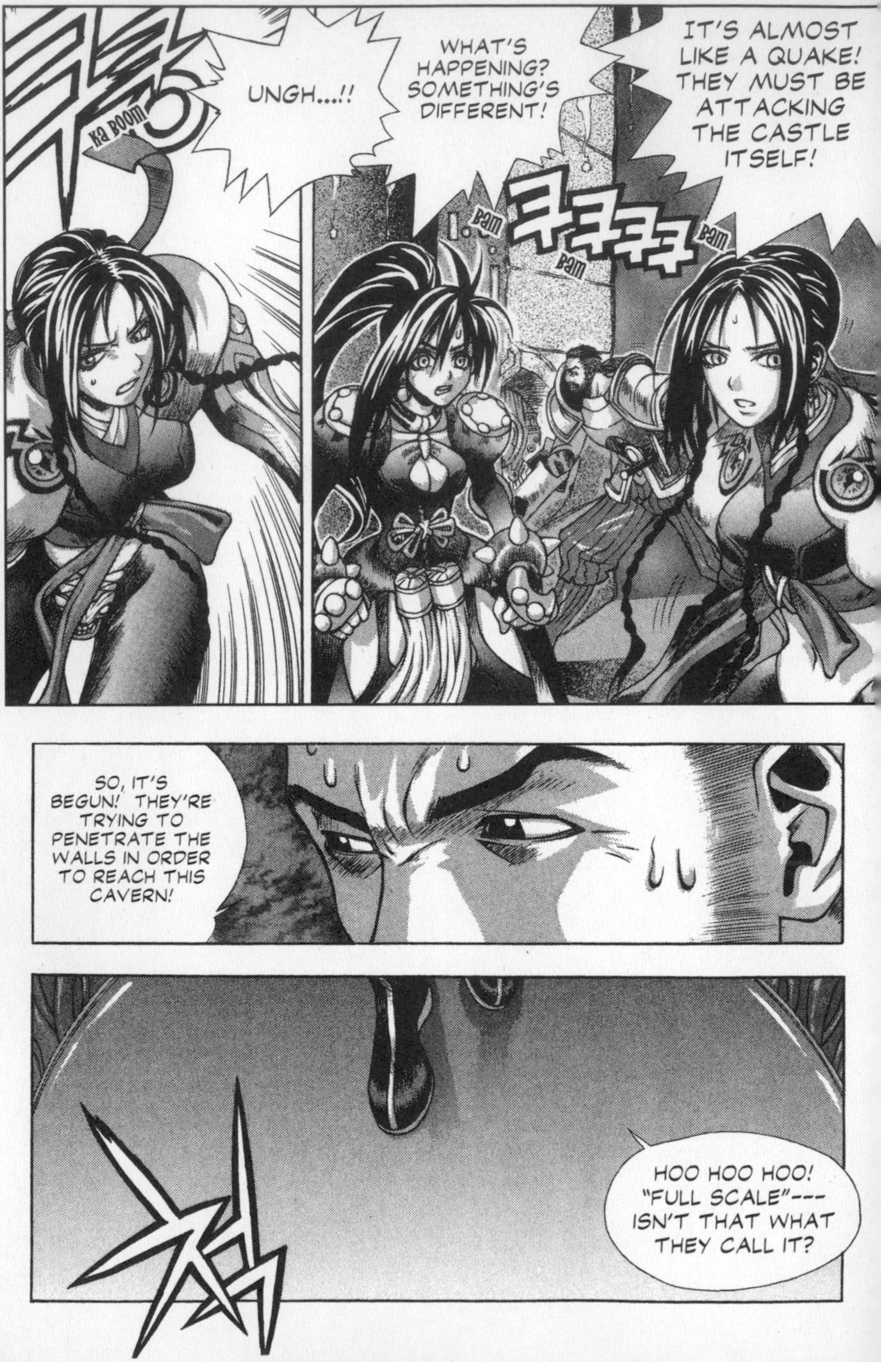
KA BOOM
UNGH...!!
WHAT'S HAPPENING? SOMETHING'S DIFFERENT!
IT'S ALMOST LIKE A QUAKE! THEY MUST BE ATTACKING THE CASTLE ITSELF!
BAM
BAM
BAM
SO, IT'S BEGUN! THEY'RE TRYING TO PENETRATE THE WALLS IN ORDER TO REACH THIS CAVERN!
HOO HOO HOO! "FULL SCALE"--- ISN'T THAT WHAT THEY CALL IT?

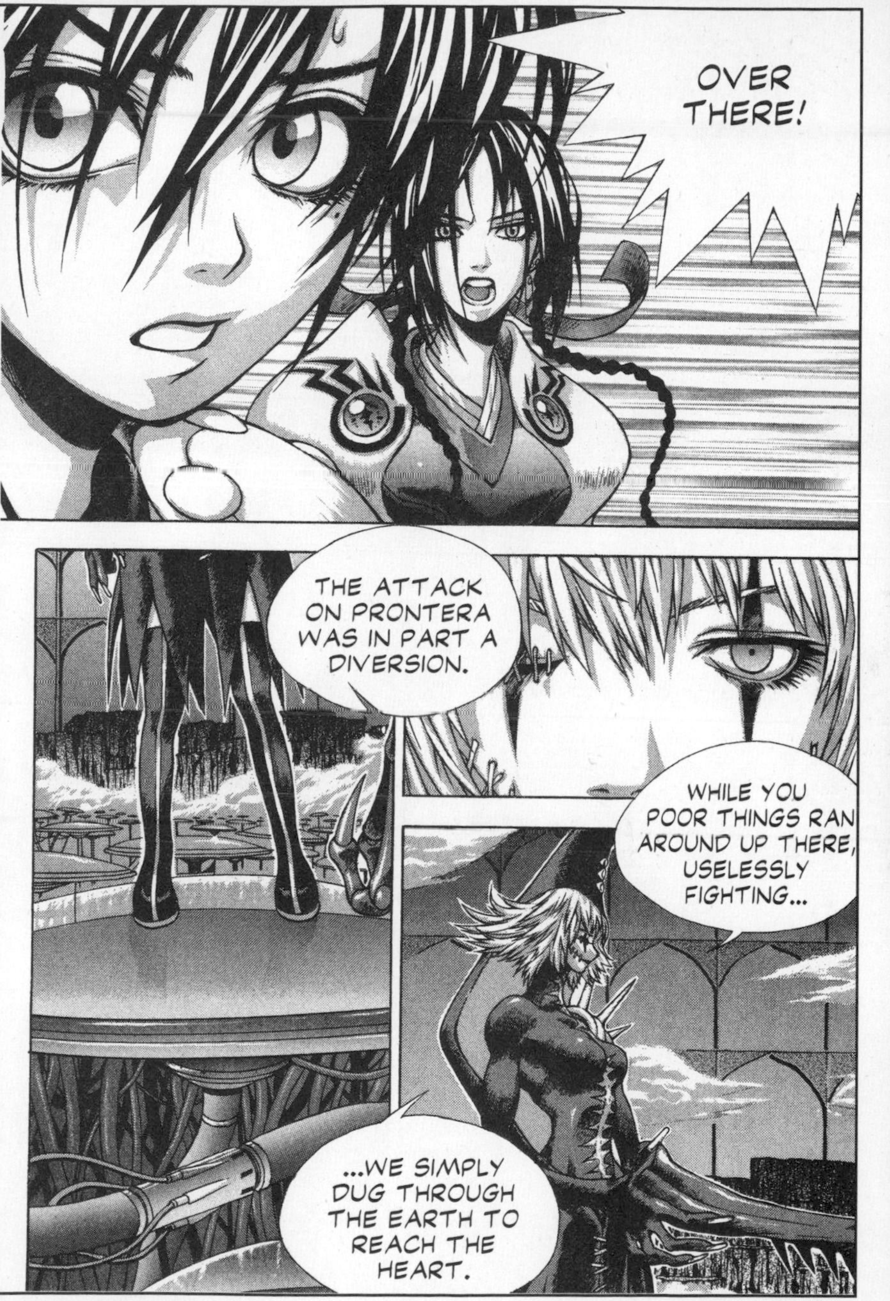

OVER THERE!
THE ATTACK ON PRONTERA WAS IN PART A DIVERSION.
WHILE YOU POOR THINGS RAN AROUND UP THERE, USELESSLY FIGHTING...
...WE SIMPLY DUG THROUGH THE EARTH TO REACH THE HEART.

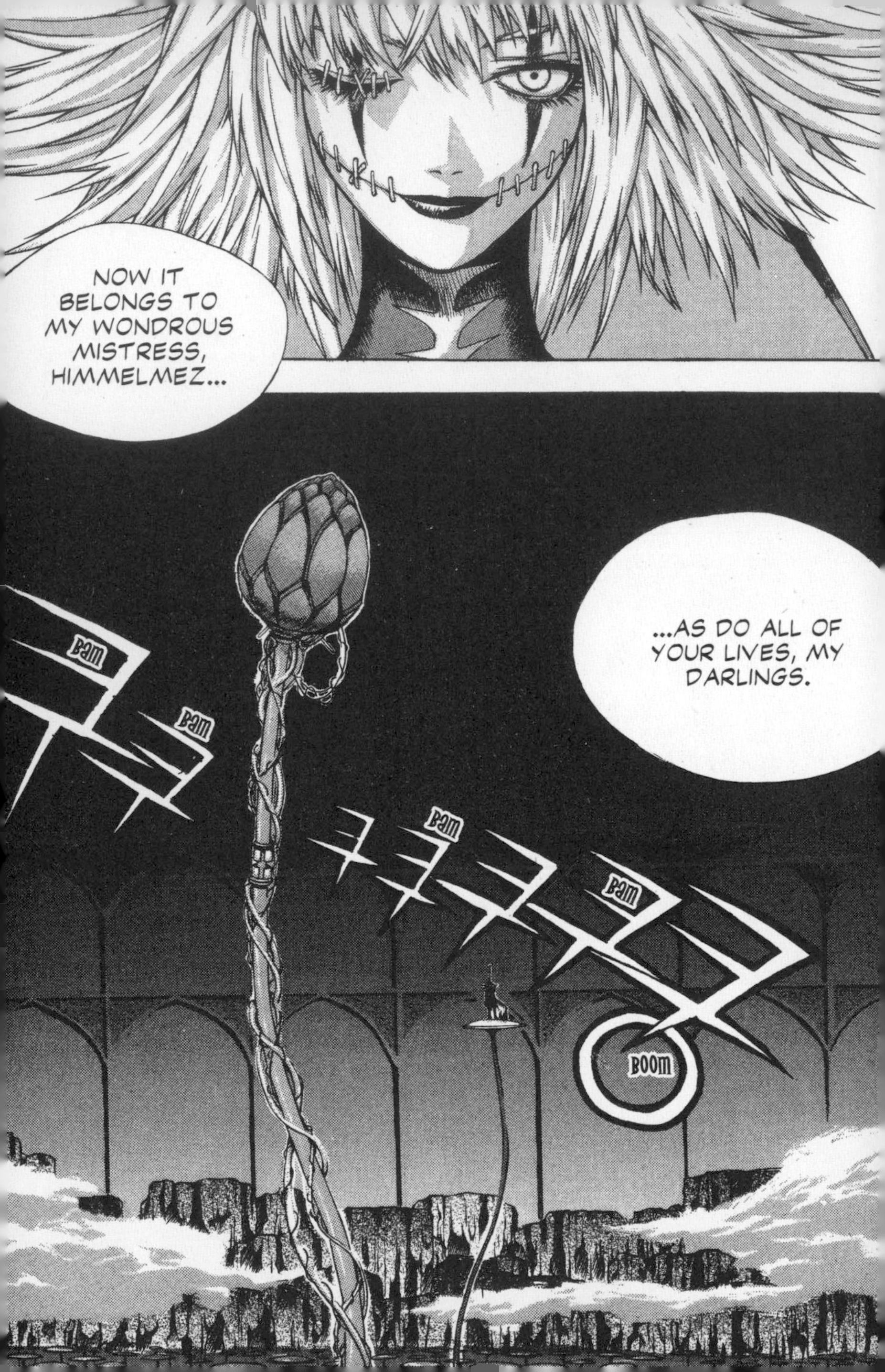
NOW IT BELONGS TO MY WONDROUS MISTRESS, HIMMELMEZ...
...AS DO ALL OF YOUR LIVES, MY DARLINGS.
BAM
BAM
BAM
BAM
BOOM

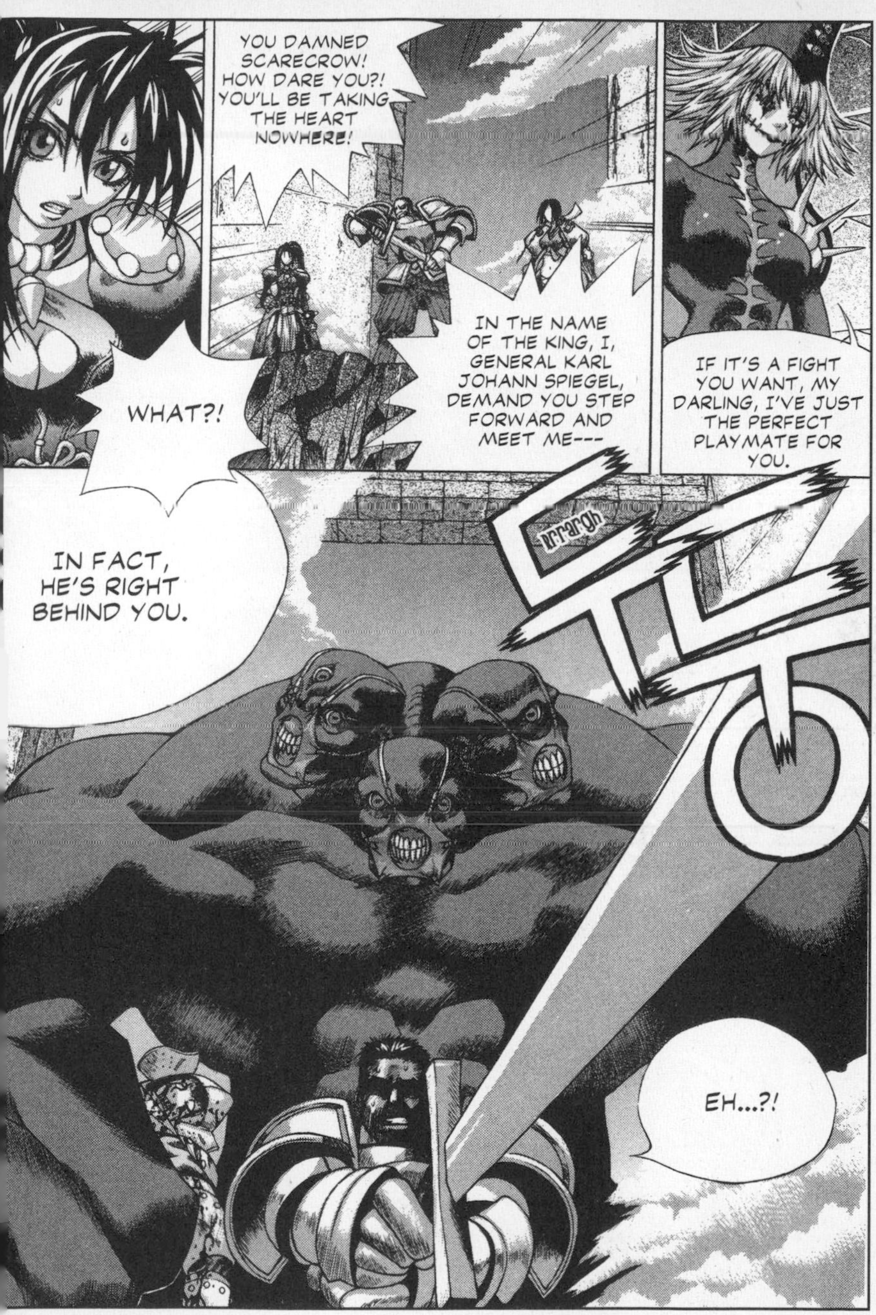
WHAT?!
YOU DAMNED SCARECROW! HOW DARE YOU?! YOU'LL BE TAKING THE HEART NOWHERE!
IN THE NAME OF THE KING, I, GENERAL KARL JOHANN SPIEGEL, DEMAND YOU STEP FORWARD AND MEET ME---
IF IT'S A FIGHT YOU WANT, MY DARLING, I'VE JUST THE PERFECT PLAYMATE FOR YOU.
IN FACT, HE'S RIGHT BEHIND YOU.
Rrrargh
EH...?!

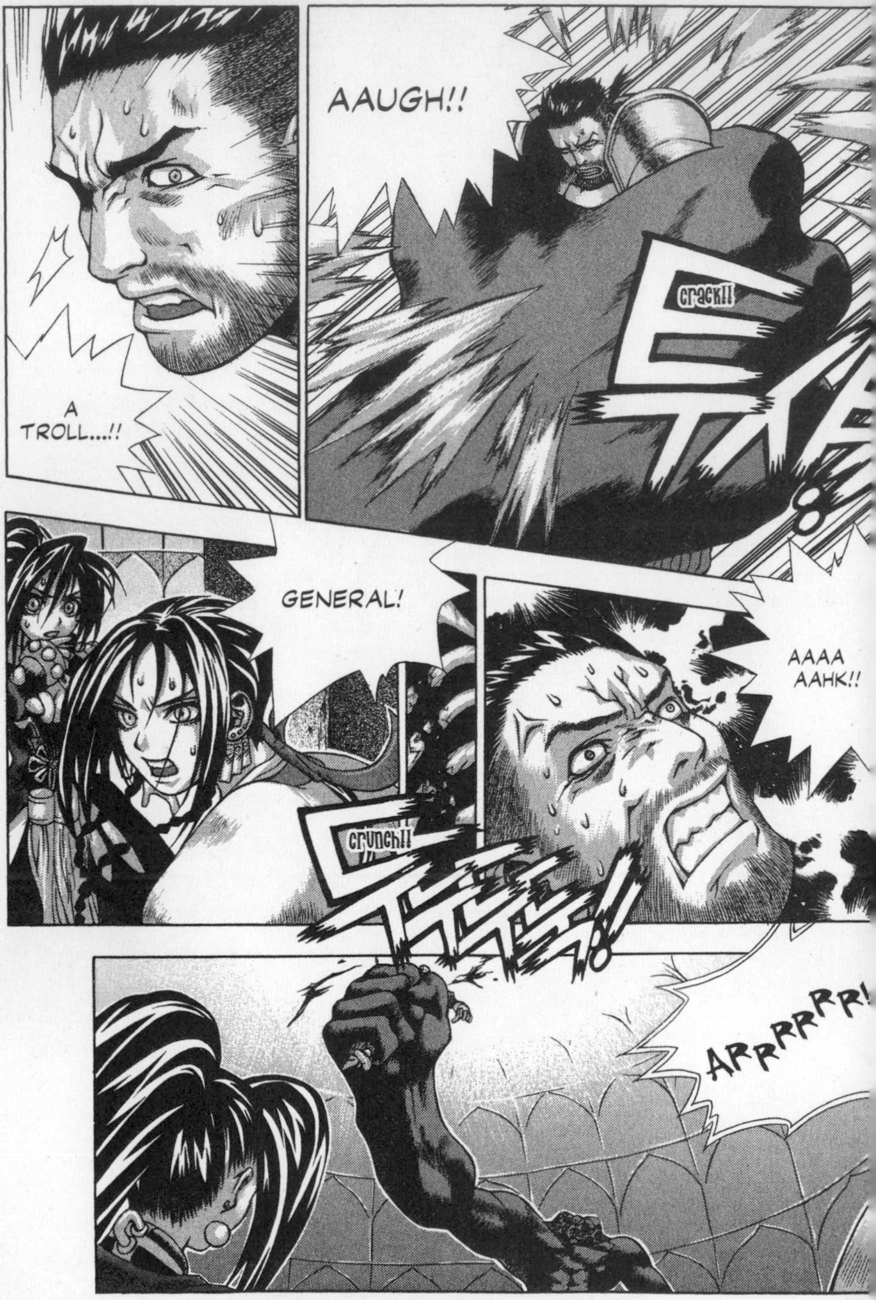
A TROLL...!!
AAUGH!!
CRACK!!
GENERAL!
AAAA AAHK!!
CRUNCH!!
ARRRRRR!

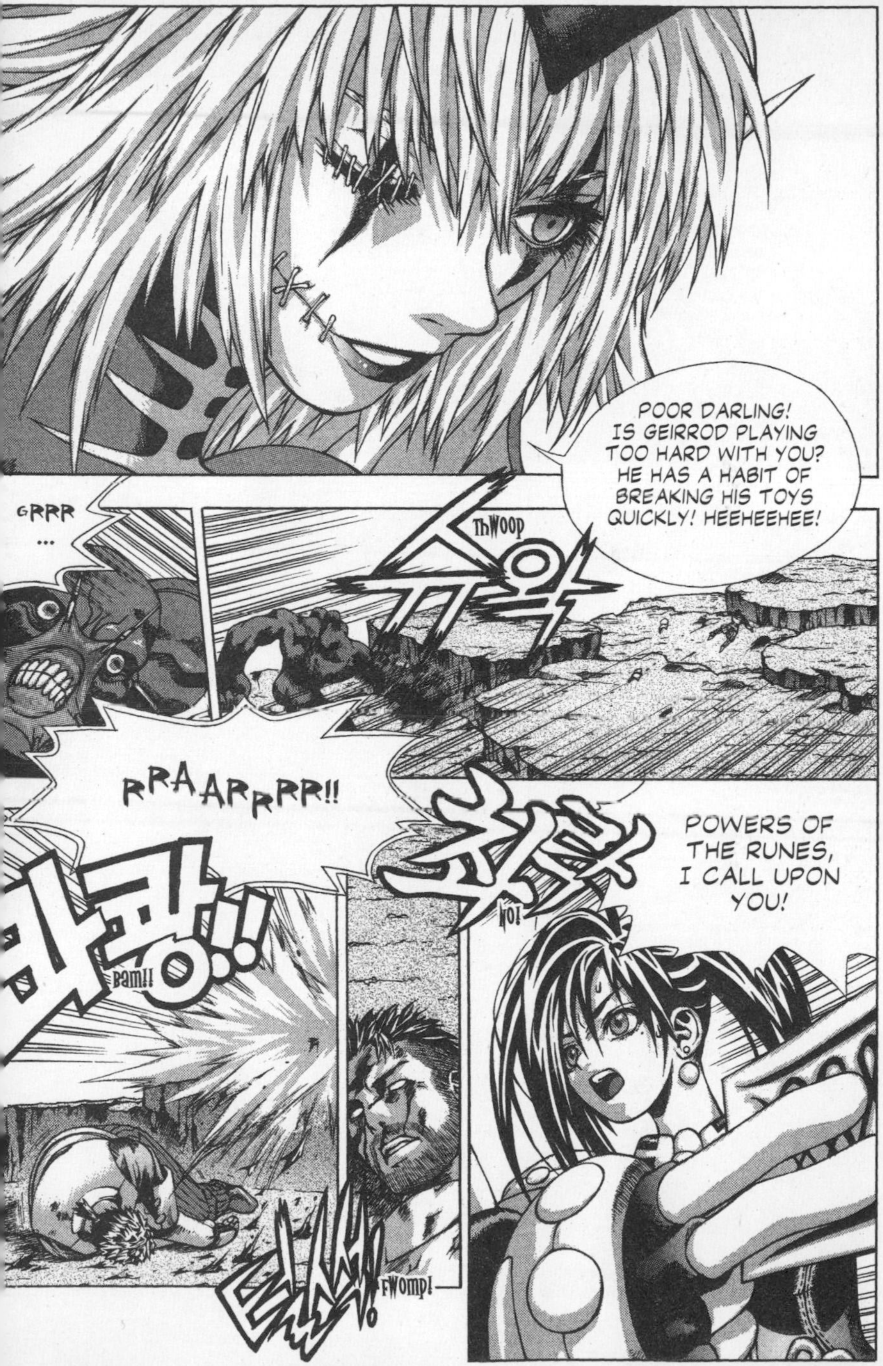
POOR DARLING! IS GEIRROD PLAYING TOO HARD WITH YOU? HE HAS A HABIT OF BREAKING HIS TOYS QUICKLY! HEEHEEHEE!
GRRR ...
ThWOOP
RRAARRRRR!!
BAM!!
FWOMP!
WO!
POWERS OF THE RUNES, I CALL UPON YOU!

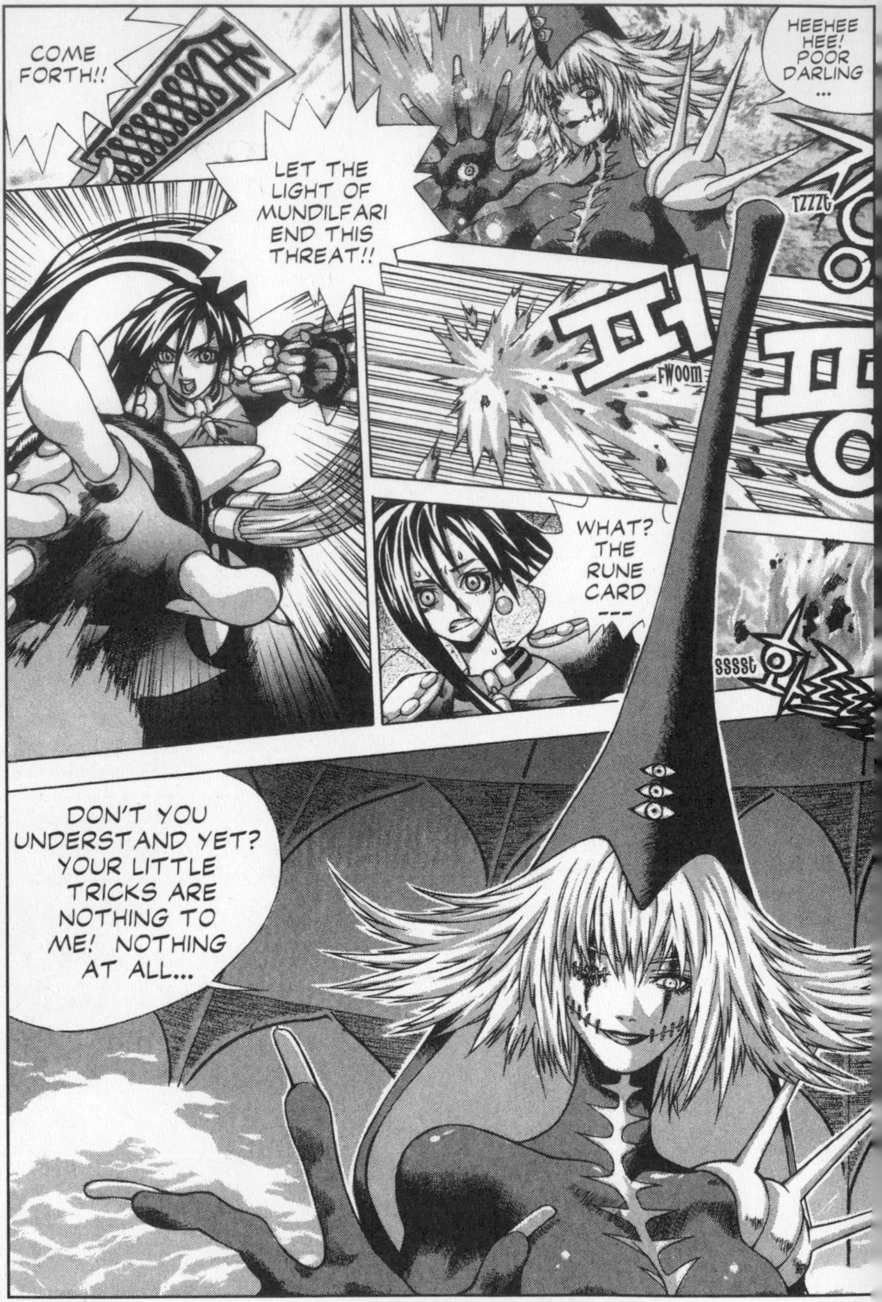

COME FORTH!!
HEEHEE HEE! POOR DARLING ...
TZZZT
LET THE LIGHT OF MUNDILFARI END THIS THREAT!!
FWOOM
WHAT? THE RUNE CARD ---
SSSST
DON'T YOU UNDERSTAND YET? YOUR LITTLE TRICKS ARE NOTHING TO ME! NOTHING AT ALL...

RAGNARÖK
라그나로크
IN TO THE ABYSS

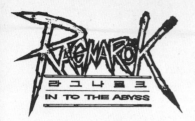

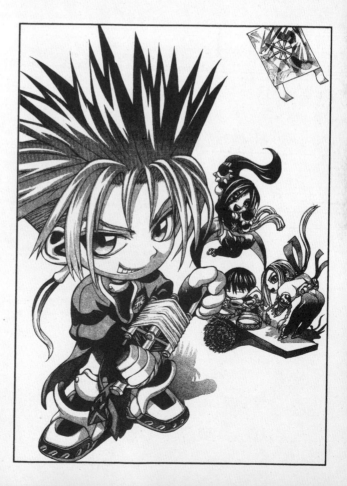

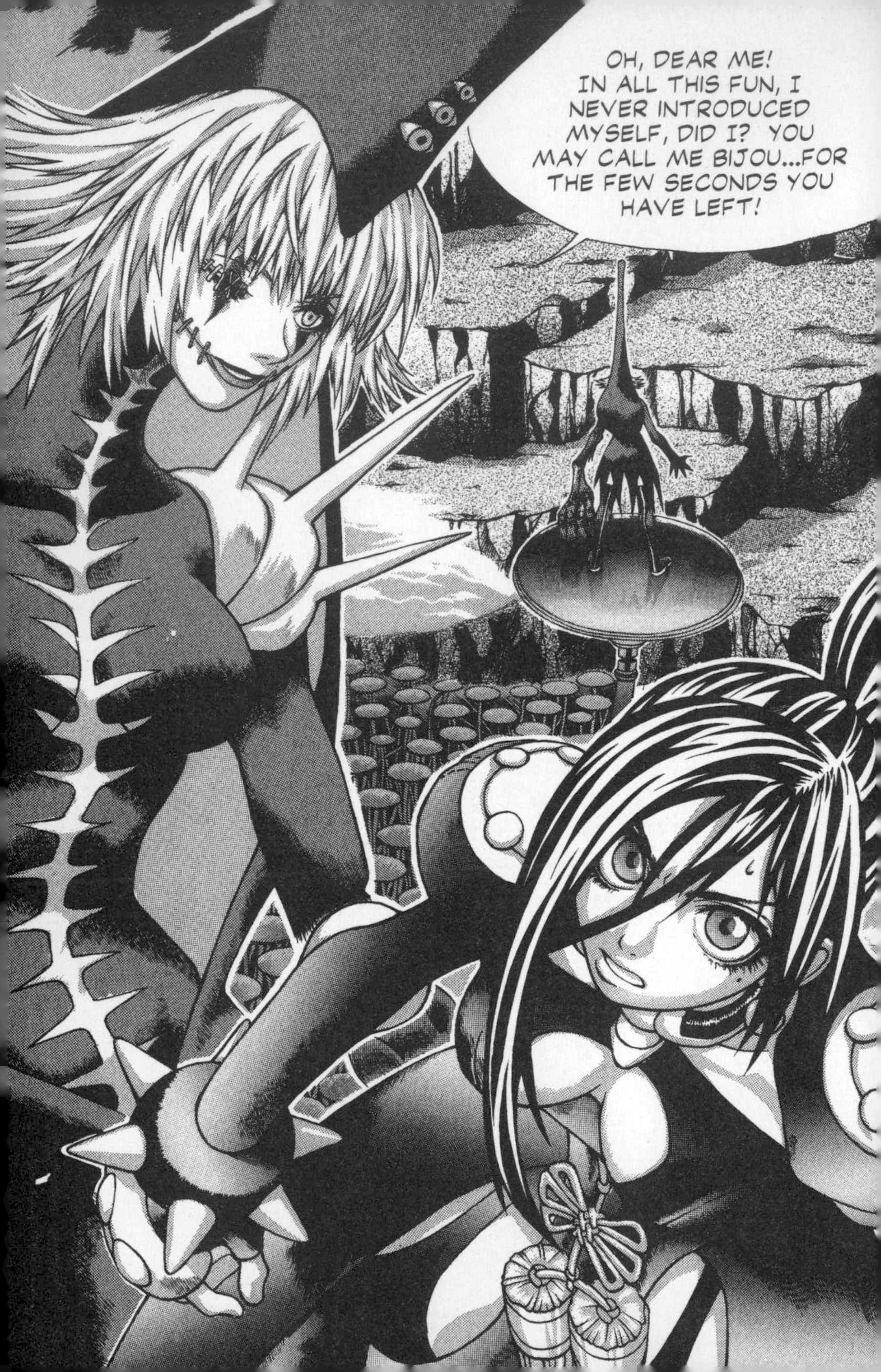
OH, DEAR ME! IN ALL THIS FUN, I NEVER INTRODUCED MYSELF, DID I? YOU MAY CALL ME BIJOU...FOR THE FEW SECONDS YOU HAVE LEFT!

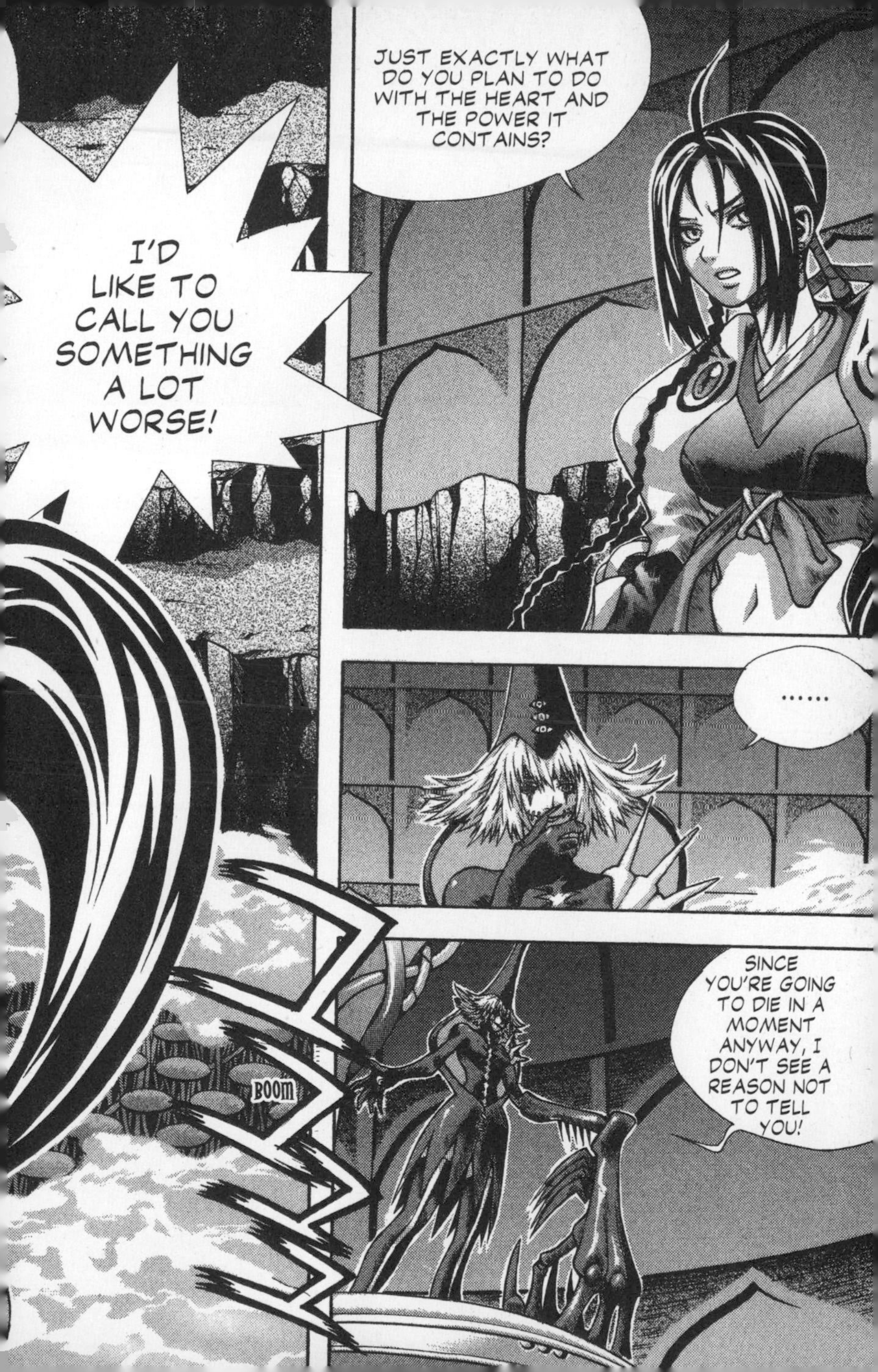
I'D LIKE TO CALL YOU SOMETHING A LOT WORSE!
BOOM
JUST EXACTLY WHAT DO YOU PLAN TO DO WITH THE HEART AND THE POWER IT CONTAINS?
......
SINCE YOU'RE GOING TO DIE IN A MOMENT ANYWAY, I DON'T SEE A REASON NOT TO TELL YOU!

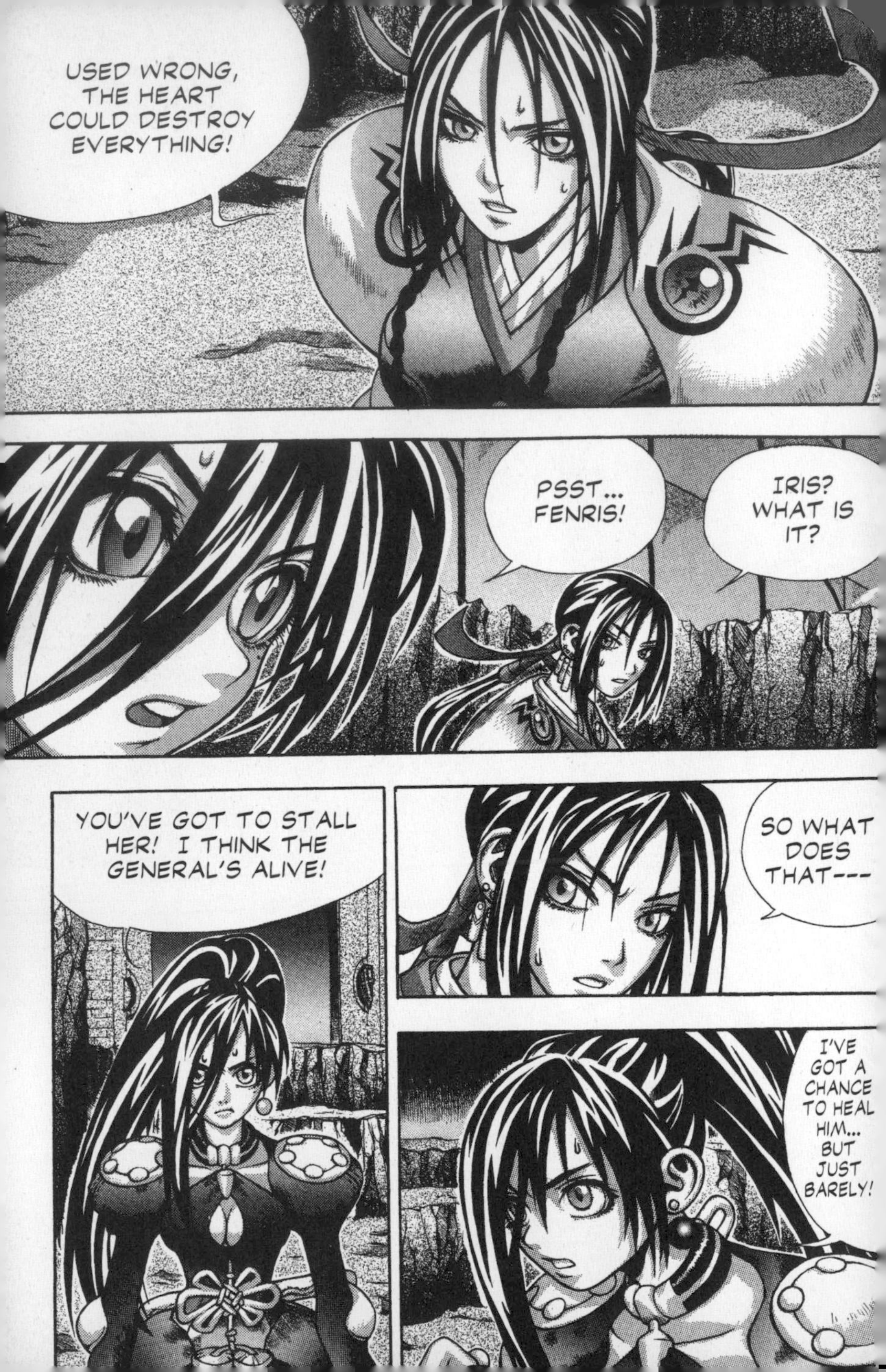
USED WRONG, THE HEART COULD DESTROY EVERYTHING!
PSST... FENRIS!
IRIS? WHAT IS IT?
YOU'VE GOT TO STALL HER! I THINK THE GENERAL'S ALIVE!
SO WHAT DOES THAT---
I'VE GOT A CHANCE TO HEAL HIM... BUT JUST BARELY!

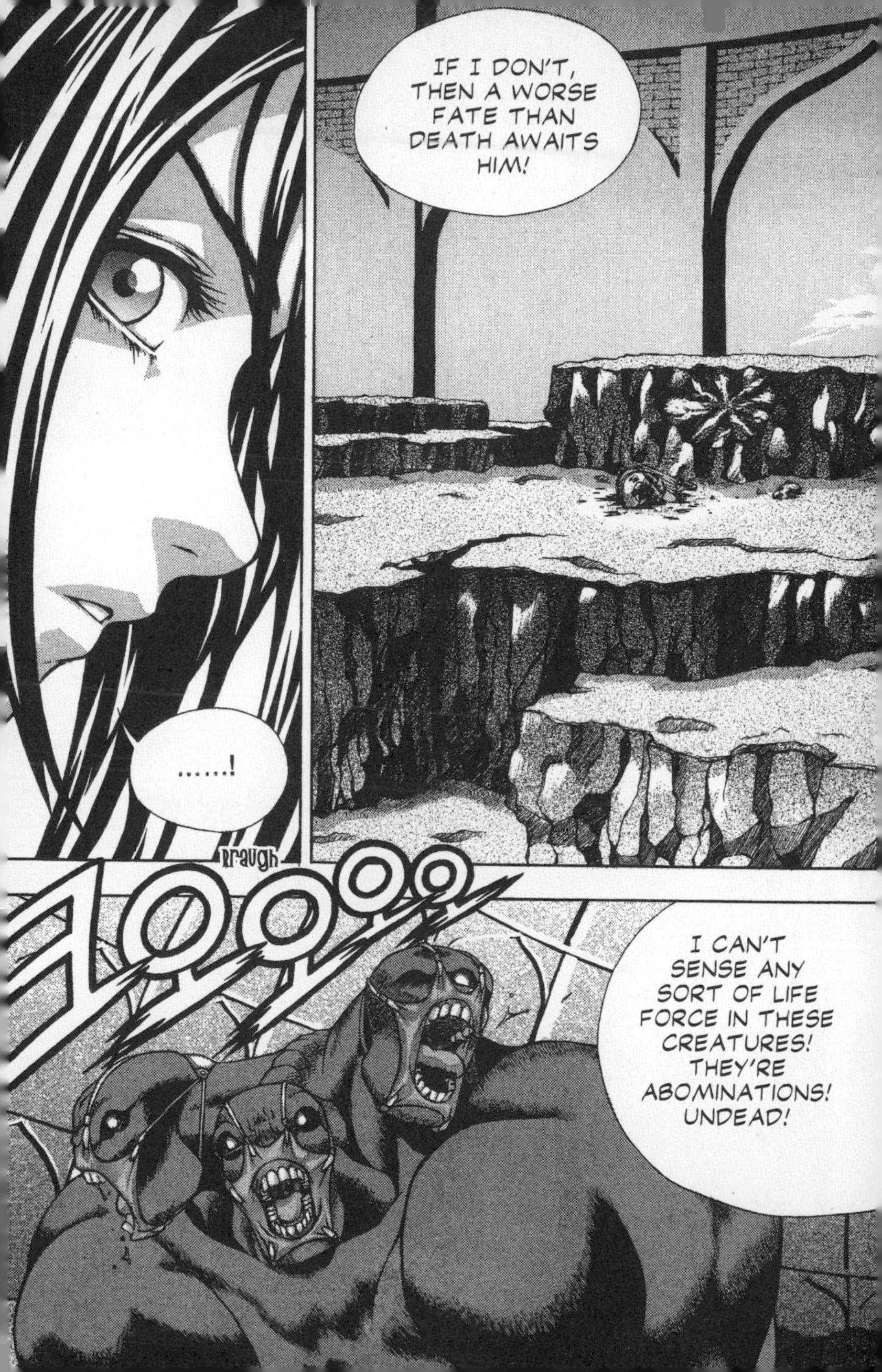
IF I DON'T, THEN A WORSE FATE THAN DEATH AWAITS HIM!
......!
BRAUGH
ZOOOOO
I CAN'T SENSE ANY SORT OF LIFE FORCE IN THESE CREATURES! THEY'RE ABOMINATIONS! UNDEAD!

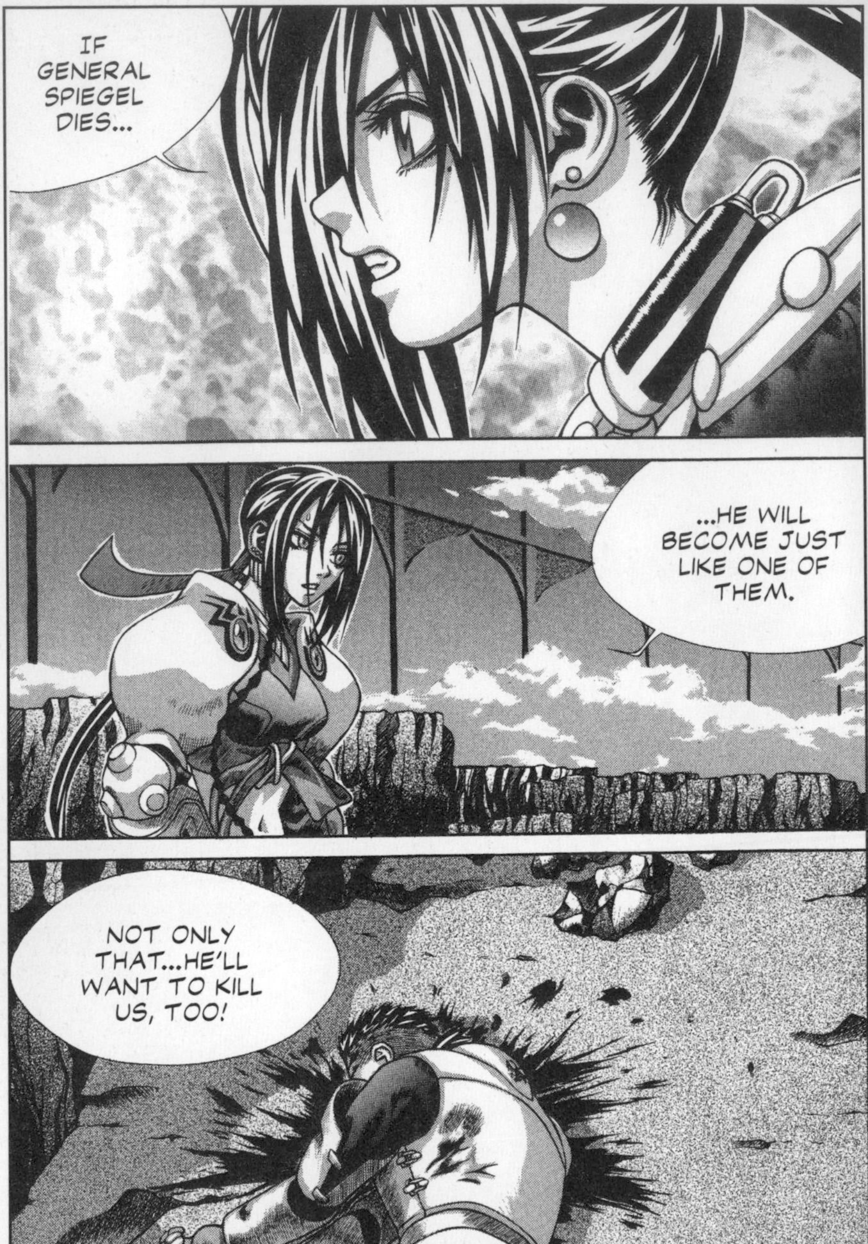
IF GENERAL SPIEGEL DIES...
...HE WILL BECOME JUST LIKE ONE OF THEM.
NOT ONLY THAT...HE'LL WANT TO KILL US, TOO!

BUT WE NEED TO GET PAST THAT WITCH FIRST!
HEE
HEE
IF WE WORK TOGETHER, WE'VE GOT A CHANCE, FENRIS.

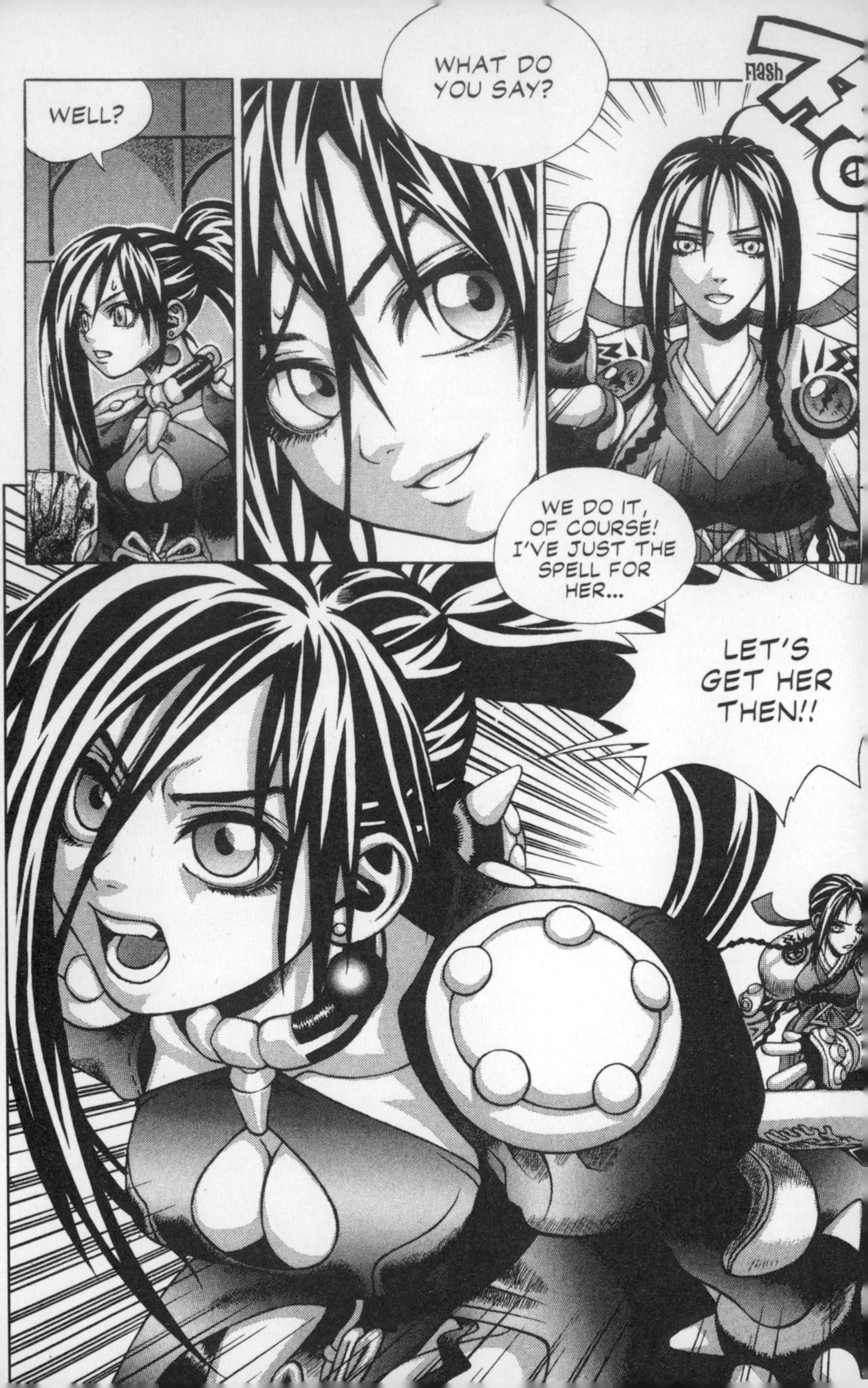
WELL?
WHAT DO YOU SAY?
FLASH
WE DO IT, OF COURSE! I'VE JUST THE SPELL FOR HER...
LET'S GET HER THEN!!

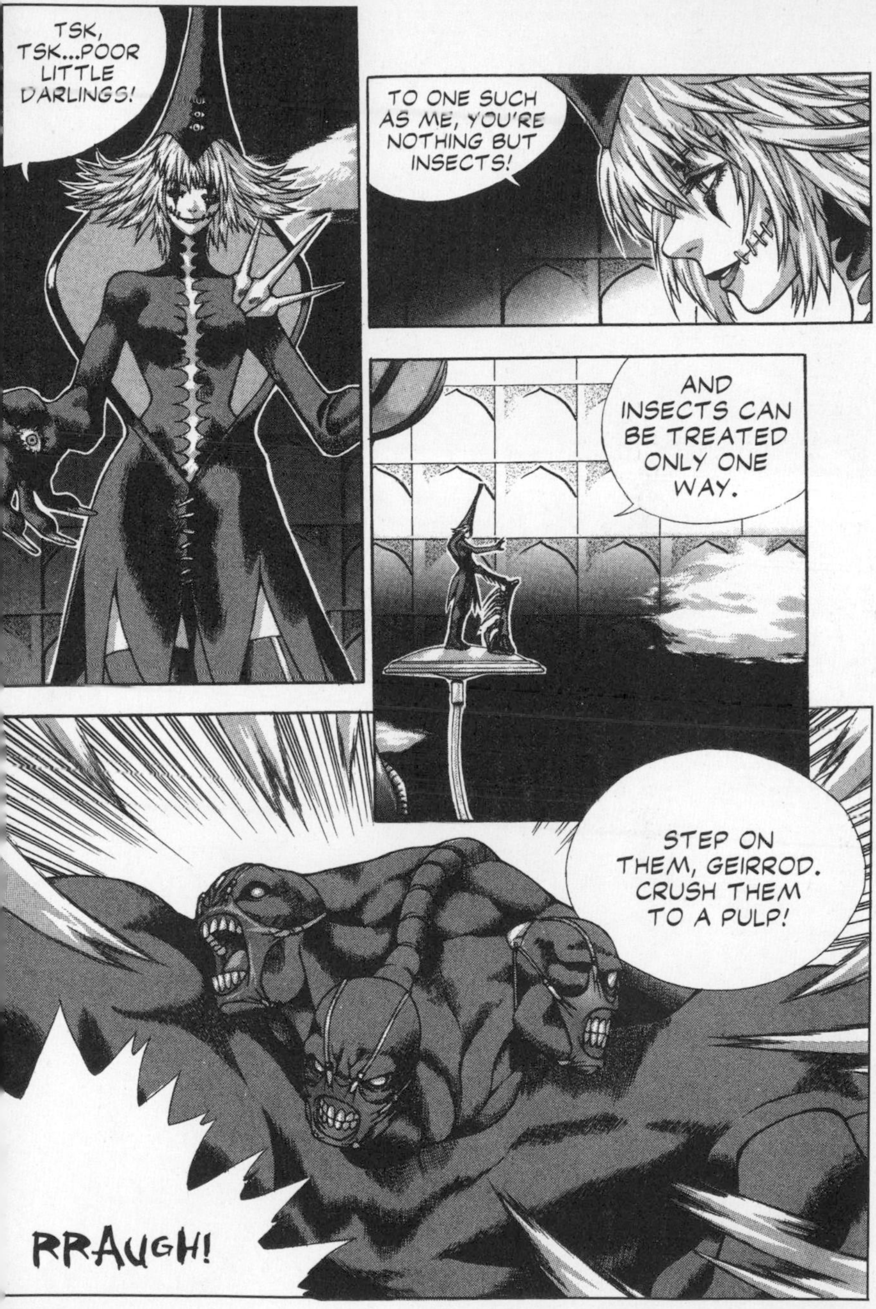
TSK, TSK...POOR LITTLE DARLINGS!
TO ONE SUCH AS ME, YOU'RE NOTHING BUT INSECTS!
AND INSECTS CAN BE TREATED ONLY ONE WAY.
STEP ON THEM, GEIRROD. CRUSH THEM TO A PULP!
RRAUGH!

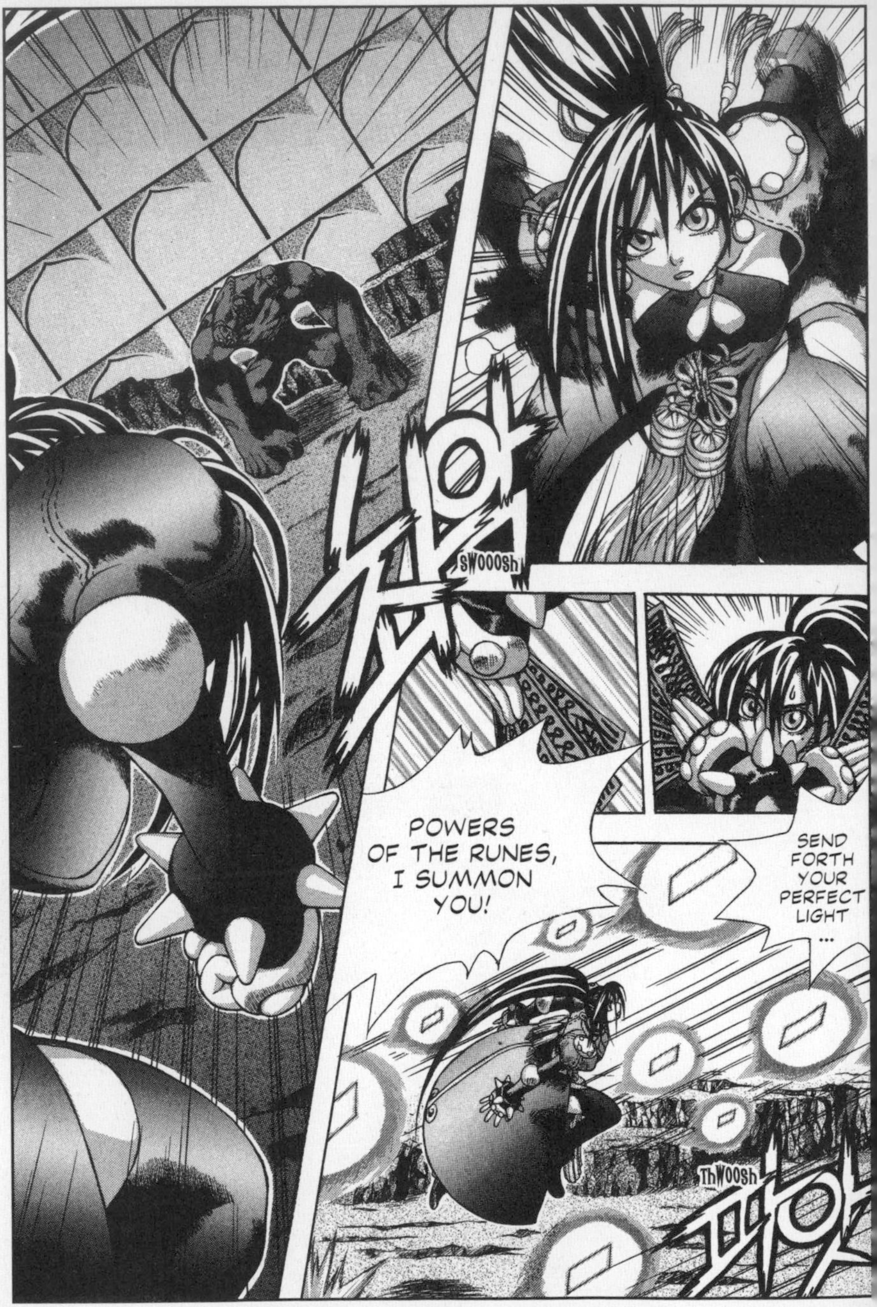
SWOOOSH
POWERS OF THE RUNES, I SUMMON YOU!
SEND FORTH YOUR PERFECT LIGHT ...
THWOOSH

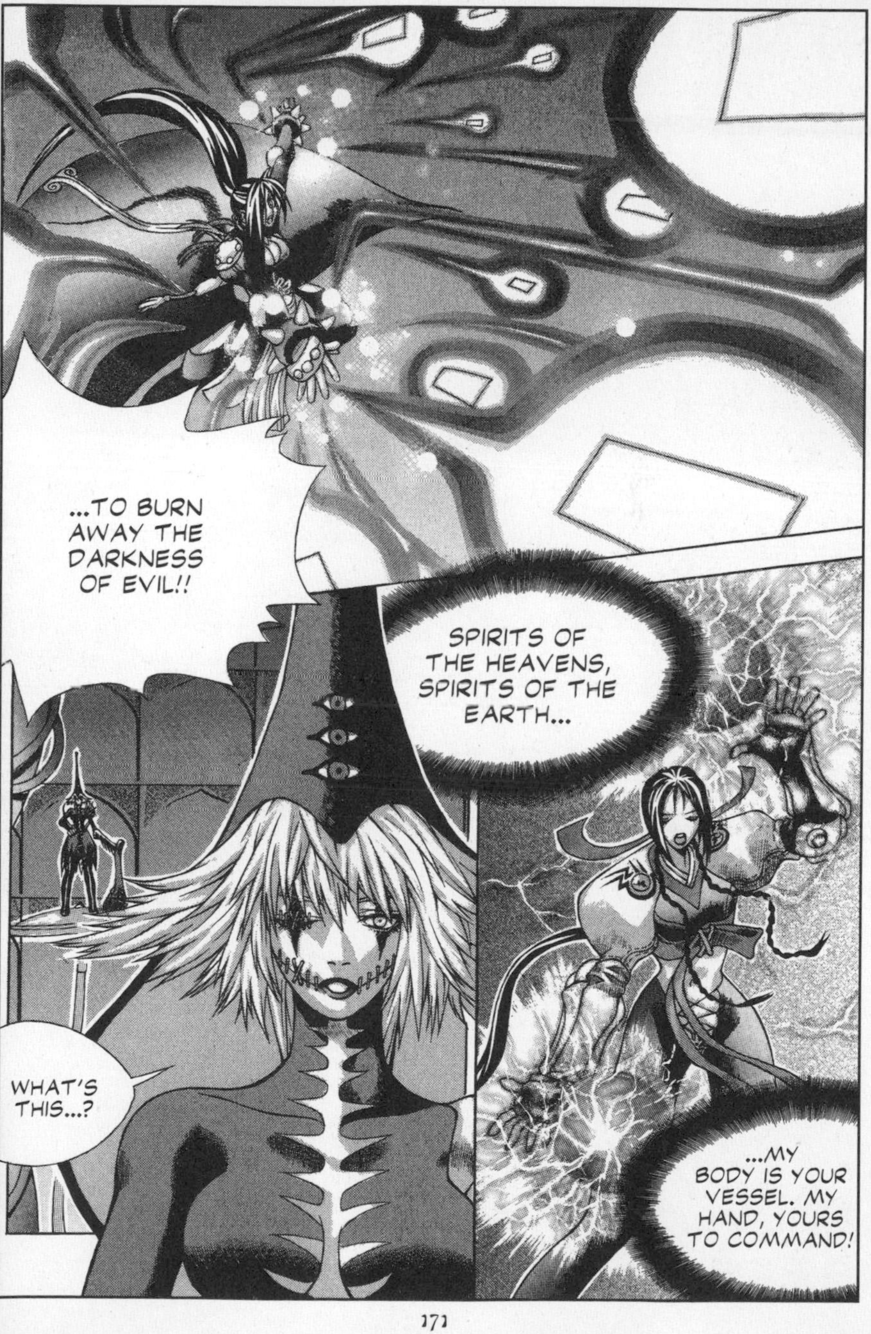
...TO BURN AWAY THE DARKNESS OF EVIL!!
WHAT'S THIS...?
SPIRITS OF THE HEAVENS, SPIRITS OF THE EARTH...
...MY BODY IS YOUR VESSEL. MY HAND, YOURS TO COMMAND!

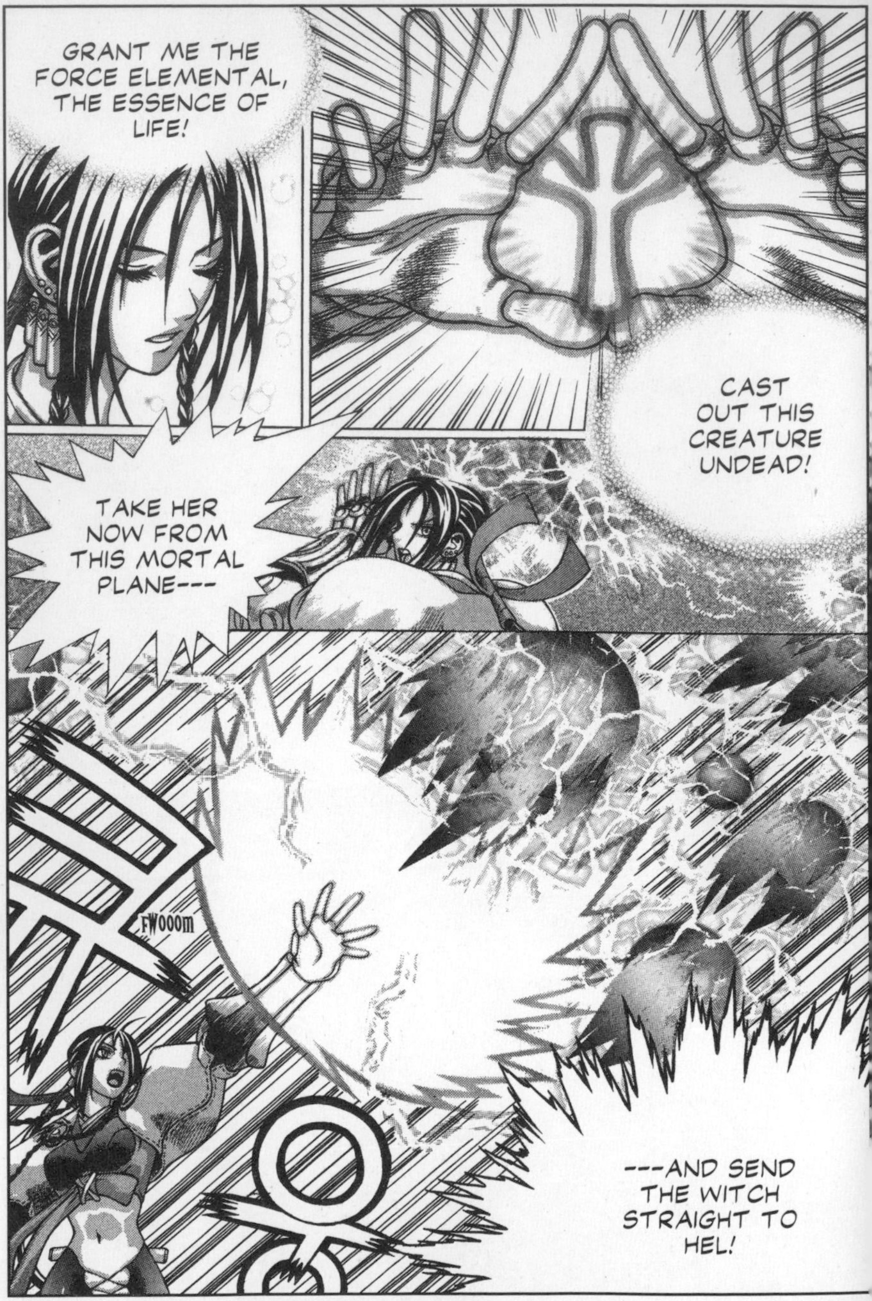
GRANT ME THE FORCE ELEMENTAL, THE ESSENCE OF LIFE!
CAST OUT THIS CREATURE UNDEAD!
TAKE HER NOW FROM THIS MORTAL PLANE---
FWOOOM
---AND SEND THE WITCH STRAIGHT TO HEL!

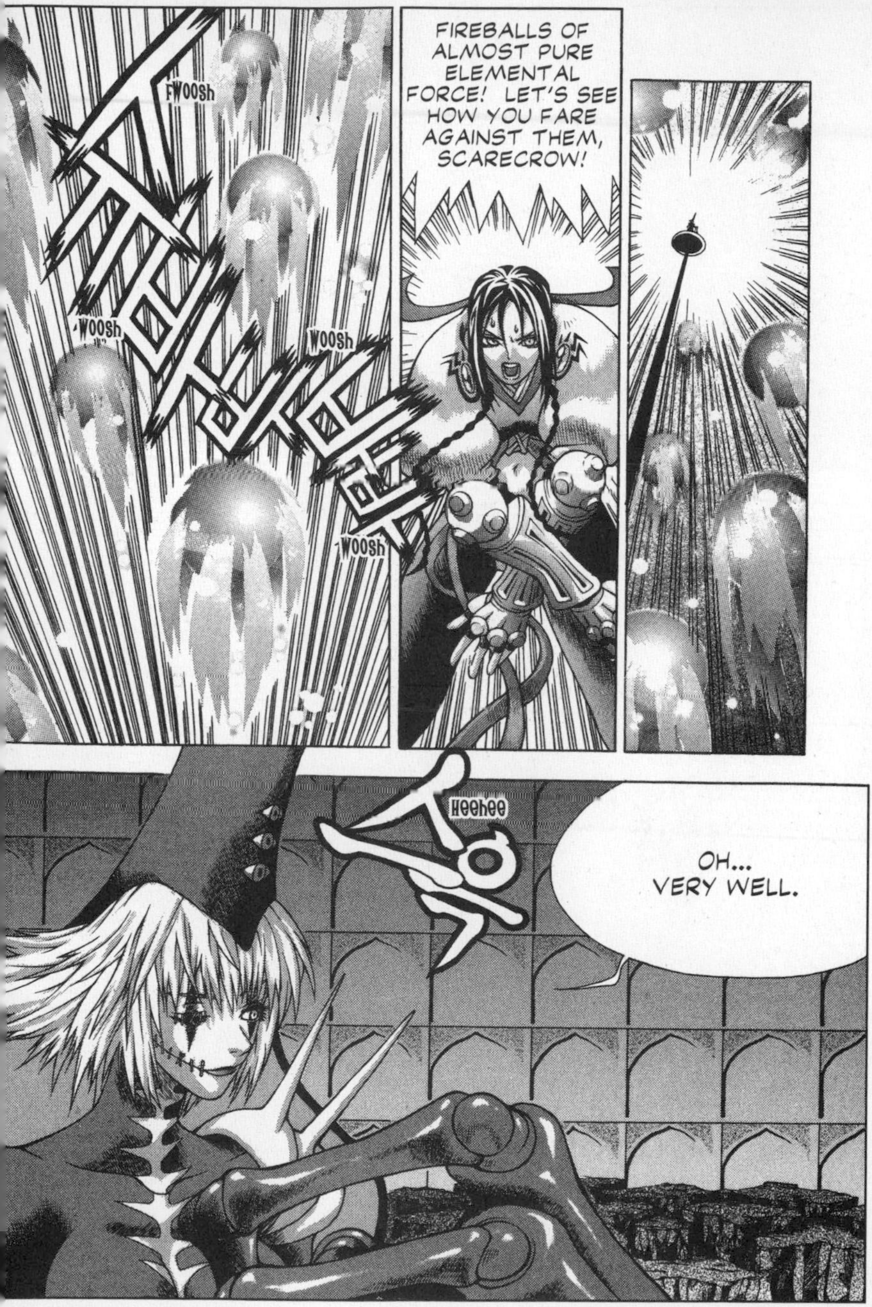
FWOOSH
WOOSH
WOOSH
WOOSH
FIREBALLS OF ALMOST PURE ELEMENTAL FORCE! LET'S SEE HOW YOU FARE AGAINST THEM, SCARECROW!
HEEHEE
OH... VERY WELL.

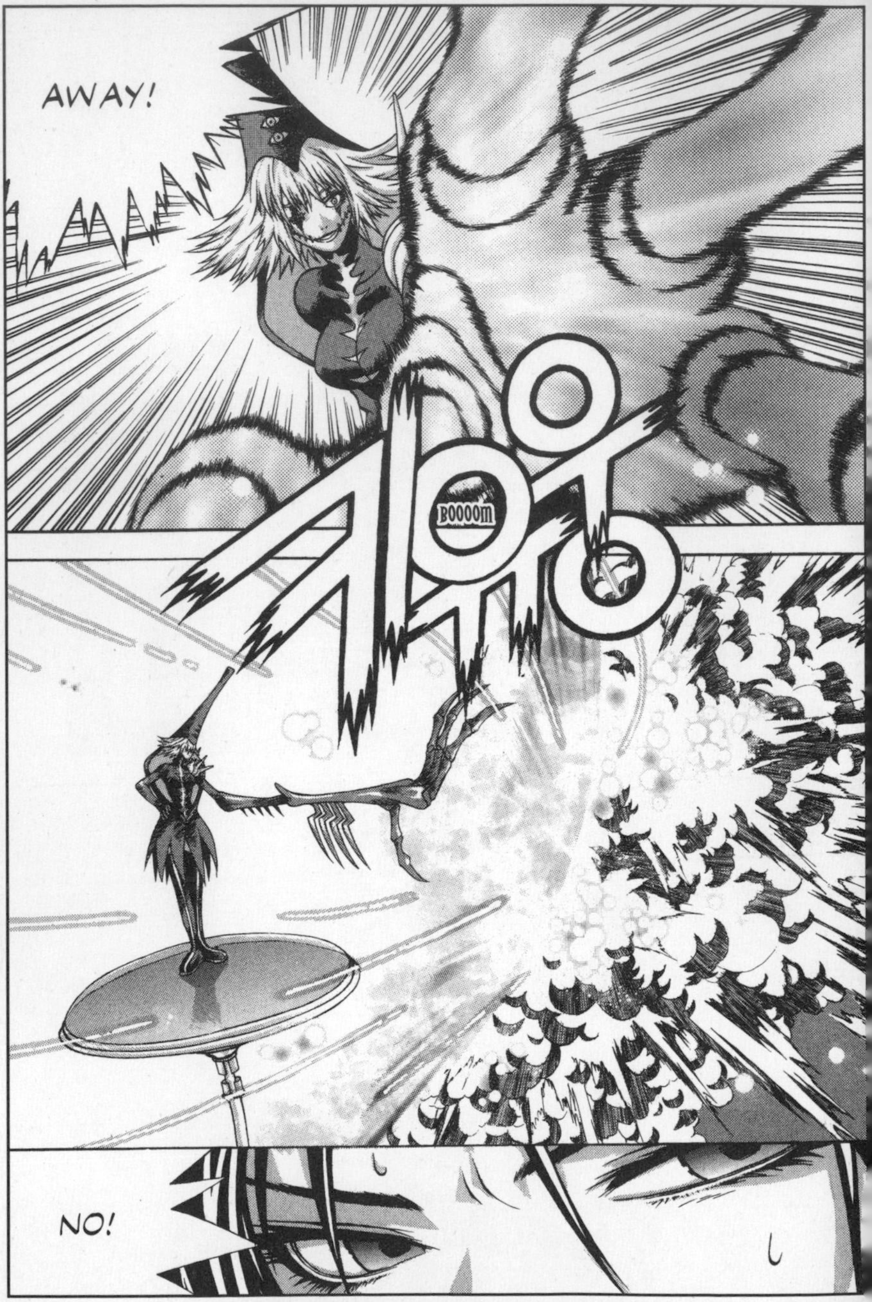
AWAY!
BOOOOM
NO!

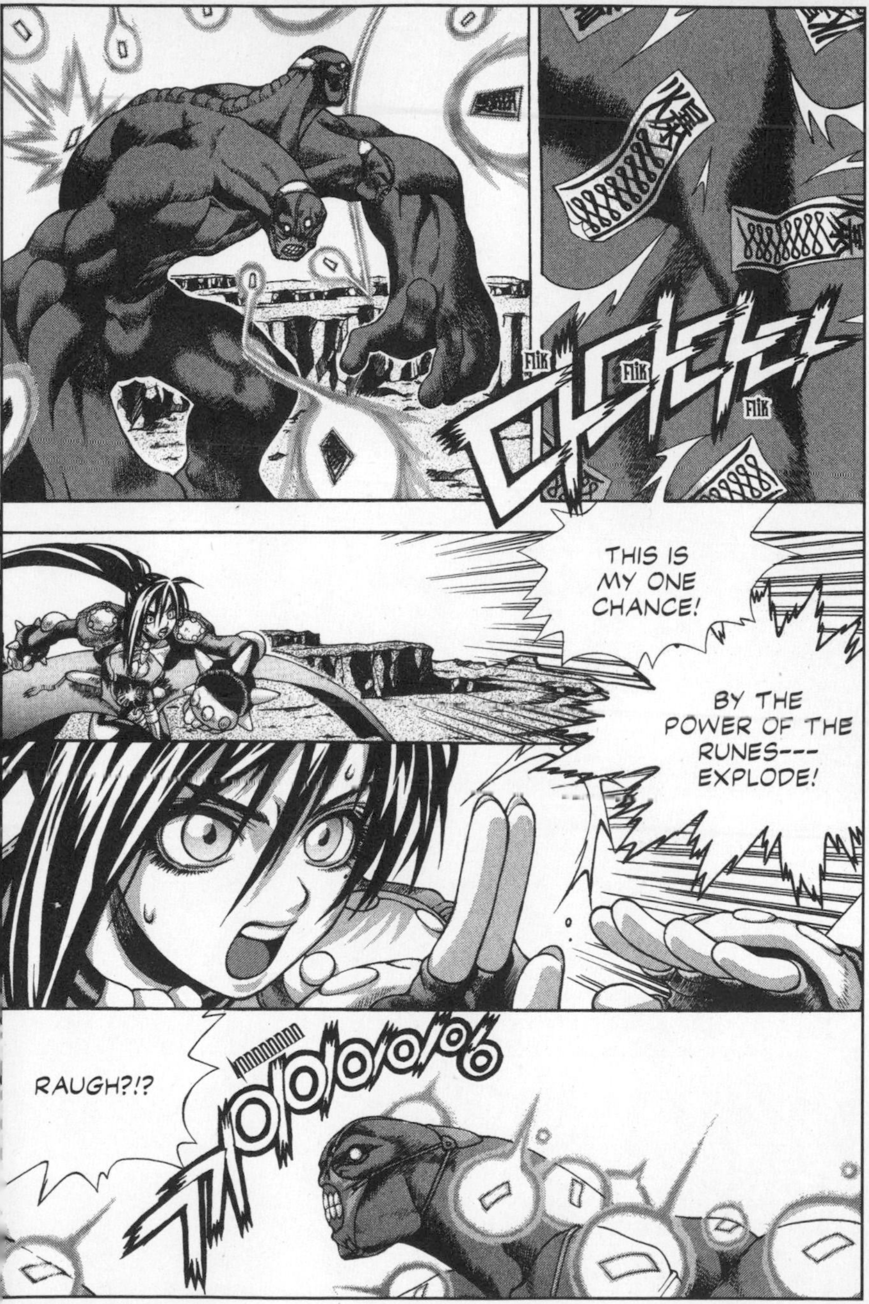
Flik
Flik
Flik
THIS IS MY ONE CHANCE!
BY THE POWER OF THE RUNES--- EXPLODE!
RAUGH?!?

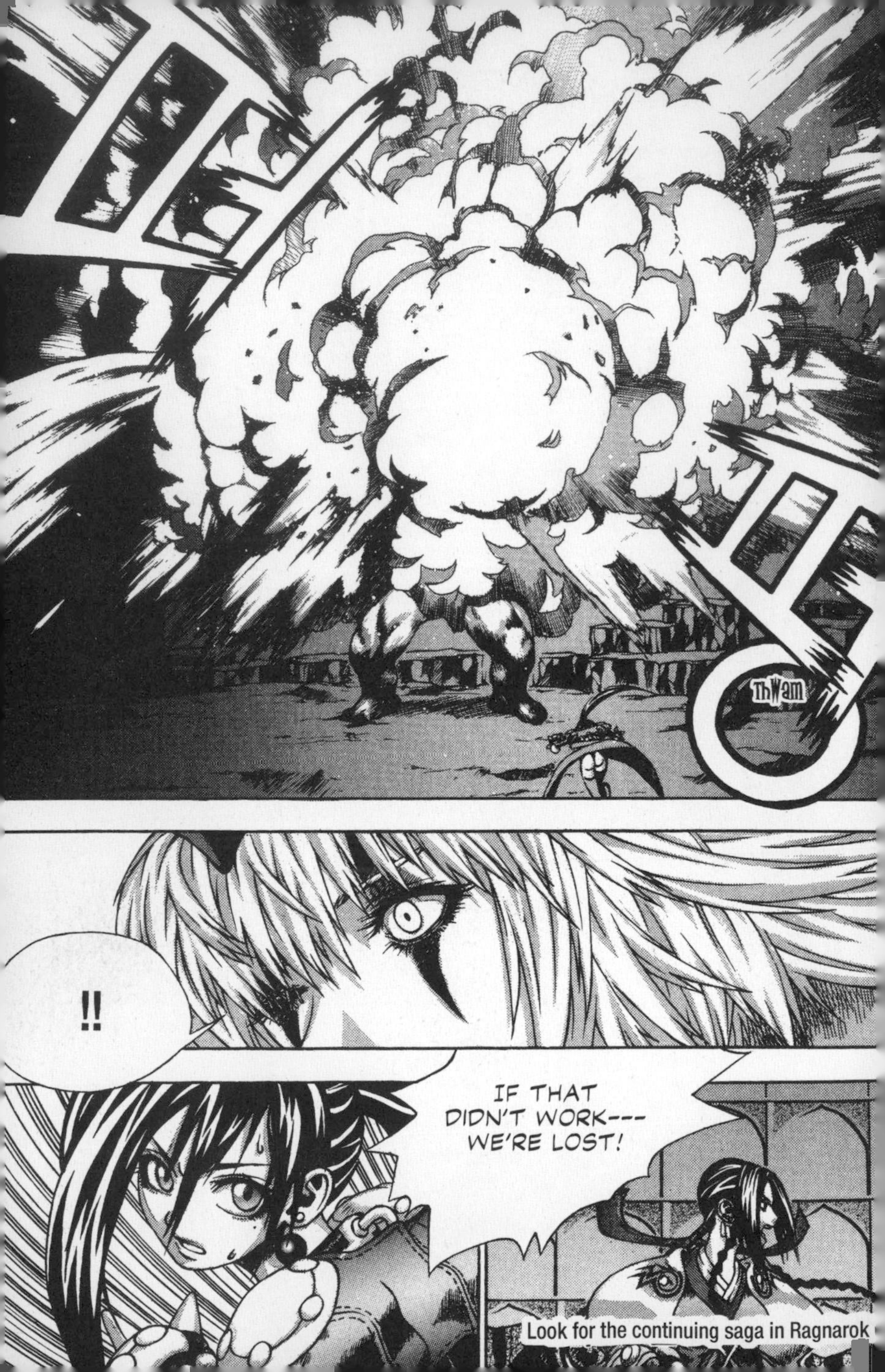
ThWam
!!
IF THAT DIDN'T WORK--- WE'RE LOST!
Look for the continuing saga in Ragnarok

## Special Collection

# RAGNARÖK

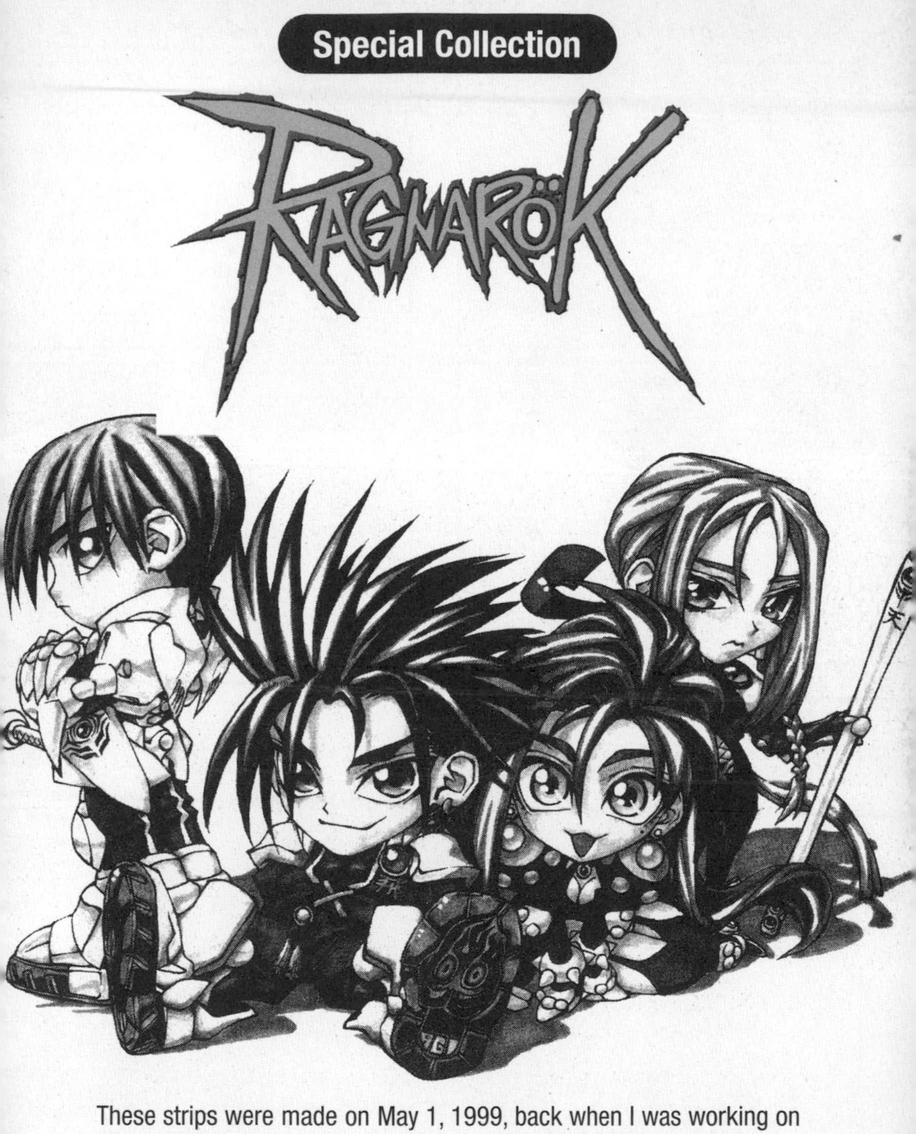

These strips were made on May 1, 1999, back when I was working on the events of *Ragnarok* volume 4. Written under the "Nights" pen name, the events of the comic world were recorded in a magazine called "Lolita Cookie". Only 300 copies were published, so I have included them here so that everyone else can read them.

## Behold the Mandrake!

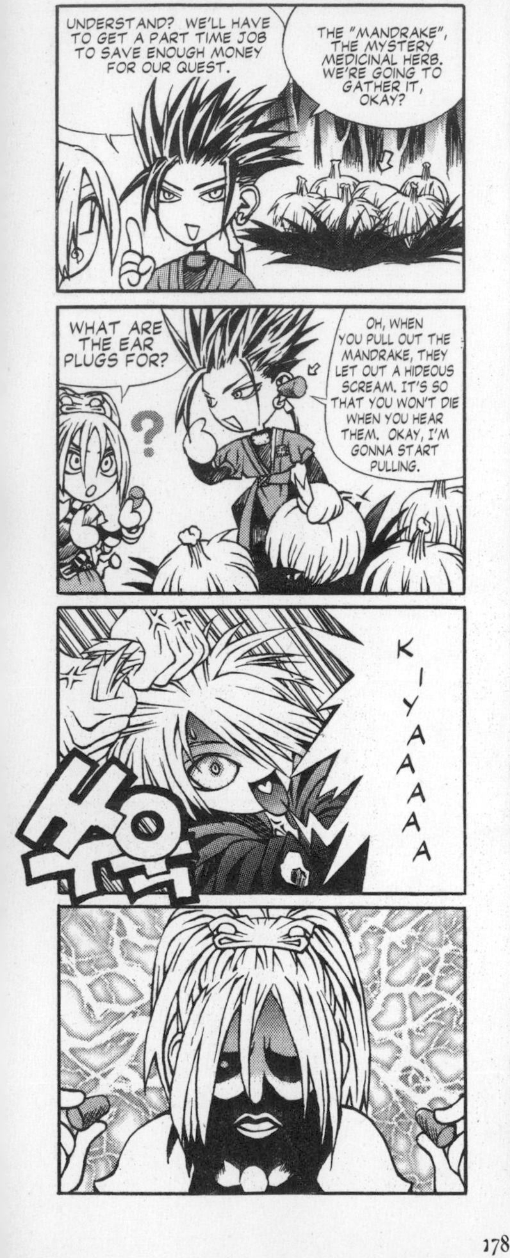
UNDERSTAND? WE'LL HAVE TO GET A PART TIME JOB TO SAVE ENOUGH MONEY FOR OUR QUEST.
THE "MANDRAKE", THE MYSTERY MEDICINAL HERB. WE'RE GOING TO GATHER IT, OKAY?
WHAT ARE THE EAR PLUGS FOR?
OH, WHEN YOU PULL OUT THE MANDRAKE, THEY LET OUT A HIDEOUS SCREAM. IT'S SO THAT YOU WON'T DIE WHEN YOU HEAR THEM. OKAY, I'M GONNA START PULLING.
KIYAAAAAA

## Skurai's Just Desserts

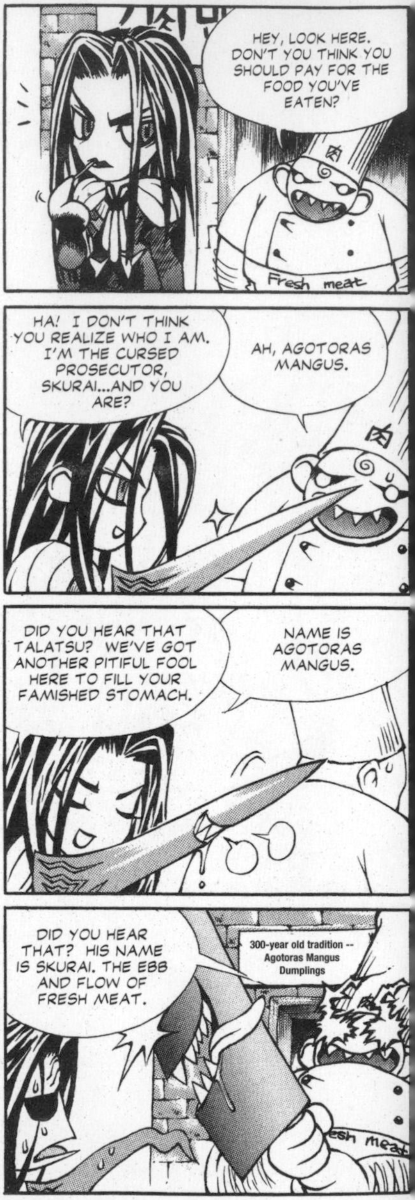
HEY, LOOK HERE. DON'T YOU THINK YOU SHOULD PAY FOR THE FOOD YOU'VE EATEN?
Fresh meat
HA! I DON'T THINK YOU REALIZE WHO I AM. I'M THE CURSED PROSECUTOR, SKURAI...AND YOU ARE?
AH, AGOTORAS MANGUS.
DID YOU HEAR THAT TALATSU? WE'VE GOT ANOTHER PITIFUL FOOL HERE TO FILL YOUR FAMISHED STOMACH.
NAME IS AGOTORAS MANGUS.
DID YOU HEAR THAT? HIS NAME IS SKURAI. THE EBB AND FLOW OF FRESH MEAT.
300-year old tradition -- Agotoras Mangus Dumplings

## Loki's Vision

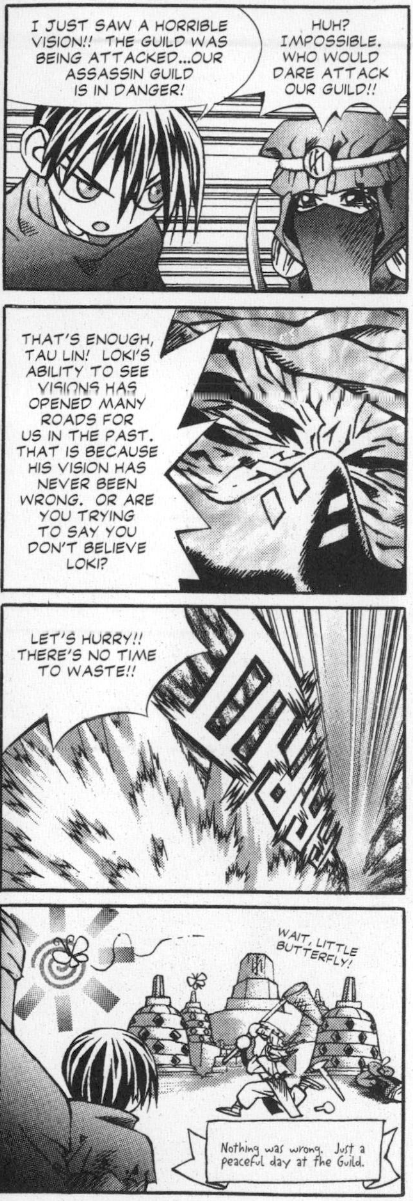
I JUST SAW A HORRIBLE VISION!! THE GUILD WAS BEING ATTACKED...OUR ASSASSIN GUILD IS IN DANGER!
HUH? IMPOSSIBLE. WHO WOULD DARE ATTACK OUR GUILD!!
THAT'S ENOUGH, TAU LIN! LOKI'S ABILITY TO SEE VISIONS HAS OPENED MANY ROADS FOR US IN THE PAST. THAT IS BECAUSE HIS VISION HAS NEVER BEEN WRONG. OR ARE YOU TRYING TO SAY YOU DON'T BELIEVE LOKI?
LET'S HURRY!! THERE'S NO TIME TO WASTE!!
WAIT, LITTLE BUTTERFLY!
Nothing was wrong. Just a peaceful day at the Guild.

## Loki's Vision: Take Two

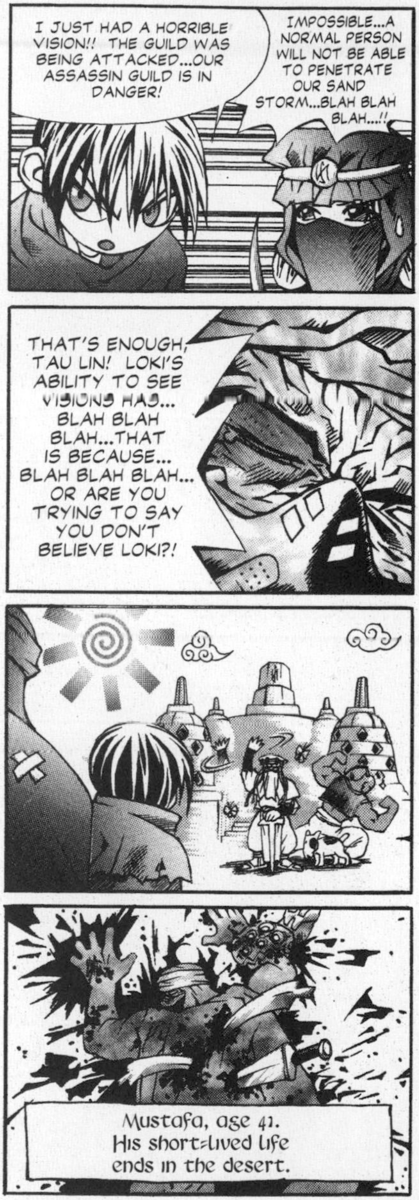
I JUST HAD A HORRIBLE VISION!! THE GUILD WAS BEING ATTACKED...OUR ASSASSIN GUILD IS IN DANGER!
IMPOSSIBLE...A NORMAL PERSON WILL NOT BE ABLE TO PENETRATE OUR SAND STORM...BLAH BLAH BLAH...!!
THAT'S ENOUGH, TAU LIN! LOKI'S ABILITY TO SEE VISIONS HAS... BLAH BLAH BLAH...THAT IS BECAUSE... BLAH BLAH BLAH... OR ARE YOU TRYING TO SAY YOU DON'T BELIEVE LOKI?!
Mustafa, age 41.
His short-lived life ends in the desert.

## My Type of Man

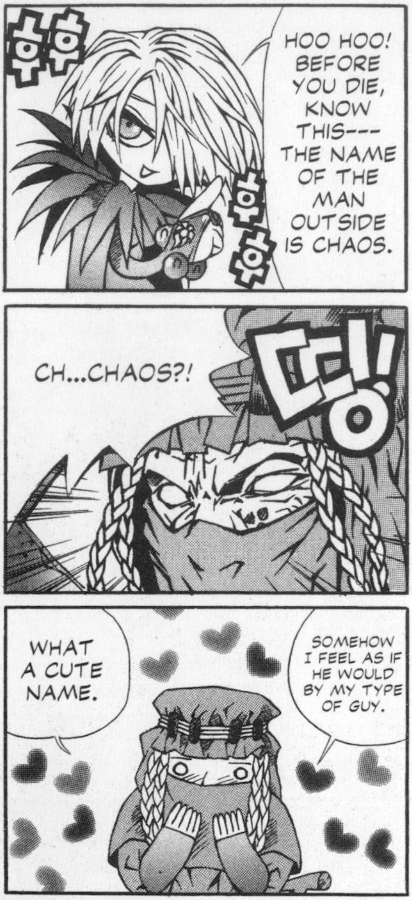
HOO HOO! BEFORE YOU DIE, KNOW THIS--- THE NAME OF THE MAN OUTSIDE IS CHAOS.
CH...CHAOS?!
WHAT A CUTE NAME.
SOMEHOW I FEEL AS IF HE WOULD BY MY TYPE OF GUY.

## Famous Last Words

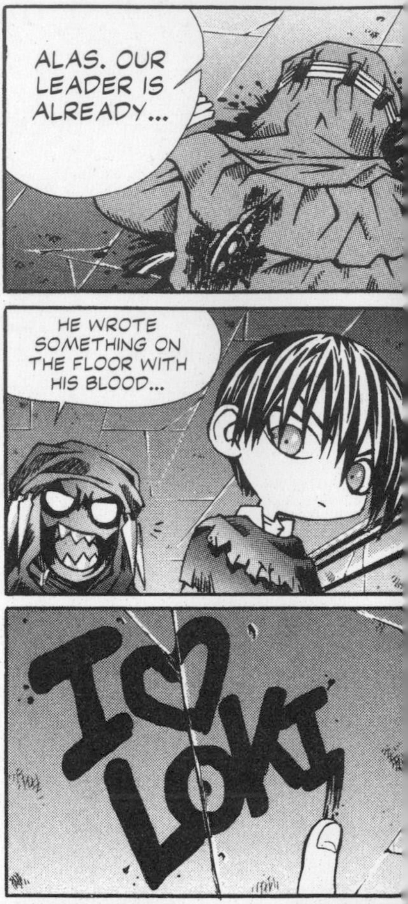
ALAS. OUR LEADER IS ALREADY...
HE WROTE SOMETHING ON THE FLOOR WITH HIS BLOOD...
I ♥ LOKI

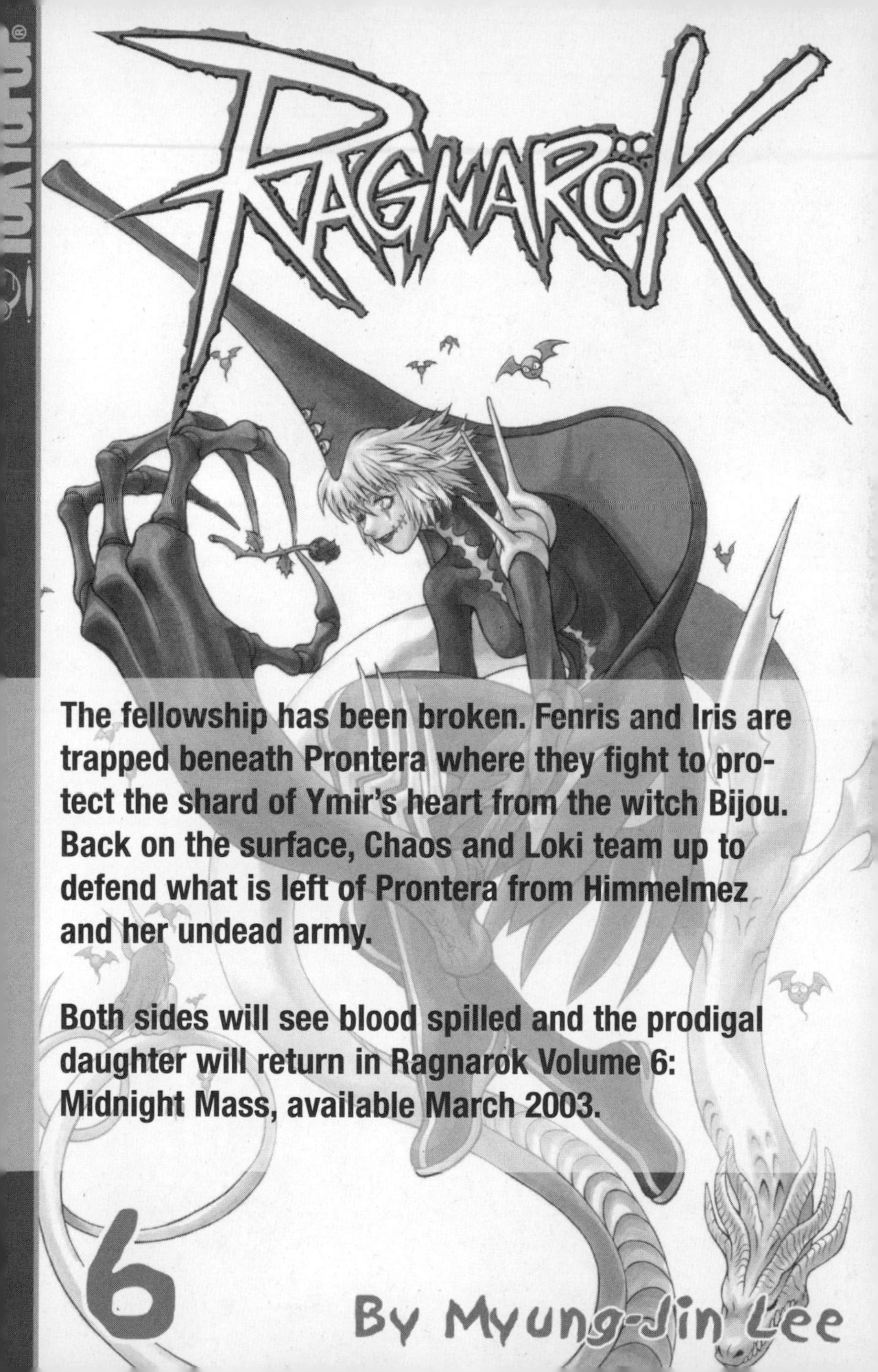
TOKYOPOP®
RAGNARÖK
The fellowship has been broken. Fenris and Iris are trapped beneath Prontera where they fight to protect the shard of Ymir's heart from the witch Bijou. Back on the surface, Chaos and Loki team up to defend what is left of Prontera from Himmelmez and her undead army.
Both sides will see blood spilled and the prodigal daughter will return in Ragnarok Volume 6: Midnight Mass, available March 2003.
6
By Myung-Jin Lee

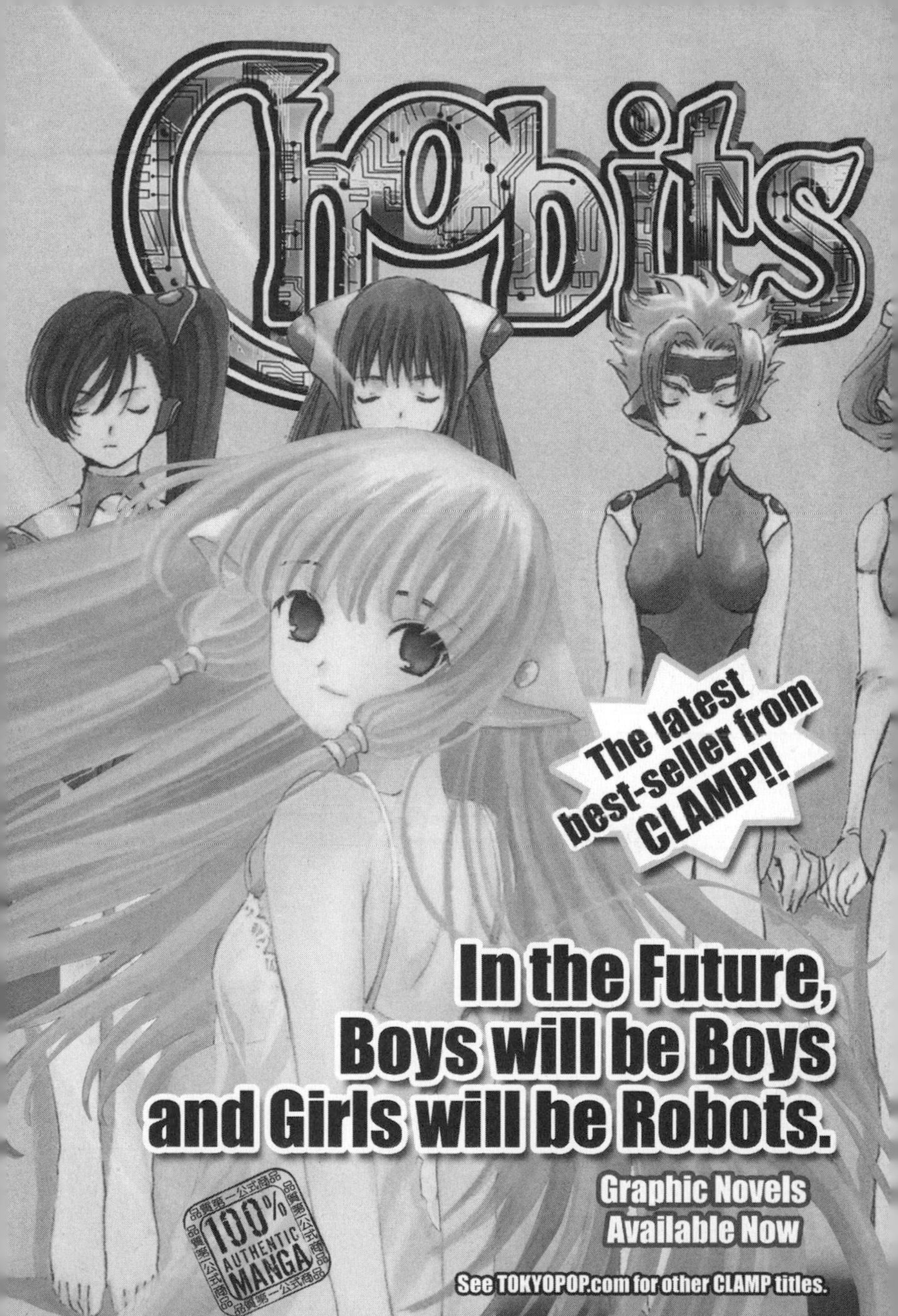
Chobits
The latest best-seller from CLAMP!!
In the Future, Boys will be Boys and Girls will be Robots.
Graphic Novels Available Now
100% AUTHENTIC MANGA
See TOKYOPOP.com for other CLAMP titles.

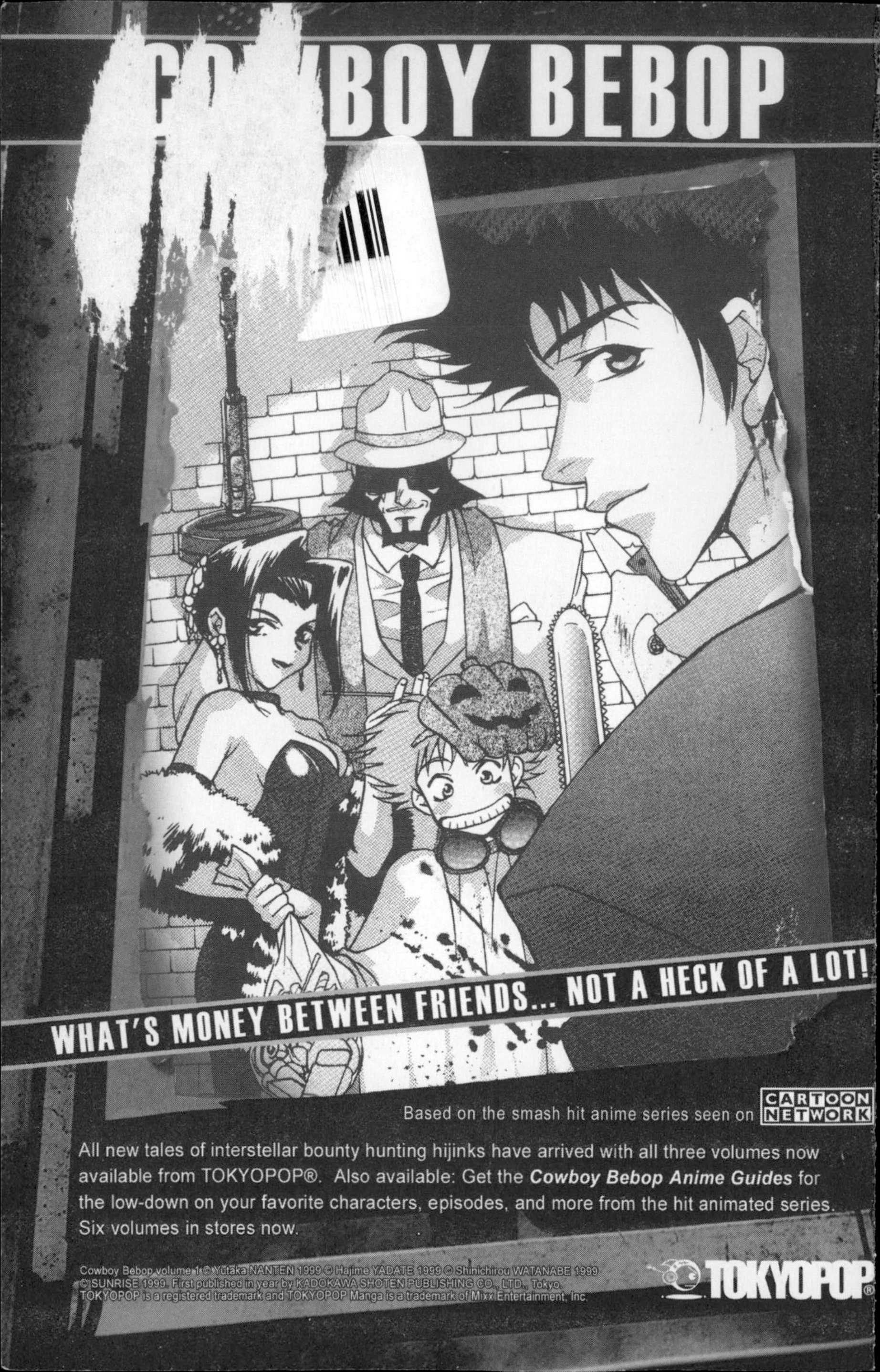
COWBOY BEBOP
WHAT'S MONEY BETWEEN FRIENDS... NOT A HECK OF A LOT!
Based on the smash hit anime series seen on CARTOON NETWORK
All new tales of interstellar bounty hunting hijinks have arrived with all three volumes now available from TOKYOPOP®. Also available: Get the Cowboy Bebop Anime Guides for the low-down on your favorite characters, episodes, and more from the hit animated series. Six volumes in stores now.
Cowboy Bebop volume 1 © Yutaka NANTEN 1999 © Hajime YADATE 1999 © Shinichirou WATANABE 1999 © SUNRISE 1999. First published in year by KADOKAWA SHOTEN PUBLISHING CO., LTD., Tokyo. TOKYOPOP is a registered trademark and TOKYOPOP Manga is a trademark of Mixx Entertainment, Inc.
TOKYOPOP